JN334784

竹原義二の住宅建築

Yoshiji Takehara

Residential

Yoshiji Takehara: Residential Architecture

First published in Japan on April 10, 2010
Third published on March 20, 2018

TOTO Publishing (TOTO LTD.)
TOTO Nogizaka Bldg., 2F,
1-24-3 Minami-Aoyama, Minato-ku,
Tokyo 107-0062, Japan
[Sales] Telephone: +81-3-3402-7138 Facsimile: +81-3-3402-7187
[Editorial] Telephone: +81-3-3497-1010
URL: https://jp.toto.com/publishing

Author: Yoshiji Takehara
Photographer: Yutaka Kinumaki
Publisher: Toru Kato
Art Director: Tetsuya Ota
Printer: Dai Nippon Printing Co., Ltd.

Except as permitted under copyright law, this book may not be reproduced, in whole or in part, in any form or by any means, including photocopying, scanning, digitizing, or otherwise, without prior permission. Scanning or digitizing this book through a third party, even for personal or home use, is also strictly prohibited.
The list price is indicated on the cover.

ISBN978-4-88706-310-5

竹原義二の住宅建築

Architecture

目次
Contents

006
序文　Introduction
完結しない建築へ ──── 竹原義二
Towards an Incomplete　Yoshiji Takehara
Architecture

138
寄稿　Essay
竹原城の謎 ──────── 藤森照信
The Enigmatic Epistle　Terunobu Fujimori
of Yoshiji Takehara

296
寄稿　Essay
「建築」家・竹原義二 ──── 花田佳明
An Architect's Architect:　Yoshiaki Hanada
Yoshiji Takehara

作品
Works

028
101番目の家
House No. 101

056
住吉山手の家
Sumiyoshi Yamate House

076
東広島の家
Higashi Hiroshima House

094
広陵町の家
Koryocho House

114
新千里南町の家
Shinsenri Minamimachi House

146 比叡平の家 Hieidaira House	228 岸和田の家 Kishiwada House
156 蓬莱・玄のアトリエ Horai Atelier Kuro	242 乗鞍の家 Norikura House
170 箱作の家 Hakotsukuri House	258 富士が丘の家 Fujigaoka House
188 明石の家 Akashi House	270 大川の家 Okawa House
208 岩倉の家 Iwakura House	306 作品データ Information on Works
218 額田の家 Nukata House	316 略歴 Profile

完結しない建築へ
Towards an Imcomplete Architecture

竹原義二　　Yoshiji Takehara

007 | Towards an Incomplete Architecture

建築との出会い

私の建築への旅は、閑谷学校との出会いから始まる。

　閑谷学校は1668年に備前藩主池田光政が津田永忠に命じて開いた儒学に基づく士庶共学の学校である。岡山から備前焼の里、伊部の町へ入り、霧の立ち込める山あいの曲がりくねった道を抜けると、山と谷に抱かれた閑谷学校がその姿を見せる。芝に覆われた地面、石橋の架かる拌池の奥に一段上がった野石積みの土留めが控え、畦道の上にかまぼこ型の石塀がそそり建つ。校門より隆起する石塀は曲線を描きながら地を這い、校地を一巡し、龍のように昇りつめ、山の奥へとその姿を消す。延長765mにも及ぶ石塀は、亀甲型に切り出された水成岩の石が人の背丈ほどにスキマなく積み上げられ、1本の草も生えずに今日までその姿を見せている。幾何学模様が風景と溶け合い、場に緊張感を与え、周囲に張りつめた変わらぬ空気を漂わせる。

　建物は講堂・小斎・習芸斎・飲室・文庫と配置され後ろに火除山が控える。講堂の東北に儀式所としての聖廟、その東に一段下がって閑谷神社、石塀を隔てて椿山がある。平行に配置された聖廟と閑谷神社は、地面に高低差がつけられ、意図的な「ズレ」が仕掛けられている。さらに建物を取り囲む漆喰塀の高さが微妙に変えられ、ふたつの塀の間にとられた「スキマ」には微妙な「間合い」がはかられる。閑谷神社から塀を通し、聖廟を見た時に初めて

Encounter with Architecture

My journey towards architecture began with the encounter with the Shizutani School. The Shizutani School was established in 1668 by Nagatada Tsuda under the orders of Mitsumasa Ikeda, the feudal lord of the Bizen domain, as a mixed school for commoners based on Confucian learning.

　The school is nestled amidst the valleys and mist-wreathed mountains along the winding road to Ibe village, famed for its Bizen-yaki ceramics. On a broad spreading lawn, behind a *hanchi* (a type of pond imitating ones in ancient China) spanned by a stone bridge, a stone retaining wall supports an elevated field, and a stone fence finished with a half-round top rises beside a narrow path. This wall climbs from the school gate in a snaking line, winding dragon-like around the school grounds before disappearing into the depths of the hills beyond. 765m in length, the head-height wall is built of blocks of sedimentary rock, cut to shapes resembling the scutes of a tortoise's shell and fitted together so finely that not a single plant sprouts from its joints. The geometric pattern merges into the landscape, bringing a sense of tension to the site and a sharp aura to its surroundings.

　The school consists of the lecture hall, study, class rooms, refectory, and library, while beyond the Hiyokeyama hill waits. The spirit of Confucius is venerated in the *seibyo*, a ceremonial space to the northeast of the lecture hall, and on a lower level to its east is the Shizutani shrine, while beyond rises Tsubakiyama hill, separated by the stone fence. Although the *seibyo* and the Shizutani shrine are parallel to each other, there has been an intentional "shift" through being situated at different levels. Furthermore, the height of the

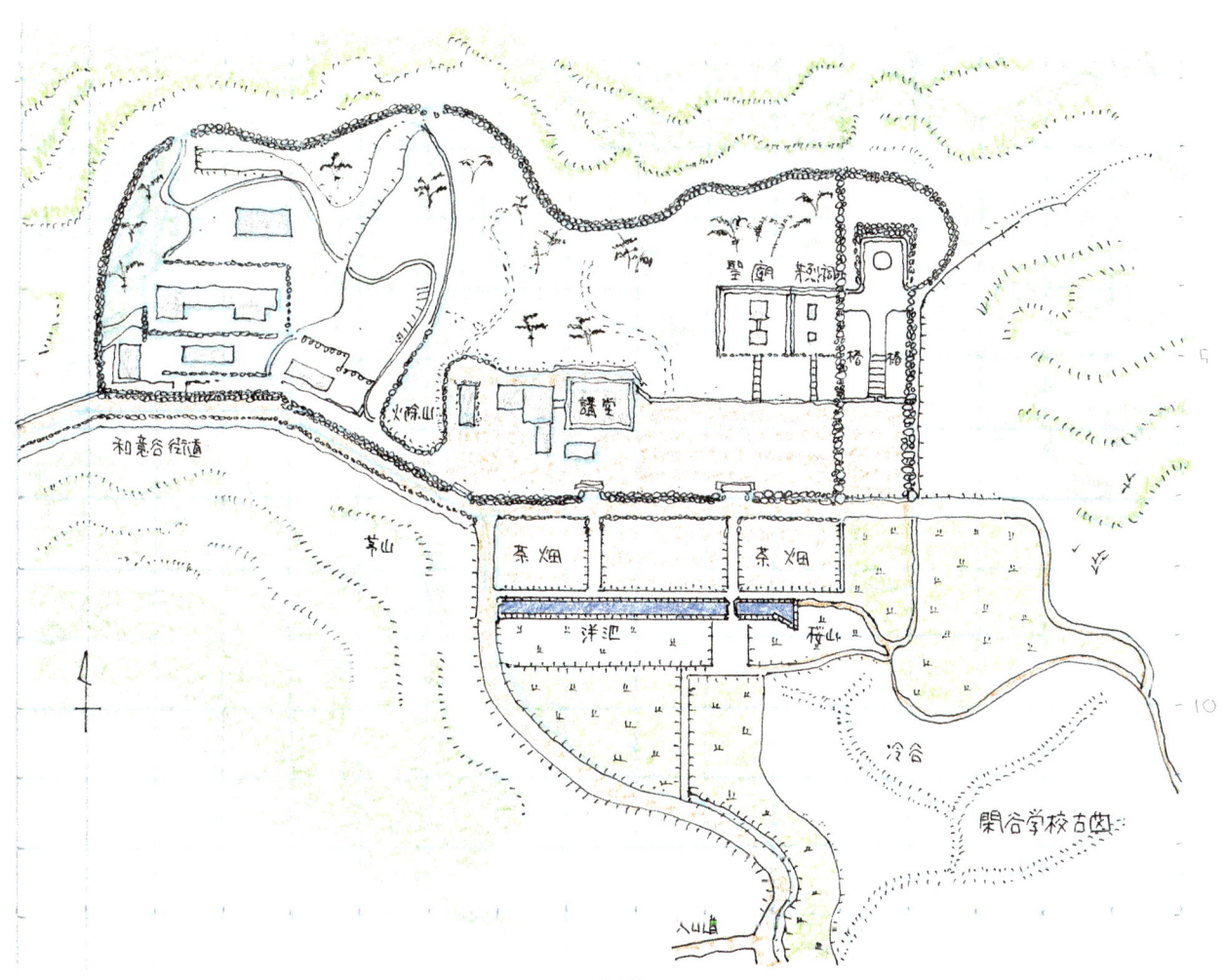

閑谷学校
The Shizutani School

その「ズレ」をとらえ、「スキマ」から視線が連続していくことを知る。
　火燈窓の連続する静寂な講堂、習芸斎、飲室の板の間に座り込むと、地面・石塀・軒・山の稜線は開口部を通して重なり合い、内と外の連続が透明感を漂わせる。この時、エレヴェーションで捉えた地面と基壇、屋根と山の関係を思い起こし、内においても外においても絶妙な高さで視線が結ばれていることに気がつく。
　閑谷学校は素材に対する意識が高い。屋根は備前瓦で葺かれ、色ムラのある不揃いな瓦の表情が漆喰塗の壁に深い陰翳を落とし込む。漆喰で塗り回された壁の足元は無垢板や敷瓦で押えている。雨に打たれ濡れ色になり、陽が射すと光と影に彩られ、自然と素材がこの場を讃える。不揃いな素材が独特のカタチを伴い、床・壁・天井・屋根を躍動的に構成する。素材美とその構成美に目を配り、空間から細部のディテールまで、張りつめた透明感がある。そこには閑谷の精神を感じずにはいられない。
　場のもつ力を引き出し、その脈絡に沿ってなりたつ建築。石積みの有機的な形態が建築の幾何学的な構成とみごとに調和する。これほどまでに自然と建築が融合している様を見たことがない。磨き込まれた板の間に座り、静寂な空間に身を沈め、外を見渡す。そして地面に跳ね返る雨の音、軒内へとしみ込む虫の声、肌を撫でる風の音に耳を澄ます。その場はまるで時間が止まったようである。
　建築の思考に立ち止まる時、私は再び閑谷を訪れる。刻々と移ろい行く時間の中で、時が

plaster fence surrounding the building has been subtly varied, and a fine gap has been placed between the two walls. One first becomes aware of this upon catching sight of the *seibyo* on the other side of the fence from the shrine, as the view continues through the gap.

　When seated upon the silent wooden floor, running beneath rows of bell-shaped *katomado* windows through the lecture hall, study and refectory, the outlines of the ground, stone fence, eaves, and mountains visible through the apertures overlap each other, and the connections between inside and outside create a sense of transparency. A such moments, the elevational relationships become evident between the ground and the building's base and between its roof and the mountains beyond, and you realise that this height is the perfect level at which interior and exterior sightlines join, whether seen from inside or out.

　The Shizutani School is highly conscious of materials. The roof is covered in Bizen tiles, whose irregular arrangement and mottled colouring lend character to the deep shadows they cast on the plaster walls. The base of these walls are protected by undressed timber boards and flat tiles. When it rains the materials darken; when the sun shines they are embellished by light and shade – nature and materials ennoble the place. Each independent material brings its own distinctive form and detail to the floors, walls, ceilings, and roof, forming a vibrant whole. Attention is paid to the beauty of materials and composition, and a lucid transparency pervades all from the overall space to the smallest detail. One can't help feeling the spirit of Shizutani in these things.

　This is an architecture which draws on the power of its place, and emerges through following its lines of energy. The organic form of the masonry harmonizes with the geometrical

過ぎるのも忘れ、また新たな感銘を受け、閑谷を後にする。この建築が今でも私の心をとらえて離さないのは、そこに学ぶべき空間の本質が隠されているからであろう。

意地の都市住宅

師である石井修(いしいおさむ)の事務所から独立し、10作目となる「北楠葉の家(きたくずは)」(1982年) で棟梁・中谷禎次(なかたにていじ)と出会う。腕利きの大工を率いる棟梁とその後2作品ほど協働し、18作目で棟梁の自邸「粉浜の家Ⅱ(はま)」(1985年) を手掛けることになる。大阪市内に残る戦前から残る木造5軒長屋の2軒目、間口3.5m、奥行9mの9坪の極小敷地は、接道問題や長屋の切り取り方など厳しい条件を数多く抱えていたが、計画開始から2年の時を経て建替えを実現させた。

閉塞する極小敷地にあえて強い壁を建ち上げ、割り貫かれた開口に左右ふたつの扉を設ける。訪れる人はこの場で戸惑い、立ち止まる。そこに時間的な「間(ま)」が生まれる。都市にたちはだかる壁は都市に棲み込む意志を表現する。扉を開けて中へ入ると、そこはまだ外部空間である。この空間を「間室(かんしつ)」と呼ぶ。機能諸室で100%満たすのではなく、明確な機能をもたないが都市と住まいの緩衝帯として存在する「間(ま)」。そこは内なる外部、すなわち中間領域としての「間(ま)」でもある。格子戸に透かされた光、壁に切り取られた空、都市の中で忘れかけていた自然を再体験する。それは建築に導かれた抽象的な自然である。

さらにモジュールを操作して室と室の合間に最小限のヴォイドを挿入し、それと直交するよ

structure of the building. I have never seen any place in which nature and architecture are so well united. Sit down on the polished floor, settle back into a serene space, and survey the world. Listen for the sound of raindrops on the ground, the singing of insects resonating inside, and the sound of wind stroking your skin. In this place it feels as if time has stopped.

Whenever my thinking about architecture is blocked, I revisit Shizutani. I forget the passing of time even as it ticks away, and after I am deeply moved yet again I take my leave of Shizutani. The reason why this architecture still exerts its hold on me is because it conceals the essentials of space itself.

An Urban House with Grit

I first met the master carpenter Teiji Nakatani through the Kita Kuzuha House (1982), my tenth project after I became independent from the architectural practice run by my professor, Mr Osamu Ishii. After this project, I collaborated with his team of skillful carpenters on two other projects, and the eighteenth project, Kohama House II (1985), became his own house. This was the rebuilding of the second of a row of five *nagaya* terrace-houses that were built before the war, on a tiny 9 *tsubo* (30m²) plot 3.5m wide and 9m deep. The project was beset with difficulties, such as achieving the requisite setbacks and separation from the street and neighboring houses, but we managed to complete the project two years after it began.

In spite the small, hemmed-in site, we decided to erected a heavy perimeter wall and set doors in two openings cut into its right and left sides. Visitors would reach this point and stop in confusion. This yields a temporal pause, or "*ma*." The walls of the city reveal the intentions

うに二方向階段をしつらえる。階段は上下を連絡する装置であると共に、空間を水平垂直につなぐヴォイドとして捉えられる。二方向階段は層を分断する廊下を介さずして各室への独立した動線を確保し、またその劇的な構成が都市の舞台装置に見立てられる。

住空間を囲いとる外殻と対照的に、内部に現された架構には棟梁の手技を結集し、その合間に降り注ぐトップライトの光が、閉塞する空間を満たしていく。極限の光の下に高密度に迫る内部空間であるからこそ彷彿としてくるテクスチュアを追い求め、極小空間をラワンベニヤで包み込む。ラワンベニヤはその色合いが力強い架構と調和し、ざらついた木肌が光を適度に吸い込み、味わい深い表情を見せる。ロッド単位で使い、木目や色合いに目を凝らし、慎重に張り方向や順番、目地幅を決め、糊張りして仮釘の跡が残らないように優しく打つ。時が経ち、飴色になったラワンベニヤは優しく極小空間を包み込み、明度差を和らげてくれる。

日常生活を営むための空間という使命を負いながら、極限のスケールの中に非日常性を組み込んでいく。こうして大胆な発想をもち込むことによって、都市住宅は本当の豊かさを知ることとなる。

of its inhabitants. On opening the door and entering we find that we are still in an outdoor space. We call this space the "*kanshitsu*," or "interval room". Such a space without clear purpose acts as a buffer zone between the city and the dwelling, something missing from dwellings where the whole building is filled with functionally defined rooms. It is an interior exterior, or in other words a liminal realm. The nature that has been forgotten in the city can be rediscovered in the light filtering through the lattice door and the sky framed by the wall. It is an abstract nature guided by architecture.

Furthermore, by manipulating modules, we introduce a minimum void between rooms and perpendicular to this furnish a two-way staircase. The staircase is a device not only for connecting above and below, but also functions as a void bridging the space both horizontally and vertically. The stair serves to keep independent access to each room without requiring a separate corridor, and its theatrical arrangement resembles a stage set in the city.

In contrast to the outer shell wrapping the dwelling, the skills of the master carpenter were bestowed on the inner spaces, which are filled with light flooding through apertures above, alleviating the cramped urban situation. In that interior space compressed by its high density context we looked for a material whose texture would respond to its extreme illumination, so we wrapped the tiny space with lauan plywood. The colour of the plywood harmonizes with the powerful structure, and its rough surface gently absorbs the light, yielding a rich expression. We applied the plywood in standard one-rod lengths, paying close attention to the wood grain and colour, carefully defining the panels' orientation, sequence, and width of joints, and fixing them in place meticulously leaving no trace of nails. As time goes by the

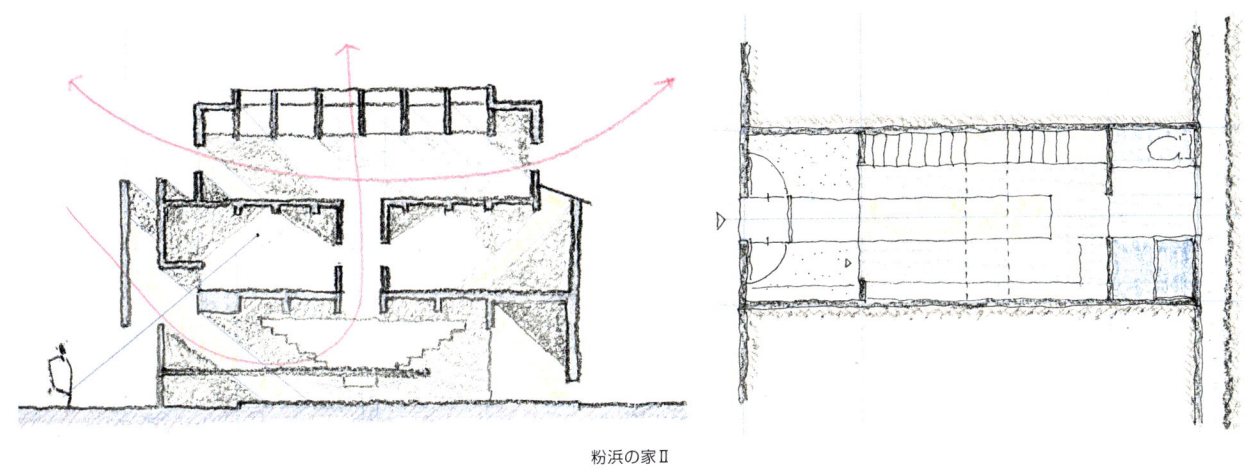

粉浜の家 II
Kohama House II

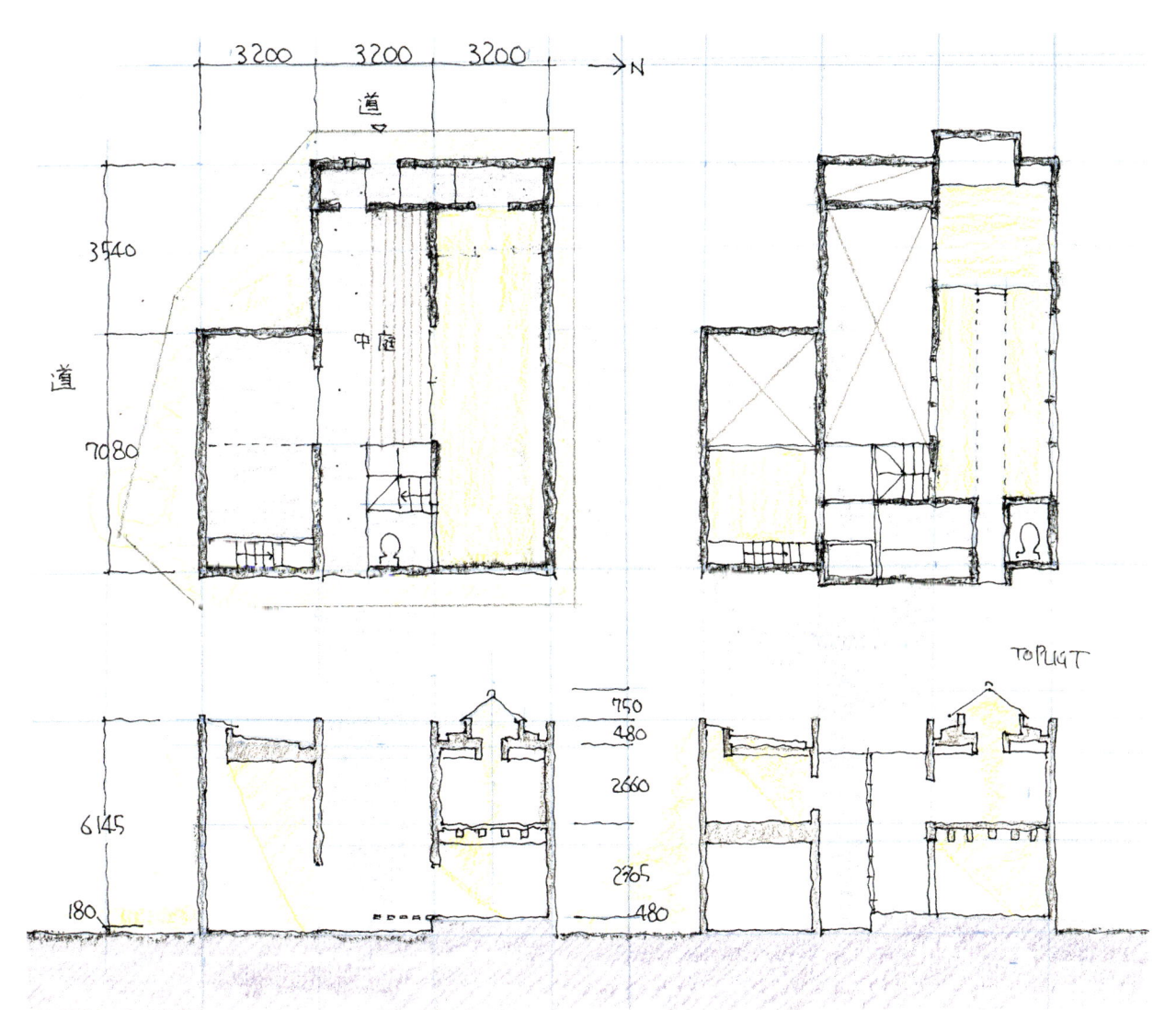

塗屋造の家
Nuriyazukuri House

013 | Towards an Incomplete Architecture

間合い

間口に少しゆとりがでてくると、平面を分割し、もう少し豊かな「間」を挿入することが可能になる。「塗屋造の家」(1987年)ではひと続きに連続する壁で都市から住まいを囲い取り、平面を東西に3,200mmずつに3分割し、外部を介してふたつの室を対峙させた。屋外の室として曖昧に定義される「外室」は、室と室に「間合い」をつくり、多様な住まい方を可能にする。内・外・内の関係をより緊密にするのは、ふたつの内部のレヴェル差と開口部の操作、内外に連続する床仕上げ、内外共に土佐漆喰で塗り込めた壁とヴォイドに連続する架構の構成である。内と外を曖昧にすることで空間は溶け出し、対峙する室同士も連帯感を増していく。

「間合い」とは、剣術にたとえるならば、剣と剣の先が触れるか触れないかの瞬間を表す。相手が一歩引けば「間合い」を詰め、一歩出れば「間合い」をとる。空間と時間をまたぎ、ある一定の間隔を保ちながら、それぞれが常に「間合い」をはかる相対関係にある。3,200mmという間口寸法は4畳半を基準に、人が動き、モノを置く寸法を加えた幅である。室としてほどよく機能しながら、内外の関係を密接かつ曖昧にし、その「間合い」に緊張感をもたらす。ここで導き出したスケールは身体的な基準寸法として重要な意味をもつ。

こうした都市と住まいの関係は外周の塗壁と内部の太軸の架構の対比で構成される。内外共に土佐漆喰で塗り込めた壁は、散漫な都市環境に馴染むような表情の壁とした。内部空間

honey-coloured lauan plywood gently embraces the space and softens its brightness.

In fulfilling the mission for a space for daily life, at this minimal scale, something extraordinary emerges. Through bold conception, urban dwelling can find true richness.

Ma'ai - The Fitting Interval

When there is sufficient space at the frontage, it becomes possible to introduce a richer "*ma*" (space or interval) through dividing up the plan. In the Nuriyazukuri House (1987), the dwelling was separated from the city by an encompassing wall, the plan was divided east-west into three areas of 3200mm each, and two rooms were positioned faced each other across an open external space. An ambiguously defined "outdoor room" creates a suitable interval (*ma'ai*) between the two rooms, allowing for diverse modes of dwelling. What makes the relations of in-out-in even closer is the difference in the levels of the two inner spaces and how their frontages are configured. A consistent floor finish links outside and inside, and a surface finish of Tosa plaster integrates wall and void both outside and within. Spaces dissolve into each other through the blurring of inside and outside, building a sense of continuity between the rooms.

"*Ma'ai*" can be compared to the point at which the tips of two swords are about to touch one another in swordplay. If the opponent withdraws a step, the *ma'ai* is released; a step forward, the *ma'ai* is taken. Both parties maintain a certain spacing between them in both space and time, continually balancing the *ma'ai* of their mutual relation. The frontal dimension of 3200mm is based on a four-and-half tatami mat room, enough space for people

は開口部を絞り込みながら空間に光の密度差をつくり、それに呼応するように壁の色合いや押え方を微妙に変えている。互いの色合いは光と影を交錯させながら混じり溶けていく。出隅や開口の取り合いも見切りを入れずに塗り回し、吹抜の壁を漆喰で表裏一体に一気に覆いつくすことで、自立する壁の存在を強調し、空間に連続性をもたせる。

分棟型平面

都市の「余白」と緩やかに接続すると、ひとつのヴォリューム、1枚の屋根の下に展開する囲い込み型の平面が解体され、分棟型平面へと拡がりを見せる。それまでは壁・ヴォリューム・屋根の自立を使い分け、内外の未分化な見立ての分棟型平面に留めていたが、「広陵町の家」（1997年）でついにヴォリューム・屋根共に分節した、完全な分棟型平面が実現する。重要なのはあくまでこれらが廻遊式住居の様相を残していることである。ヴォリュームとしては自立するが、機能的には完結しないことにより、外部を介在した動線をやむなくする。介在する庭や路地空間は、棟と棟の間合いをはかりながら、外界から光や風をもたらし、雨ざらしとなり、土足のまま残された「余白」の空間は新たな住まいの受け皿となる。一見不便にも見えるが、そこには家族以外の他者をも自在に受け入れ、外界へと溶け出した豊かな生活がある。

to move around and have some things. While fully satisfying the room's functional requirements, the *ma'ai* brings closeness and ambiguity to the inside-outside relationship, and achieves a sense of tension. The resulting scale has an important meaning as a dimensional standard geared to the human body.

This relationship between the city and the dwelling is formed from the contrast between the surrounding plaster wall and the bold structural elements of the interior. The wall, fully rendered on both sides with Tosa plaster, is able to blend into its diffuse urban environment. The interior space generates variations in the density of light while narrowing its openings, and in response to this the colourings and modulations of the walls subtly vary. The colours blend into each other through an intertwining of light and shade. Rather than differentiating the edges and openings, plaster was applied consistently to both sides of the walls to the void, emphasising the independent presence of the wall itself, and bringing continuity to the overall space.

Distributed Plan

Once it has been loosely attached to the liminal spaces of the city, the dwelling, which typically unfolds in a single volume under a single roof, can now be taken apart and spread out into a distributed or *bunto-gata* plan. Initially we limited ourselves to treating the wall, volume, and roof independently, yielding some possibilities for distributed plans in which inside and outside are undivided, but in the Koryocho House (1997), we divided the volume and the roof, fully achieving this configuration. What is important here is that these dwellings

ズレとスキマ

建築は物理的にある一定のヴォリュームをもつ。そこへ「間」を挿入し、相対する関係に「間合い」をつくるとき、私はあえて「ズレ」をつくる。「ズレ」によって生じた「スキマ」には、厚み、奥行き、拡がりが生まれ、方向性を示唆し、そこへ光や風、雨、そして人の意識までもが流動する。視線や動線の「ズレ」は意識的な「間合い」を喚起し、様々なシーンを展開する。部材や素材のディテールにおける「ズレとスキマ」は空間構成を際立たせ、人の意識を巧みに導く。この「ズレ」によってシーンが巡り始め、「間合い」は静から動へと展開する。

　ヴォリュームと余白、内と外、ズレとスキマが複雑に交錯するにつれ、架構による空間表現、壁による空間表現がより明確になり、素材や構造と空間の相関性がいよいよ高まってくる。

重層する廻遊式住居

狭小の都市住宅以後、時代と共にもう少し大きなヴォリュームの住宅を手掛けることが多くなった。それぞれの敷地にはゆとりが出てくるが、同時に町も過密化し、敷地境界線という概念が次々と都市を分断する。庭や路地を共有することがもはや困難になり、塀の出現により都市の「余白」は打ち消されていく。また、平屋を基本とした日本の伝統的な住空間は、内と外の緩衝帯となる「中間領域」を取り入れ、空間の奥行きや開放性を獲得しながら、そこ

retained their circulation, or *kaiyusei*. Although each element stands independently as a volume, functionally they remain incomplete on their own and have to be mediated by circulation pathways through outside space. The gardens and alleys introduce *ma'ai* spacings between buildings, bringing light and wind from outside, and turn these weatherbeaten and trampled residual spaces into receptacles for new forms of dwelling. Although it may appear inconvenient at first sight, such spaces are open to those others beyond the family unit, enabling a richer life through such connections to the outside world.

Shifts (*zure*) and Gaps (*sukima*)

Architecture has a certain physical volume. When introducing spaces (*ma*) and relative intervals (*ma'ai*) into such a volume, I purposefully make inconsistencies and shifts (*zure*). The gaps (*sukima*) generated a result create thickness, depth, and expansion, suggest direction, and cause flows of light, wind, rain and even our human attention. These *zure* form misalignments of vision and movement, rousing our consciousness of *ma'ai* and yielding various scenes. The shifts and gaps at the level of the details of elements and materials render conspicuous the spatial structure, and adroitly guide our awareness. Scenes unfold from these *zure*, and they transform *ma'ai* from static to fluid.

　With the intricate imbrication of volume and void, inside and outside, and *zure* and *sukima*, the spatial expression of structure and walls becomes clearer, and the interrelation between space and structure or materials becomes closer.

に通り路地や土間、縁などの動線を組み込む「廻遊式住居」を形成してきた。しかし、現代の過密化する都市では、必然的に上下に住空間が積み上げられ、延床面積という概念がこうした住宅の「余白」を排除し、豊かな「廻遊性」も失われてしまった。

そこで私は都市の「余白」を住宅の内に埋め込むことから始める。室のヴォリュームを最小限に抑え、家と家のスキマ、庭、空地や路地など、本来都市に内在していた様々なスケールの「余白」を重層する住空間に内包する。

「余白」には不均質で多様な空間の質を与える。この時、いかに外なるものを引き込むかが重要になる。たとえば中庭やヴォイドといった外部そのものを取り込む、また光や風といった外部環境を内部に引き込む、さらには素材やテクスチュアによって外部表現を与えるということである。逆に室と室を内部動線的につないで緩やかな一室空間を形成し、廊下や階段などの独立した動線を外部に晒していくこともできる。この多様な「余白」を立体的に紡いでいったとき、重層する都市の住まいに内と外の交錯する豊かな「廻遊性」を取り戻し、時間や季節、家族や都市の移り変わりを受け止め、生活に拡がりを与える。

ほぼ同時期に計画された「真法院町の家」(1992年)「山坂の家Ⅰ」(1992年)「住吉山手の家」(1993年)の3作は、建物で敷地を囲い取り3層に重層する空間に外室や路地、ヴォイドや立体的な動線を複雑に引き込んだ住宅である。敷地条件や周辺環境によりその構成を異にするが、地階に地面と関係を強く結ぶ座の空間、地上階にはヴォイドや中庭、テラスのような外

Dwellings of Multi-layered Circulation.

After the completion of the tiny urban residence, as times changed I came increasingly to be involved on houses of larger volume. Although each plot of land had more space, at the same time the density of the urban context increased, and the concept of the site boundary became increasingly a dividing line from the city. It became almost impossible to share garden and alleys, and the introduction of fences erased the liminal spaces of the city. The traditional dwelling spaces of Japan were based upon the single storey bungalow or *hiraya*, which incorporated a buffer zone as an "in-between space" between interior and exterior. This not only secured the depth and openness of the space, it also established an circulation path linking alleyways, *doma* spaces with earth floors, and verandas, forming a "circulation dwelling". However, in the high-density context of the contemporary city, the vertical stacking of residential space has become unavoidable, and the domination of the concept of total floor area has eliminated such liminal spaces and the rich circulation that they afforded.

This is why I began embedding such liminal spaces into the house itself. Keeping the volume of rooms to a minimum, I incorporate, at various scales, the liminal spaces which used to exist in the city – such as the gaps between houses, gardens, vacant lots, and alleys – into multi-layered dwelling spaces.

I apply heterogenous and diverse spatial qualities to these liminal spaces. It is important here to consider how to bring inside what normally exists outside. For example, we can incorporate exterior elements, such as courtyards and voids, into the interior; we can bring

部空間と対峙する家族室、最上階に個室が配され、上下をつなぐ複数の階段が複雑な動線を仕掛け、躍動的に視線をつなぐ。場の脈絡を再解読し、都市に棲む魅力を引き出した「重層する廻遊式住居」というひとつのプロトタイプを示唆する。

つなぎの間

こうした現代の住まいに内と外、他者との「間合い」を取り戻すための第3の空間を意識的に組み込む。それは特定の機能をもたないが、ふたつの領域、場所をつないで距離を調整する「つなぎの間」である。「つなぎの間」は単に室と室の間に設けられた部屋ではない。そこは人と人が出会う場であり、「間合い」をはかる場である。空間としても時間としても「間」を取り合い、時に互いを取り込み合う。その住宅の空間構成によって、内、外、中間領域と、その質を変えながら、室と室との距離・幅・奥行・高さ・レヴェル・方向性などが巧みに操作され、まさに人の意識を描写する変幻自在な空間である。「つなぎの間」は「間」と「廻遊」の起点となり、さまざまなシーンをつなぎ留める。

逃げのない建築

時は巡り2000年、私は100の建築を携えて再び原点に立ち還る。時代と共に希薄になる場の力・平面・空間・寸法・素材・構造・技術・家族・そして人、私たちにとって住宅とは一体何

inside external environmental factors such as light and wind; and moreover we can give an exterior expression to the interior by applying certain materials and textures. Alternatively, we can create a single loosely defined interior by linking different rooms through internal connections, or we can expose independent lines of circulation, such as corridors and staircases, to the outside. When spinning out these various liminal spaces in three dimensions, a circulation (*kaiyusei*) that interweaves inner and outer spaces is re-introduced into multi-layered urban living spaces, and it becomes possible to respond to the transitions of time, season, family, and the city itself, broadening the scope of daily life.

The following three projects, Shinpoincho House (1992), Yamasaka House I (1992), and Sumiyoshi Yamate House (1993), which were designed at almost the same time, were all built as three-story buildings that occupied the entire site, incorporating outdoor rooms, alleys, voids and three-dimensional circulation paths into their composition. Although the compositions differ depending upon site conditions and their surrounding environments, there are features in common. A seating position that strongly ties the basement floor to the ground plane; courtyards and voids at the ground floor; terrace-like exterior spaces facing family rooms; individual rooms on the upper level; and several staircases linking things vertically to provide intricate circulation paths and lively visual connections. These projects suggest one prototype of a "dwelling of multi-layered circulation," that reinterprets the history of local place and draws out the appeal of urban living.

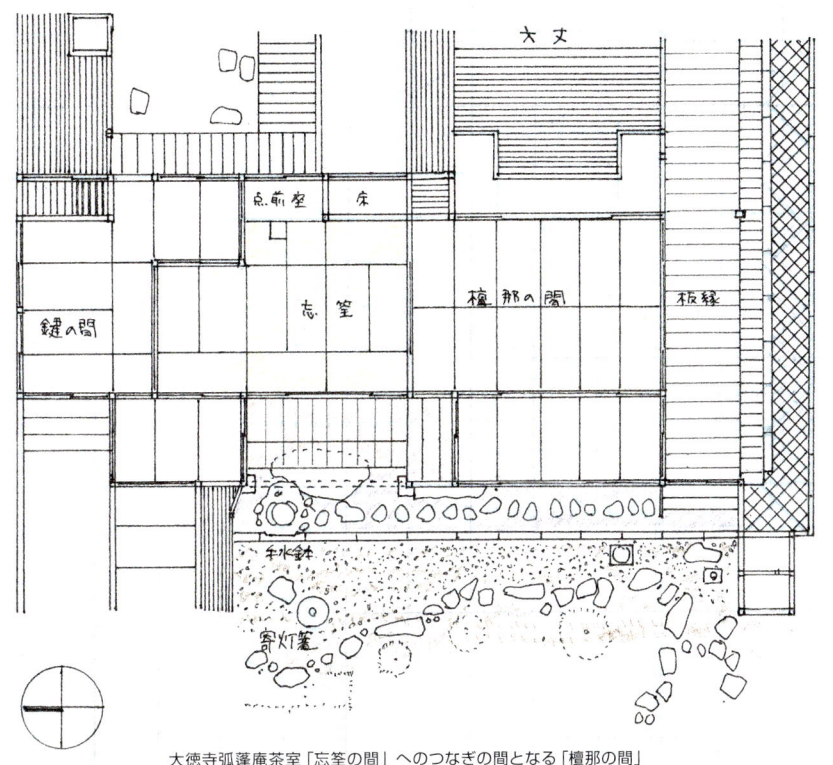

大徳寺弧蓬庵茶室「忘筌の間」へのつなぎの間となる「檀那の間」
The *dannna-no-ma* connecting to the *bosen-no-ma* in the Kohoan teahouse at Daitokuji Temple, kyoto

Connecting Space

In order to restore the *ma'ai* mediating inside, outside, and other people, we consciously bring "third space" into the contemporary dwelling. Such space does not have a specific function, but is a "connecting space" which bridges and adjusts the distance between two different domains and places. The "connecting space" is not simply a room between other two rooms. It is a space where people meet each other and calibrate the *ma'ai* with others. It is a space in which one can take distance or engage, both temporally and spatially. It is a protean space reflecting our consciousness, adjusting the qualities of interior, exterior, or threshold realms by manipulating distance, width, depth, height, level and orientation between rooms. Such "connecting space" is the source of both *ma* and *kaiyusei* and links various scenes.

Architecture without Compromise

In the year 2000, after having completed one hundred buildings, I came full circle, back to my starting point. The power of place, plan, space, dimension, materials, structure, skill, family, and human beings – all these have become more invisible as time passes. What, exactly, is a dwelling for us? In order to find an answer to this question, I resolved to build my own dwelling – my 101st project.

When building your own house, there is no-one to make demands of you. There is just the will to face architecture completely. One must always maintain one's self-possession – the vagueness that comes from involvement of others or losing track of things under a pile of

なのであろうか。私は101作目にして自邸をつくる決意をした。

　自邸とは誰からの要求もない建築である。ただ徹底的に建築と向き合う意志だけが存在する。他者の存在によって曖昧になり、思いの渦の中に埋没してしまうものを、常に自分の手中に捕らまえながら、そこには一切の逃げが許されない。逃げのない建築。それはこの場と建築の在り様をすべて剥き出しにしていくことから始まる。可能な限り要素を純化しながら、生々しくぶつかり合うその様に、住宅の本質を見極める契機となる。

　「101番目の家」は100㎡の狭小敷地に建つ。100㎡とは概ね3層程度で4人家族が快適に住み続けることができる必要最小限の面積とされ、日本の都市住宅において重要な意味をもつ。間口7m奥行き15m、前面道路より1層分沈み込む東西に細長い狭小敷地に、「都市に住まう」ということに徹した逃げのない建築をつくり出す。最小限のスケールの中であらゆる要素が1：1でせめぎ合い、重層する廻遊式住居を極限まで突き詰めることを決意する。

1×1

場×建築	ヴォリューム×余白
内×外	ズレ×スキマ
平面×断面	間×廻遊
空間×構造	構造×素材

distractions – none of these excuses apply here. An architecture without compromise. It begins with the complete baring of the way this place and architecture exists. Purifying as much as possible, nakedly confronting existential reality, it is an opportunity to determine the essence of the house.

　House No. 101 is built on a tiny plot of land of 100m². 100m² is about the minimum space necessary for a family of four to live comfortably in a house of three stories, and it has a significant meaning for urban housing in Japan. On a long narrow site of 7m frontage and 15m depth oriented east-west, and with a fall of one level, we built a house whose ultimate purpose is "to live in the city". At this minimal scale, in which every element is multiplied by each other, we seek to pursue the limits of the dwelling of multi-layered circulation.

1×1

Place × Building	Volume × Liminal Space
Inside × Outside	Shift × Gap
Plan × Section	*Ma × Kaiyu*
Space × Structure	Structure × Material
Framework × Details	Wood × Concrete
Strength × Transparency	Independence × Continuity
Openness × Closure	Frame × Window
Horizontal × Vertical	Articulation × Connection
Wall × Column	Front × Back

骨格×ディテール　　木×コンクリート
力強さ×透明感　　　自立×連続
開放×閉鎖　　　　　躯体×マド
水平×垂直　　　　　分節×連結
壁×柱　　　　　　　表×裏
光×闇　　　　　　　天×地
家×家族　　　　　　職人×建築家　……

　こうした建築における対比構造がコントラストを見せながら、一対に掛け合わされて建築を築き上げるとき、単体でははかり知れない力が互いに引き出され、新たな次元へと昇華する。

棟梁の自邸「粉浜の家Ⅱ」から私の自邸「101番目の家」へ

私は棟梁・中谷禎次というひとりの棟梁と出会い、手でモノをつくる職人と、モノを考え出す建築家の1対1の関係の重さを知る。建築家は土地を吟味し、そこから建ち上がる建築の有り様を思い描くことはできるが、自分の手でつくることはできない。思いを1本の線に託して図面に刻み込み、その意志を汲み取る職人たちがいて建築は成り立つ。ここでもう一度考える。手間暇を掛ければより良いものになるということぐらい、本当は職人自身がよく知ってい

Light × Darkness　　　Heaven × Earth
House × Family　　　　Craftsman × Architect

If these binary oppositions within architecture are able to multiply one another to forge an architecture while still revealing their differences, they collectively draw out immense power, sublimating to a new dimension.

From the House of the Master Carpenter (Kohama House II) to my own house (House No. 101)

Through the encounter with the craftsman Teiji Nakatani, I learnt the significance of the one-to-one relationship between the craftsman, who creates something by hand, and the architect, who generates the idea of a thing. Although the architect can investigate a site and imagine how a building might exist on it, he does not have the skill to build it with his own hands. Architecture exists because of craftsmen who can interpret the intentions behind the drawings, each line of which is an inscribed thought. And think it once again. The more time you spend the better it becomes, and the craftsmen themselves know this. They therefore ask again whether it is really a worthwhile job to do or an architecture to pursue. We architects then have to answer these questions. We must continually seek out potentials in each other, colliding with each other. From this process, new techniques are born.

　And then the contest between craftsman and architect, "one-to-one", through their respective private houses, begins once again.

る。だからこそそれが本当に求めるべき仕事か、求めるべき建築かどうか、職人たちは問い直す。私たちはその問いに答えられなければならない。常に互いの可能性を求め、ぶつけ合うこと。それによってまた新たな技が引き出される。

　そして棟梁と建築家、ふたりの自邸を巡る「1対1」のせめぎ合いが再び始まる。

混構造の表現

かつての民家がもっていた剥き出しの骨格の力強さには「棲み続ける」意志が込められている。これを現代の都市の住宅に読み替え、「101番目の家」では構造をすべて剥き出しにし、空間を支える骨格だけで内部空間を構成した。それは「木」と「コンクリート」が「1対1」の関係で絡み合う混構造によって表現される。

　木とコンクリートという素材を1対1の関係で捉えた時、そこには新たな木造の表現が求められる。コンクリートに負けない無垢の木は、檜や杉といった針葉樹の素木づくりでも、銘木の数寄屋づくりでもなく、荒々しい表情をもった広葉樹でなければ表現できない。堅くて色艶のある広葉樹は1本1本強い個性があり、鉄のように重く、圧倒的な存在感をもつ。この広葉樹の木を打ち放しのコンクリートと同じように内外一体に現し、大断面木造の架構で表現した。広葉樹の柱梁は、製材所に置いてあったままの不揃いの断面寸法で使用し、色艶の異なる13種類の木をランダムに使い分ける。かつての民家がそうであったように、素材のありのままの

Expressing Mixed Structure

In the power of the naked framework of the old Japanese *minka*, one perceives the will to "keep on living." Re-interpreting this for the contemporary urban dwelling, we left the structure of House No. 101 exposed, so that the definition of the interior space was made via its supporting framework. This was expressed by a "one-on-one" intertwining of wood and concrete into a mixed structure.

　In order to appreciate the relationship between wood and concrete on a "one-to-one" basis, it becomes necessary to find new form of expression for timber construction. Neither *shiraki-zukuri* using softwoods such as Japanese cypress (*hinoki*) or cedar (*sugi*), nor *sukiya-zukuri* using precious woods can give the robust expression necessary to compete with concrete that hardwoods sourced from broadleaf trees can. Hardwoods are hard and clear, each different from the another, heavy as iron, and have a overwhelming presence. We used these hardwoods in heavy sections both inside and outside, in the same way as off-form concrete. Hardwood beams and columns were used just as they were displayed at sawmill, in diverse dimensions, and thirteen different kinds of wood in all their variations of colour and complexions were used at random. As the old *minka* teach us, materials are best when used just as they are. As for the concrete, we used broad cedar boards for rough-cast formwork, embedding it with the timber's acerbic taste and expression. This is how we get wood and concrete to form an equal "one-to-one" relationship.

　At a stroke, the dependent relationship between wood and concrete in mixed structures

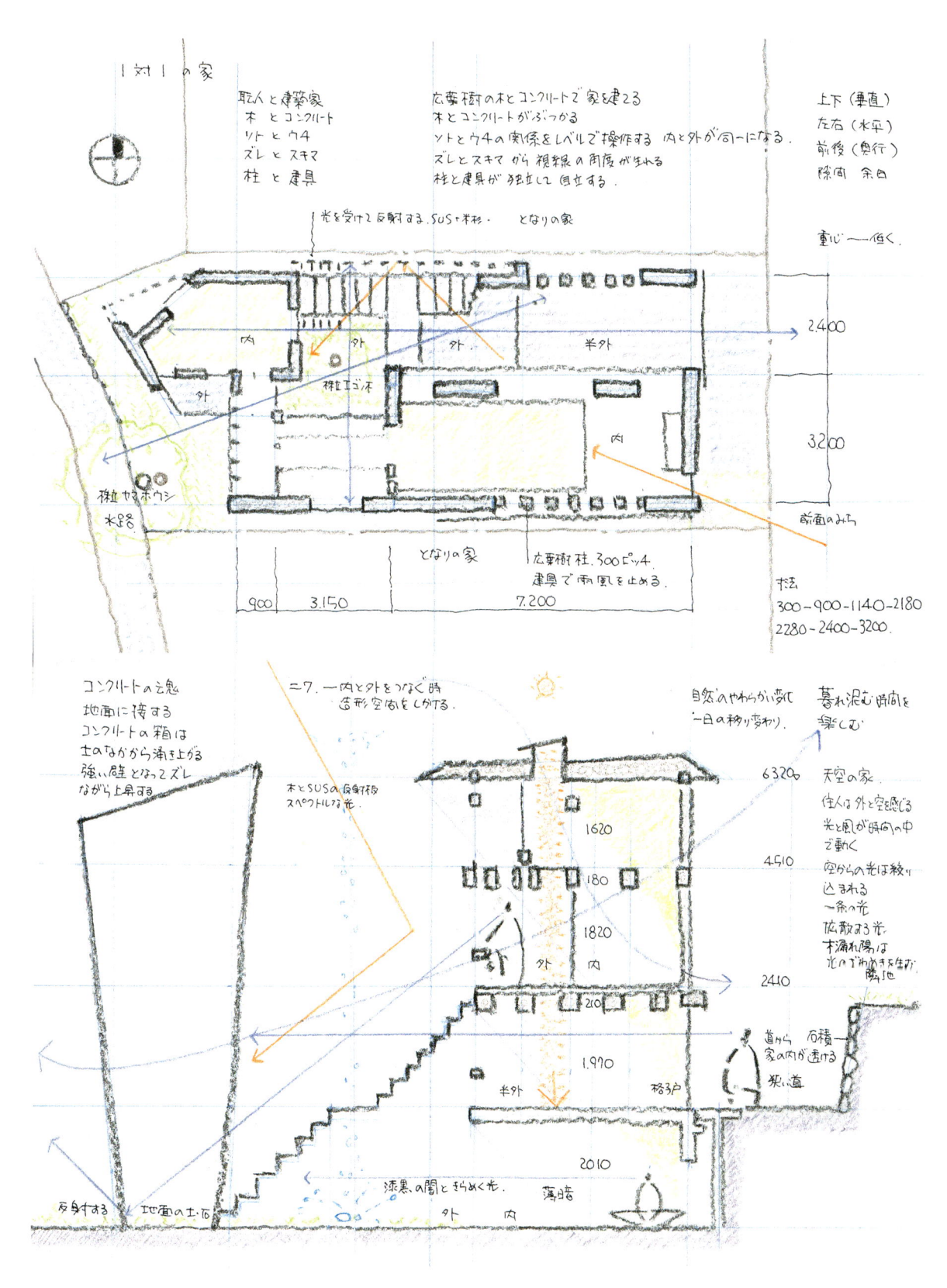

101番目の家
House No. 101

姿を生かしている。一方コンクリートは乱幅の杉板型枠を暴れさせて打ち、木の灰汁や表情を映し込んだ。こうして木とコンクリートが素材として1対1の関係を獲得する。

　そして木とコンクリートの混構造における従属的な関係を一旦白紙に返し、複雑な入れ子状にして1対1の関係を結ぶ混構造を考え出した。鋼のように硬い広葉樹は鑿(のみ)が立たず、道具を何度も欠く。鉄のように重い広葉樹は手で担ぎ上げることができない。捻(ねじ)れながら育つ広葉樹は真っ直ぐな長尺材が取りづらい。路地の入り組んだ都市空間に運び込める材寸にも考慮し、2層分の通し柱をずらして継いだ合わせ柱、合わせ梁で3.5層分にわたる架構をつくり出した。架構のズレとスキマはすべて開口部として透過され、力強い骨格に支えられながら透明度の高い空間がたち現れた。その奥に最後の礎として水路際に5角形にせり上がるコンクリートボックスを突き刺し、場と建築の結び目をつくり出している。

　広葉樹の大断面木造とコンクリート造の混構造、荒々しい素材のぶつかり合いという構造表現をそのまま空間に表現することは容易ではない。仕上げをせず、すべてが剥き出しになるということは、職人にとっても逃げがまったく許されないということである。新たな構法はそのまま空間のディテールとなり、そこには数えきれないほどの手仕事の痕跡が刻まれている。不整形なコンクリートの型枠から広葉樹の大断面木造の架構まで、棟梁・中谷禎次率いる職人たちは見事にこの仕事を成し遂げた。

was dissolved, and we worked out an approach that adopted a complex nested arrangement to establish a one-to-one relationship. Hardwoods are as hard as steel, chisels are useless, and our tools often chipped and failed. Hardwoods are as heavy as iron, and impossible to shoulder. They twist as they grow and thus are difficult to find in long lengths. We took account of the logistics of the narrow urban alleyways in determining the lengths we used, and so the structure for the three-and-a-half storey building consisted of a combined elements using two shifted double-height columns tied with a cross-beam. The resulting *zure* and *sukima* of the structural frame are expressed as openings, yielding a powerful skeleton that is yet highly transparent. At the rear, a pentagonal concrete channel serving as a waterway is revealed and used as a foundation, a final knot binding architecture and place.

　It was not easy to achieve spatial expression through the direct confrontation of two rough materials – broad-section hardwood timber construction and concrete – in a mixed structure. Choosing to forgo finishes and exposing everything fully uncovered also meant that no compromises were available for the craftsman. The new construction method itself formed the detailing of the space and left the traces of the manual labour of countless hands. From the irregularly-shaped frame for the concrete, to broad-section hardwood timber structure, the craftsmen, guided by the master craftsman Teiji Nakatani, accomplished their task splendidly.

An Architecture of Incompletion

Volume and liminal space, *zure* and *sukima*, *ma'ai*, competing dimensions, heterogenous space, the changes in family and environment – I inquire into all of these things and return

完結しない建築

ヴォリュームと余白、ズレやスキマ、間合い、せめぎ合う寸法、不均質な空間、変わり続ける家族や環境……様々な思考を突き詰め、曖昧な日常の中に緊張感を取り戻す。しかし私は突き詰めた思考の先に、完結しない建築を追い求めている。変幻自在な「間」の構成、行き止まることのない「廻遊性」は閉塞する都市に風穴を空ける。これらを体現させる構造、素材も同じである。その時代そこにあった素材や技術を継ぎ接ぎながらつくられてきた古建築は、不揃いであることや粗さを許容し、剥き出しの素地のままでも美しく深い味わいをもった骨格や表情を今に見せる。均質にする技術、綺麗に磨く技術を追い求めるあまり見失われていく構造美や素材美を、私は現代の手仕事によって取り戻していきたいと考えている。それは未完であることを出発とし「手の痕跡」によって見出される本当の豊かさなのではないだろうか。力強い骨格の中に緊張感と透明感が現れ、その中を時が巡り、ゆっくりと風化しながら、深みを帯びる住まい。それは都市に再解読された民家の在り様であり、住まいの原点となるであろう。

すべては無に始まり有に還る。何も無いところから場の脈絡を紡ぎ出し、たくさんの人の手の痕跡によってカタチを有し、生き続ける。そんな建築の在り様を追い求め続けている。

tension back into the vagueness of everyday life. However, this all boils down to the pursuit of an architecture of incompletion. The composition of protean ma and the ceaseless circulation inherent in *kaiyusei* opens a space through which the closed city can breathe. Likewise with the structure and materials that embody these things. Through their close linkages to the materials and techniques of a certain time and place, old buildings accept the unrefined and the raw, revealing to us today the beauty and deep appeal of the structure and expression of architecture in its naked state. Through my manual labours, I have attempting to retrieve the beauty of structure and material – long overlooked in the pursuit of techniques of homogenisation and cosmetic appeal. Such beauty should be understood as deriving from incompletion, and that real richness is to be found in the "traces of the hand" A dwelling in which a powerful frame reveals tension and transparency, and slowly weathers and gathers depth as time passes. This is the character of the minka re-interpreted for the city, and the very origin of dwelling.

All that is begins from nothing and emerges into being. The lineaments of place are spun out from a realm of nothingness, and gather form and are given continued existence from the traces of many hands. That is the nature of the architecture I perpetually pursue.

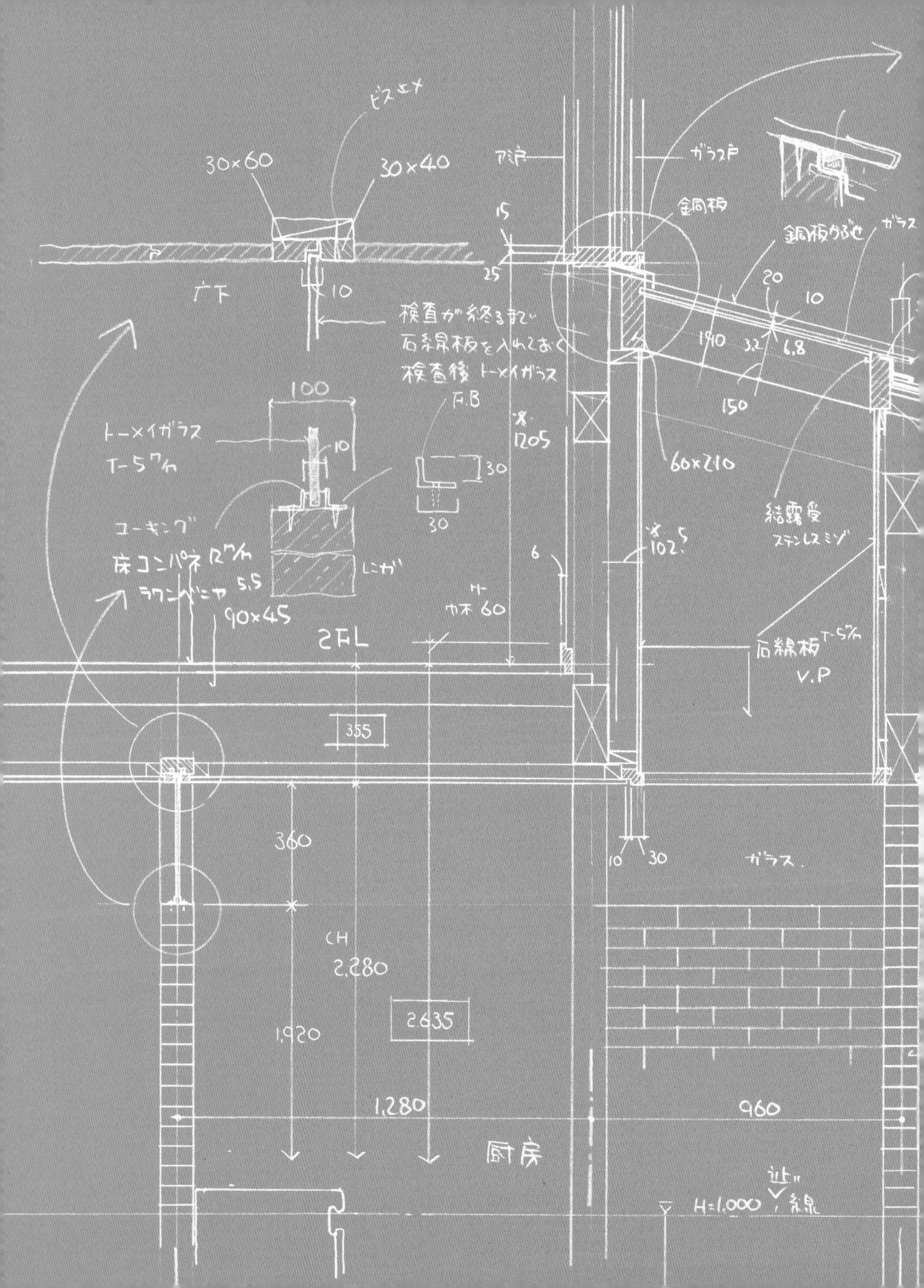
ビス止メ
30×60
30×40
10
検査が終るまで
石綿板を入れておく
検査後 トーメイガラス
100
トーメイガラス
T-5ミリ
10
FB
30
30
コーキング
床コンパネ 12ミリ
ラワンベニヤ 5.5
レンガ
90×45
2FL
アミ戸
ガラス戸
15
25
銅板
銅板かぶせ
ガラス
20
10
140
3.2
6.8
150
1205
60×210
102.5
6
結露受
ステンレスミゾ
石綿板 T-5ミリ
V.P
355
360
10
30
ガラス
CH
2,280
2,635
1,920
1,280
960
厨房
H=1,000

Works

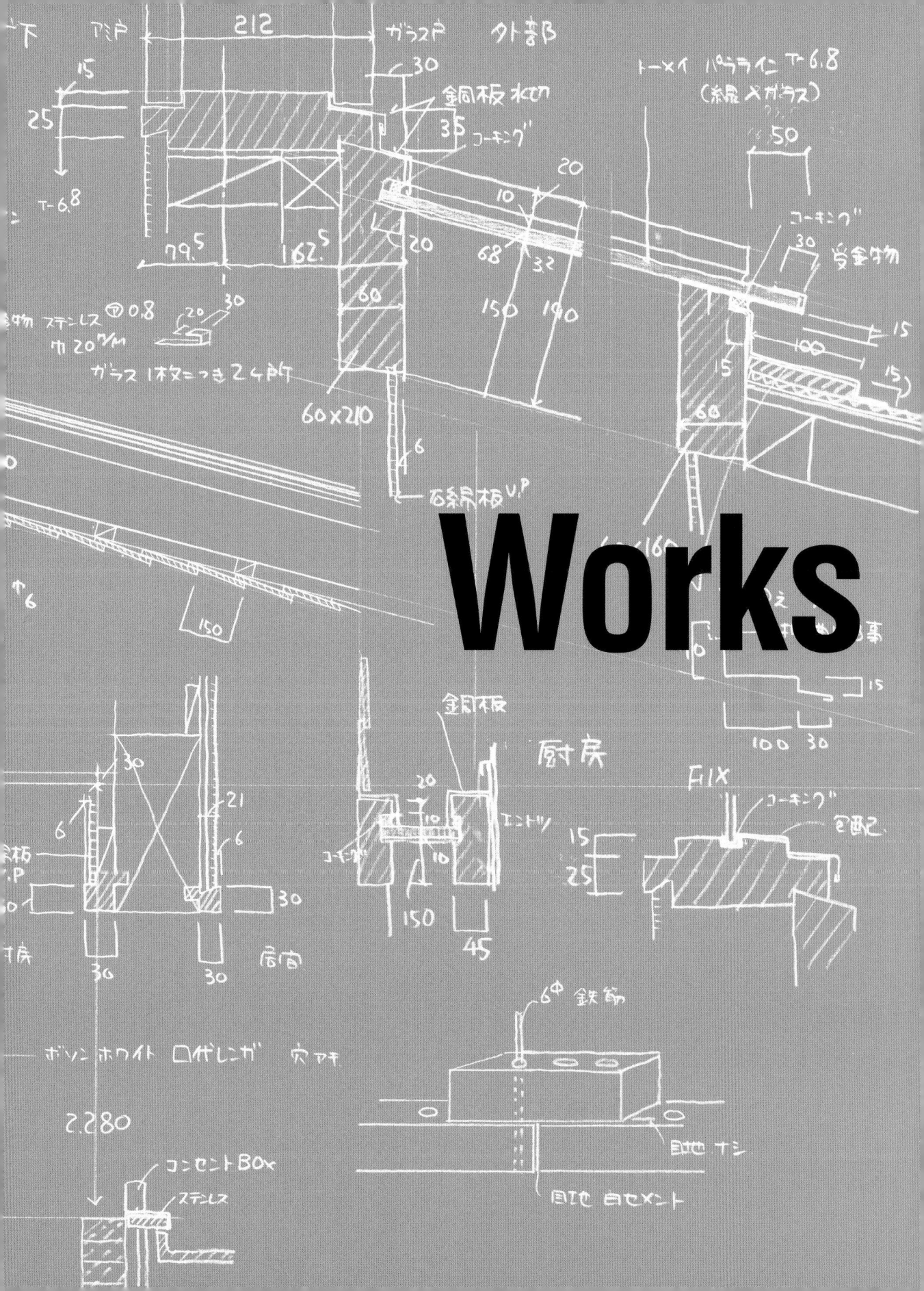

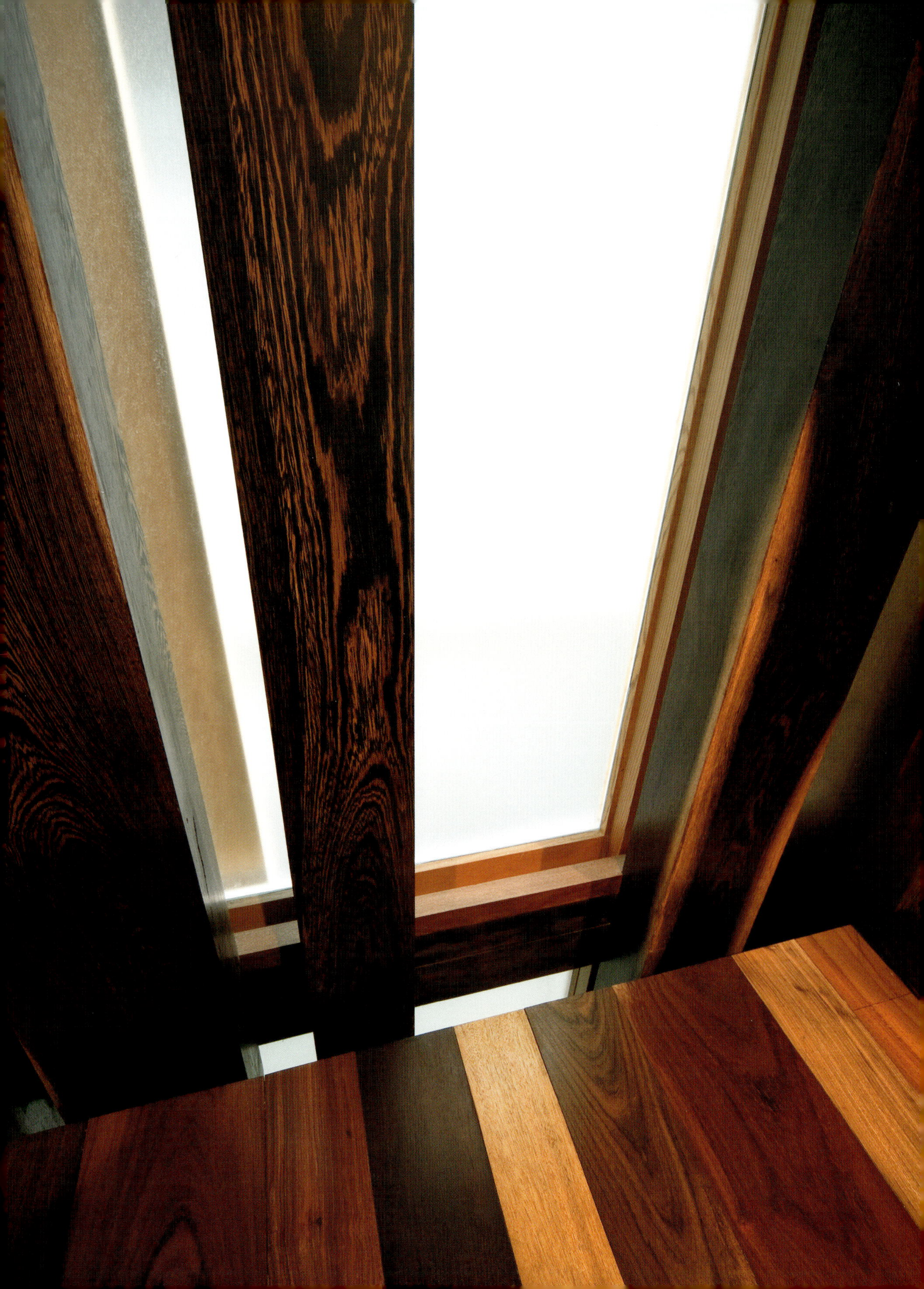

離発着する飛行機、空を跨ぐ高速道路を望む、緩やかな下り坂の終着点。T字路の突き当たりに「101番目の家」が建つ。新旧の建物が渾然一体となる都市の中に、車がやっとすれ違うほどの路地空間が現れ、背丈の高さに積まれた石垣がカーブを描き、視線の先へ消えていく。間口7m奥行き15m、東西に細長い敷地は前面道路より1層分沈み込み、家々のひしめき合う奥の水路までつながる。表と裏、場の様相のコントラストがこの建築の建ち方を決定付ける。

　100㎡の狭小敷地にヴォリュームと余白が1対1の関係を結ぶ。風が西から東へ通り抜け、太陽が東から西へ最も長い弧を描く敷地形状を活かし、あえて北側に中庭を挿入する。スケールを抑え込まれた北の庭にバウンドする光が、南の部屋へ安定した光を届けている。余白として挿入された中庭は地階から天空まで突き抜け、光や雨が地下深くまで降り注ぐ。

　内と外の1対1のせめぎ合いは間口を南北に2分割する1本の軸線に込められる。1階は南側間口3,200mmの内部空間と北側間口2,400mmの外部空間に分割され、2階ではその寸法が中間領域を介し反転する。点在する内室とそれをつなぐ外室で構成された平面は「ズレ」と「スキマ」によって雁行し、複雑な廻遊式住居を形成する。

　構造を露出させ、内外を仕切る壁を設けず、骨格以外のすべてを開放することで、都市にそそり建つ力強いボックスの中に透明感を取り戻す。地下1階・地上2.5階のボックスを広葉樹の大断面木造とコンクリートの混構造で構成し、入れ子状に組み込むことで、木とコンクリートが1対1の関係で絡み合う、緊張感ある空間が生まれた。階高を極限まで抑え、道路から2.5層分の高さにとどめたエレヴェーションは、坂の上から望む彼方の景色を町に残す。そして水路へ続く地面から五角形にせり上がるコンクリートボックスを突き刺し、場と建築を結び付ける。

　力強い骨格に裏付けられた重層する廻遊式住居は、狭小敷地に内外が玉手箱のように展開し、あらゆるものの1対1の関係の中に緊張感と透明感を取り戻していく。

101番目の家
House No. 101

At the end of a sloping road near a T-junction with a view of airplanes taking off and landing, stands House No. 101. The long narrow lot with a frontage of seven meters and a depth of 15 meters is sunken one story beneath the frontal road and continues toward a waterway in the rear. The strong contrasts of the lot determined the form of the residence.

　The 100-metersquare of land has a one-to-one ratio between volume and empty space. To make the most of the lot, with wind blowing from west to east, and the sun arcing from east to west, the courtyard was inserted on the north side. The light, ricocheting into the north garden, enters the southern rooms in a more stable form. The courtyard, functioning as "empty space," shoots up from the ground floor into the open sky, and light and rain sink deep into the ground.

　This one-to-one clash between interior and exterior is interrupted by an axis line that splits the frontage in half from north to south. The first floor is divided into an inner 3,200-millimeter frontage on the south side and an outer 2,400-millimeter one on the north side, while on the second floor, these dimensions are reversed. The plane, structured around a scattering of inner rooms connected by outer rooms, has an echelon form created through "gaps," and the residence has a complex "stroll style."

　With an exposed structure and no walls to divide the interior and exterior, everything is open save for the framework, creating a sense of transparency in this box that towers over the city. The complex structure of large-sectional wood from broad-leaved trees and concrete in the 2.5 above-ground floors and one below-ground floor engenders a sense of tension due to the one-to-one relationship between the wood and concrete, combined in a nested form. By controlling the height of each floor, the elevation sustains the distant scenery ; and by piercing the concrete box that gradually rises in a pentagonal shape, the structure is linked to the site.

　This "stroll-style" residence, on a narrow lot in which the interior and exterior have been carefully developed, recovers a sense of tension and transparency through the one-to-one relationships it encompasses.

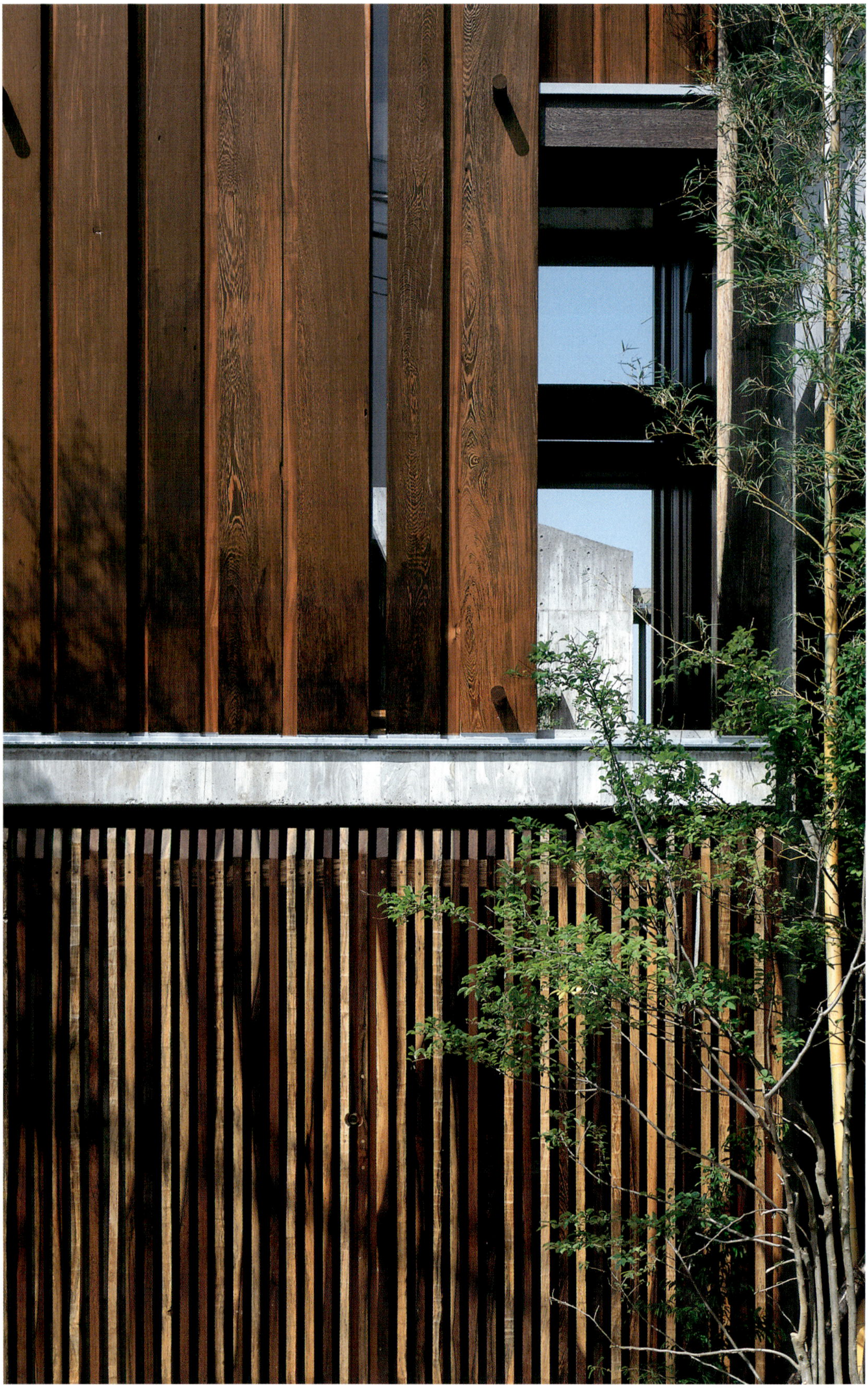

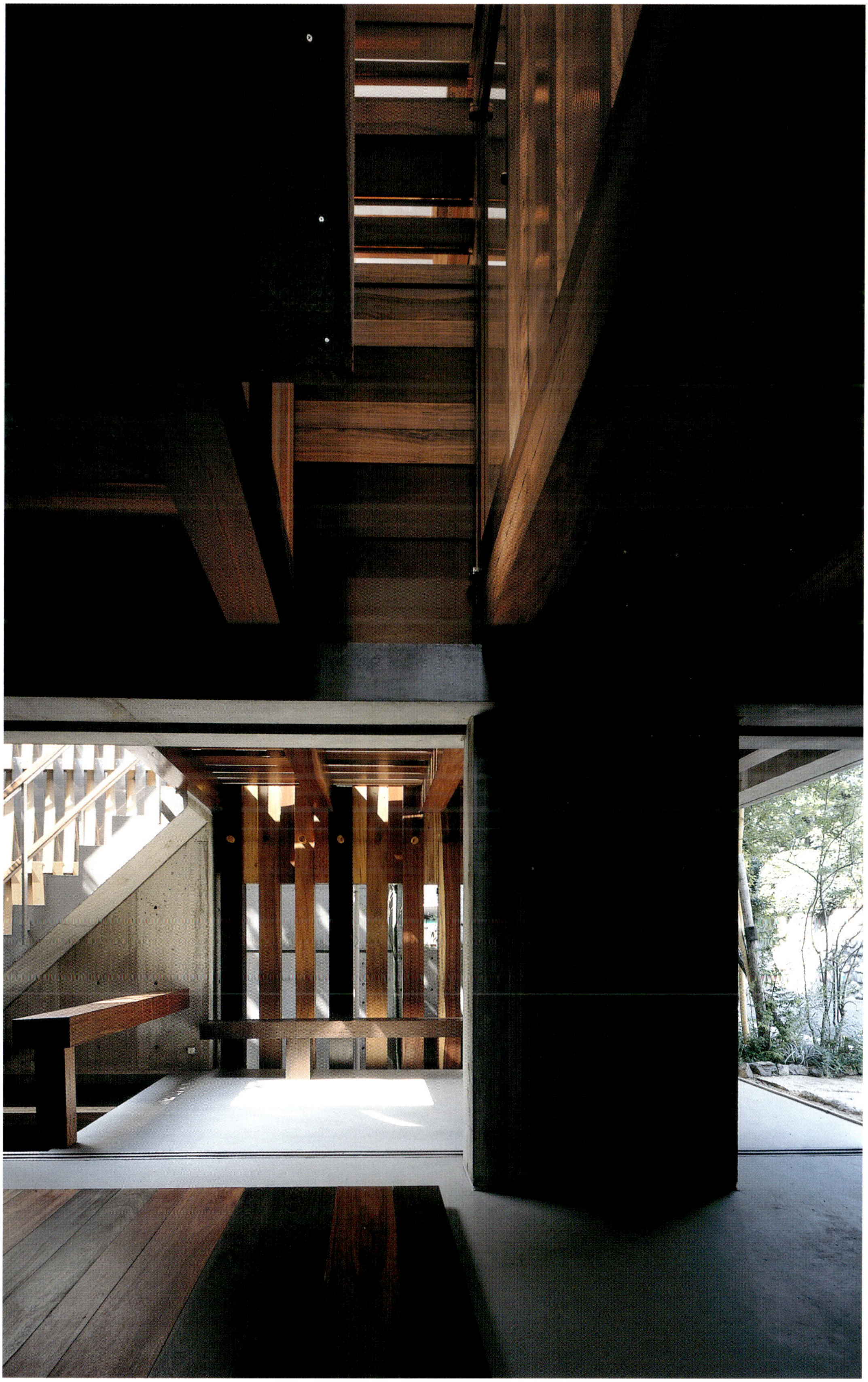

左：天地3層分に貫くヴォイドは中庭となり、周囲を吹きさらしの外部廻廊が巡り、点在する内室をつなぎ留める。
右：地階から通し柱のスキマに上層からの列柱を抱き合わせることで、3層分の木軸架構を実現した。抱き合わせ部分は外側にRCの梁が控え、列柱の外側を走る建具だけが内外を仕切る。

Left: The void, which penetrates to the third story, functions as the courtyard, and the exterior corridor, exposed to the periphery, surrounds and connects the scattered inner rooms.
Right: By bundling the colonnades on the upper story with the gaps between the colonnades that rise up from the basement, a three-story wooden-shaft frame is realized. The exterior of the bundled section is restrained by reinforced concrete beams and only the fittings on the outside of the colonnades divide the interior and exterior.

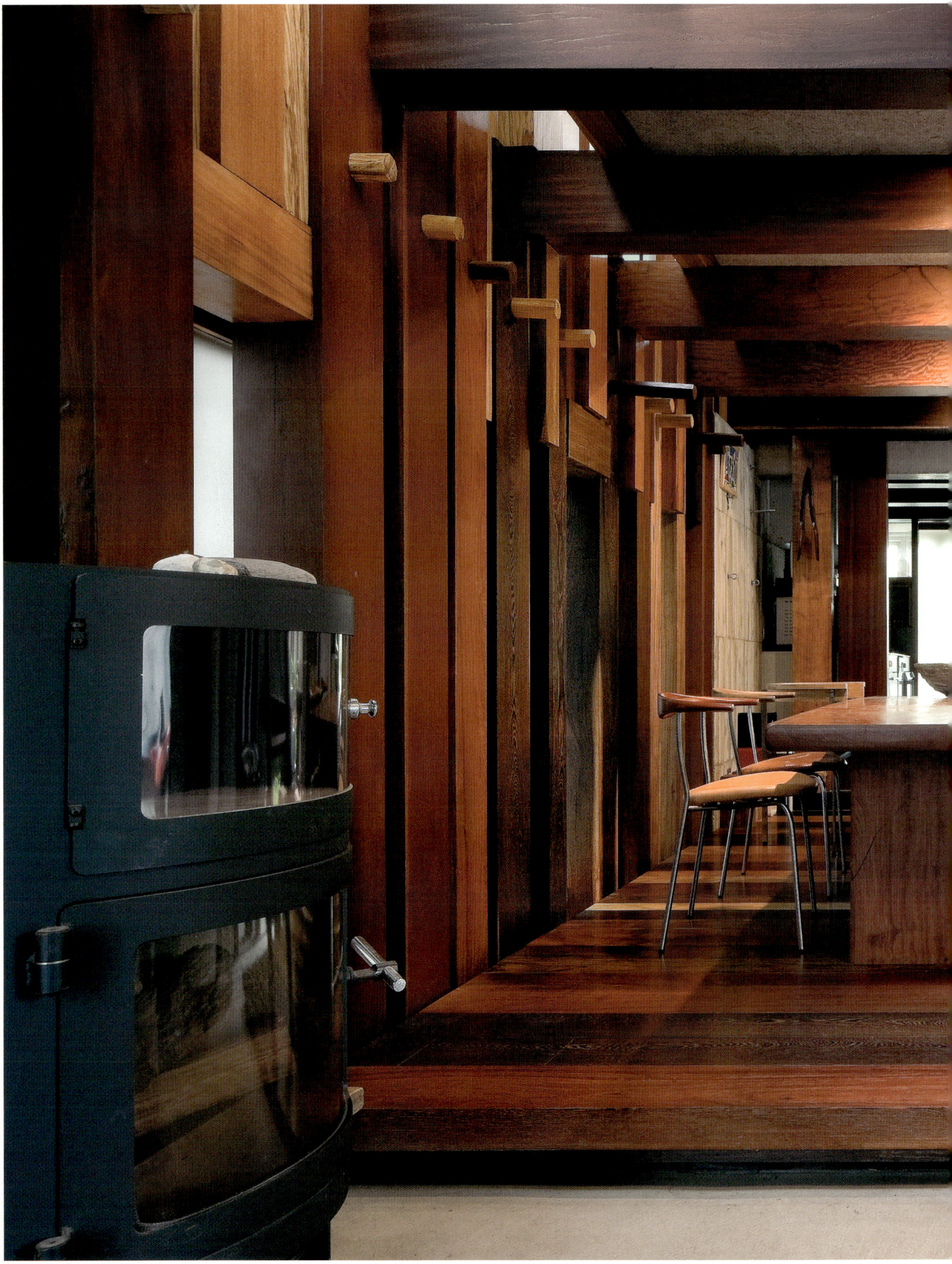

035 | House No. 101

前頁：内2から厨房を見通す／土間と床はわずか60mmの段差で結界をつくる。幅3,200mm、梁下1,980mmの極限まで抑え込まれたスケールが、東西の抜けに奥行きを見せる。

上：内2南を見る／RCの壁柱、広葉樹の列柱、建具の構成に混構造のズレを見る。

下：北に庭をもつ分棟型平面の中に内室を点在させ外室でつなぐ。内と外は1：1の関係をもち極限の寸法でせめぎ合い、内外入り乱れた廻遊式住居を呈する。

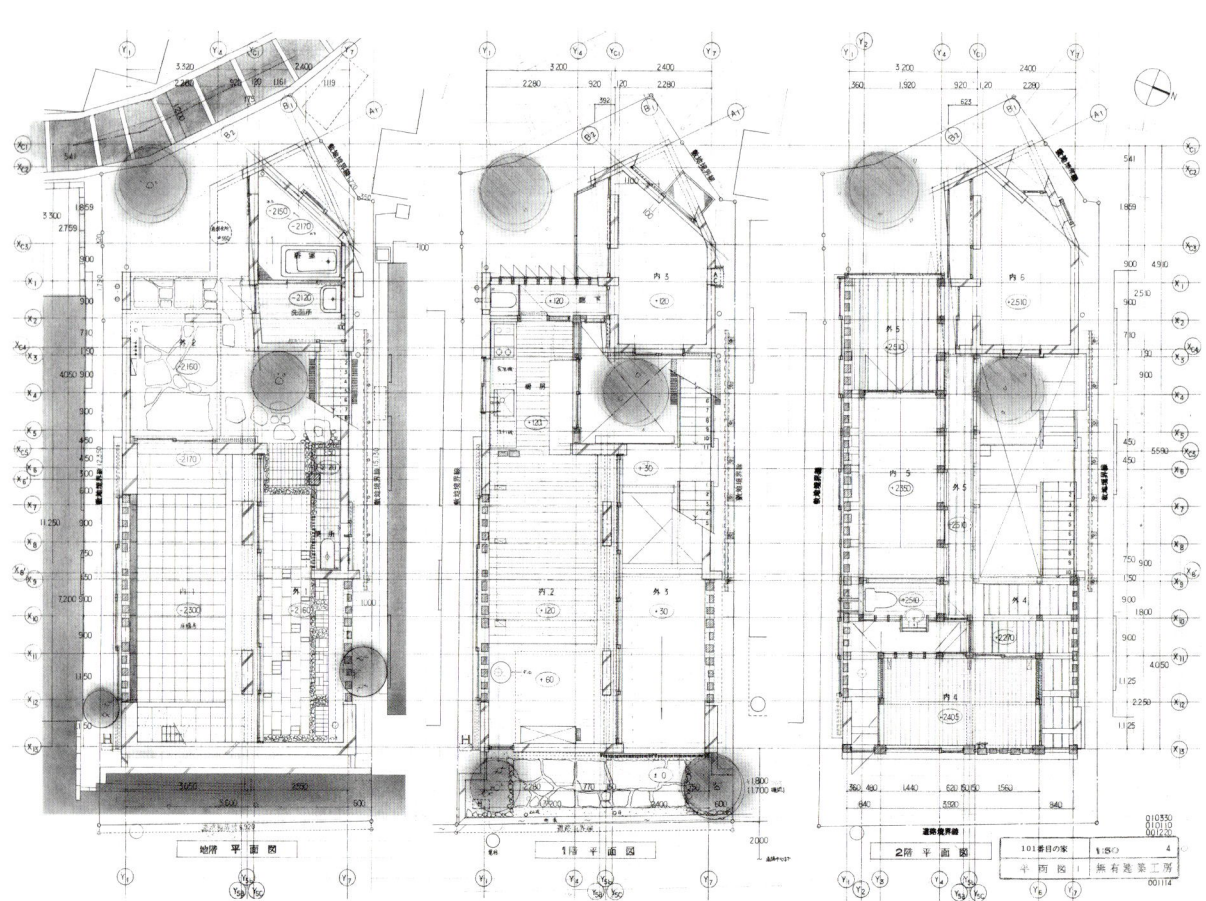

各階平面図・屋根伏図　Floor and roof plans

pp. 34-35: View through the kitchen from Interior 2— The unfloored area and the floor are divided by a mere 60mm difference in level. The scale, tightly limited to a width of 3,200mm and 1,980mm below the beams, creates a sense of depth in the east-west gap.

Above: South Interior 2— View of the gaps in the mixed structure of the reinforced-concrete wall columns, wooden colonnades made from broad-leaved trees, and fittings.

Below: In the *buntogata* plane, with a garden on its north side, the scattered inner rooms are connected by the outer rooms. With a one-to-one ratio, the maximum dimensions of the interior oppose those of the exterior to create a complex, "stroll-style" residence.

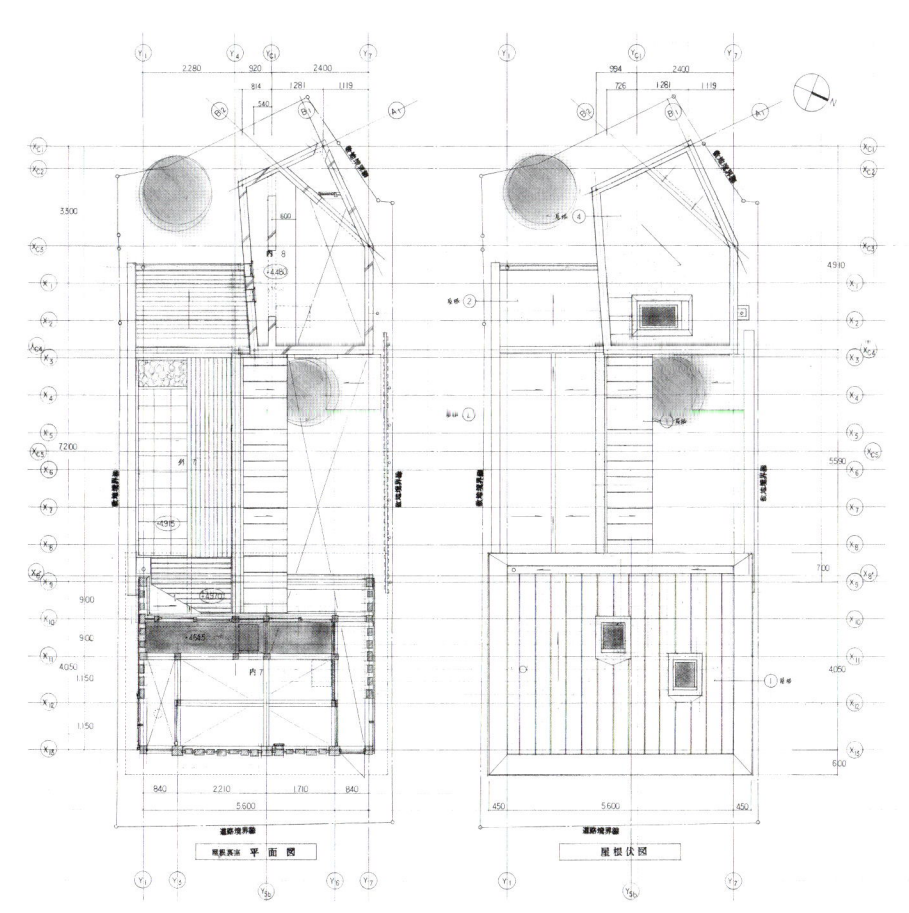

House No. 101

左：内4と内5は緊密なヴォイドによって間合いをもつ。ここからはしごで内2と連絡する。
右：2枚のRC壁を介し内2と外3が対峙する。構造が剥き出しになり、構造壁以外の壁をもたず、建具だけで内外が仕切られ、力強さの中に透明性が現れる。

Left: A distance is maintained through the tight void between Interior 4 and Interior 5; and a ladder connects this space with Interior 2.
Right: Mediated by two reinforced walls, Interior 2 and Interior 3 stand in opposition to each other. The structure is exposed and without any walls, except the structural wall, the interior and exterior are divided only by the fittings, giving rise to a sense of transparency in the strong inner space.

House No. 101

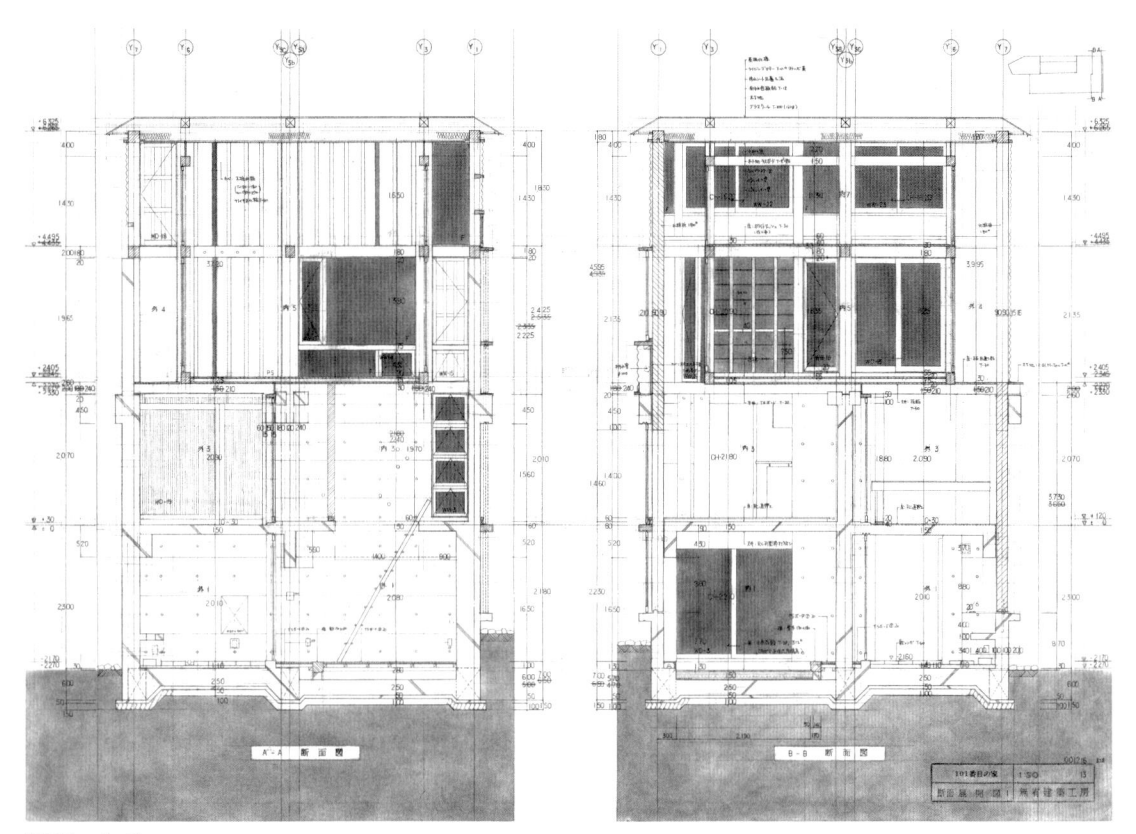

断面図　　Section

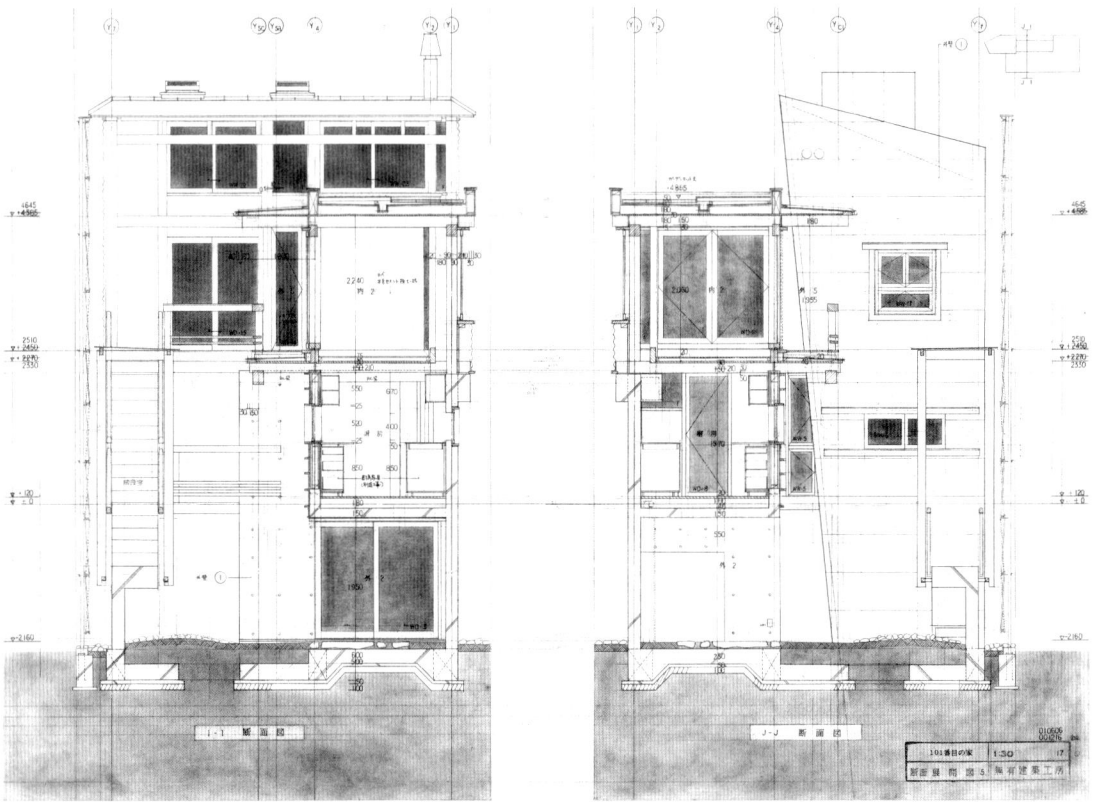

断面図　　Section

040

041 | House No. 101

上：北側の庭に射し込む光を南の室へバウンドさせる反射塀。淡く鈍い光を放つ半艶仕上のステンレス板と、光を吸い込み陰翳をつくる粗肌の米杉板を編み込む。
下：地階から階段を見上げると、外4を介して天空まで視線が抜ける。

Above: Preceding page— A reflecting wall refracts the light that pours into the garden on the north side into the room on the south side. The space is a mixture of faint, thick sheets of light given off by half-gloss, stainless-steel panels and light-absorbing shadows created by the rough surface of red-cedar panels.
Below: Looking up at the stairs from the basement, the line of sight passes through Exterior 4 to the sky.

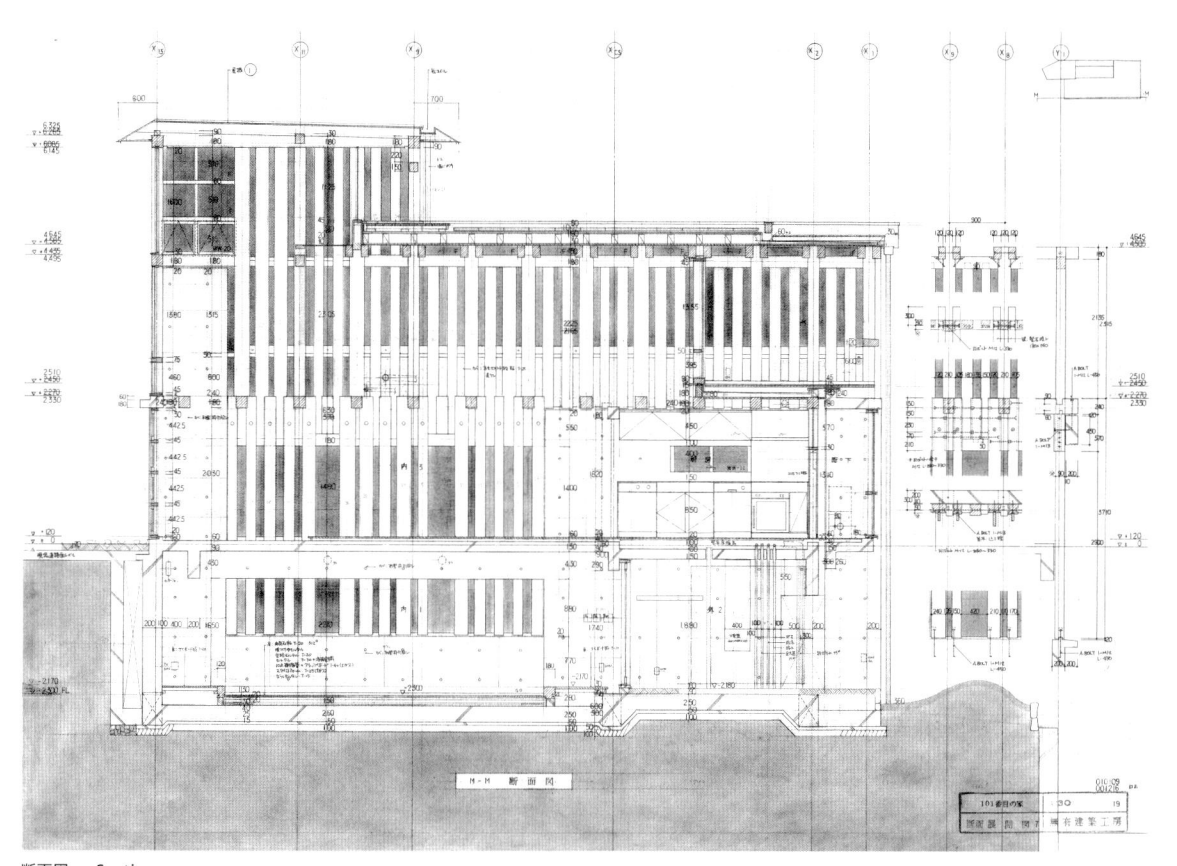

断面図　　Section

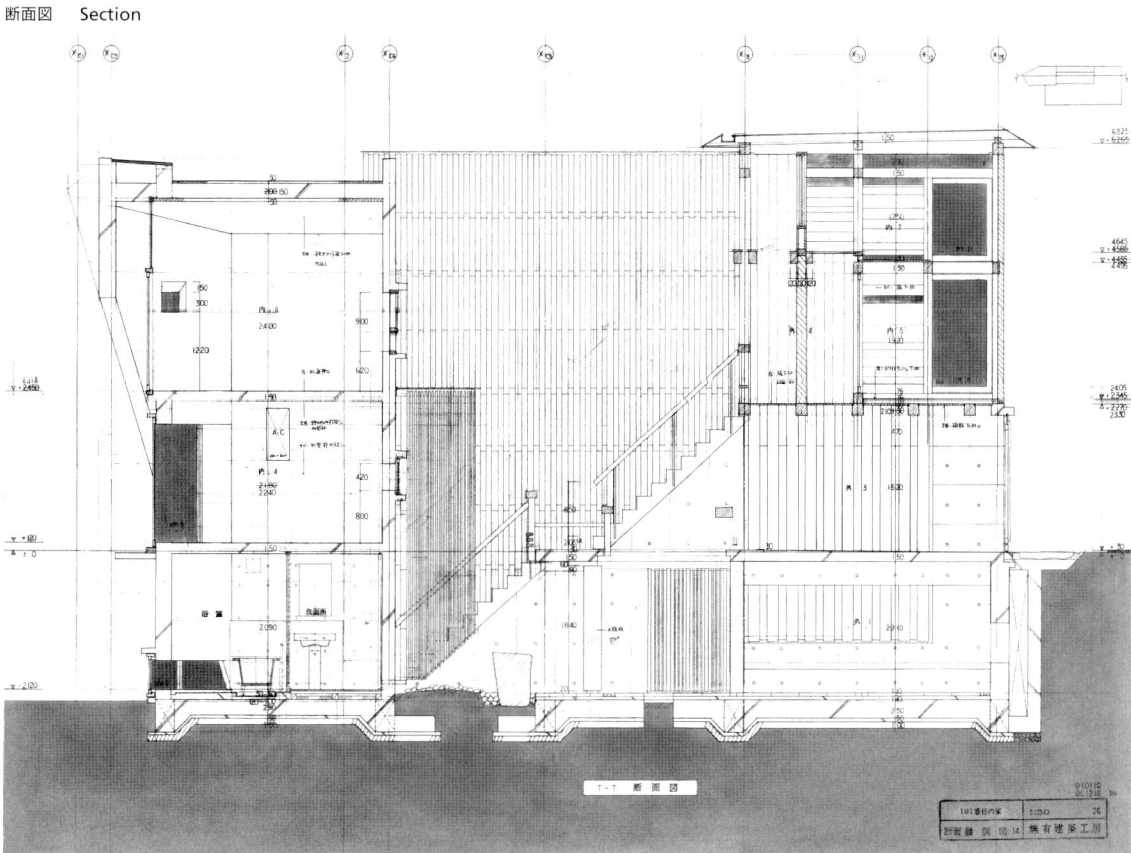

断面図　　Section

043 | House No. 101

右：平面のズレにより外廻廊が雁行し立体的な廻遊動線が視線を交錯させる。正面に捉えるのは水路際の地面より3層分せり上がる五角形のRCボックス。

044

By means of a gap in the plane, the exterior corridor is staggered and a three-dimensional, "strolling" flow line creates a complex line of sight. A pentagonal, reinforced-concrete box rises up three stories from the basement next to the waterway to control the facade.

内3より中庭を介して外4を見通す・見返す／内室をつなぐ外室に、視線と風が抜ける。
ボックス状の外観とは対照的に、内部は立体的な架構が住空間を開放する。

Looking back at Exterior 4 through the courtyard from Interior 3: The line of sight and wind pass through the exterior room that links the inner rooms. In contrast to the box-shaped exterior view, a three-dimensional frame imbues the living space with a sense of openness.

House No. 101

048

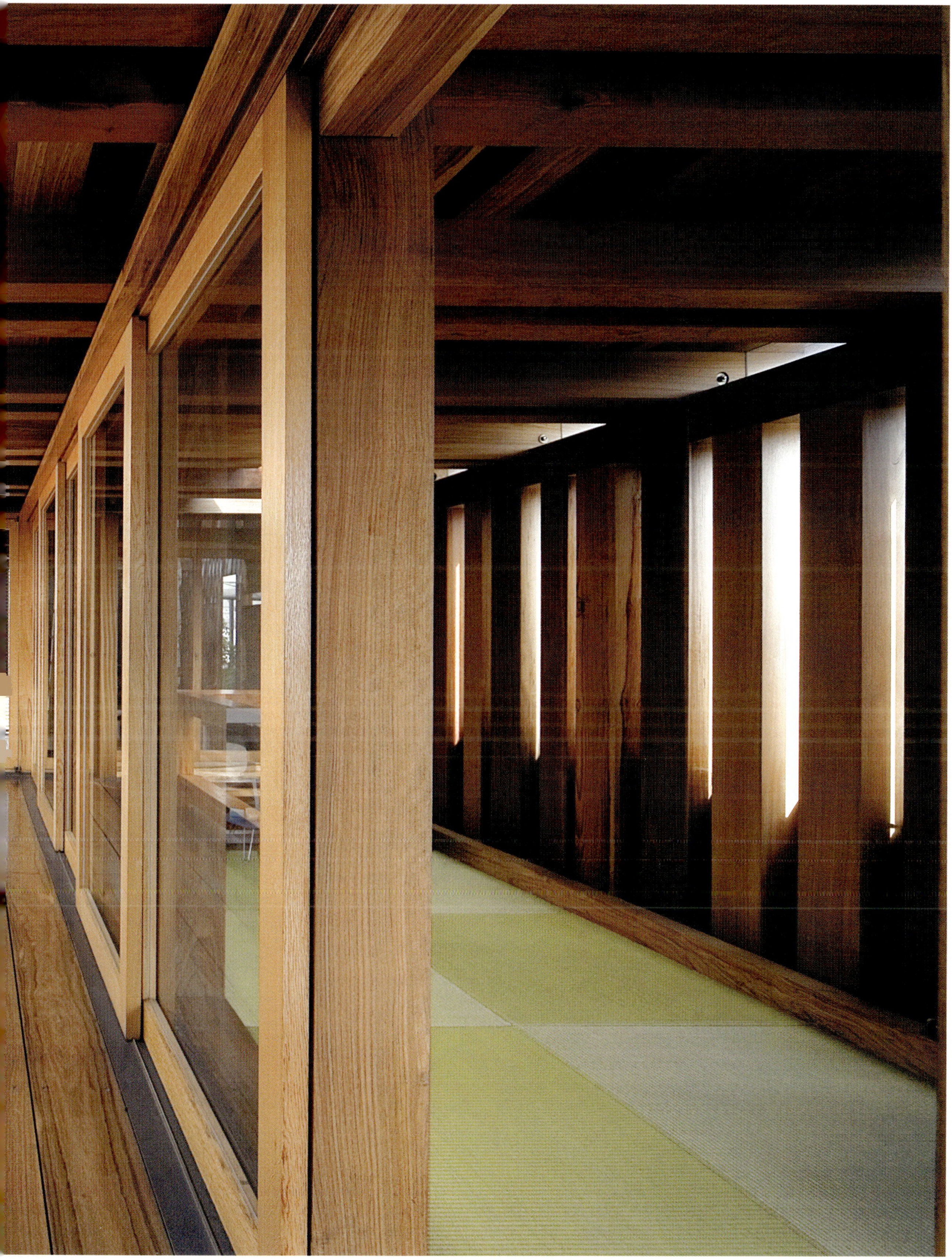

48-49頁：外5は内5と中庭の中間領域となる。内5の床を落とし込み、逆スラブとすることで、床梁が外5との結界を結ぶ敷台となる。建具はその外側を動く。

下：外観／RCの基壇に木造のボックスが載り、1:1.5の可分数のプロポーションをもつ。樹種の異なる不揃いな断面寸法をもつ広葉樹の列柱壁は、エレヴェーションに深い陰翳を見せる。

pp. 48-49: Exterior 5 serves as an intermediary space between Interior 5 and the courtyard. By sinking the floor of Interior 5 and reversing the slab, the floor beams form a raised entrance barrier between Exterior 5 and the outside world. The fittings move along the exterior.

Below: Exterior view— The wooden box, standing on a reinforced-concrete platform, has a fractional proportion of 1:1.5. The wall colonnades, made of a variety of broad-leaved trees with irregular sectional dimensions, create deep shadows on the elevation.

内5南側の列柱は1階からの通し柱で、床梁とのスキマから下階の気配が伝う。落とし込まれた床に座ると神輿のような浮遊感が漂う。外6から都市の裏側へ景色が抜ける。

Through columns rising from the first story on the south side of Interior 5 allow a glimpse of the lower floor through the gaps in the floor beams. Seated on the sunken floor, one has a sense of floating akin to a portable festival shrine. The back side of the city can be seen from Exterior 6.

上：内1より外2を見る／三和土（たたき）土間の地面にバウンドする光が薄暗い洞窟のような空間に緊張感を与える。
下：路地空間を装う外1に突如突き抜けるヴォイドから光が降り注ぐ。外1と内1はRCの骨格を介して寄り添い、外2へ外部空間が雁行する。

Above: View of Exterior 2 from Interior 1— Light ricochets off the surface of the earthen floor imbuing the cave-like space with a sense of tension.
Below: Light pours in from the void that abruptly pierces Exterior 1 along the alley. Exterior 1 and Interior 1, mediated by a reinforced-concrete frame, are nestled together and the exterior space is staggered toward Exterior 2.

1段沈み込む内1と外1はRCの壁柱と垂壁を介して対峙する。奥に見える列柱は2階床まで延び、平面・断面共に入れ子状になった混構造が見える。

Mediated by the colonnaded wall and hanging partition wall, Interior 1, sunken one step, and Exterior 1 stand across from each other. The columns visible in the rear extend to the second-story floor to create a complex structure with a nested form of planes and sections.

054

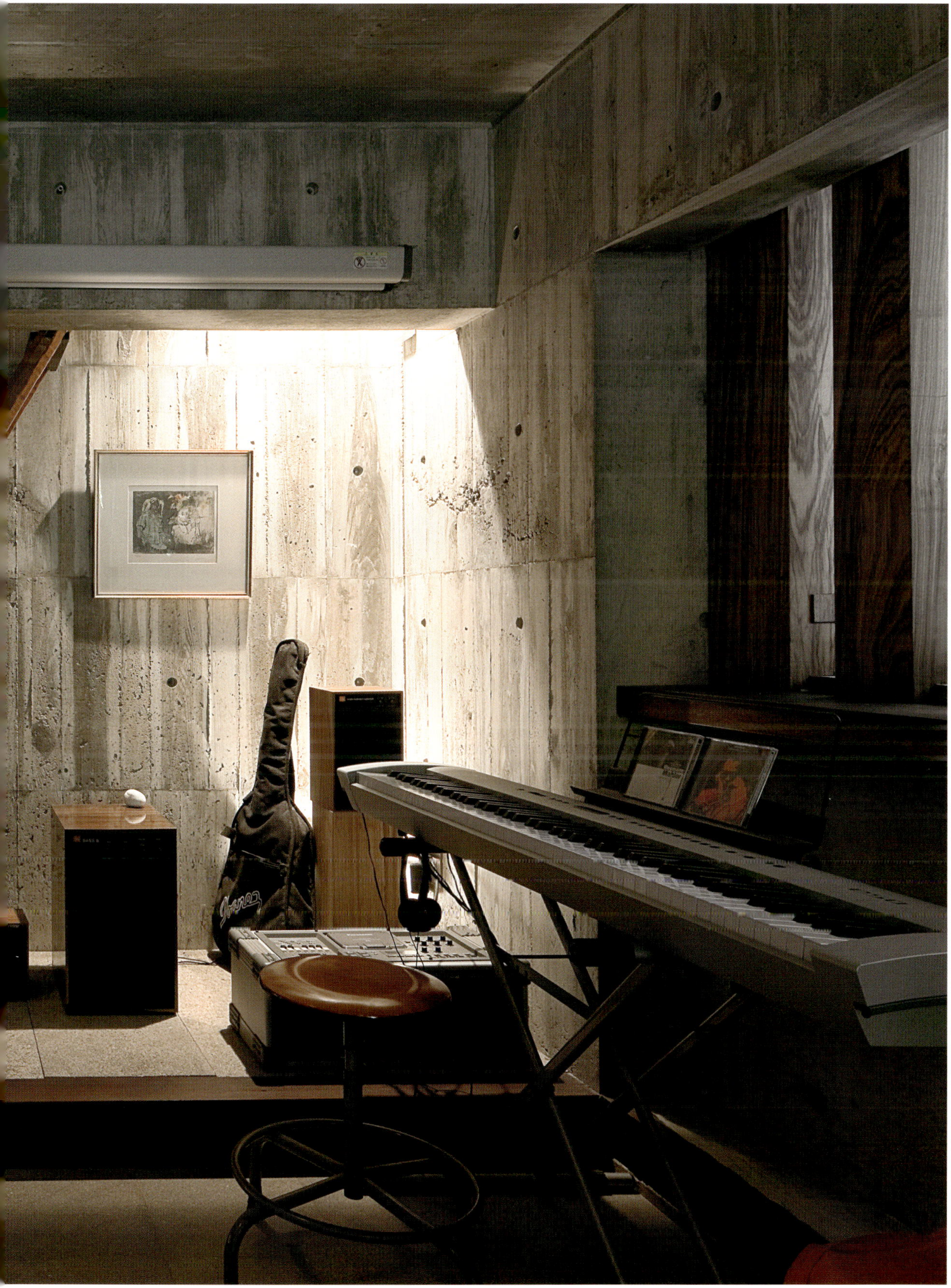

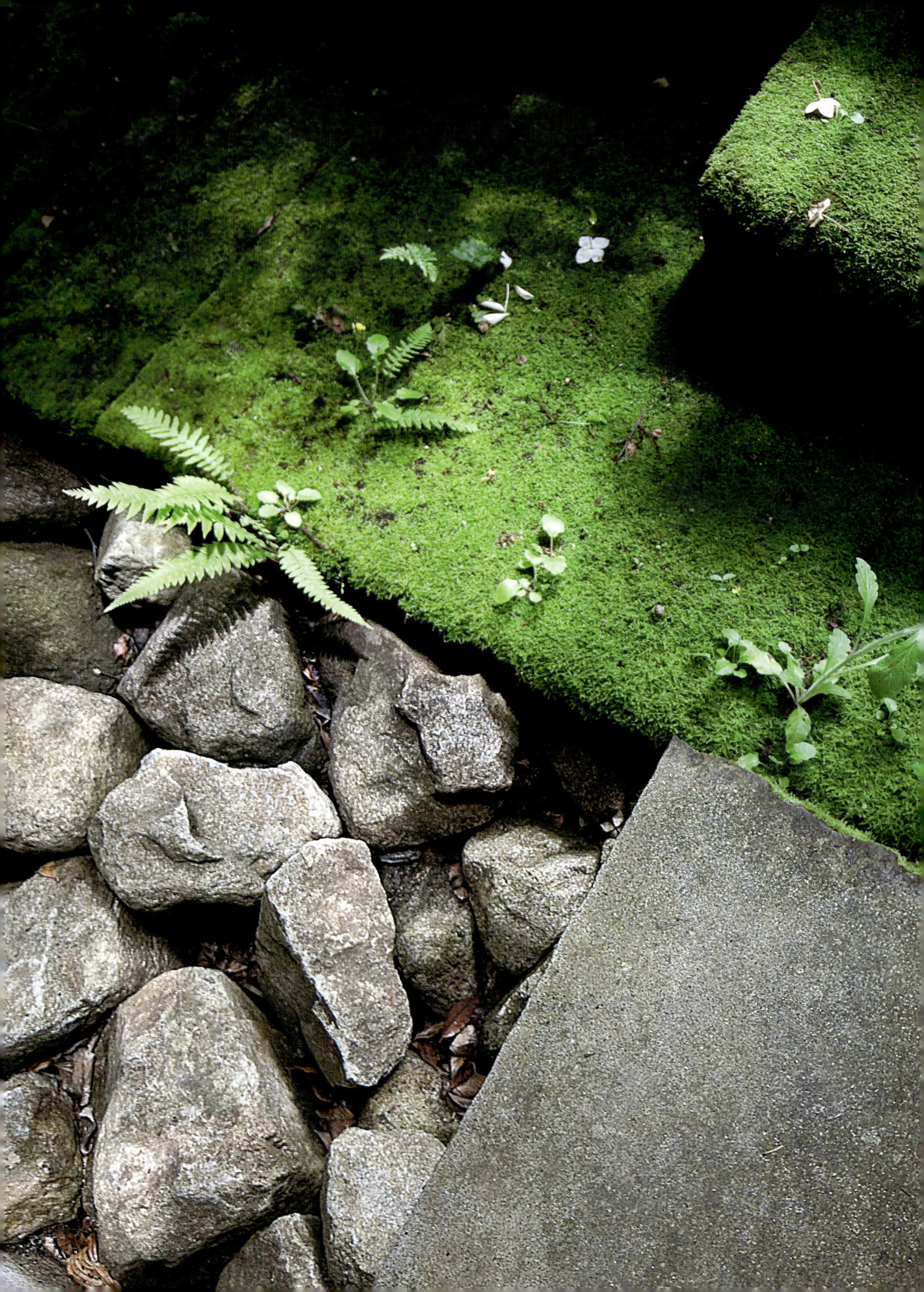

神戸市北東部の山手、御影石玉石積みの古い塀が坂道沿いに連続する閑静な住宅街の中に建つ。少しゆとりのある郊外のこの町も、家々が連なることで都市の「余白」の空間は打ち消され、豊かな内と外の関係を持続することが難しくなりつつある。日本の都市空間は区画の大小に関わらずどこも同じような状況を辿り続け、残された「余白」にさえ背を向けるように、住まいも箱の中に閉ざされていく。住まいを取り巻くあらゆるものに対して適切な「間合い」をもった「余白」をつくることは、日本の都市の住まいにとっての主題とも言える。

　この住宅も敷地をなぞるように自立する壁で一旦領域を囲い取っているが、室のスケールをできるだけ抑え込みながら、前面道路の傾斜に沿って北側へ2mのレヴェル差をもった敷地に「余白」としての中庭を埋め込み、機能的ではない路地、土間、廻廊などの空間を幾重に重ねることで、多様なシーンを展開させた「廻遊式住居」を形成する。

　南北の境界と平行に配された平面のヴォリュームと、東西の境界線に沿って建つ自立壁のわずかな角度のズレは、スキマの空間にパースペクティヴを生み出し、外界との緩衝帯となりながら、アプローチや階段といった立体的な路地空間が巡らされる。内部空間でありながら、その裂け目にもたらされる光の操作によって、さながら外部空間を彷彿とさせる。道路から地階へと落とし込まれた中庭の立体的なデッキは、都市空間の舞台装置に見立てられ、そこへ降り注ぐ光や雨が、重層する空間に共鳴することで、心地良さと共に緊張感をもたらす。

　内部空間は中庭を囲い取るようにコの字型に配し、沈み込んだ中庭に外階段や廻廊を絡ませ、内と外の狭間に幾重にも動線を重ね合わせている。これらの間にわずかな床のレヴェル差をつくり込み、視線の高さや見え隠れを複雑に変化させ、内と外のしつらえを曖昧にすることで日常生活の中に豊かな空間体験を呼び覚ます。コートハウスを原型としながら展開していく「廻遊式住居」は都市の中で身を委ねることができるひとつの住形式となるであろう。

住吉山手の家
Sumiyoshi Yamate House

A wall made of stone stands along this slope in the hills of Kobe. In this area, rows of houses negate the "empty space" of the city, making it increasingly difficult to maintain a relationship between interior and exterior. Every urban area in Japan faces similar problems and there seems to be no choice but to enclose a dwelling inside a box. Creating an "empty space" with a sufficient amount of "distance" in regard to everything that surrounds a house is now the main theme of urban dwelling.

　This residence is also enclosed by a free-standing wall that traces the outline of the lot, but while controlling the scale of the rooms and embedding a courtyard as an "empty space" on the lot, with a two-meter level difference following the incline of the frontal road to the north, this "stroll-style residence" was created with a diverse range of scenes by adding layers to functionless spaces such as alleys and corridors.

　The volume of the plane, parallel to the north-south boundary, and the subtle disparity of the angle of the free-standing wall on the east-west boundary line emphasize the perspective of the gap in the space, creating a buffer with the outside world and surrounding the three-dimensional alley space which encompasses the approach and stairs. Though an interior space, by manipulating the light that is allowed in through the gap, it bears a close resemblance to an exterior space. The three-dimensional deck in the courtyard, which descends from the road to the basement, resembles a stage set, and the light and rain create both a sense of comfort and tension in the multilayered space.

　The internal space is designed to enclose the courtyard in a U-shape, and an external staircase and corridor are connected to the courtyard, superimposing multiple flow lines in the narrow space between the interior and exterior. This creates another slight difference in the level of the floor, and varies the height of the line of sight and the degree of visibility, engendering a rich spatial experience by obscuring the interior and exterior. This "stroll-style residence," though based on the archetype of the courtyard house, allows the residents to abandon themselves to the city.

058

Sumiyoshi Yamate House

060

北側の自立壁と建物のヴォリュームのスキマに生まれた由良石敷きの路地空間。自立壁の内側にズレた垂壁がトップライトからの光を絞り込み、天井高3.7mの土間空間に陰影をもたらす。突き当たりの開口部から足元にバウンドする光が薄闇の中にぼんやりと浮かぶ。

The Yura-stone-lined alley space produced by the gap between the free-standing wall on the north side and the volume of the building: Inside the free-standing wall, the staggered hanging partition wall refines the light that pours in through the skylight and creates shadows in the earthen-floor space, with a ceiling height of 3.7 meters. The light that ricochets from the opening at the other end to the floor rises hazily in the dim space.

Sumiyoshi Yamate House

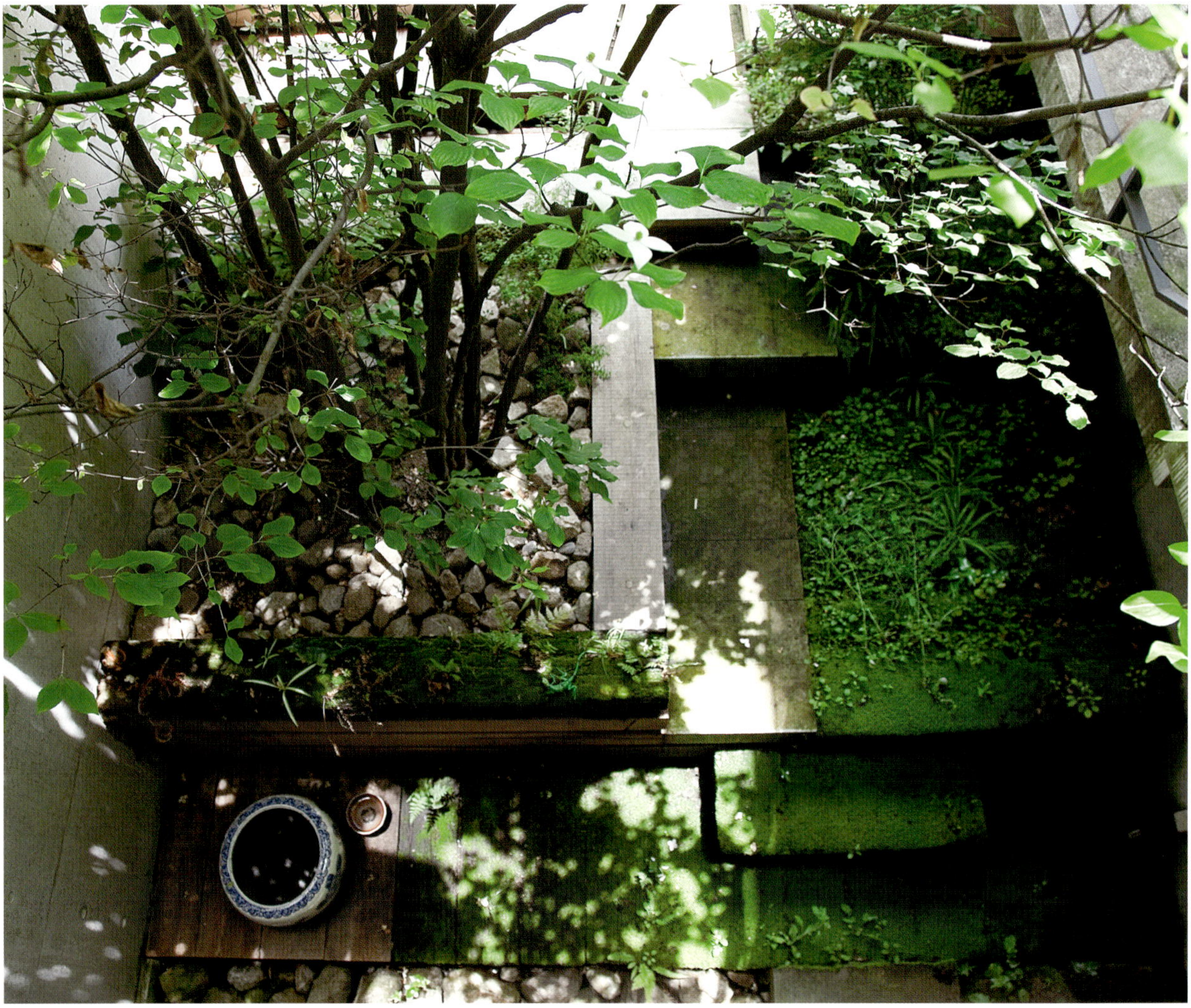

道路より1層分沈み込んだ中庭から地階土間／大小のデッキを
都市の舞台装置に見立て、立体的な中庭をつくる。

The earthen floor on the ground level as seen from
the courtyard, sunken one story below the road.
The small and large decks stand out as urban stage
sets, creating a three-dimensional courtyard.

Sumiyoshi Yamate House

064

065 | Sumiyoshi Yamate House

地階の土間へ仕上げを連続させ、建具を壁の内側に引き込むことで、中間領域が生まれ、内と外が曖昧となる。土間と和室のレヴェル差を170mmとすることで、小空間の和室に座り込んだ時の地面との視線の関係をつくり出す。

Drawing the fittings toward the inside of the wall and linking them to the finishing of the earthen floor in the basement creates an intermediary space and obscures the distinction between the interior and exterior. By including a 170-mm level difference between the earthen floor and the Japanese-style room, a link is forged between the ground level and one's line of sight when seated in the small space.

左：1階食堂南側を見る／地階から伸びる中庭の樹木は季節ごとに色づき、重層する空間の天地を結ぶ。
右：1階内室／アプローチから同じレヴェルの由良石敷きの土間空間は内外が曖昧となって、訪れる者を迎え入れる玄関であると同時に、暖炉がしつらえられ、食堂より沈み込んだ家族の居場所となる。

Left: View of south side of the first-floor dining area: The trees in the courtyard that extends from the basement change color with the seasons and form a connection to the sky and earth in the multilayered space.
Right: Inner room on the first floor—
With the same level as the approach, the earthen floor, lined with Yura stone, blurs interior and exterior, and while serving as an entranceway for visitors, acts as the family's living space, sunken below the dining area and equipped with a hearth.

Sumiyoshi Yamate House

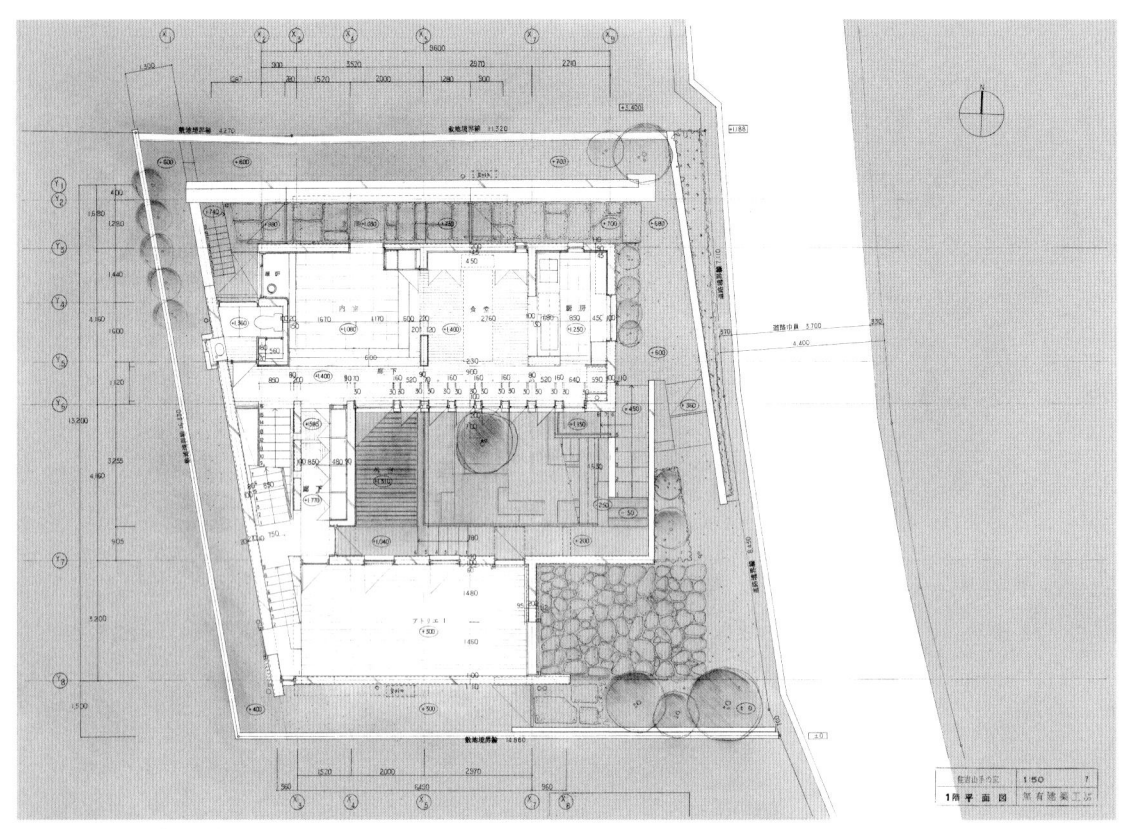

1階平面図　　First-floor plan

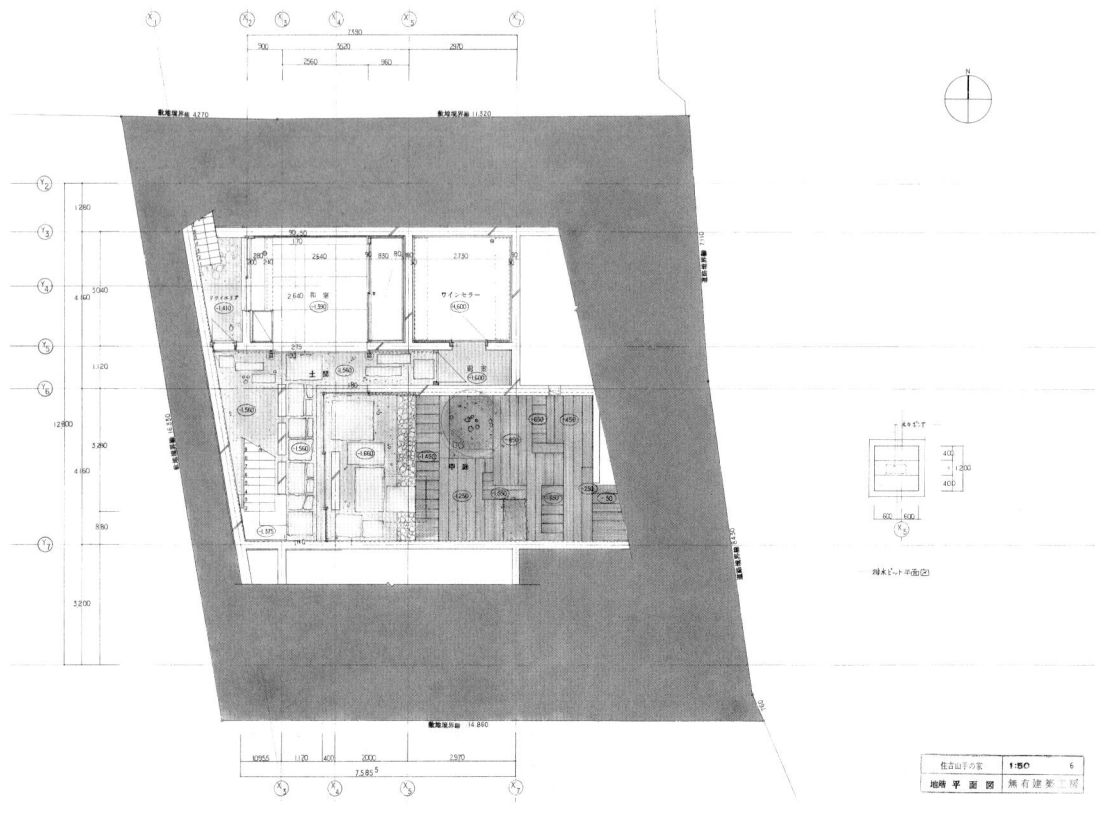

地階平面図　　Basement plan

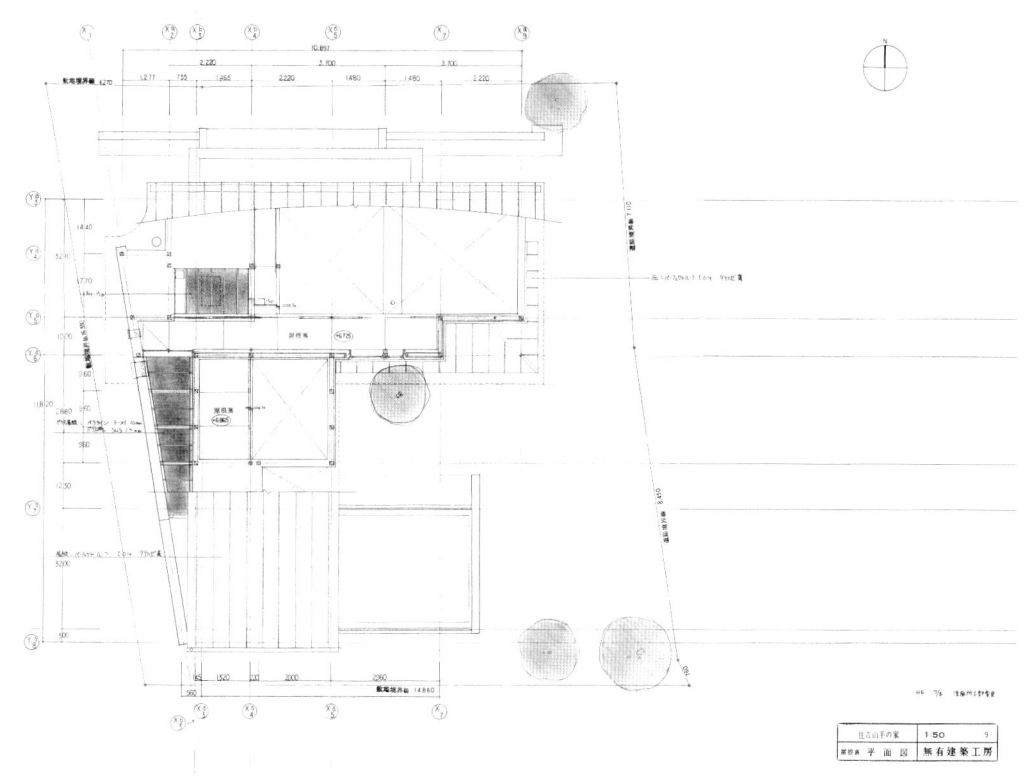

R階平面図　　Roof-floor plan

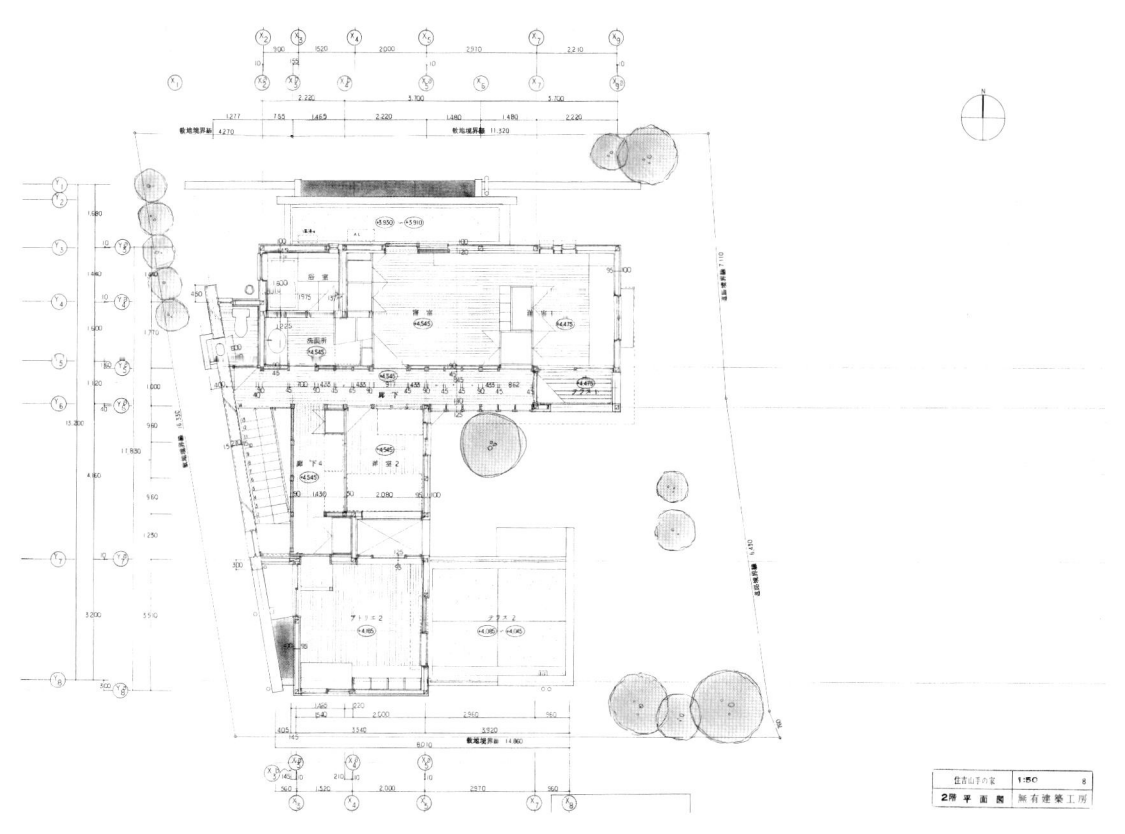

2階平面図　　Second-floor plan

071 | Sumiyoshi Yamate House

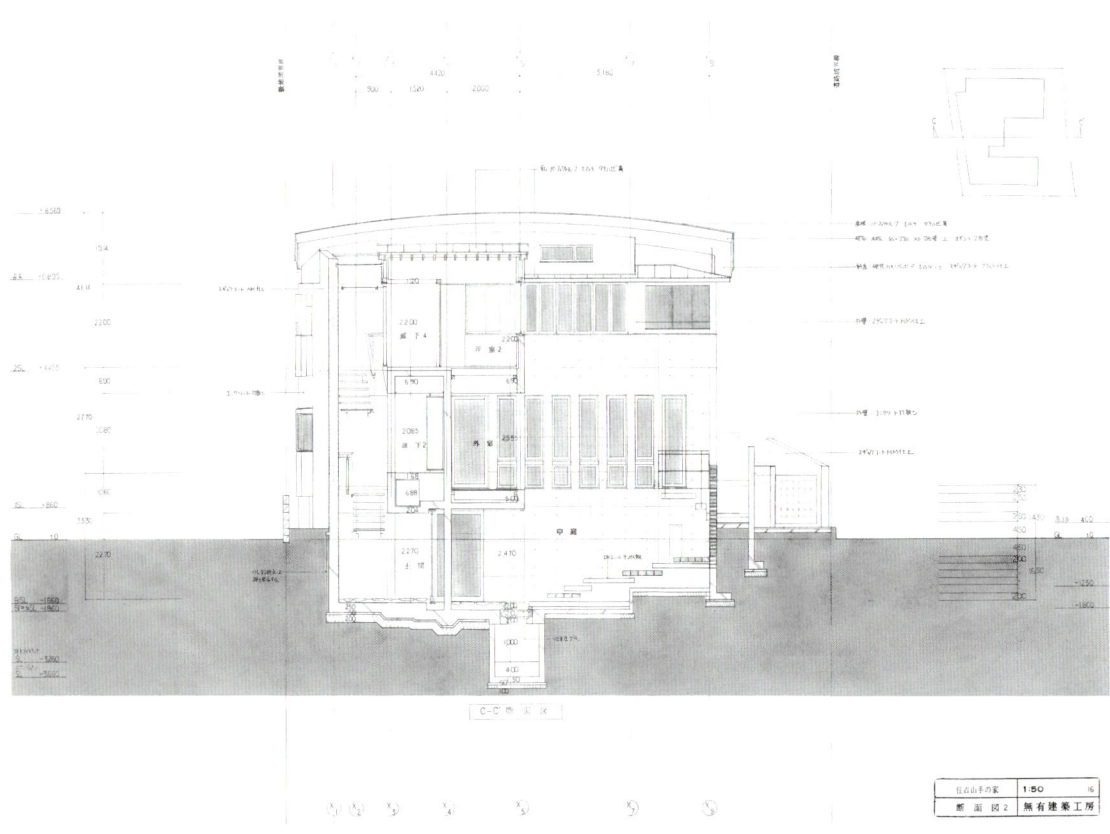

断面図　Section

072

1階西側廊下・階段／壁から自立し、2本のH型鋼のササラ桁と段板で構成されたスケルトン階段。層ごとに階段の軸線をずらし、角度の振れる壁により下階に向かってパースペクティヴのかかるヴォイドはさらなる視角の変化をもたらす。ここから家族室、半地下のアトリエ1、地階、2階へと4つの床レヴェルに複雑に接続する。

Corridor and staircase on west side of the first floor: Unattached to the wall, the skeleton stairs are constructed out of two H-shaped steel stringers and stair treads. By staggering the axis line at each level, when facing the lower floor, the perspective of the void is imbued with a varied angle of vision due to the angled wall. This gives rise to the complex way in which the family room, semi-underground Atelier 1, basement, and the four floor levels leading to the second story are linked.

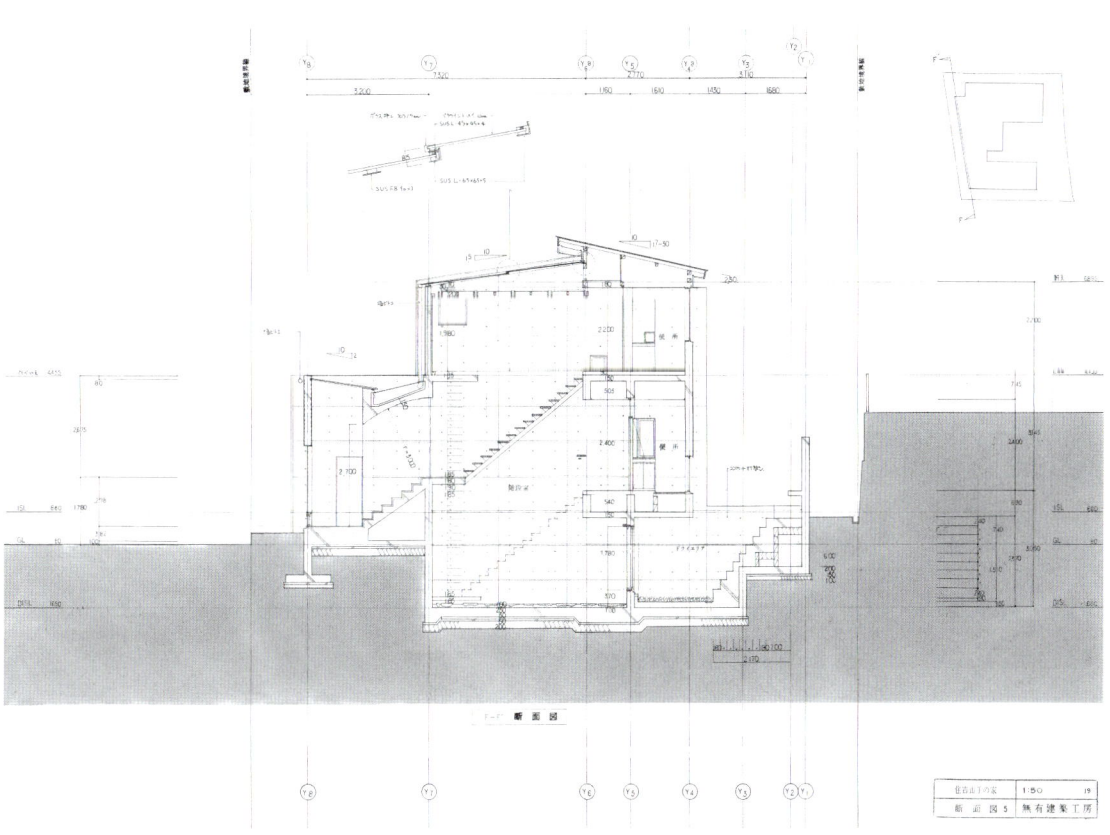

断面図　　Section

Sumiyoshi Yamate House

自立壁とヴォリュームの構成、屋根と開口部の構成により生まれた立体的なファサードは道路からの見え掛かりを抑え込み、周辺環境に適切なスケールを与える。

The three-dimensional facade that emerges from the structure of the free-standing wall and volume, and the roof and opening invites gazes from the road and is appropriately scaled to the surrounding environment.

075 | Sumiyoshi Yamate House

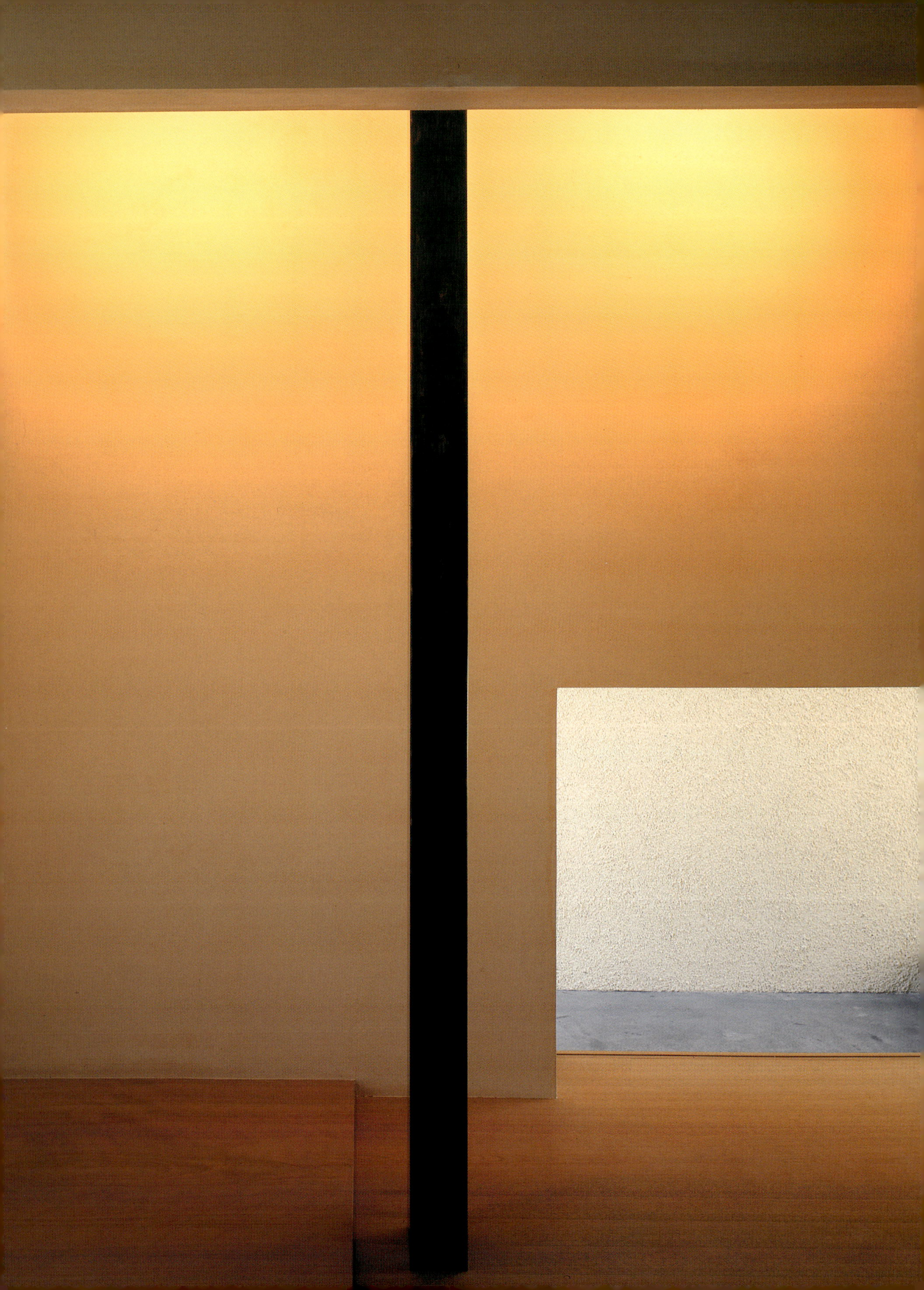

古くから酒所として名高い東広島市西条の町。市街地の少し外れに連なる里山のふもとには田園風景が拡がり、石州瓦の旧集落が点在する。賀茂学園都市構想に基づく広島大学キャンパス移転に伴い、この里山の風景も少しずつ変貌し、田畑の区画割が学生マンションに読み替えられ、ありふれた郊外の住宅地が形成されつつある。敷地は家々の続く下り坂の終着、三叉路の角地に位置し、敷地の奥にはまだ手つかずの松林が深く傾斜し、池の水面に対岸の里山の風景が映し出されている。

建物によって分断されるこの風景をたぐり寄せるように、松林から中庭、アプローチまでを南北の軸線で結び、そこから3つのヴォリュームをずらして点在させる。中央に中庭を囲む分棟型平面を思わせるが、これら3つのヴォリュームは雨掛かりのない内部としてつなぎ留められ、雁行型平面を形成する。ヴォリュームのスキマに路地や廻廊、吹抜を巡らせ、床の仕上げやレヴェルを幾度も操作する。トップライトや開口部からスキマへと射し込む光が粗塗壁のテクスチュアを彷彿とさせ、室と室の合間、室からの見え掛かりに外部への意識を誘い出している。

1層分の高さで連続する庇は家族にひとつながりの空間を意識させ、視線を地面へと誘い込むが、2階で分節された屋根は自立した個々を意識させ、天空への視線の抜け道をつくり出す。それぞれの室は自立したヴォリュームをもち、外部と直接的に接続する「離れ」の様相を帯びているが、一旦2階の家族室を介して行き来するように動線が仕掛けられている。床レヴェルを違えることで目線を交錯させることなく、対峙交差する内部空間を透かして奥の里山へ景色が連続する。漆喰を塗り込めた空間に現された架構は、長く延びる空間から裏の松林から遠くの里山へ続く景色を切り取り、坂道に切り立つ断面のスケールを調整する。のびやかな壁と屋根の稜線は視線の方向性を示唆し、壁から自立する柱がその間合いをはかる。内外の「間合い」と家族の「間合い」が見立ての分棟型平面の中に内在しているのである。

東広島の家
Higashi Hiroshima House

Not far from the Saijo district of Higashi Hiroshima is an expansive rural area at the base of a woodland that is dotted with tile-roofed houses. After a university relocated here, the woodland has gradually disappeared, and many of the fields now contain student apartments, giving the area the look of an ordinary suburb. This residence stands on a corner lot at a junction of three streets that terminate at the bottom of a house-lined slope. In the rear, at a steep incline, is an untouched pine forest and a pond that reflects the opposing woodland.

The dwelling, drawing together this disjointed landscape, connects the pine forest to the courtyard and the approach via the north-south axis line, and disperses three volumes at different points around the lot. In the center, surrounding the courtyard is a *buntogata* ("divided-ridge-style")plane, and the volumes are linked by an interior passage with an echelon form. In the gap between the volumes are an alley, corridor, and atrium, and a number of adjustments have been made to the floor finish and level. The light streaming in from the skylight and openings is reminiscent of the texture of a roughly coated wall, and the intervals between the rooms draw one's attention outside.

The eaves, continuing at the height of the first story, create a sense of a single space and family, drawing one's line of sight to the ground, but the articulated roof on the second floor creates a sense of something autonomous, and the sky is visible through a gap. Each of the rooms has its own volume and is tinged with a "distance" that is directly linked to the exterior. This effect is created by the flow line, which comes and goes via the second-floor family room. By altering the floor level, the scenery continues to the rear of the woodland and clear through to the opposing interior space without disturbing one's gaze. The structure that emerges in this plastered space seems to frame the scenery that extends from the elongated space to the rear of the pine forest into the distant woodland and control the scale of the steep incline of the road. The relaxed walls and the ridge line of the roof help orient one's line of sight, and the free-standing columns are arranged in a well-spaced manner. The "distance" between the interior and exterior, and the family, is an inherent part of the *buntogata* plane.

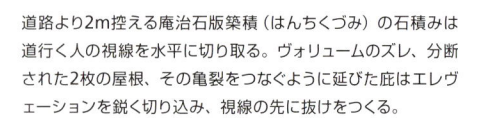

道路より2m控える庵治石版築積（はんちくづみ）の石積みは道行く人の視線を水平に切り取る。ヴォリュームのズレ、分断された2枚の屋根、その亀裂をつなぐように延びた庇はエレヴェーションを鋭く切り込み、視線の先に抜けをつくる。

A wall of stacked Aji stone, two meters from the road, horizontally limits the line of sight from the outside. The staggered volume, divided roofs, and the eaves, which seemingly connect the cracks, cut through the elevation sharply and create a gap at the end of the line of sight.

Higashi Hiroshima House

080

Higashi Hiroshima House

玄関にしつらえられた3畳の小座敷に座り込むと、内法の抑えられた開口部から中庭と周囲に拡がる松林が見え隠れする。

When seated in the small, three *tatami*-sized room in the entranceway, the courtyard and the pine forest that extends around the lot come in and out of view from the opening, which has controlled internal dimensions.

083 | Higashi Hiroshima House

1本の真壁柱によって3畳の小座敷は庭を借景とした床に見立てられる。低く抑えられた開口部からバウンドした光が漆喰塗の壁に包まれた翳りのある空間を優しく満たす。

Through the use of a single *shinkabe*-type column, the small, three *tatami*-sized room resembles the alcove, providing a borrowed landscape of the garden. From the low, controlled opening, light gently envelops the shadowy space within the plaster-coated walls.

Higashi Hiroshima House

廊下3北方向を見る／ヴォリュームの亀裂に生じたスキマはトップライトからの光と粗壁のテクスチュアによって内外を曖昧にする。

North view of Corridor 3: The gap that arises out of the cracks in the volume blurs the line between the interior and exterior due to the light that pours in from the skylight and the rough-coated walls.

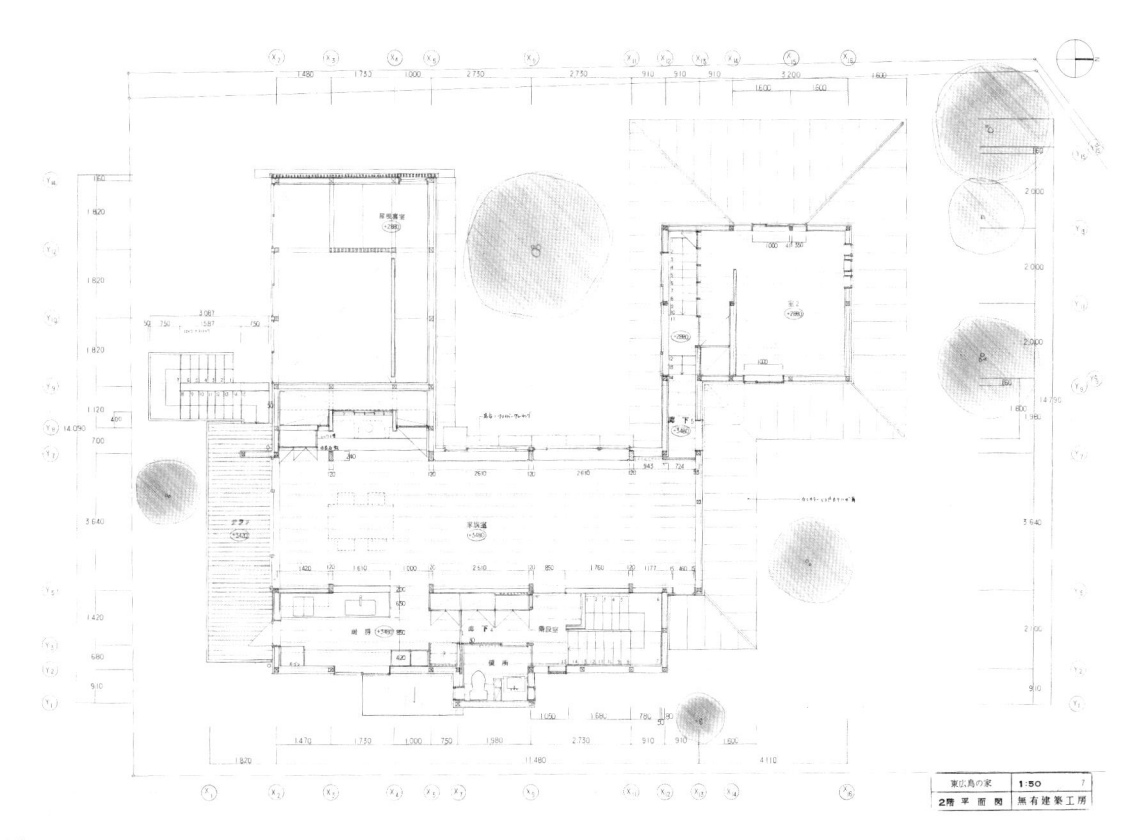

2階平面図　　Second-floor plan

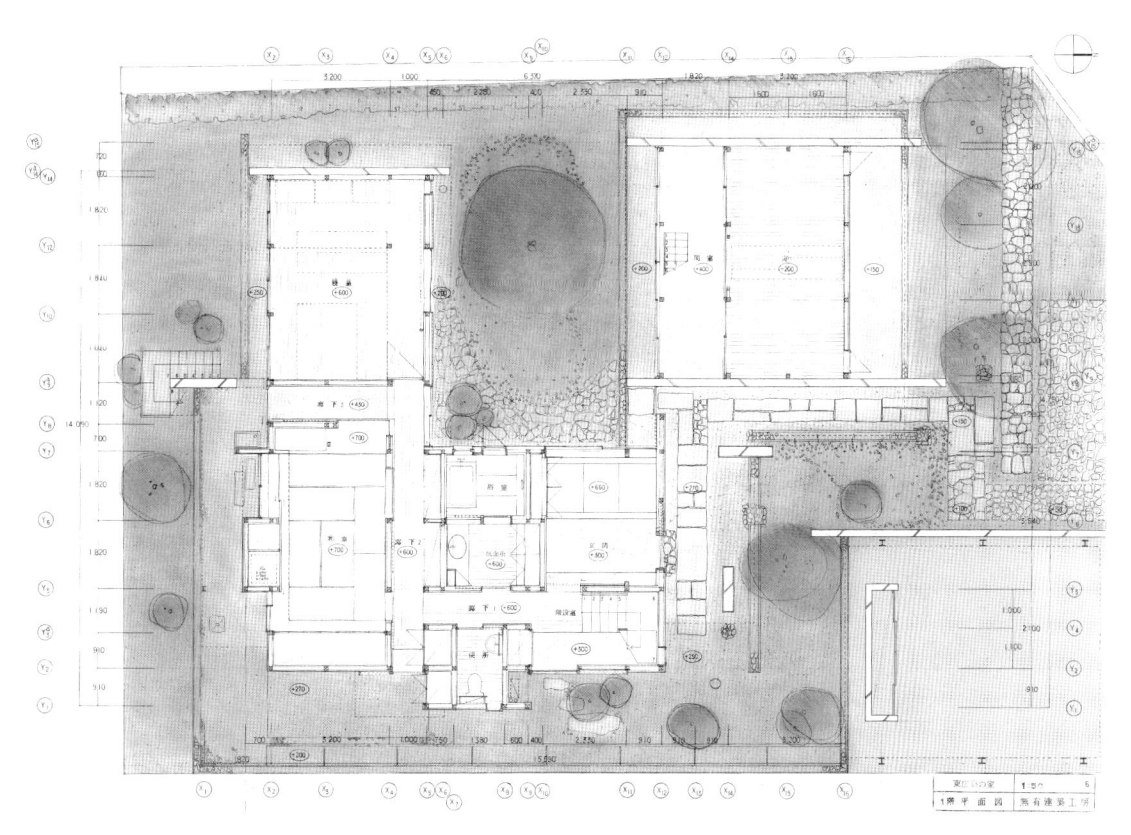

1階平面図　　First-floor plan

087 | Higashi Hiroshima House

和室床方向を見る／漆喰塗の壁の先にはトップライトのある吹抜空間とテクスチュアのある粗壁が控え、
ひとつながりとなった空間に内外を錯覚させる。

View of alcove in Japanese-style room: By controlling the sky-light-equipped atrium and textured, rough-coated walls beyond the plaster-coated wall, the illusion of an interior and exterior is created in the space.

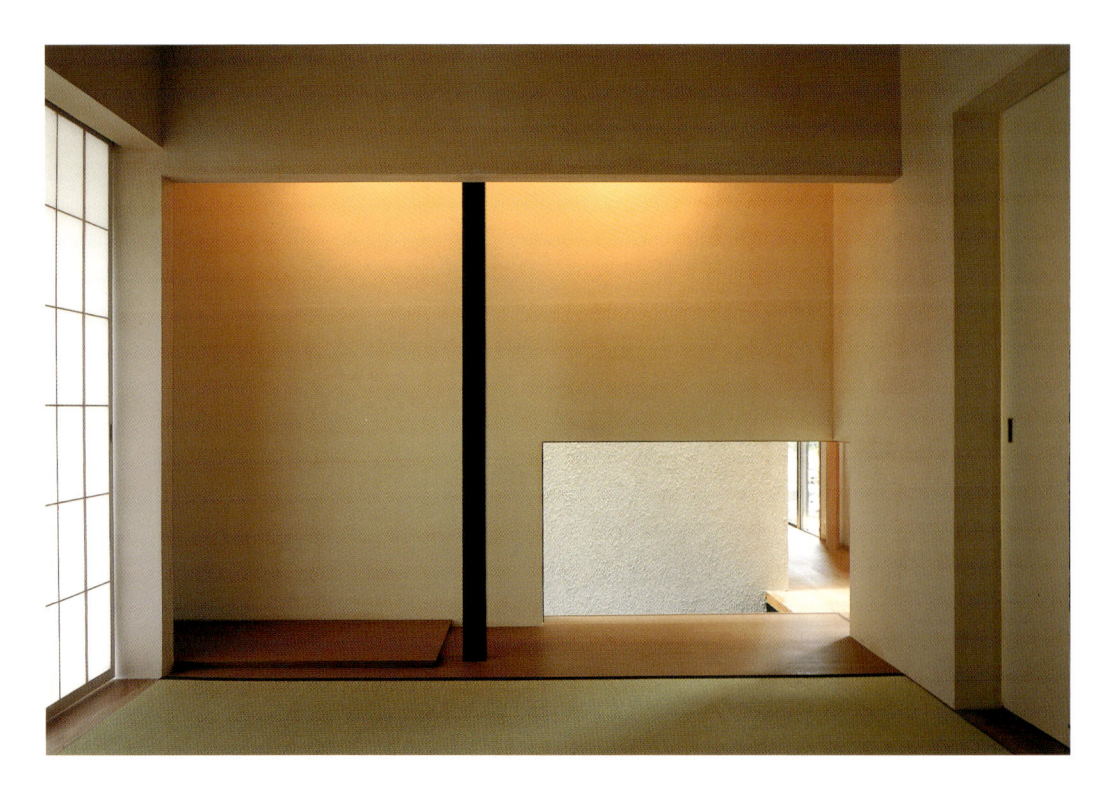

Higashi Hiroshima House

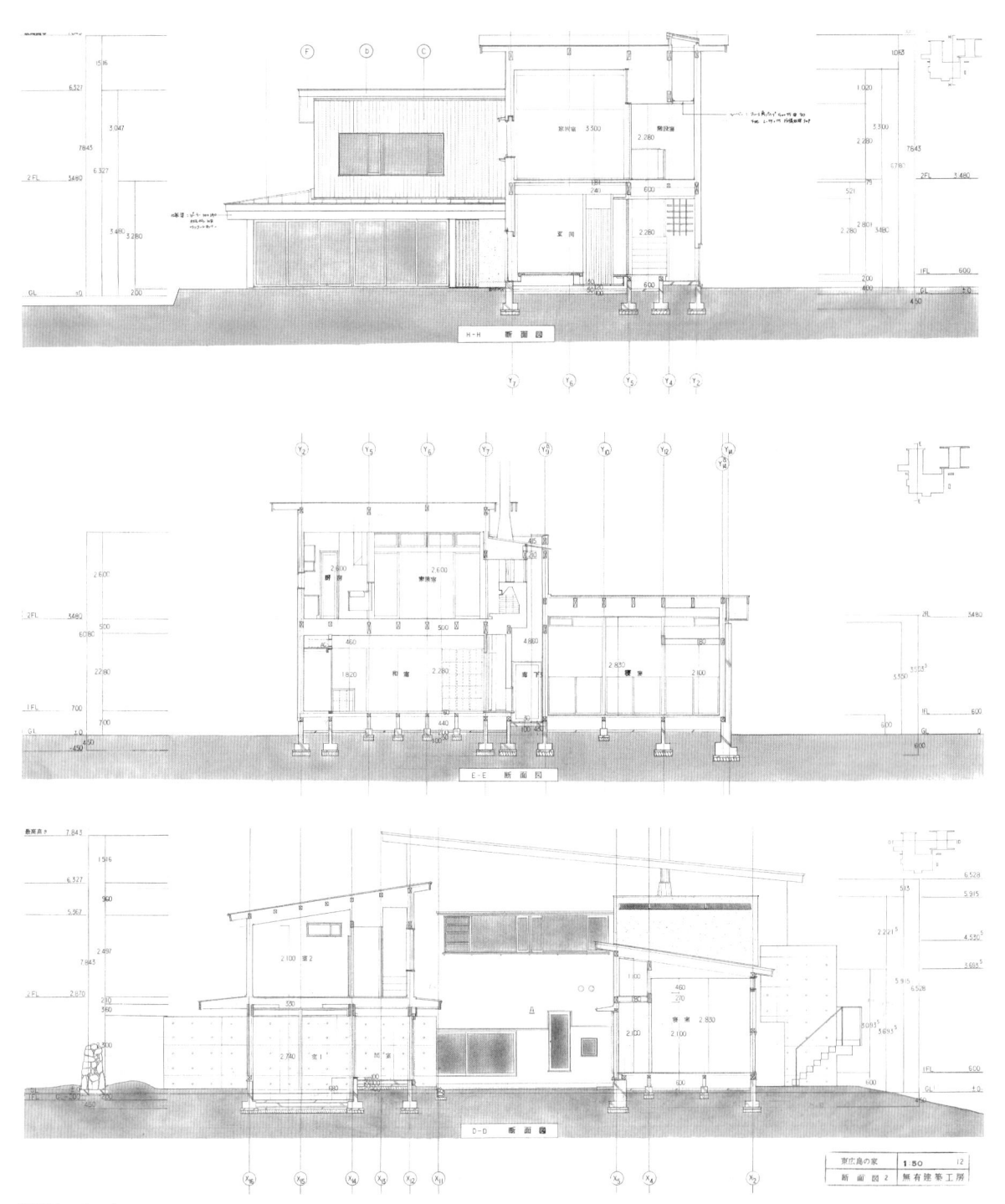

断面図　　Section

右：中庭から室内にもたらされた西陽が壁の重なりに映し出され、柔らかな塗壁の面に架構や開口部に現された線の構成が際立つ。

Right: Shining in from the courtyard, the sunlight from the west is projected in layers on the wall and creates a strong linear structure of the framework and opening on the surface of the lightly painted walls.

Higashi Hiroshima House

092

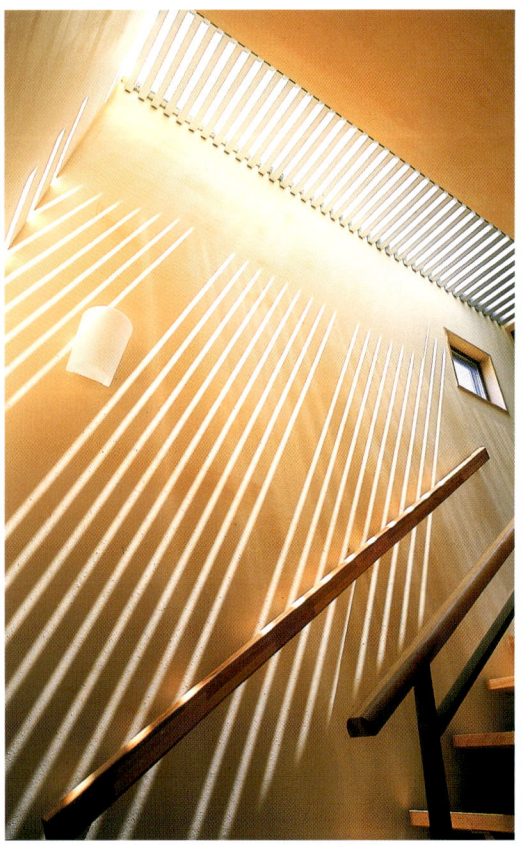

家族室西側の暖炉の上にマドがしつらえられ、光に満たされたヴォイド空間に粗壁のテクスチュアが現れると、あたかも外部のように錯覚される。

A window, located above the hearth on the west side of the family room, creates the illusion of being outside as the texture of the rough-coated walls emerges in the light-filled void.

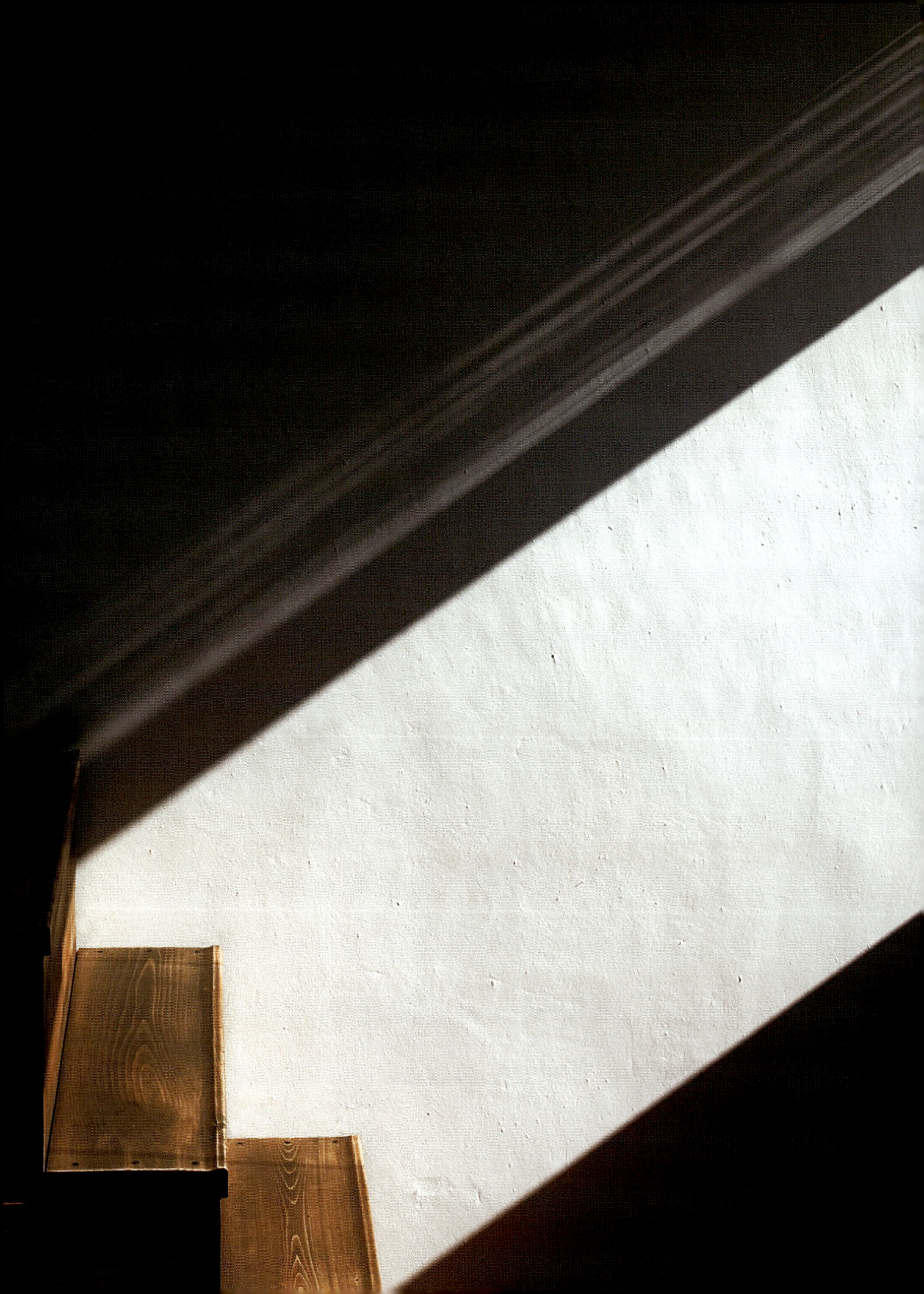

奈良県南西部、生駒山から金剛山へと連なる山並みに抱かれ、陵墓や古墳が点々と残る里山の合間に開発された郊外の住宅地の一角。緩やかな丘陵地の曲り角に佇むこの住宅は、変わり行く町並みから領域を囲い取りつつ、西方に望む山並みや里山の面影、田畑のような余白の風景を日常生活の中へと引き込むように、3棟に分棟配置され、点在する生活空間の合間を雨ざらしの外部空間がつなぎ留める。それぞれの棟は自立したヴォリュームをもつが、スケールは最小限にとどめられ、機能的には完結しない。3棟がズレながら分棟配置され、そのスキマに緊密な路地空間、ブリッジが交錯し、何をするにも内と外を立体的に行き交い、常に自然と共に生活が展開する。光や風、雨の通り抜ける路地空間の交点に結ばれたデッキは、屋根を分節された3つの内部空間と、土の匂いの残る裏側の風景との「つなぎの間」となる。

　1枚の自立壁によって道路から棟と棟のスキマへと誘われ、軒のラインによって切り取られた空と歩幅に沿って打たれた石敷きの路地空間に導かれていくと、小上がりのデッキに辿り着く。その先に待ち受ける玄関はなく、人は立ち止まり、戸惑いながらも声を掛ける。するとどこからともなく中から人が迎え出て挨拶を交わす。デッキはそのまま裏の畑へと開かれており、ここで土が付いたままの野菜を並べて座り込み、近所の人と分け合いながら、朝の集いが始まり出す。すぐ脇の厨房で採れたての野菜を料理しては、また青空のデッキで食事をする。そのまま日向ぼっこをして寝転び、夜になれば宴の場所へと変幻する。器の外へ溶け出した生活を彩るように、四季や太陽の移ろいが「つなぎの間」を満たす。

　この住宅の仕掛けはここを訪れた者にしかわからないであろう。しかしかつての民家がもっていた縁側のように、「つなぎの間」はあらゆる他者を迎え入れ、内と外、ズレとスキマを自在に行き交うにつれ、ひとつ屋根の下に覆われた「家」という概念を越えた生活が巡り始めるのである。

広陵町の家
Koryocho House

This lot is located in a suburban area developed between woodlands dotted with ancient tombs and burial mounds in a mountain range that runs from Mt. Ikoma to Mt. Kongo in southwestern Nara Prefecture. It stands at a bend in the road in a section of gently rolling hills that is enclosed in the ever-changing townscape, but the external space creates a distance between the living spaces through the distribution of the three wings in this *buntogata* ("divided-ridge-style") residence and seemingly incorporates the mountains, woodlands, and the fields to the west. While each wing has its own volume, due to their limited scale, none is functionally complete. Within the gaps between the structures are a compact alley space, an interlocking bridge, a thoroughly three-dimensional flow between the interior and exterior, and a constant development of daily life in tandem with nature. The deck, connecting the intersecting points in the alley space, which allows light, wind, and rain in, acts as a "connecting space" between the three inner spaces segmented by the roof and the opposite landscape with its earthy aroma.

　A free-standing wall invites one from the alley into the gaps between the wings, and after being enticed by the sky, the frame created by the line of the eaves, and the stone-flagged alley space designed with one's stride in mind, one arrives at the slightly raised deck. The deck opens out into the field behind it, and as the still dirt-covered vegetables are divided up between a group of seated neighbors, the morning assembly begins. After carrying some of the vegetables into the kitchen that flanks the space to cook them, one returns to the deck to eat them beneath the blue sky. Then, one curls up for a nap in the sunshine and throws a party in the same spot that night. Adding color to daily life as it flows outside the box, this "connecting space" brims with changes in season and light.

　Like the verandas that were once a part of old folk-style dwellings, this "connecting space" welcomes all types of people, and by encouraging a free flow between the interior and exterior, and the cracks and gaps, daily life here comes to transcend the concept of a "house" as something contained under a single roof.

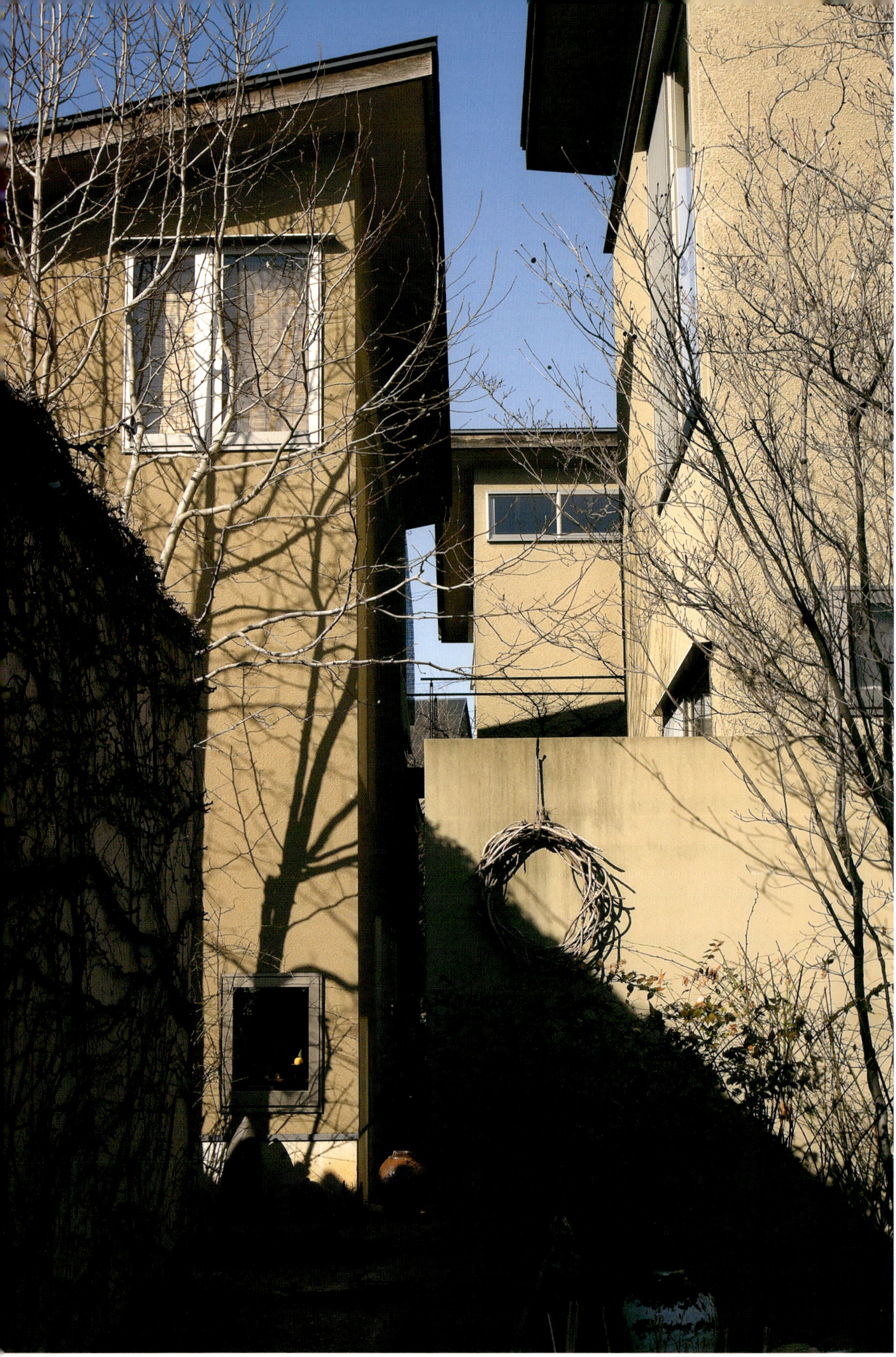

左：自立壁、分棟配置された3棟のズレとスキマに、軒のラインによって空を切り取られた緊密な2層分の路地空間が誘う。
上：路地より3棟の交点となるデッキを見る／左手の抑え込まれた開口部は躙り口となり、出迎えられた者だけがランダムに実矧ぎ（さねはぎ）されたタガヤサンの縁に腰掛け、家族室へ入り込むことができる。
下：2階のブリッジより路地を見下ろす。

Left: The compact, second-level alley space, framing the sky with the line of eaves, invites one toward the gaps between the free-standing wall and the three wings Arranged in a *bunto*-style.
Above: View of deck, the node for the three wings, from the alley— The controlled opening on the left functions like a small, tea-house door, Only one guest can enter the family room, sit on the veranda of the randomly rabbet-joined Bombay blackwood.
Below: View of alley from the second-floor bridge.

土間の家族室には手持ちの箱階段が置かれ、この寸法を元に平面と高さ寸法が決められる。抑え込まれた開口部からは路地の気配が見え隠れする。
右：ハイサイドよりもたらされた光は、大磯玉砂利と真土（まさつち）を混ぜ粗く仕上げた三和土（たたき）の土間、土佐漆喰中塗仕上げの壁のテクスチュアのコントラストを鮮やかに引き出す。

In the earthen floor of the family room, there is a portable staircase chest, on whose dimensions the plane and height of the space were based. From the controlled opening, glimpses of the alley come in and out of view.
Right: The light that pours into the room from the high sidelights brilliantly emphasizes the contrast between the roughly-finished earthen floor, made of Oiso gravel and high-grade soil, and the texture of the walls, finished with an intermediate coat of Tosa plaster.

Koryocho House

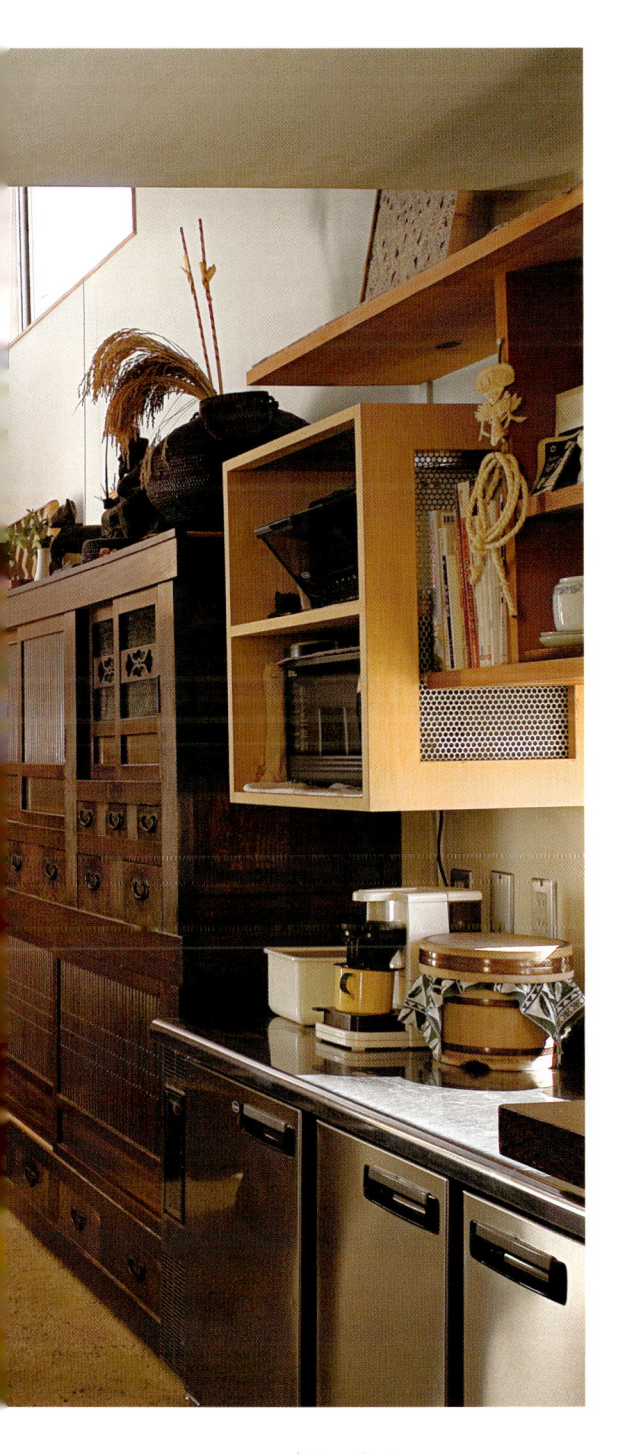

右：厨房は三和土土間によって靴のままデッキとつながる。箱階段の高さで導かれた2階の床レヴェルに対し、天井高を抑え込むことで吹抜に緊張感が生まれる。

Right: The earthen floor in the kitchen allows access to the deck without taking off one's shoes. In contrast to the floor level of the second story, based on the height of the staircase chest, the controlled height of the ceiling produces a sense of tension in the atrium.

101 | Koryocho House

左:「つなぎの間」となるデッキを介して棟と棟が斜交いにズレ、高さの異なる開口部が互いの視線を調整する。
右:室1／砂漆喰押えの壁を重ね、陰影をつくり出し、極小の空間に奥行きをなす。

Left: Mediated by the deck, which functions as a "connecting area," the wings are diagonally staggered and the disparate height of the openings controls the line of sight.
Right: Room 1— The layered, pressed-plaster walls create shadows and add depth to the extremely small space.

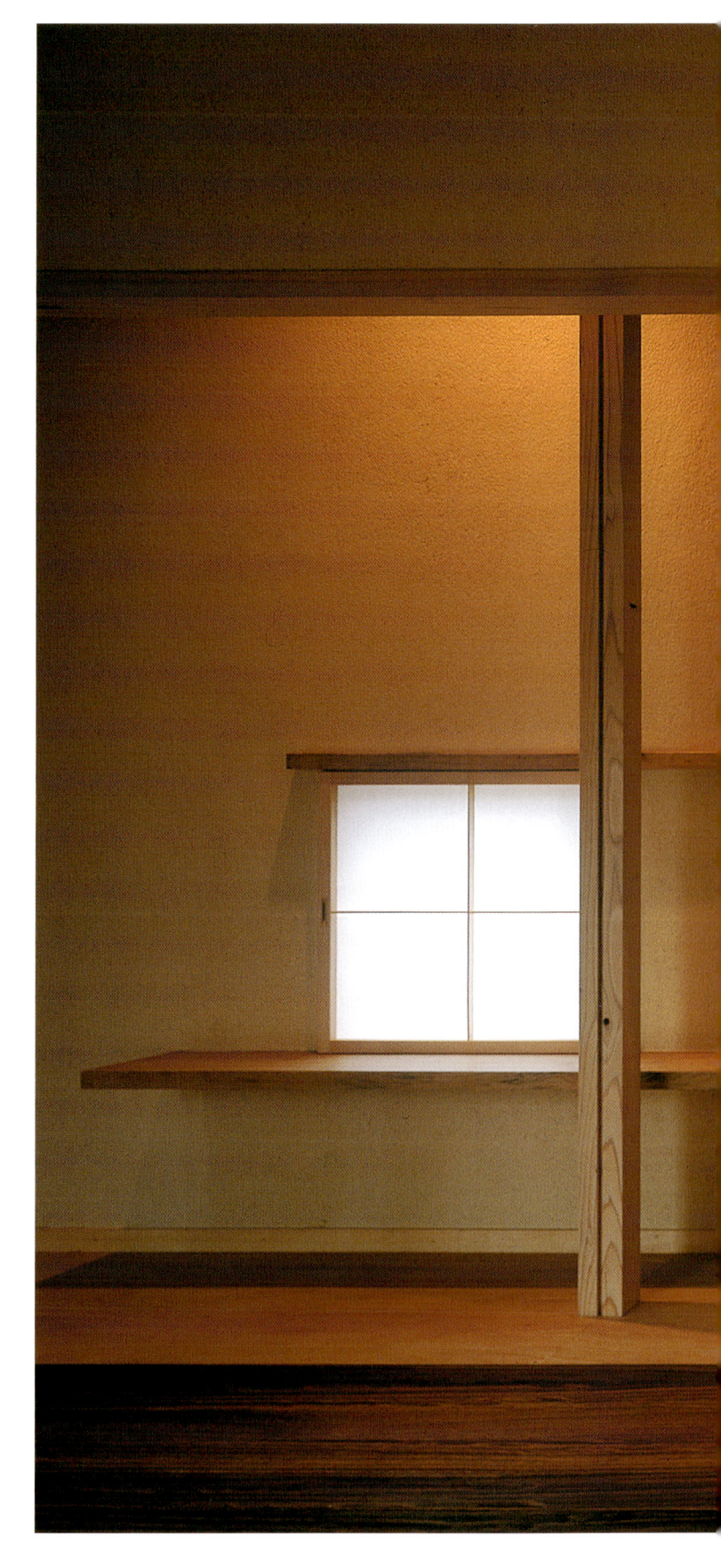

Koryocho House

室1／床の意匠、水屋、袋棚の内法の構成。

Room 1— Alcove design, cupboard, and inner dimensions of tea ceremony stand.

104

室4／古材を使った床、色粉と藁スサ入りの木ゴテ押えの塗壁で構成される粗材のテクスチュア。

Room 4 — Alcove using old pieces of wood, wood-braced plaster walls containing colored powder and straw fiber add texture to these structured rough materials.

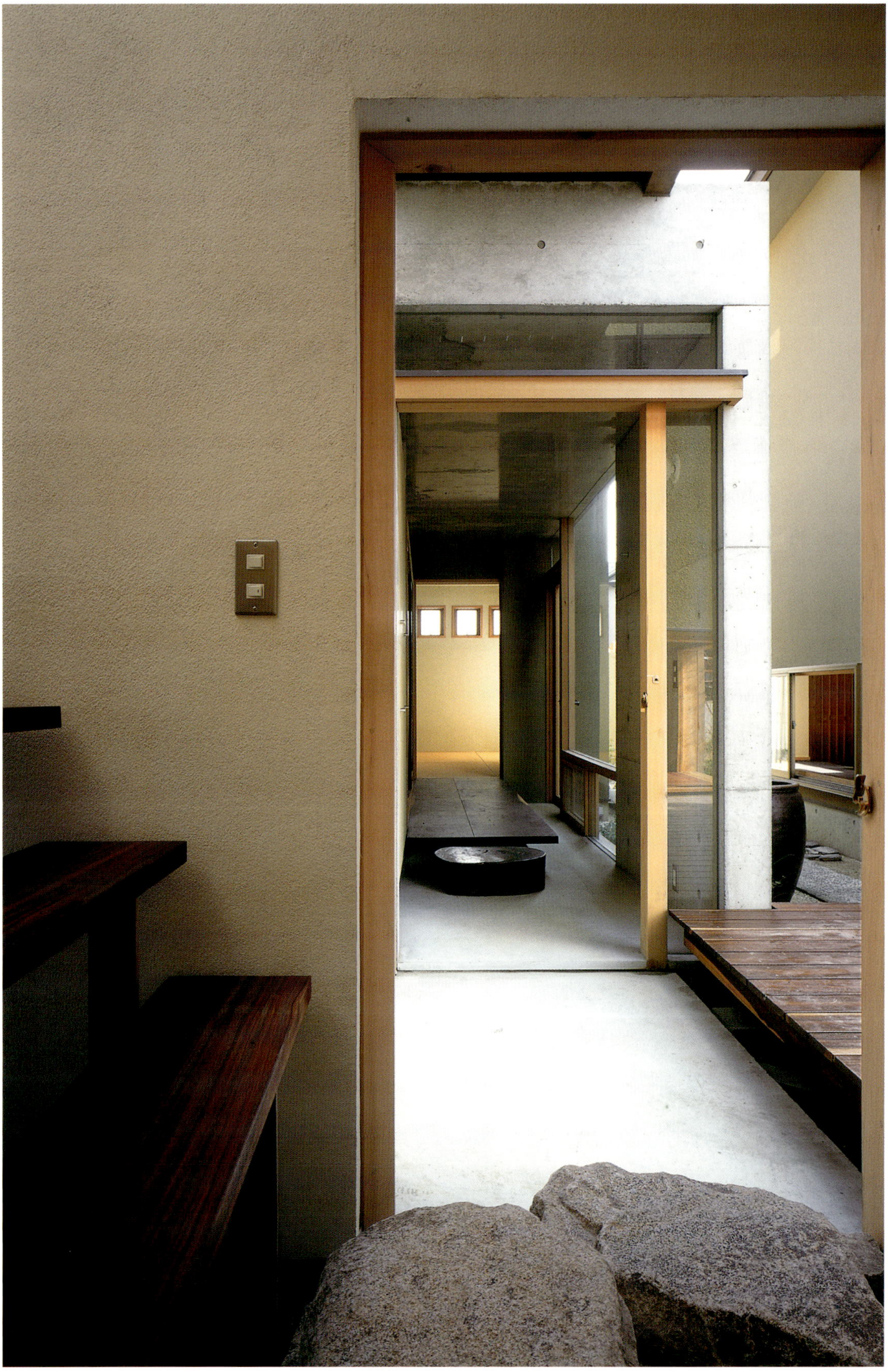

庵治石敷きの小空間にスチールのフラットバーと段板だけで構成されたスケルトンの折り返し階段が浮かぶ。
左：階段室より外部を介して室2まで見通す／庵治の自然石を置いた階段室、土間に床板を渡した廊下は、内と外の結界を示唆する。

The skeleton-frame, dog-leg stairs, constructed only out of steel flat-bars and stair treads, rises up in the small, Aji-stone-lined space.
Left: View to Room 2 through exterior of the staircase— The floorboards in the corridor that lead to the natural Aji-stone-lined staircase and earthen floor suggest a barrier between the interior and exterior.

Koryocho House

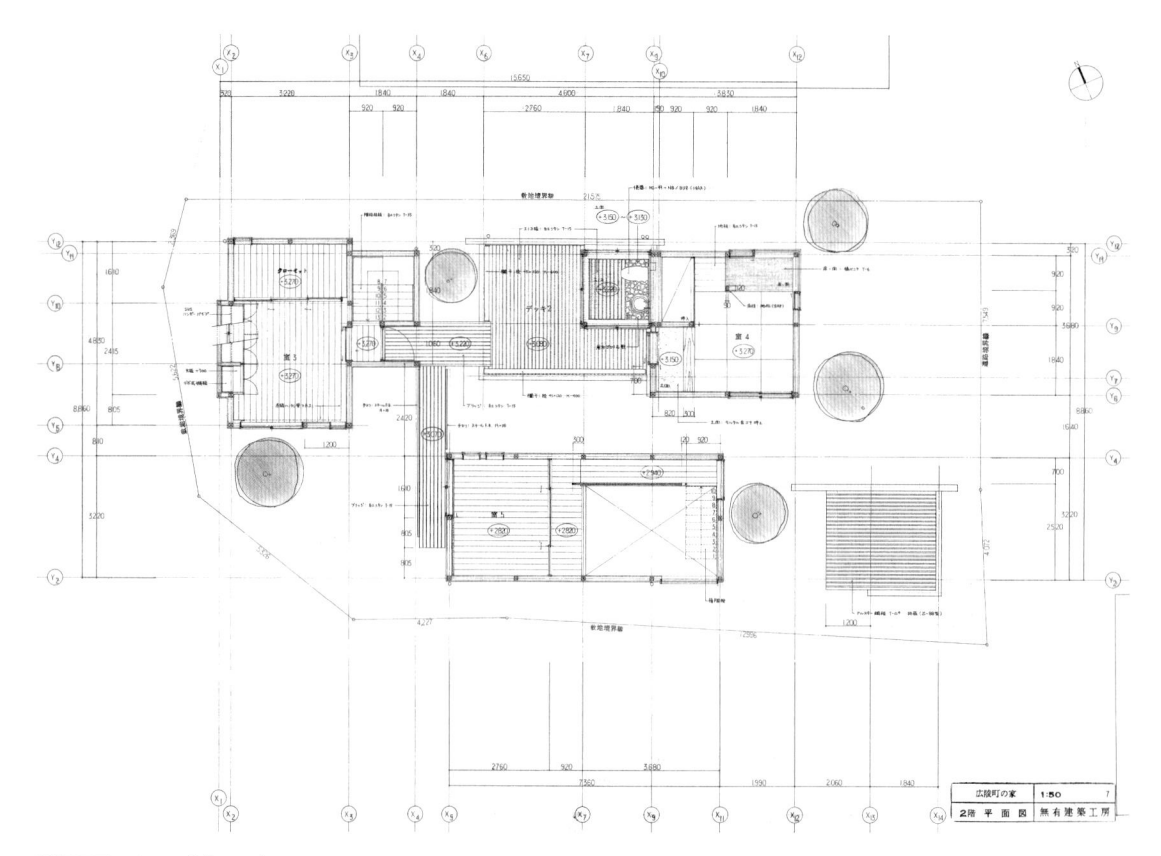

2階平面図　　Second-floor plan

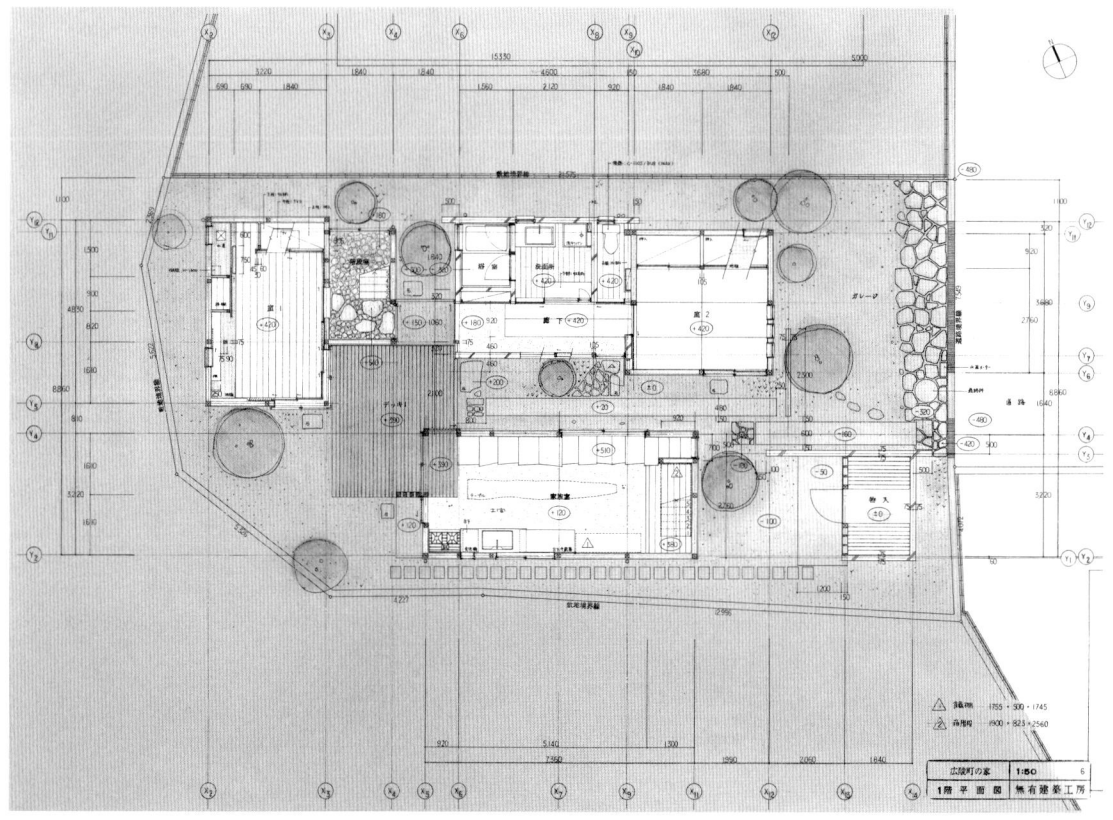

1階平面図　　First-floor plan

108

室4／開口部を絞り込み、限られた光の中で粗材のテクスチュアが彷彿とする。

Room 4: The restrained opening and limited light recall the texture of the coarse materials.

110

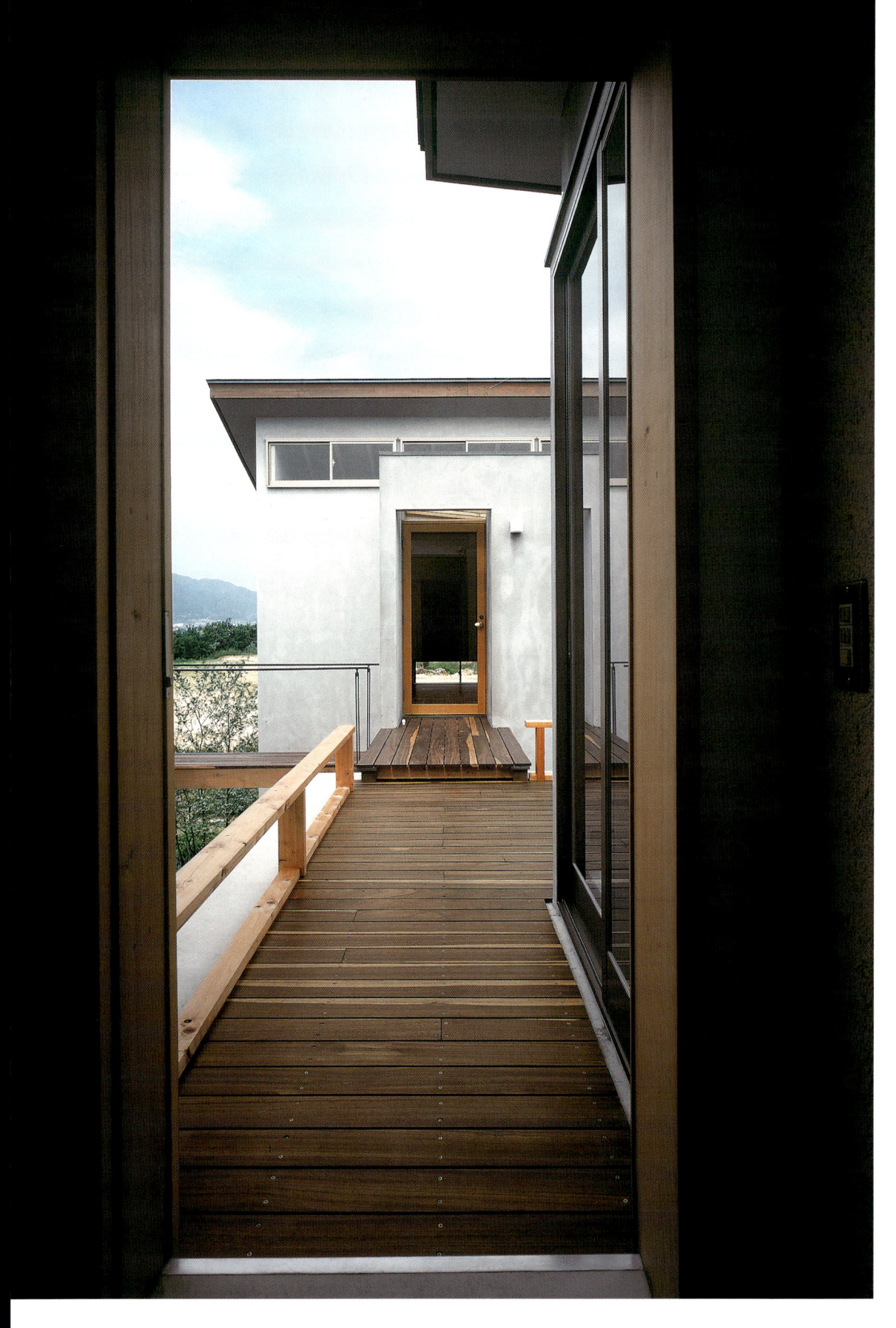

3棟は平面、屋根の高さが共にズレ、田畑や山並みの風景が残る南西方向に開かれる。棟と棟はブリッジによって雁行するようにつながり、動線と視線が交錯する。

The planes and roof height of the three wings are staggered, opening out to the southwest and affording a view of the fields and mountains. The wings are linked in an echelon structure by means of a bridge, mixing the flow lines and lines of sight.

Koryocho House

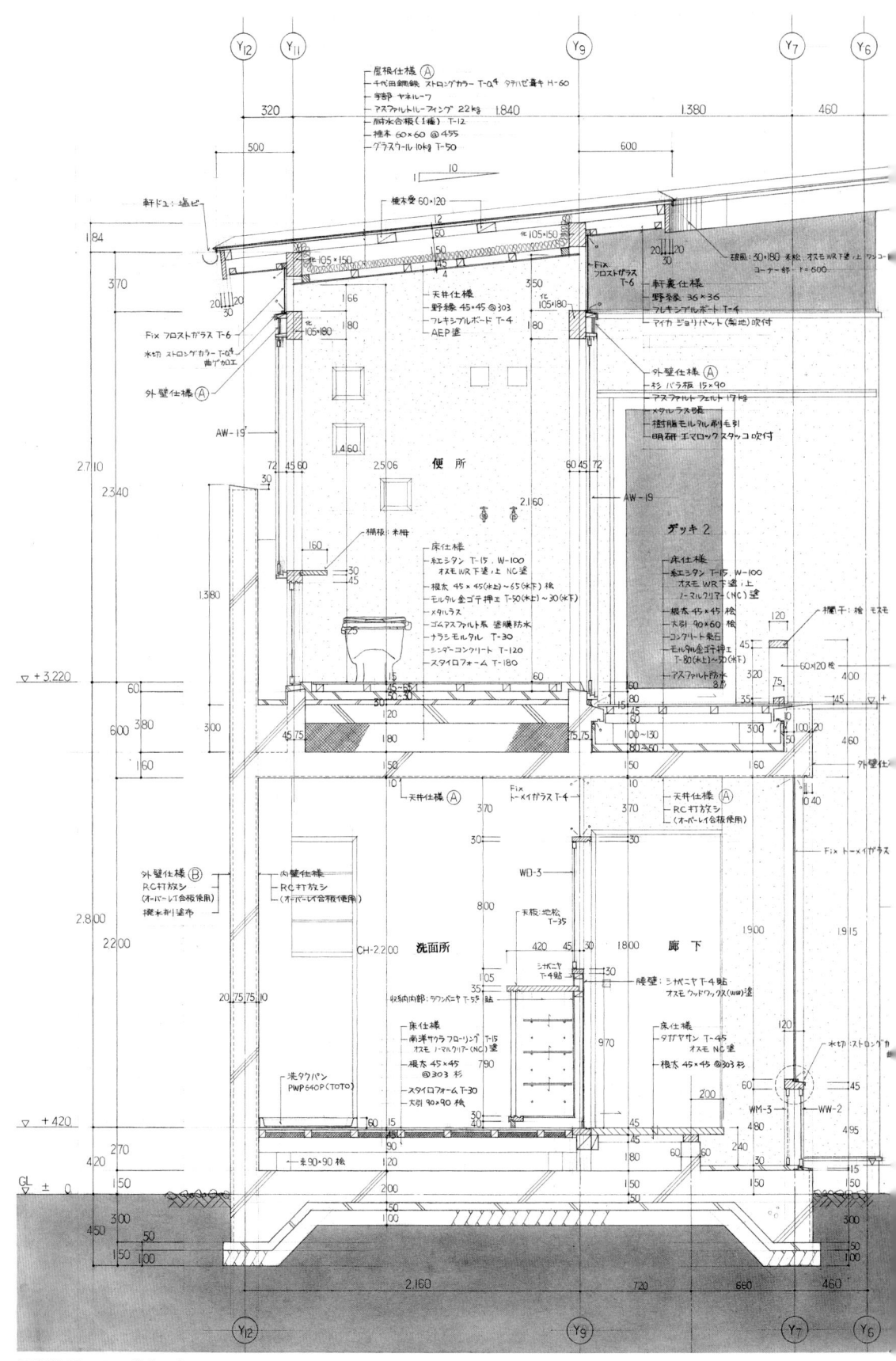

矩計詳細図　Detail drawing

Koryocho House

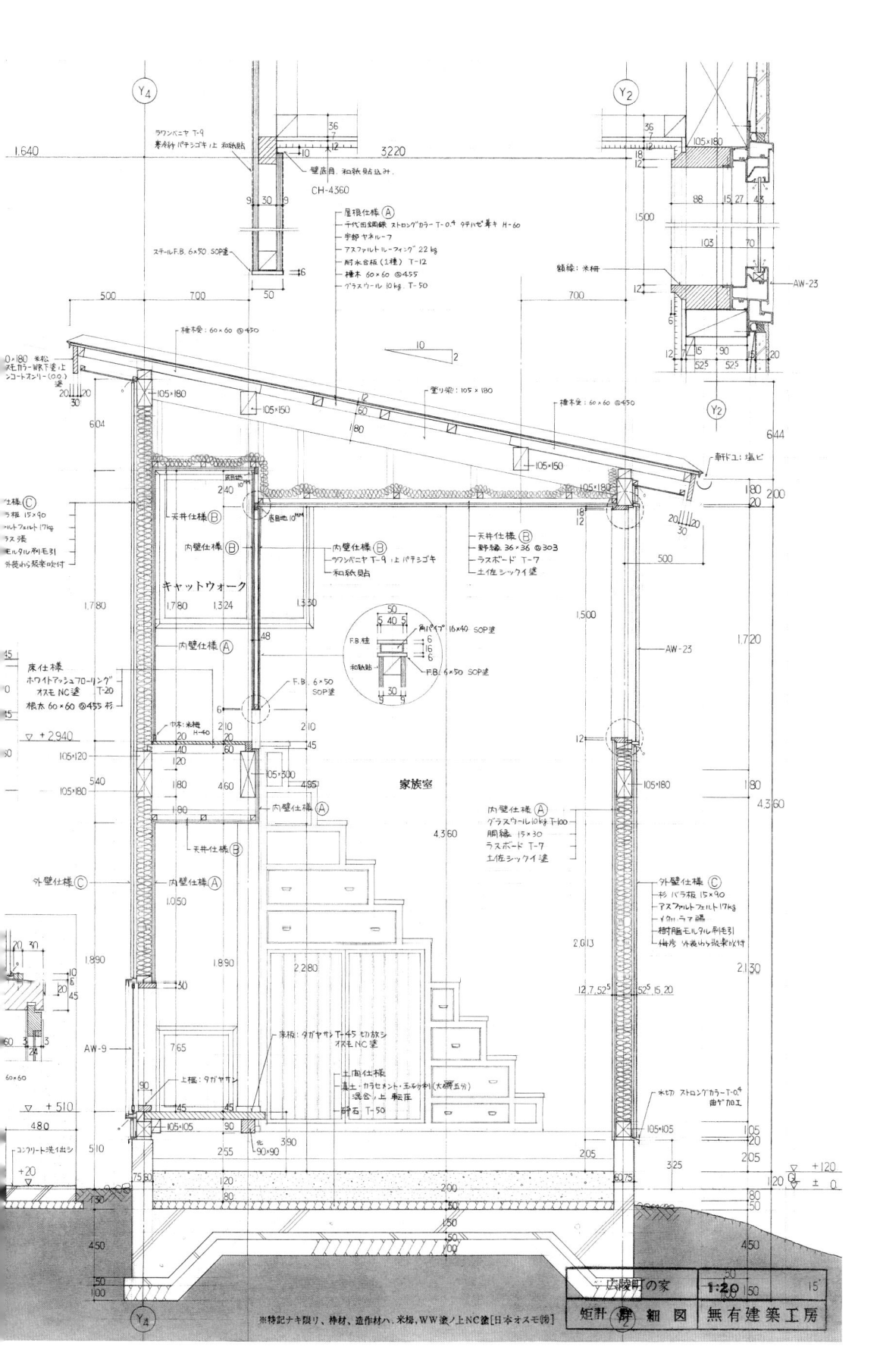

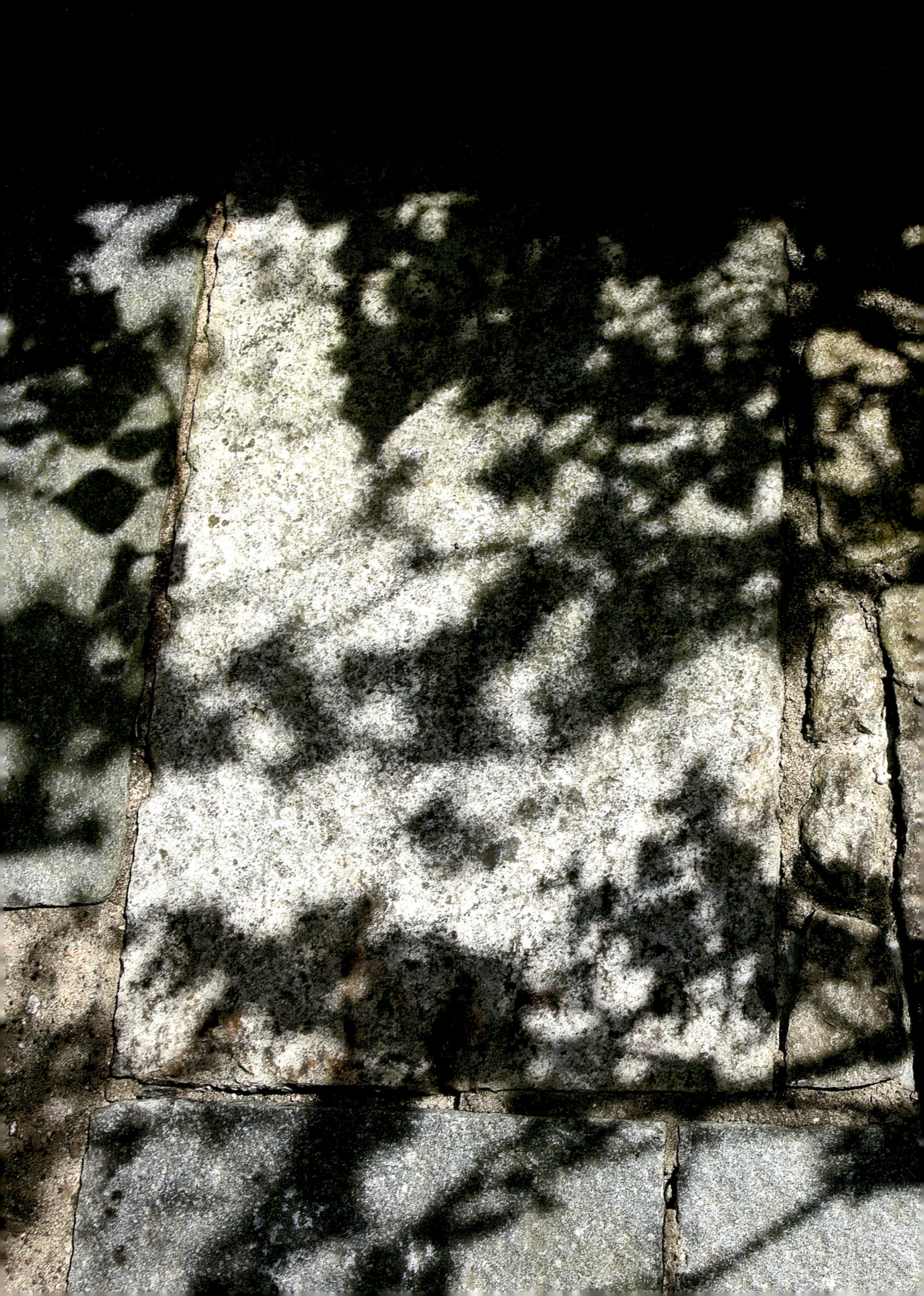

1970年代より大阪府北部に開発されたニュータウンを中心に、千里丘陵一帯にはひな壇状に造成された閑静な住宅街が拡がる。緑豊かな丘の上には擁壁を兼ねた石垣が連なり、100坪ほどのゆとりある区画割で成熟した町並みを見せる。敷地は緩やかな坂を描く十字路の角に位置する。道路より半層から一層ほど上がった地盤面を、既存の石垣を基壇に残したまま一旦掘り込み、ひな壇状にレヴェル差をつけて再造成した。南北の軸線を境に、中庭を介して対角をなす分棟型平面を配し、他者を迎え入れる2層分のパブリック棟と、住み手の安息の場となる3層分のプライベート棟をズラして対峙させ、2棟のスキマに雁行する余白を残した。多角的な動きを見せる3つの庭は、ひな壇状になった町の余白へと展開する。ズレを伴った2棟は庭、路地、ブリッジによってつながり、立体的に交錯する廻遊式平面を構成する。

　ここでは他者と住まい手が出会い、滞留する場となる「つなぎの間」がこの平面をつかさどる。前面道路より2層分の高さをもつパブリック棟をファサードに捉え、建物側面へとアプローチが潜り込む。そこにはトンネル状の路地空間が待ち構え、水を打たれた敷石が薄闇の中で鈍い光を放つ。粗く打たれた石敷きのリズムに幾度となく踏み止まり、ゆっくりとくぐり抜けると、自立壁に沿って水盤のある中庭へと誘われる。そこへ待ち受けるのは土間の巡る和室である。来客の時刻をはからい、建具を開け放ち、石に水を打つ。訪れた者は腰を掛け、中庭を見返し、水音に耳を澄ませ、水盤越しに光に満たされた南北の庭を垣間見ながらゆっくりと迎えを待つ。中へ通されると、土間の内側に障子が建て込まれ、柔らかな光に包まれた和室は座敷に変貌する。壁・建具・床のズレと重なりによって内と外を展開する和室は、住まい手と訪れる者の間合いをはかる「つなぎの間」となる。こうした曖昧な「つなぎの間」に対し、緊張感のある階段やブリッジが自在な動線をつなぎながら互いの領域を意識させる。棟を違えた廻遊式住居の中に様々な住まいの作法と仕掛けが隠されているのである。

新千里南町の家
Shinsenri Minamimachi House

In a town developed in Osaka Prefecture in the 1970s, this residential area extends in tiers across the hills. Atop the verdant region runs a stone wall that also functions as a retaining wall and a spacious, 331-square-meter plot. The sloping lot is on the corner of a crossroads. The ground level, between half a story and one story above the road, descends to a platform that remains from the stone wall and was reconstructed in a tiered formation. With the north-south axis line as a boundary, the residence, located on a *buntogata* ("divided-ridge-style") plane diagonally mediated by a courtyard, consists of a two-story guest wing and a three-story wing for the residents. These face each other in a staggered position with an echelon-shaped gap between them. The three gardens, displaying a multifaceted movement, function as "empty spaces." The wings are linked by the garden, an alley, and bridge on a three-dimensionally interlocking "stroll-style" plane.

　Controlling the plane is a "connecting space" that serves as a meeting and dwelling place for guests and residents. While the facade of the guest wing, rising some two stories above the frontal road, is visible, there is a concealed approach to the side of the building. Here one finds a tunnel-shaped alley space with paving stones sprinkled with water emitting pure light in the dim space. Stopping along the rough rhythm of the pavement, one passes slowly through until being invited into the courtyard with flower basins along a free-standing wall. Waiting here is a Japanese-style room surrounded by an earthen floor. With a guest expected, the fittings are open and water sprinkles the stones. The guest takes a seat and glances back at the courtyard, and while listening to the water, catches a glimpse of the north-south garden bathed in light beyond the basins. Passing inside, one sees *shoji* screens inside the earthen floor enveloped in gentle light that transforms the *tatami*-floored room. The room, with an interior and exterior that arises out of the gaps and layers of walls, fittings, and floors, becomes a "connecting space" for the resident and the guest. In contrast to this ambiguous space, the tension-filled staircase and bridge connect with the free-moving flow line, encouraging an awareness of each other's space. In the wings of this "stroll-style residence" are concealed a variety of methods and devices for dwelling.

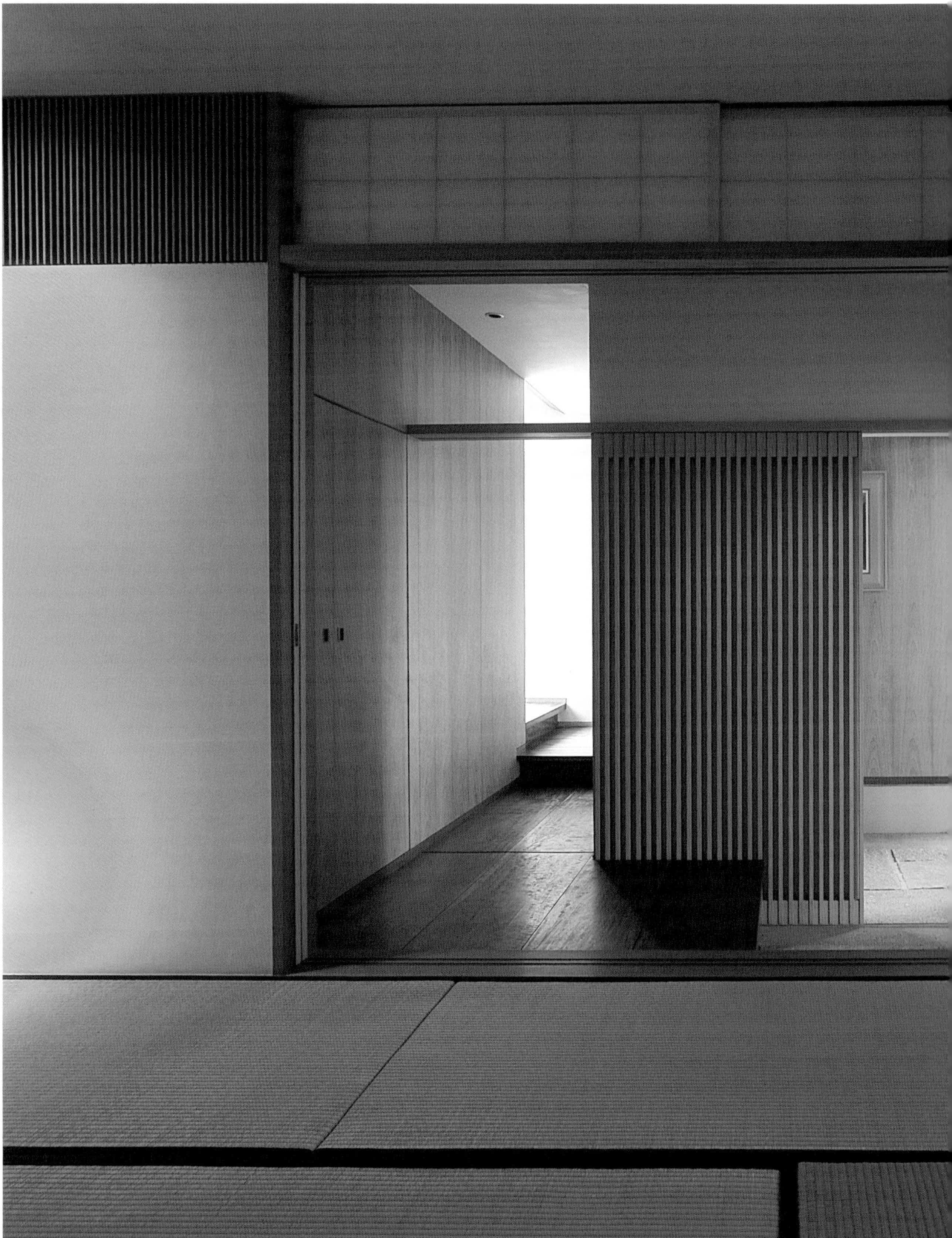

117 | Shinsenri Minamimachi House

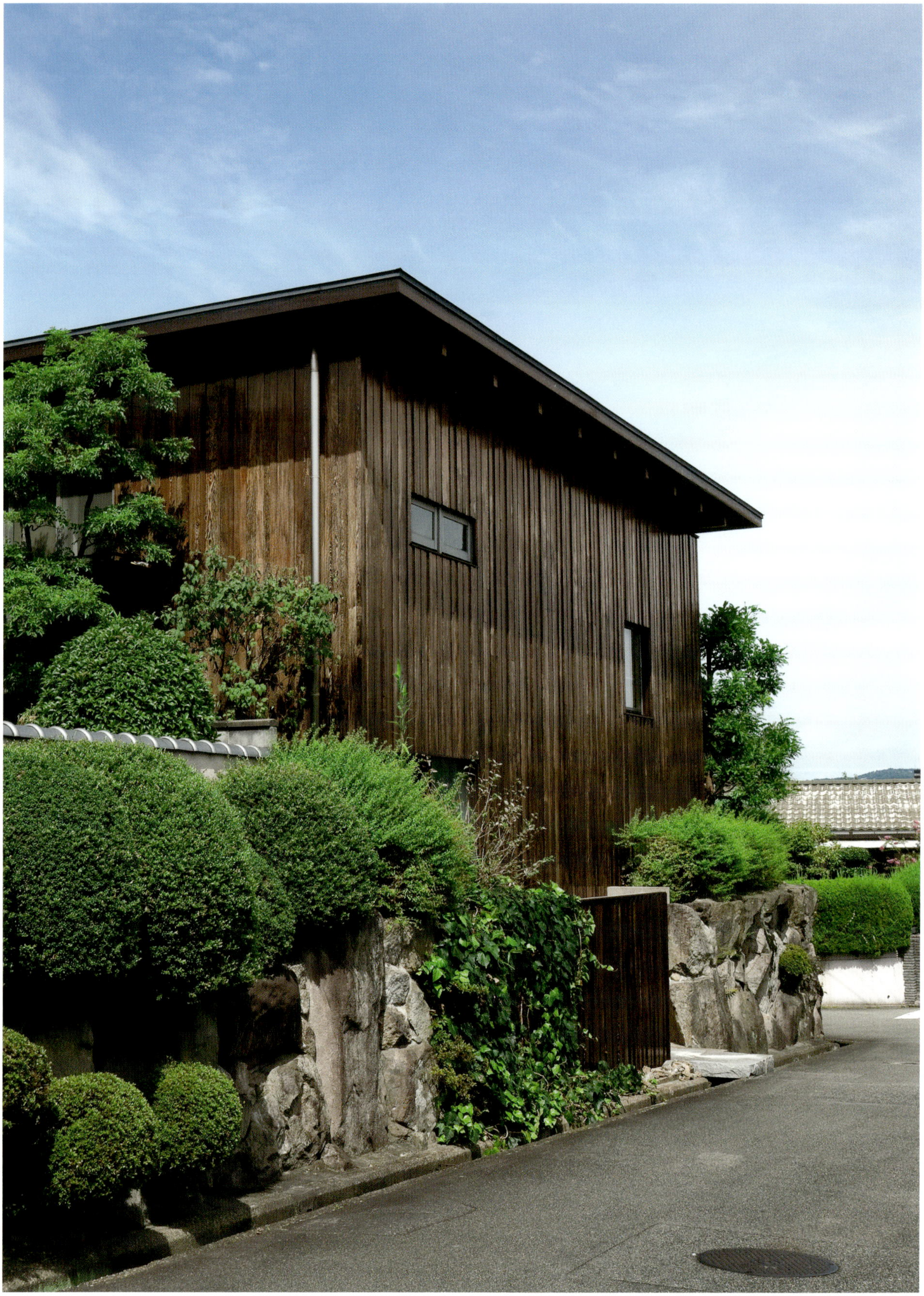

左：石積み壁の内へ控え、2層分の高さに抑えられたパブリック棟は乱厚の板張によって陰影をつくり出し、表情をもった佇まいを見せる。

Left: Contained within a stone wall, the public wing, with a controlled height of two stories, creates shadows with boards of various thicknesses and displays an expressive appearance.

右：2棟の平面と断面におけるズレによって生じた立体的な中庭には光と影が錯綜する。

Right: Light and shadow are intermingled in the three-dimensional courtyard produced by the gap between the planes and sections of the two wings.

Shinsenri Minamimachi House

左：トンネル路地より中庭を見る／薄闇に包まれたトンネル路地を抜けると、光に満ちた中庭が待ち構える。
右：水盤のある中庭／2棟の間に架け渡されたブリッジは透かされ、光や雨の雫が漏れ落ち、水盤へと反射する。

Left: View of courtyard from tunnel alley— Immediately after exiting the tunnel alley, shrouded in dim light, one comes upon the light-drenched courtyard. Right: Courtyard with flower basins— The bridge that spans the two wings is open, allowing light and misty rain to fall through, and is reflected in the basins.

中庭・路地・土間・和室の雁行の構成／自立壁で支え上げられた
ヴォリュームの足元は、建具の開閉によって自在に透かされる。

The echelon structure of the courtyard, alley, earthen
floor, and Japanese-style room: The volume,
supported by the free-standing wall, can be controlled
at will through the opening or closing of the fittings.

123 | Shinsenri Minamimachi House

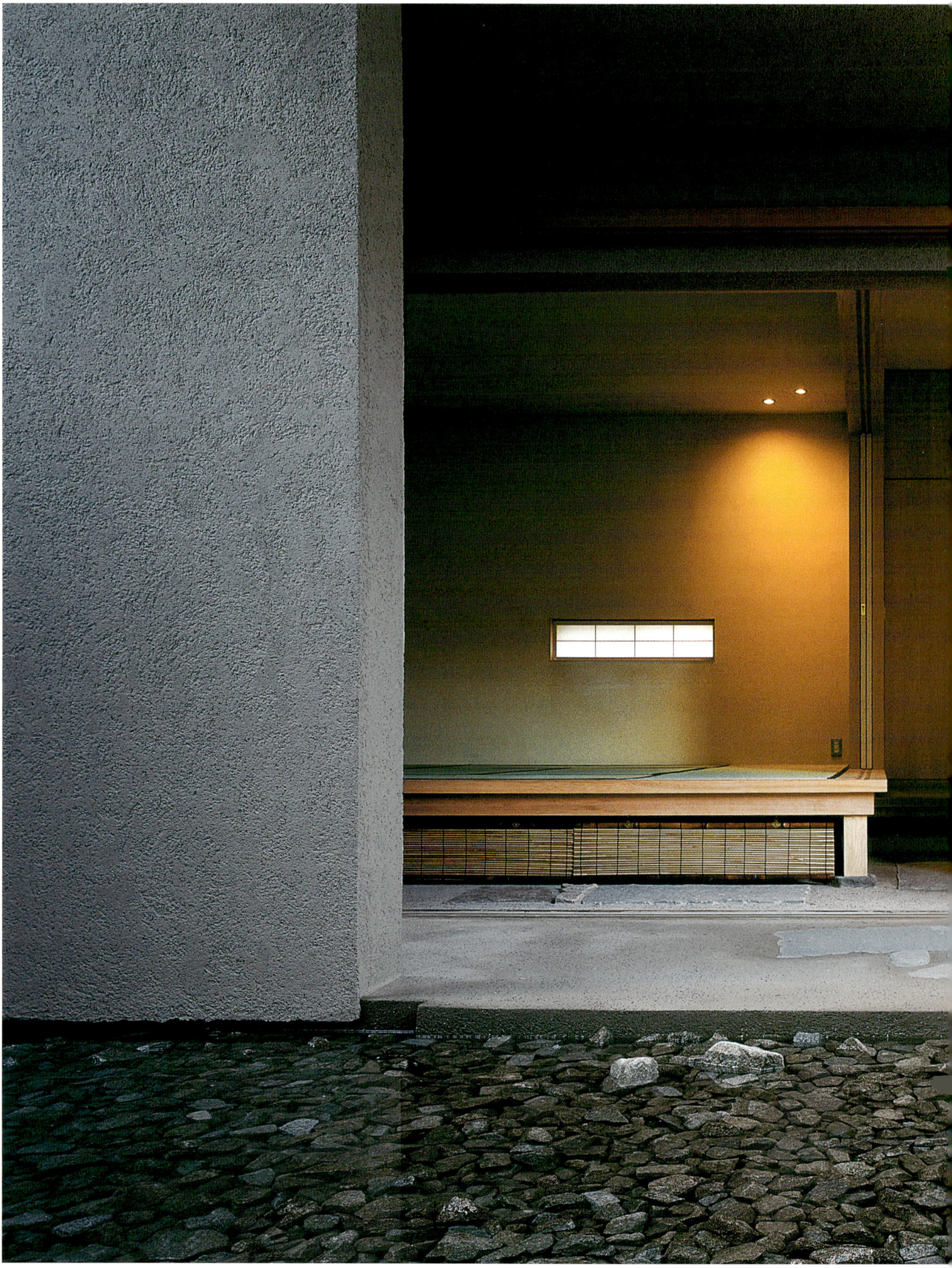

Shinsenri Minamimachi House

126

鴨居、障子、垂壁、自立壁、ガラス戸、中庭へと、内から外へ幾重も層が重なり、複雑な中間領域が生まれる。面と線で構成される内法の重なりは、視覚的な奥行きをつくり出す。

Various layers, beginning with the lintel, and continuing through the *shoji*, hanging partition walls, free-standing wall, and glass doors to the courtyard, overlap to produce a complex intermediary space. The layering of internal dimensions constructed out of planes and lines produces a visual depth.

Shinsenri Minamimachi House

薄く張られた水盤は水鏡となって、季節や天候、時刻を追って変容する情景をすべて映し出す。

The slightly risen flower basins reflect the scenery, constantly changing according to the season, weather, and time, on the surface of the water.

Shinsenri Minamimachi House

壁に沿って折り返し、トンネル状になった階段室は、
緊密な上昇感を生み出す。

The staircase, with a tunnel form that turns
back to follow the wall, creates a heightened
sense of tension.

Shinsenri Minamimachi House

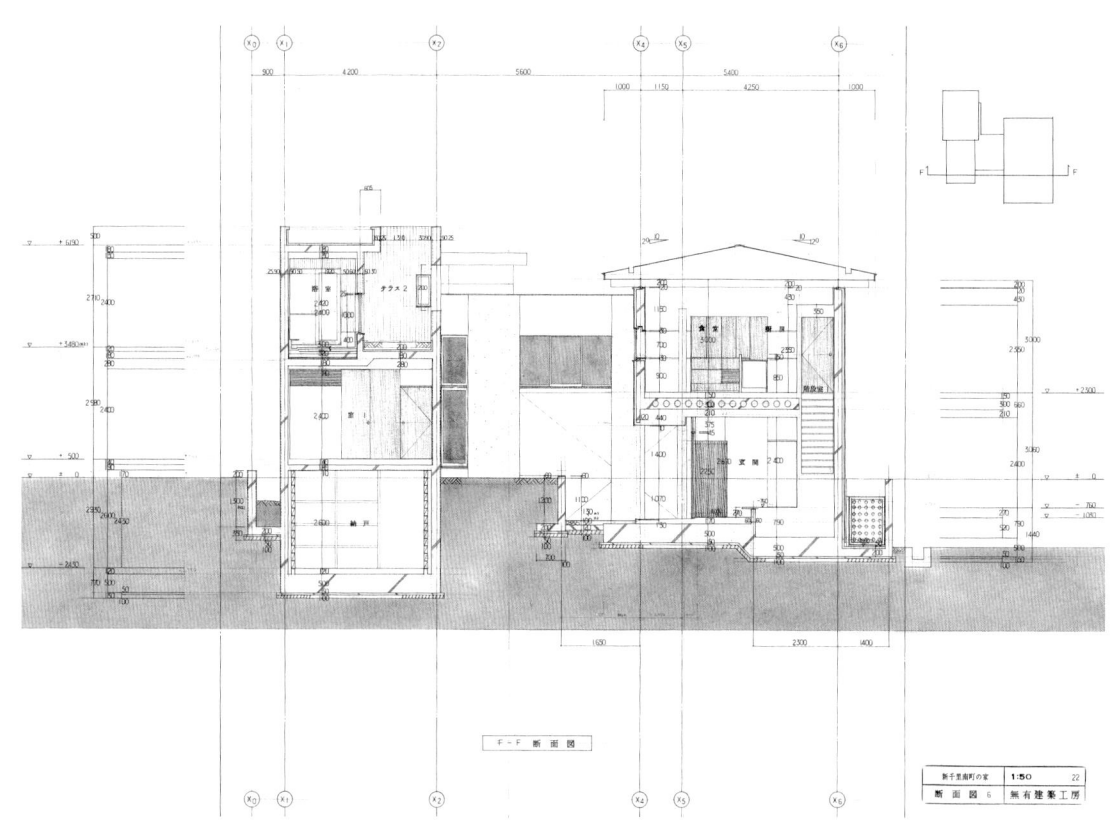

断面図　　Section

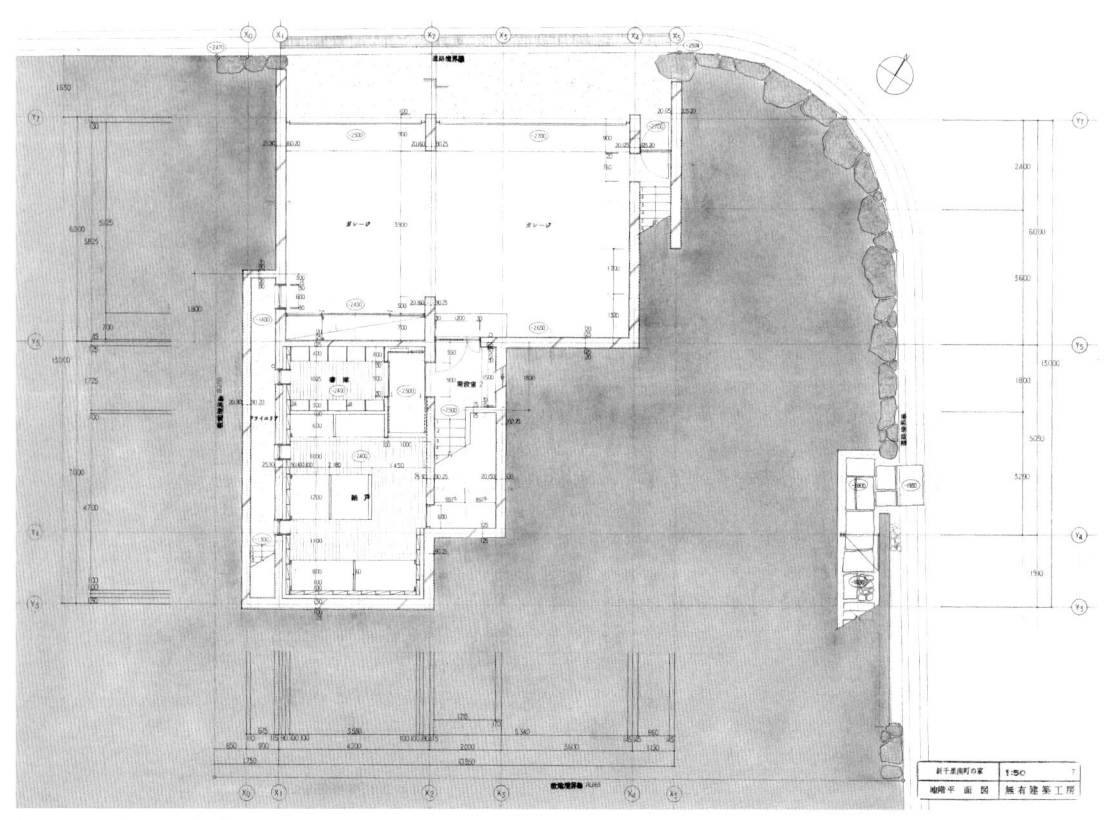

地階平面図　　Basement plan

132

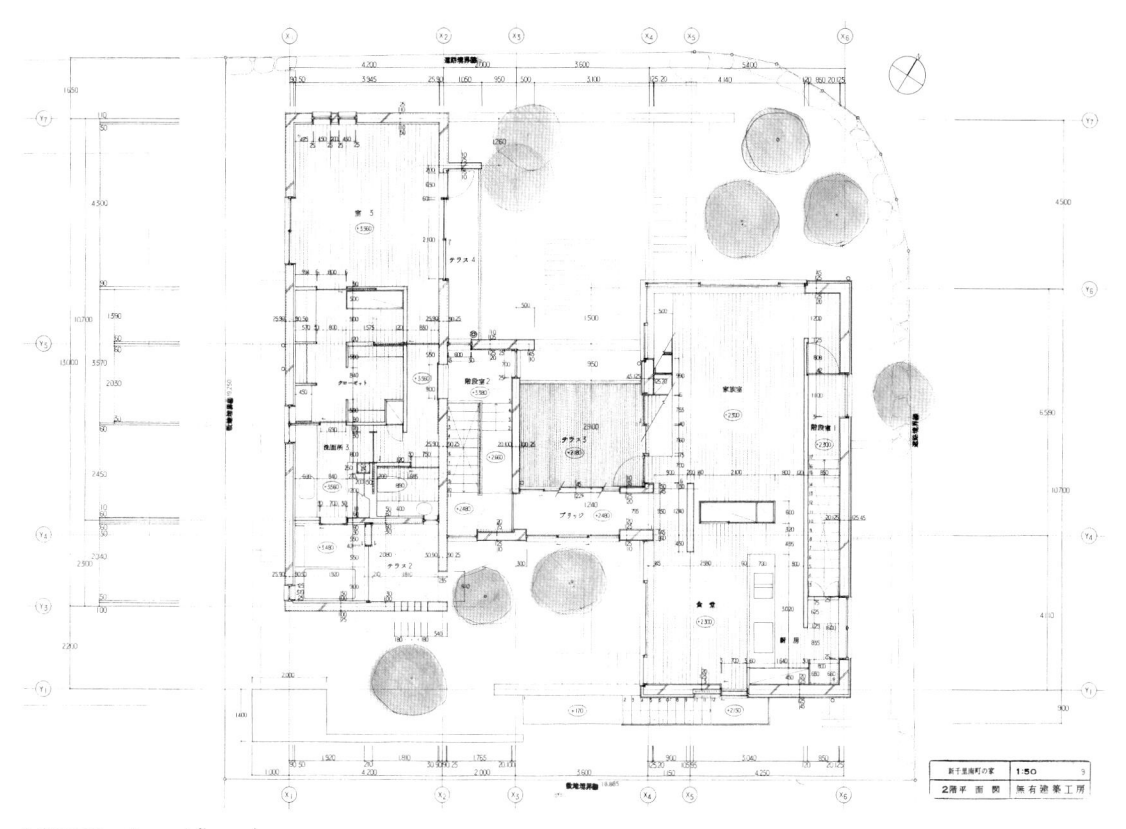

2 階平面図　　Second-floor plan

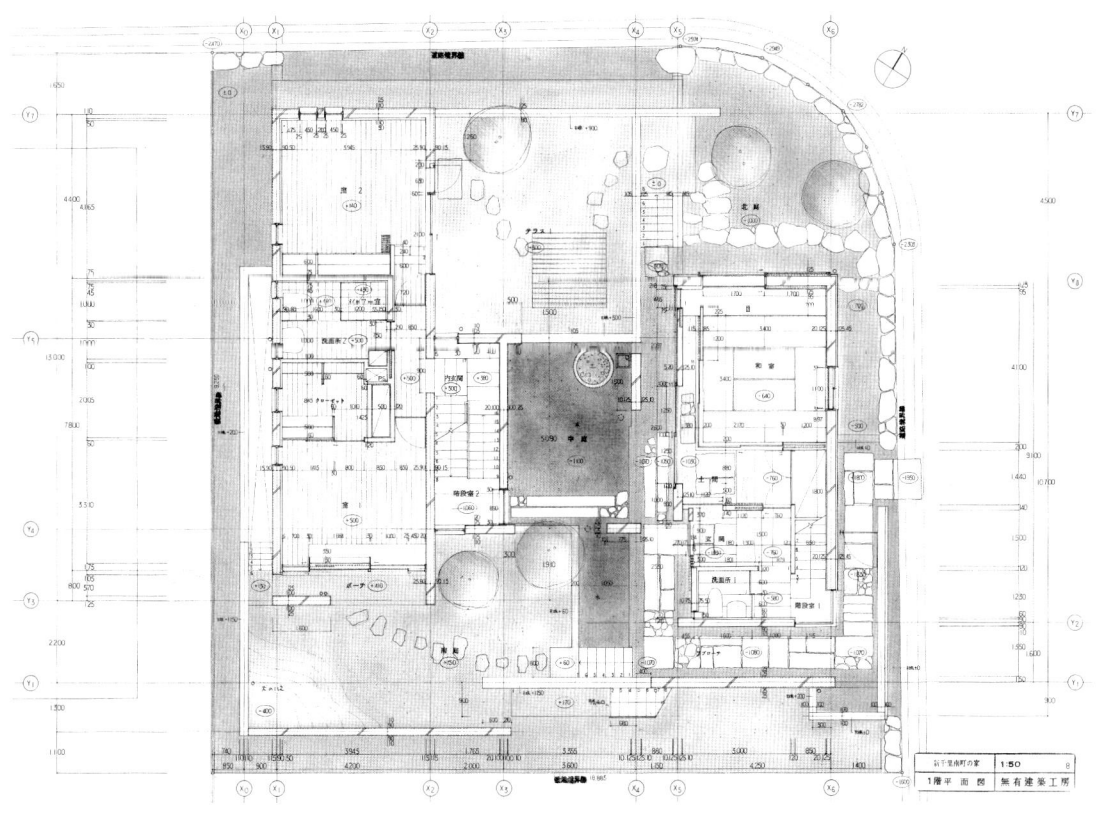

1 階平面図　　First-floor plan

Shinsenri Minamimachi House

家族室／コンクリート造の躯体に木造の屋根が架かり、漆喰塗の壁と、連続する化粧垂木の合間から光が透かされる。切り込まれた開口部が3つの庭への視線を調整し、空間に多角的な抜けをつくる。

Family room: A wooden roof spans the concrete frame and light is allowed in through the space between the plaster walls and the exposed rafters. The framed opening controls the line of sight to the three gardens and creates a multitude of gaps in the space.

135 | Shinsenri Minamimachi House

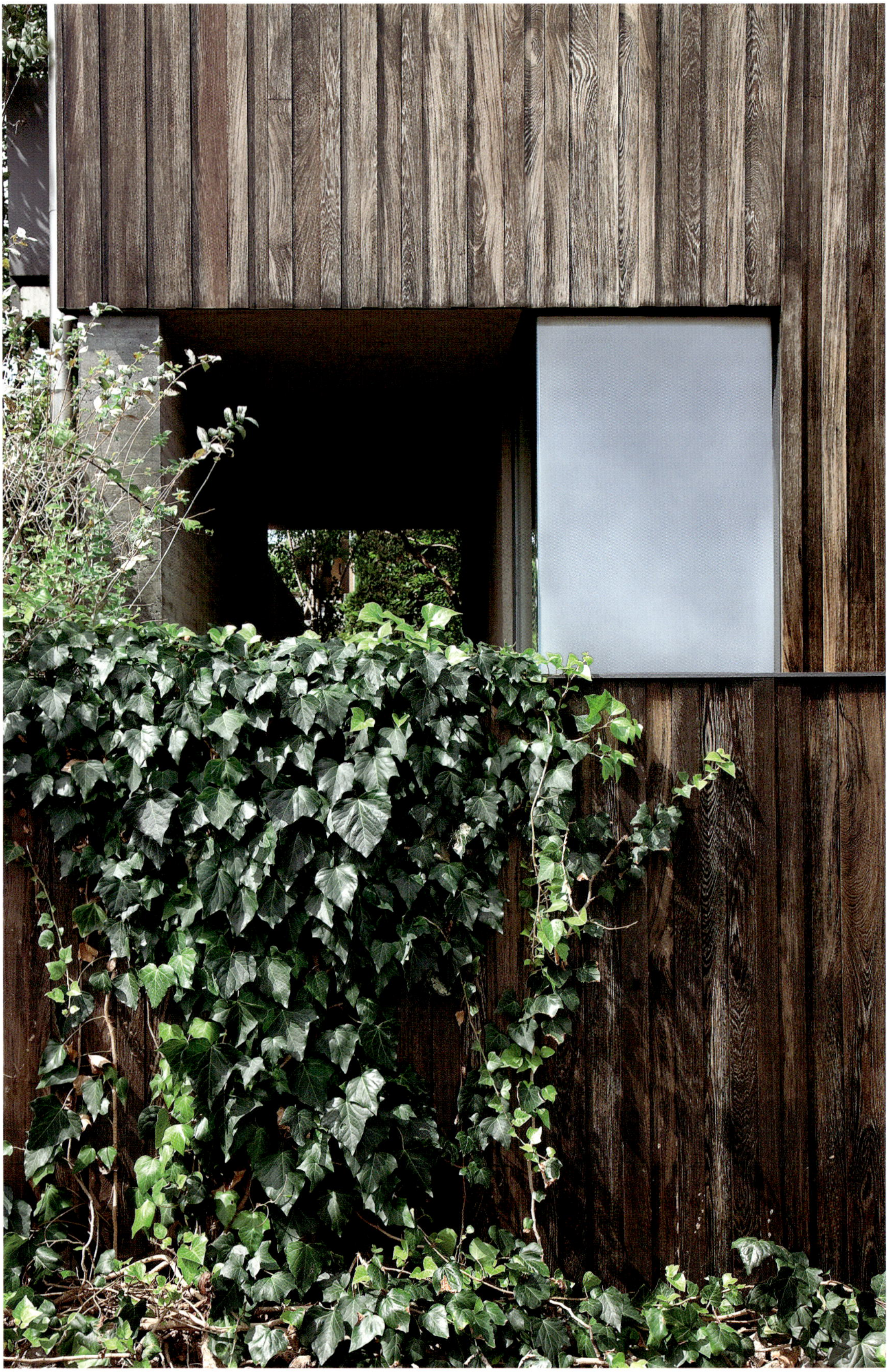

Shinsenri Minamimachi House

竹原城の謎

藤森照信　<建築史家・工学院大学教授>

　竹原義二の作品も名前も日本の建築界ではよく知られている。大阪を代表する住宅作家として広く名は通っている。
　でも、その作品や作品の属する系譜や思想や人となりについて語った例を知らないし、書かれた文も知らない。私もそのひとりで、雑誌の写真を通して独特な作風については存じているし、いろんな機会に会ってもいるが、それ以上に踏み込んだことはない。
「力作であることは使われている材料や細部の納まりから伝わってくるが、語りにくく論じにくい作風だナァ」
　という第一印象が邪魔してそれ以上に踏み込めない。言葉という道具は、トンガッタ思想やデザインを把むには適していても、誰にでもすぐわかるような目立つ先端部分をもたない存在には向いていない。
　竹原のつくる建築は、言葉をどこから侵入させたらいいのか、その門がわからない謎の城のような存在なのである。実際も城郭風で、外から眺めると広からぬひとつの敷地に棟が分立し、凹凸し、おまけに使われている材が、コンクリートにせよ石にせよ木にせよ、太くて堅そう。中はきっと、細い通路が右に行ったり左にいったり、もぐったり、渡ったり、抜けたり、突然外が見えたり、不意に光が射したりして、城郭的迷路性をはらんでいるにちがいない。
　その竹原城を訪れようと思ったのは石井修の一連の住宅を見たからだった。何年か前、石井の自邸を探訪し、この独特な作風が、その後の日本の住宅建築にどんな影響を与えたのか知りたくなった。とすれば、竹原しかいない。大学を出た竹原が入ったのが石井の設計事務所であり、設計に加わったのが石井邸にほかならないからだ。

　訪れたのは<新千里南町の家>。全体の構成は北側から眺めるとよくわかるが、中庭を挟んで左右の2棟からなり、2階部分が空中でつながれている。この敷地なら普通1棟にまとめるのに、どうしたんだろう。
　2棟に分けた結果、各棟のプロポーションは必然的に縦長になる。さらに、隣り合う縦長2棟の光景はどこかミニ開発に似てくる。日本の庭付き1戸建て住宅は、伝統的に横長、水平性を旨とし、このプロポーション感覚は戦後のモダニズム建築でも堅持されてきたし、石井修も守っているのにどうしたんだろう。
　2棟ゆえの縦長。2棟が原因で縦長は結果のはずなのだが、もしかしたら逆で、縦長のプロポーションが好きゆえに2棟に分けた可能性もある。
　2棟分立、縦長プロポーションの"どうして"以上に、私が"どうして"だったのは、構

造だった。左手は木構造の木造仕上げなのに、右手はRC造の打ち放し仕上げ。このスケールの住宅で、そう広からぬ中庭を挟んで向き合う場合、木かコンクリートのどっちかひとつに統一するのが普通だろう。

その木造棟の仕上げに使われている木の種類は何だろう。近づいてためつすがめつ眺めても、触ってわからない。木にはそうとう詳しいつもりだが、こんな仕上げ木材は見たこともない。

竹原さんにうかがうと、

「タガヤサン」

エッ、マサカ！？　タガヤサンといえば400年前の安土桃山の南蛮時代このかた「シタン、コクタン、タガヤサン」と讃えられた銘木中の銘木。はるばる東南アジアから渡来した材にちがいない。ふつう床柱に1本だけシンボリックに使う。それを板にして外壁に張っているのだ。タガヤサンで包んだ住宅は空前絶後だろう。奢侈禁止の江戸時代なら首が飛ぶ。

あきれて敷地の中に入るが、城郭的で、右に曲がったり左に折れたり、閉じたり開いたり、屋外のような屋内のようなアプローチを経て、家の中に入る。

まず応接間。土間を一方にとって、8畳敷の応接。正面の床には真黒な床柱。黒檀だ。仏壇以外で黒檀が使われているのは久しぶりに見た。しかも、こんなに太いのを角で。

黒檀の立つ床板もただものではない。東南アジアの堅木にちがいないが、これだけの巾と長さはちょっとない。

壁は硬く厚い塗りで知られる土佐漆喰。日本の伝統の塗り壁ナンバーワン。

土間が回る室内。低い位置から土間に入る光。和風をベースとした部屋のつくり。そして、堅く、厚く、太い木の扱い。この空間、昔どっかで見たことがあるぞ。もしやアレではあるまいか。影響を受けた建築家の名を聞くと、

「白井晟一」

やはり、そうか。白井の代表作＜呉羽の舎＞につながる空間だ。日本の伝統をモダンな感覚で洗った空間。使う材は、石にせよ木にせよ、太く、厚く、それもムクで見せる。

日本は古来そして今でも、世界一の木造建築の国である。そして使われる木は、檜、杉、松といった北方の針葉樹が主流である。栗のような広葉樹も使われるが、堅くはない。いずれの材も、柔らかく色も薄い。

そうした中で、400年前の南蛮時代このかた東南アジアの熱帯雨林で育った堅く色の濃い木が輸入されるようになり、古くは唐木、近代に入ってからは南洋材と呼ばれ、日本の木造建築の中で特別に貴重な材として扱われ、床柱や床床にシンボリックに使われている。

＜新千里南町の家＞の応接間の堅く色の濃い木を眺めて、ミースの空間を思った。たとえばチューゲンハット邸やバルセロナ・パヴィリオン。材料から受ける感覚が近いのだ。ミースは大理石や蛇紋岩といった石の中では柔らかいのを使い、竹原は、黒檀やタガヤサンなどの木の中では一番堅い熱帯雨林材を使う。石の柔らかいのと、木の堅いのは目に与える印象が似ているにちがいない。

木造王国日本でも、木を大理石のように見せたのは竹原が最初。そして最後になるにちがいない。熱帯雨林の伐採は強く制限され始めているからだ。

応接間の後、2階に向かうが、その階段のつくりに目が釘付けになる。思わずしゃがんでチェックすると、濃い色の熱帯雨林材の堅い踏み面には明るい色の堅い木がノンステップとしてはめ込まれている。こういう小さな材をていねいに埋め込むことを日本では象牙細工にちなみ「象嵌」と呼ぶ。今では建築ではめったに見ない精妙な細工である。

でも踏み面の象嵌にしゃがんだわけではない。階段の最初の数段は蹴上げが正面と側面の2面見えるのだが、2面の見え方が普通ではないのだ。しゃがんで確かめるとヤハリだった。2方向の"ころび"。2方向ころびの階段なんて生まれて初めて見た。これぞ、日本の大工技術の加工精度の極み。指示した建築家も建築家だが、仕上げた大工も大工。

そして2階。応接間のように床の間はじめとする伝統のつくりはなく、現代のモダニズムでまとめられているが、使われている材料の別格と施工の精妙は応接間と階段で経験したとおり。

この家を一巡して、頭に刻まれたのは木と施工のことばかりだった。空間の構成や造形は基本的にはモダニズムを踏まえているから既知といっていい。

現代建築を訪れて、使われている木をはじめとする石やコンクリートといった材料がこれほど雄弁な例は初めてだった。空間の構成、造形、光と闇の演出、構造や設備、それらの要素を押しのけて、まず素材が迫ってくるのだ。それも多種多様な素材が迫ってくる。

だから私も、木のことばかり述べてきたのだが、マテヨ、こうした私の竹原建築へのアプローチは、日本の伝統的建築鑑賞法の血脈を引いているんじゃあるまいか。
「家ぼめ」である。
近代以前から、日本では、とりわけ、しかるべき家の主人たるものの間では家ぼめ能力が不可欠とされた。知人が住まいを新築し、オープニングに迎えられた時、ふたつのことが大事だった。ひとつはご祝儀。お金や酒や米や砂糖や魚などの食料を持参すること。そしてもうひとつは、新築された家をほめなくてはいけない。ここで建築についての素養が必要になる。
どうほめればいいか。使われいる材料と施工の精度をほめる。"床材は紀州の檜の四方柾ですね"とか"床板はケヤキの無節のタマモクですね"とか"これだけ太いタガヤサンよく手に入りましたなあ"とか"柱と壁のチリギワに隙が毛筋ほどもない"とか。近代以前の建築においては、スタイルや平面計画や構造や設備などの要素はどの家もそう変わらないから、施主の熱意と建築的素養と財力によって大いに変わり得る材料と施工の精度をほめる。
私は、まず入った応接間で熱帯雨林材の多様にあきれ、2階への階段の"2方へのころび"に感嘆したが、これは伝統の家ぼめ以外の何ものでもあるまい。
当然のように、モダニズム成立以降の建築界では、家ぼめはタブーだった。材料と施工ではなく、その上位にあるとされるデザインや空間の構成、平面や構造技術を評価すればいい。材料と施工なんてデザインや空間のわからんシロートの言うこと。竹原建築初体験で、自分の目の反応にわれながらあきれ、「家ぼめ」とは何なのか考えた。
"材料"と"施工精度"、このふたつを"物"と"手"と言い換えてみればどうか。にわかに竹原建築の立つ景色が変わり、近代ではなく、人類にとっての建築誕生の光景が広がりはしないか。人類はそのスタートにおいて、木や石や土といった材料を選び、ふたつの手で組み立てて建築としたのだ。
竹原の建築は、材料と施工精度に肝所がある。それ以外にはない。そのことが、モダニズムとともに成立した今の建築評価からズレを起こし、名と作品は知られても、言葉にしにくい建築家にしてしまったのではないか。
21世紀の建築のあり方を考えるとき、もし、これまでの20世紀建築が行き詰っているとするなら、人類の建築の始原に思いを馳せるのはムダではあるまい。そこには、物と手のふたつからなる建築の光景が広がっているのだ。

The Enigmatic Epistle of Yoshiji Takehara

Fujimori Terunobu
Professor of Architectural History, Kogakuin University

Yoshiji Takehara – both his name and his works – are well known amongst architects in Japan. He is one of the leading figures of residential architecture in Osaka.

However, not many of them know much about his works, nor the lineage, thought, and person behind them, nor anything written about his works. I am no exception, and although I know his unique style from photos on magazines and I have met him on different occasions, I have not explored further.

My first impressions can be summed up as follows: "These are fine works, judging from the way materials are used and how the details are put together, but the style seems difficult to talk about or discuss." This has prevented me from delving deeper into his works. Although words can be employed to capture 'edgy' ideas and thoughts, they are not necessarily appropriate for describing things with less outstanding characteristics.

It is hard to find an opening for words to enter Takehara's architecture – it is like a castle of riddles with a hidden entrance. His buildings are indeed often castle-like – looking from outside you may see separate towers clustered on a single site, in different heights in various materials such as concrete, stone, or wood, which all look thick and hard. One could imagine that the inside would be like a labyrinth with narrow winding alleys going right and left and diving underground, flying across space like bridges and penetrating walls, suddenly taking you outside or being lit up unexpectedly.

It was after visiting houses designed by Osamu Ishii that I decided to visit the Takehara castle. A few years ago, I visited Ishii's own house, which made me curious to find out what sort of impact that its unique design might have had on later residential design in Japan. If so, Takehara would have been the only one. It was Ishii's practice that Takehara joined after graduation, and it was Ishii's house that he was involved with designing.

What I visited was the Shinsenri Minamimachi House. The overall structure can be well grasped when looking from the north, consisting of two towers sandwiching a courtyard which are connected to each other on the second floor. One would normally build one building on this site. Why did he build two instead?

The division into two towers necessarily results in each having proportions oriented vertically. Moreover, two towers standing next to one another reminds you of *mini-kaihatsu*, the micro-scale housing developments often encountered at the suburban fringe. Traditionally, a single-family house with a garden in Japan tends to be built with a wide frontage and oriented horizontally. Postwar modernist architecture firmly maintained a sense of such proportions, including by Osamu Ishii. So what happened here?

Verticality results from the twin towers – these towers must be the cause of this verticality, and yet it could well be the other way around that he built two towers because he liked vertical proportions.

What puzzled me even more than the two separate towers was the structure. The left tower is built using timber construction with a wood finish whereas the right one is built using reinforced off-form concrete construction. For this scale of dwelling, with two towers facing each other with a smallish courtyard in between, one would normally unify the construction method to either timber or concrete.

What kinds of woods were applied as finishes for the wooden tower? I didn't have any clue, even after close scrutiny and touching it. I consider myself pretty knowledgeable about wood, yet I have never seen this kind of wood finish before.

When asked Takehara, the answer was "*Tagayasan*" (Siamese Senna or Cassod Tree in English). Impossible! Ever since the Nanban trade during the Azuchi Momoyama period 400 years ago, *tagayasan* has been one considered of the three most precious woods, as eulogised in the expression "*sitan, kokutan, tagayasan.*" Without a doubt it must have travelled far, all the way from south-east Asia. It use is normally reserved for symbolic purposes, such as the post in the *tokonoma*. And yet here they were made into wooden boards and applied to the external walls. This must be the only house ever finished with *tagayasan*. Under the prohibitions of the sumptuary laws of the Edo period you would have lost your head for this.

Astounded, I entered the site, following the labyrinthine winding path which turned right and left, closed down and opened up, felt sometimes inside, sometimes outside, until I finally entered the house.

First of all, there is the reception room. A 8-mat tatami reception room with a *doma* (earthen floor) space to one side.

Ahead lies an inky-black alcove post. In ebony. I have rarely seen ebony used except in *butsudan* (the Buddhist family altar). But here it is a hefty chunk of wood.

The floor on which the alcove post stands is also unusual. No doubt this is also hardwood timber from south-east Asia, but it is rare to have it in such widths and lengths.

The walls are finished with Tosa plaster (*shikkui*), famous for being hard and trick. The premier finish for traditional plaster walls in Japan.

The *doma* continues into the interior. The *doma* is illuminated by low windows. Rooms are based on traditional Japanese lines. Also the way the architecture deals with hard, thick, bold wood. But I am sure I have seen this space before. Could it be that? When asked who he was influenced by, "Sei'ichi Shirai" comes the reply. Aha, so that's it! This is is a space that pays homage to Shirai's masterwork 'House in Kureha.' A traditional Japanese space refreshed with a modern sensibility. Whether stone or wood, materials are thick, bold and stripped bare.

From ancient times to today, Japan has been the standard bearer for wooden architecture. Softwoods from the northern areas, such as *hinoki*, cedar, and pine have been the main materials. Some broadleafs such as chestnut has been also used but they are not that hard. In any case, these timbers are all soft and blond.

About 400 years ago, during the Nanban period, hard, dark timber from trees grown in the south-east Asian rainforest started to be imported into Japan. Such woods, which used to be called *karaki* or in modern times *nanyo-zai*, have been regarded as a precious material in the traditional wooden architecture in Japan, and were reserved for symbolic elements such as the alcove post or floor.

As I was looking at the dark hardwood near the drawing room of Shinsenri Minamimachi House I found myself thinking of spaces by Mies van der Rohe. For example, Villa Tugendhat or the Barcelona Pavilion. This is because you get a similar feeling from the materials. Mies uses soft stones such as marbles and serpentines, whereas Takehara chooses among the hardest of rainforest hardwoods, such as ebony or *tagayasan*. The visual impression from soft stones and hard timbers are undoubtedly similar.

Although Japan is the kingdom of wooden architecture, Takehara must have been the first architect to make wood look like marble. And no doubt the last. This is because restrictions on the logging of tropical rainforest are being increasingly tightened.

Proceeding upstairs from the reception room, one's eyes are riveted by the way the staircase is made. I could not help squatting down to take a closer look, and found that pieces of light-coloured hardwood are set seamlessly in the stair treads made of dark rainforest hardwood. We call this technique of carefully inlaying small pieces *zogan*, named after ivory crafts. Such exquisite workmanship is rarely seen in architecture these days.

However, the reason I squatted down was not to look at the stair treads. It was to look at the risers. Both the front and the sides of the first few risers were visible, but they looked strange. When I looked closer, I confirmed my suspicion that they were 'tilted', in both directions Never in my life have I seen a staircase tilted in two directions at once. This must be the height of Japanese craftsmanship. I cannot believe that there exists an architect who could have ordered this, nor a craftsman who could manage to get it done.

On to the second floor. Here there is nothing traditional like the *tokonoma* in the reception room. It is executed according to the manner of contemporary modernism, but the experience of the exceptional materials and craftsmanship on the second floor is no different to that of the reception room or staircase.

What was etched in my mind while going through this house was wood and craftsmanship. The spatial structure and formal design are based upon modernism and thus well-known. But I had never seen a more eloquent use of material in contemporary architecture, whether of timber, stone, or concrete. Spatial structure, formal design, play of light and shadow, structure, services – all these are pushed aside by the materials. It is the materials that overwhelm you, in all their wide variety.

That is why I have been talking only about wood – but come to think of it, the way I approach Takehara's architecture is in line with the traditional way of appreciating architecture in Japan.

This is called *iebome*, or 'house-praising'.

Before the modern period in Japan, it had long been regarded as an essential skill amongst respectable society to be able to praise a house. There were two important things to remember if you were invited to an opening of a new house by your acquaintance. One was a congratulatory gift. You would have to bring money or food such as sake, rice, sugar, or fish. The other was praising the new house. For this you needed architectural knowledge.

How to praise? You could compliment materials and fine craftsmanship. "Straight-grained on all four sides! This must be *hinoki* from Kishu!"; or "How smooth is the grain of these *keyaki* floorboards, without the usual gnarls!"; or "How did you manage to find *tagayasan* this thick?"; or "The gap between column and wall is as finer than the thickness of a strand of hair!" and so on. Before the modern period, there was not much variation among aspects such as style, plan, structure, and equipment to distinguish one house from the other. It was in the aspects of material quality and the levels of craftsmanship that the owner's passion, architectural connoisseurship, and wealth were reflected, and so it was these things that were praised.

So my surprise, on entering the house, at the variety of rainforest timbers used in the reception room, and my admiration of the two-way tilt to the staircase leading upstairs are no different from the traditional 'house-praising'.

Naturally, with the emergence of modernism, 'house-praising' became taboo in the architecture world. It was only necessary to review design, spatial structure, plan, and structural techniques, these being regarded as superior to materials or craftsmanship. Materials and craftsmanship were seen as subjects for non-professionals who neither understand design nor space.

I could not help being surprised at my own reaction to my first experience of Takehara's architecture, and I thought about what 'house-praising' actually means. Why not call 'materials' and 'fine craftsmanship' as 'matter' and 'hands' respectively. Suddenly, the setting in which Takehara's architecture is built changes from the modern era to that moment when human beings first gave birth to architecture. In the beginning, human beings took materials such as wood, stone, and earth, put them together with their hands, and called it architecture.

The key to Takehara's architecture is materials and fine craftsmanship. Nothing else. This is why the terms of architectural evaluation that emerged with modernism fail to gather much purchase upon it. And this may well be the reason why, even though his name and works are well-known, he has been an architect who has been difficult to grasp through words.

When we think of what a 21st century architecture might be, and if we regard the architecture of the 20th century as having come to a dead end, then it would do us well to cast our minds back to the very origins of architecture. Here we find a vision of architecture made from just two things: matter and hands.

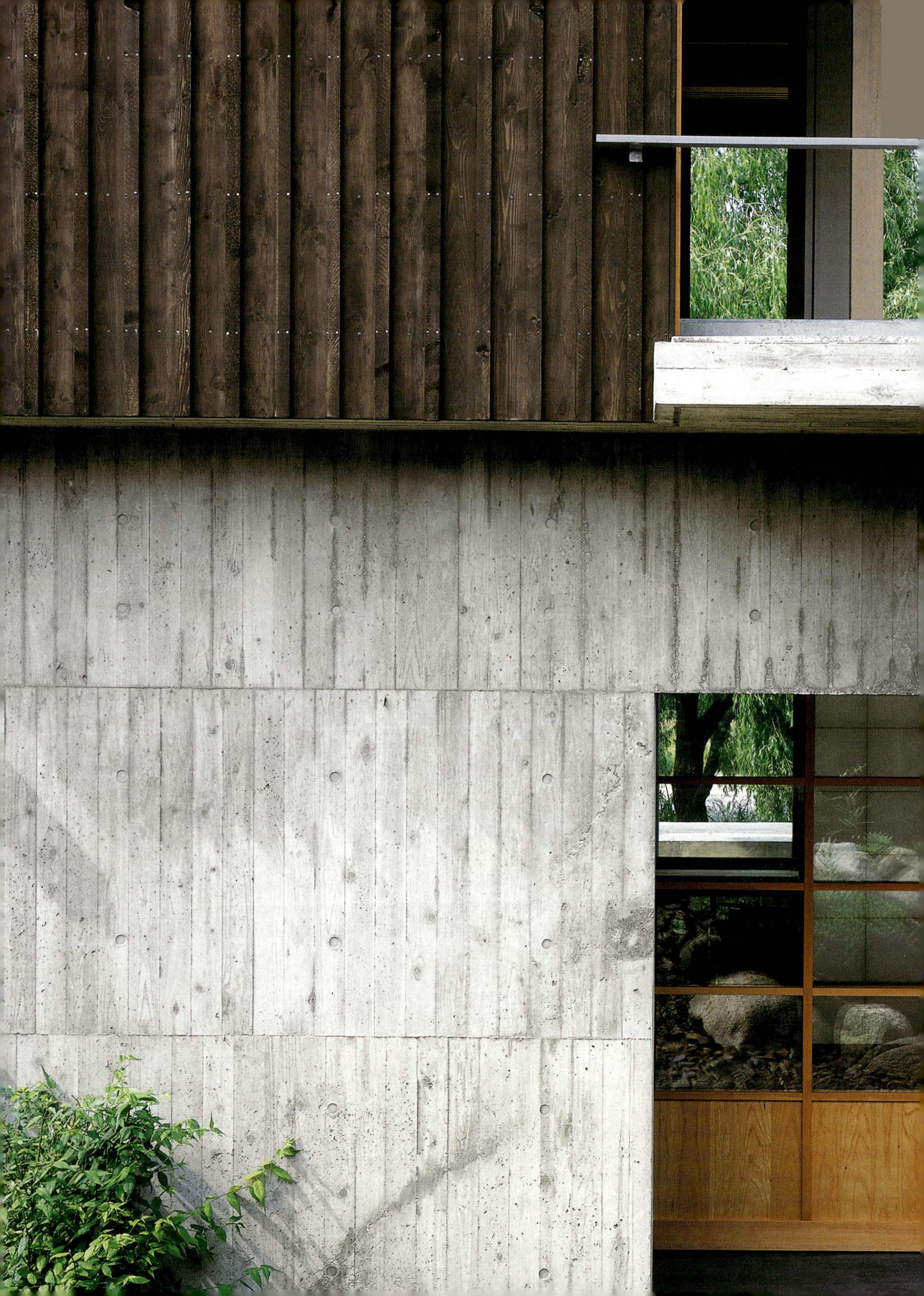

京都市から大津市にまたがる比叡山の中腹、標高370mに位置するこの町は、1970年代頃から避暑の別荘地として開発された。現在では住宅が建ち並び、比叡山を中心とした景色の中にひとつのニュータウンを形成する。先代より受け継がれたこの敷地はもとより南に庭が配され、石組みや岩肌を覆いつくす苔がこの庭を豊かなものにしていた。歳月が培ってきたものに手を加えないように配慮し、寒さの厳しい気候条件から、以前は北風を遮るように壁で分断されていた南側の庭と北側に望む比叡山の景観を積極的に取り込みながら、環境に呼応する住まいへと変貌を遂げた。

南北の壁に開口部を穿ち、内と外の緩衝帯となるよう、室の外周に廻廊を巡らせる。殻とその内なる皮膜で平面が構成され、廻廊の狭間に浮かぶ室はほどよいスケールをもつ。廻廊を介して自在に動く二重の建具は、季節に応じた空気の流れを調整する。廻廊に巡る小壁・垂壁・腰壁・現しの柱の構成は、内と外の視覚的な間合いをはかり、その領域をより意識させる。

地面と接する1階は庭に面する壁に開口部を穿ち、敷居を設け、その内に建具を引き込むことで「またぐ」という行為を促し、意識的な結界をつくり出す。このとき廊下は囲い取られた廻廊として、方向性をより意識させる。北面は太鼓障子と襖が静かに光を透過し、道路からの視線をかわしている。宙に浮かぶ2階は庭に面する南側には結界を設けず、水平スラブによって景色を連続させた。内に纏う太鼓障子と外に纏うガラス戸が中間領域をつくり、床のレヴェル差によって庭への視線をさらに切り込み、素材の切替えによって内と外を曖昧にする。このとき垂壁と自立する柱は距離感をつくり出し、庭の様相を身近に引き寄せる。北面は垂壁や腰窓を重ね、比叡山の稜線だけを水平に切り取り、静穏な空気を醸し出している。

内と外の関係性、環境に呼応する中間領域の多様性が、廻廊となって紡ぎ出されたとき、住空間に様々なシーンを展開するであろう。

比叡平の家
Hieidaira House

Hieidaira was developed as a resort area on Mt. Hiei in the 1970s at an elevation of 370 meters, and a new town is now taking shape. This lot originally included a garden with a south orientation that was distinctive for its lush moss. As the property had long been neglected and the climate was so cold, a variety of changes were made, including the creation of a garden on the south side (previously partitioned off by a wall to block the north wind) and the adoption of the mountain scenery on the north side.

Passing through the opening in the north-south wall, one finds a corridor outside one room that acts as a buffer zone between the interior and exterior. The plane consists of a shell and an inner membrane, and the room, rising up in the narrow space between the corridors, is modest in scale. The two-layered fittings, mediated by the corridor, regulate the flow of air according to the season. The structure of the upper small walls, hanging partition walls, waist-high partition walls, and visible columns that surround the corridor create a visual interval between the interior and exterior.

The first floor passes through an opening in a wall that abuts the garden, creating a threshold, drawing the fittings inside, and erecting a conscious barrier. At this point, the enclosed corridor heightens one's sense of direction. On the north facade, the *taiko shoji* (paper-covered sliding doors) and *fusuma* are permeated by gentle light, discouraging a direct line of sight from the road. Without erecting a barrier to the south side, which faces the garden, the second floor, suspended in midair, is linked to the scenery by means of a flat slab. The *taiko-shoji* interior and the glass-door exterior produce an intermediary space, and due to the level difference, the line of sight to the garden is limited. Here, the hanging partition walls and free-standing columns evoke a sense of distance, and draw the aspect of the garden toward the viewer. Layered with hanging and waist-high partition walls, the north facade horizontally frames Mt. Hiei's ridge line.

The relationship between the interior and exterior, and the diversity of intermediary space in response to the surrounding environment gives rise to a variety of scenes as one makes their way through the residence.

148

左：廊下2より室1を見る／垂壁と小壁の構成により光の密度が変幻し、斜交いに視線が抜ける。
右：室1西側の自立壁の間より廊下3を見る／高さの異なる開口部を重ねることでマドとして景色を切り取りながら、空間そのものを囲い取り、廻廊の様相を見せる。

Left: View of Room 1 from corridor—Due to the structure of the vertical hanging walls and overhead walls, the density of the light is constantly changing, and the line of sight passes through diagonally.
Right: View of Corridor 3 from between the free-standing walls on the west side of Room 1—The juxtaposition of openings with different heights frames the scenery like a window, encloses the space itself, and displays the aspect of the corridor.

1階間室／廻廊の交差点に「つなぎの間」となった間室。廻廊より一段沈み込み、垂壁に包まれた筒状の吹抜となって平面と断面を曖昧につなぐ。

"Connecting space" in the node between the first-floor intermediary room and the corridors: Sunken one step below the corridor, the area takes the form of a tubular atrium enclosed by vertical hanging walls and connects the plane and section in an ambiguous manner.

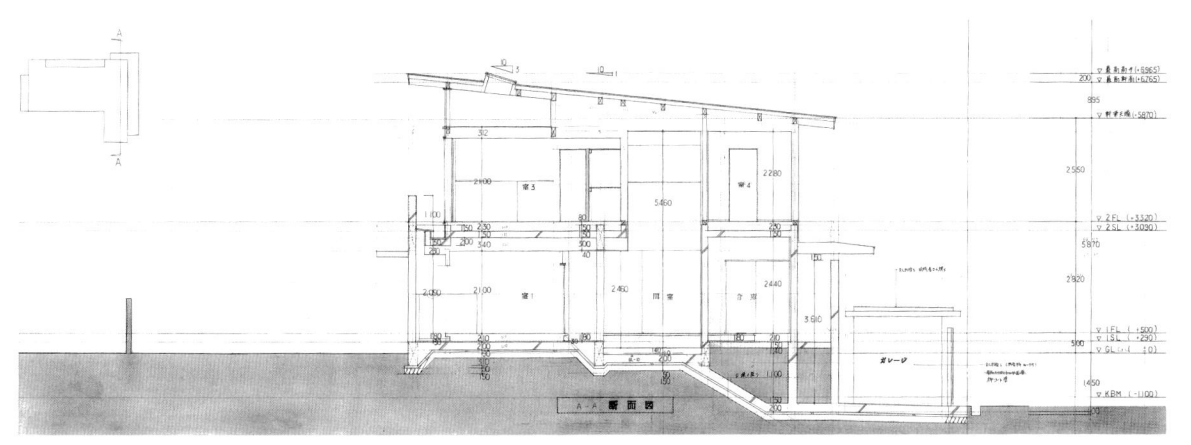

断面図　Section

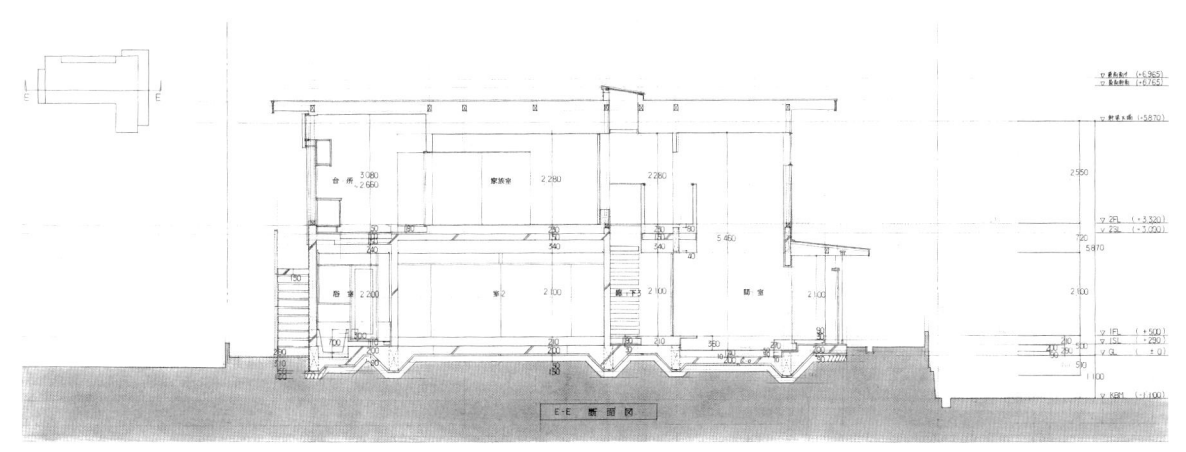

断面図　Section

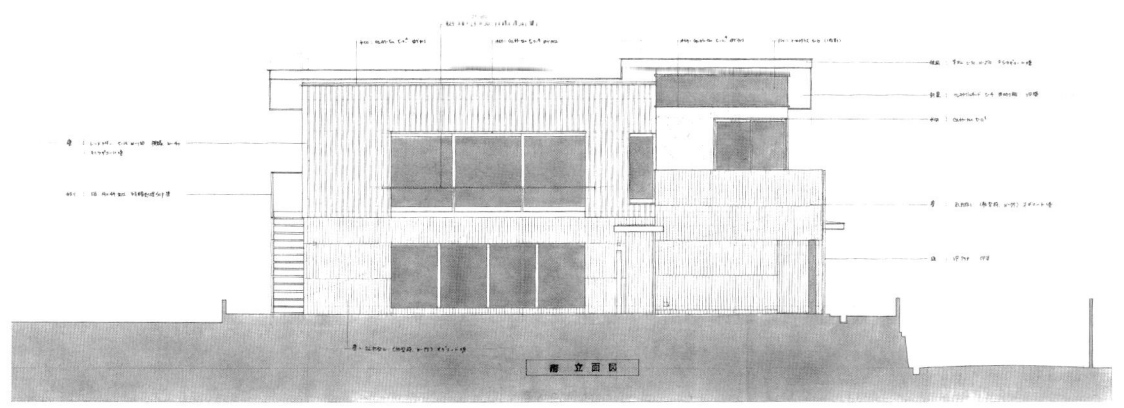

立面図　Elevation

151 | Hieidaira House

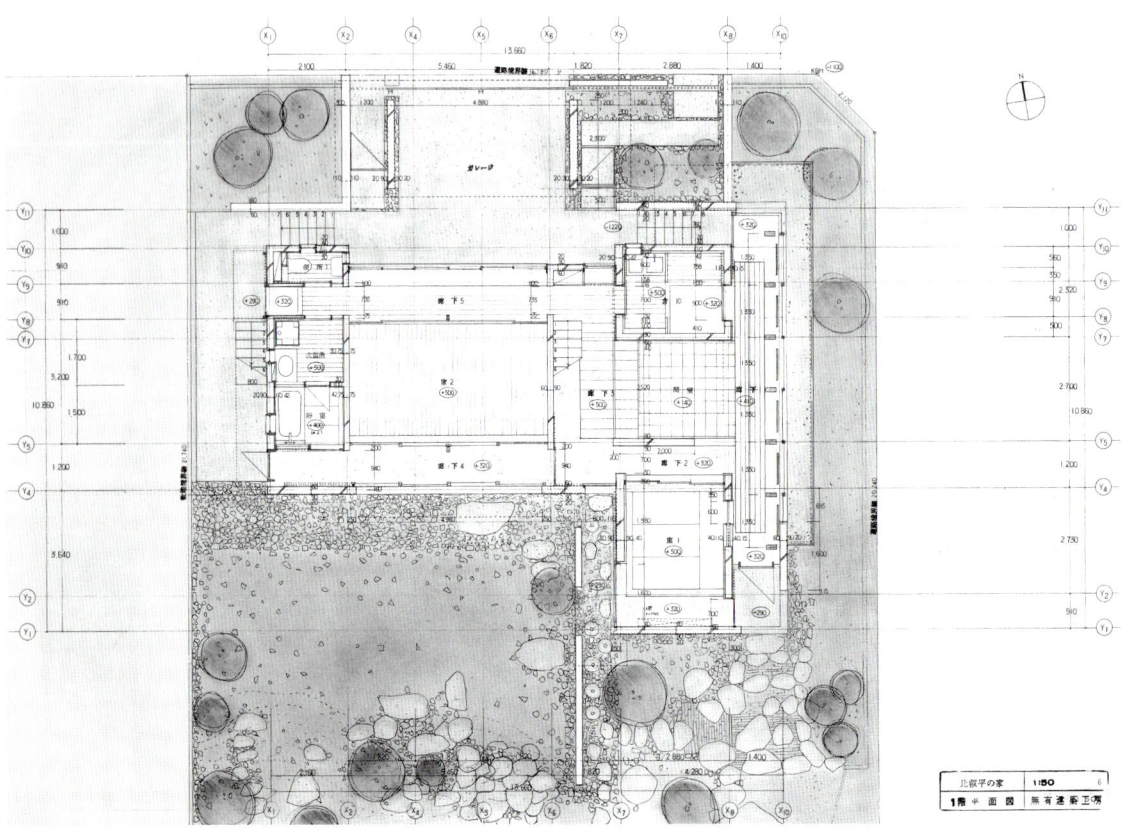

1階平面図　　First-floor plan

152

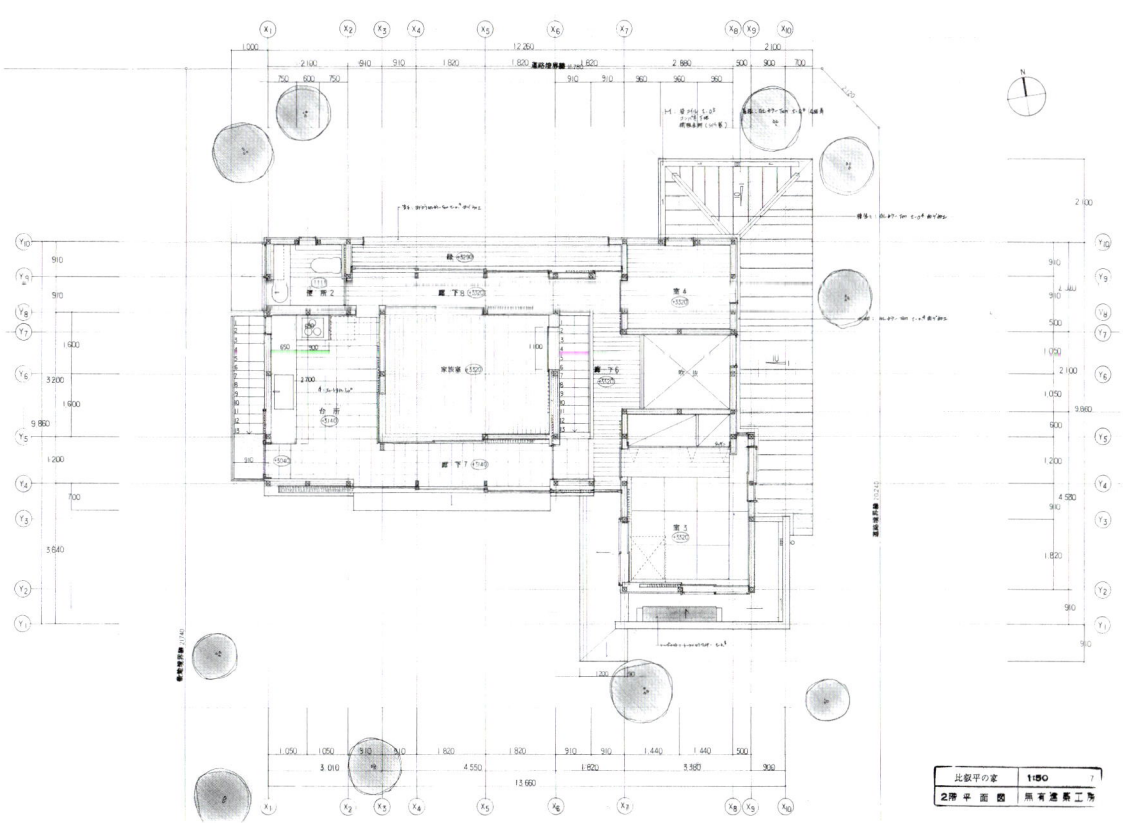

2 階平面図　Second-floor plan

153 | Hieidaira House

前頁：2階家族室／室と廻廊の床レヴェルと仕上げ、垂壁や小壁の構成、二重の建具や柱の建ち方が、曖昧な空間の領域を示唆し、庭へと続く視線を調整する。
左・右：室2と庭は敷居によって足元に結界を結び、建具を内側に走らせることで内外の様相を反転させる。足元と内法の構成が視線を徐々に抑え込み、南の庭から北の比叡山までの景色をより印象的に囲い取る。

Preceding page: Second-floor family room—The finishing of the floor levels between the room and the corridor, the structure of the vertical hanging walls and overhead walls, and the dual-layering of the fittings and columns creates an ambiguous space and controls the line of sight that leads to the garden.
Left and right: Due to the threshold, a foot-level barrier is created between Room 2 and the garden, and by installing the fittings on the interior, the aspect of the interior and exterior are inverted. The structure of the barrier and the internal dimensions subtly limit the line of sight, enclosing an impressive landscape that stretches from the garden in the south to Mt. Hiei in the north.

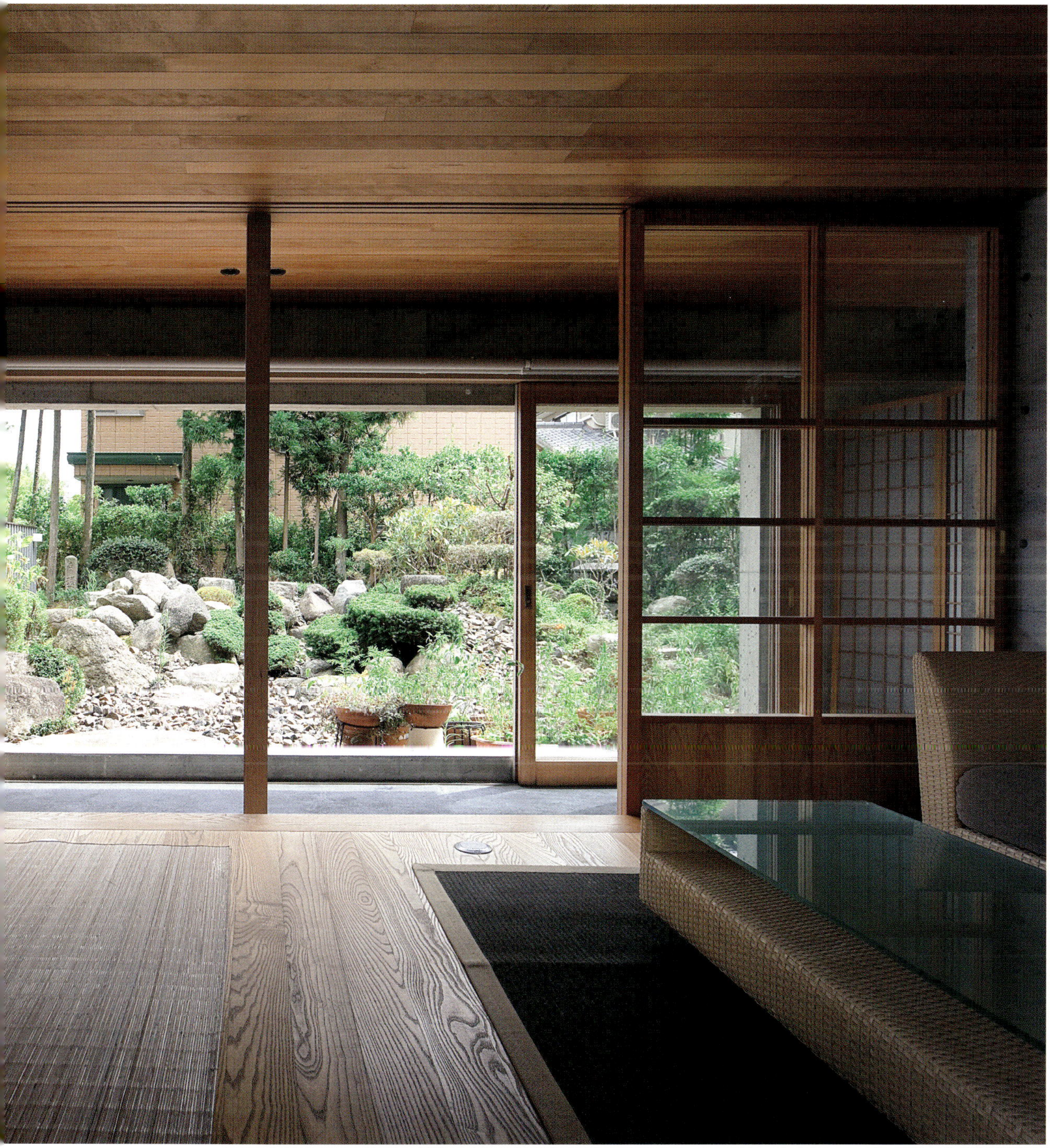

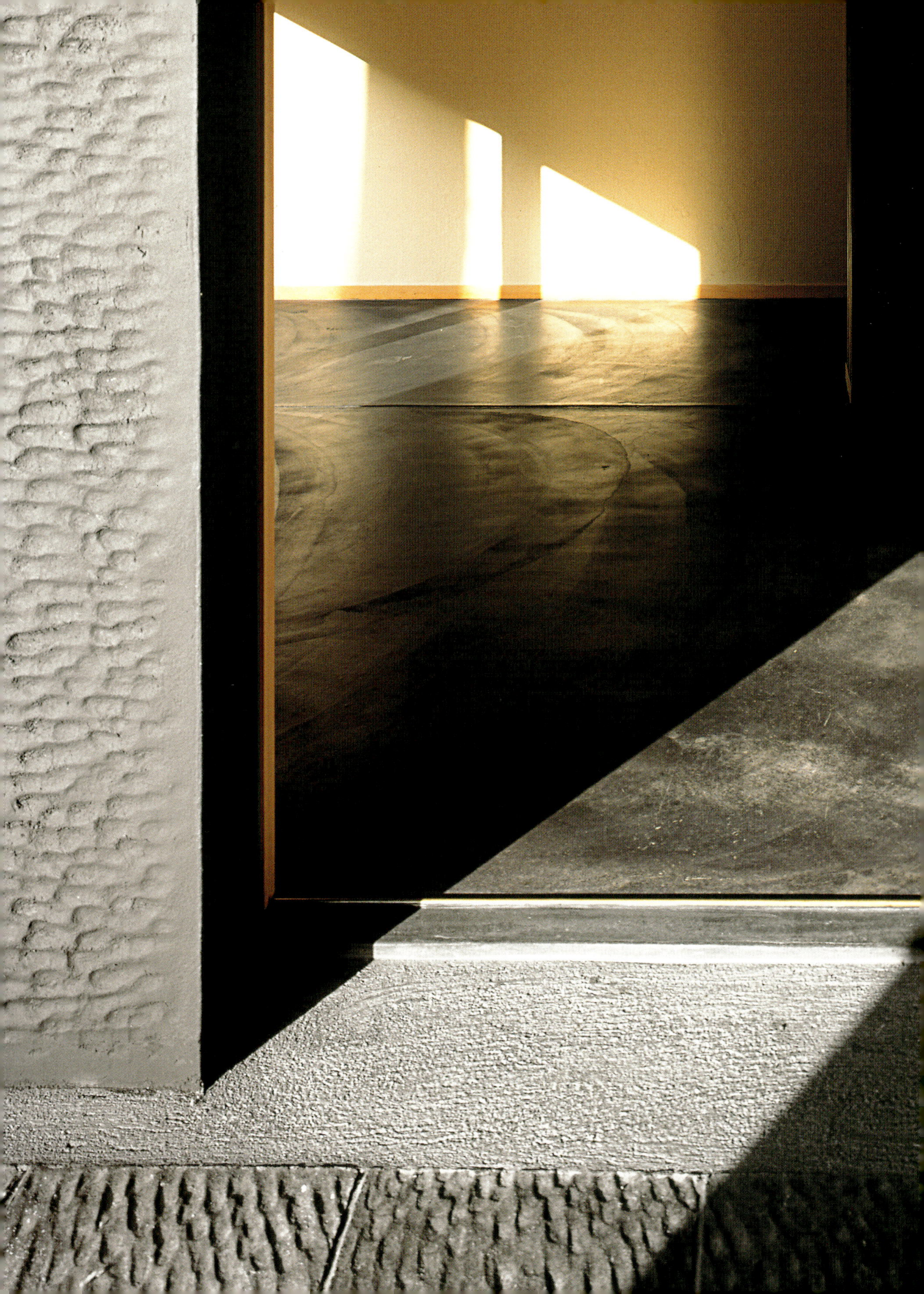

敷地は琵琶湖を見下ろす蓬萊山の中腹、標高265mの傾斜地に位置し、琵琶湖の湖面越しに伊吹山を背景とした近江八幡、安土の町並を望む。北側は石積みの残る美しい棚田が比叡山系へとつながり、人為と自然が融合した壮大なロケーションを見せる。ここに陶芸家のアトリエと居を構え、土と真摯に向き合い、創作と日常が自然へ回帰するための場をつくり出した。

間口37m、奥行12mの細長い敷地は八屋戸川の谷筋に向かって9mの急斜面をなす。斜面に対し水平な床を最大限確保できるように床レヴェルを決定し、動線が間延びしないようにヴォリュームの外へ階段を突出させ、レヴェルを半階ずらし、地階・1階・1.5階の3つのレヴェルからアプローチできるようにした。地階はコンクリートの直方体を斜面より突き出し、基壇を構成する。床スラブ、低く抑えられた庇が描く水平線は傾斜する地面に拮抗し、ひな壇状のヴォリュームがエレヴェーションを切り込む。

坂の上に配された玄関より3畳の小座敷をしつらえた室1へ通される。ここはアトリエと家族室の中間階に位置し、他者と住まい手、制作活動と日常生活の「つなぎの間」となる。草庵茶室のように玄く塗り込めた小空間は、太鼓障子から透過する光をぼんやりと纏い、薄灯りの中で向き合う土と陶は色彩と質感を微細に変幻させる。一方アトリエは木造大断面の列柱にラワンベニヤ張の壁とコンクリート直押えの床で構成し、土と建築が素地のまま対峙する。内法を抑え込む垂壁と1枚の自立壁が止めどなく続く視線を受け止め、自然を感じながら程よく作品と向かい合うことができる。列柱の足元には敷土台が横たわり、外廻廊との結界を結ぶ。浮遊感を漂わせる水平スラブの上に場の重心が与えられる。

東西に延びる外壁の表裏に折り返す階段は、動線的・視覚的なレヴェル差を調整しながら、意識的な内外を錯綜させる。最上階のテラスより景色を一望し、天地の稜線に身を委ねたとき、日常と創作、そして自然が三位一体となった豊かな生活を再認識するであろう。

蓬萊・玄のアトリエ
Horai Atelier Kuro

Situated on the side of Mt. Horai at an elevation of 265 meters, this lot boasts a view of Mt. Ibuki, rising up beyond the shores of Lake Biwa. On the north side are terraced rice paddies with stone walls on this magnificent site that synthesizes artifice and nature. The atelier/residence was designed for a ceramicist who wanted to return to a natural environment.

With a frontage of 37 meters and a depth of twelve meters, the long, thin lot lies on a steep, nine-meter incline facing a river ravine. After determining a level that would provide maximum security for a flat floor, the stairs were allowed to protrude outside the volume to prevent the flow line from extending, and by staggering the level half a story, it was possible to create an approach consisting of three levels (basement, first floor, and 1.5 floor). The horizontal lines of the floor slab and the low, controlled eaves produce an antagonism with the slanted ground level, and the tiered volume cuts through the elevation.

A small room with its entrance positioned at the top of the slope leads into another room. The intermediary staircase, between the atelier and the living space, serves as a "connecting space" between creative and daily activities. The small space, painted black like a tea house, allows dim light to permeate the *shoji*, and the ceramics are constantly enveloped in subtle changes of color and quality. The atelier is constructed out of wooden colonnades with lauan-veneered walls and a pressed concrete floor. Limiting the internal dimensions of the hanging partition walls and making the free-standing wall look as if it continues forever provides the artist with a comfortable working atmosphere. At the base of the colonnades lies a mudsill that acts as a barrier to the exterior corridor. The gravity of the space is centered above the "floating" flat slab.

The staircase regulates the level difference in the flow line and visually blurs the interior and exterior. The top-floor terrace offers a commanding view of the landscape, and as one becomes absorbed in the ridge line between heaven and earth, one's thoughts turn to the fundamental elements of a full life: everyday activities, creative pursuits, and nature.

地階をつくるコンクリートの基壇の上に2層分の木造がセットバックして載る。スラブ、庇、屋根が構成する水平ラインはエレヴェーションを切り込み、のびやかな視線を遠景へと誘う。
右：ポーチ床に敷き詰められたタイル、束石に使われたのは陶芸家自らの作品。

On a concrete foundation, which forms the basement, the two-story structure is positioned in a setback style. The horizontal lines created by the slab, eaves, and roof, cut through the elevation, inviting an extended line of sight into the far distance.
Right: The tiles and stone struts lining the porch floor are an example of the resident ceramicist's work.

159 | Horai Atelier Kuro

160

161 | Horai Atelier Kuro

谷筋へ9mのレヴェル差をもつ前面道路。敷地や建築の余白、廻遊する視線の先に作品が佇む。土をはじめとする創作活動が自然を背景にした日常生活の中に溶け込んでいる。

There is a nine-meter difference in level between the frontal road and the river ravine. One's line of sight "strolls" toward the work standing in the empty space between the land and the structure. The resident's creative activities, centering on clay, blend together with daily life in this natural setting.

163 | Horai Atelier Kuro

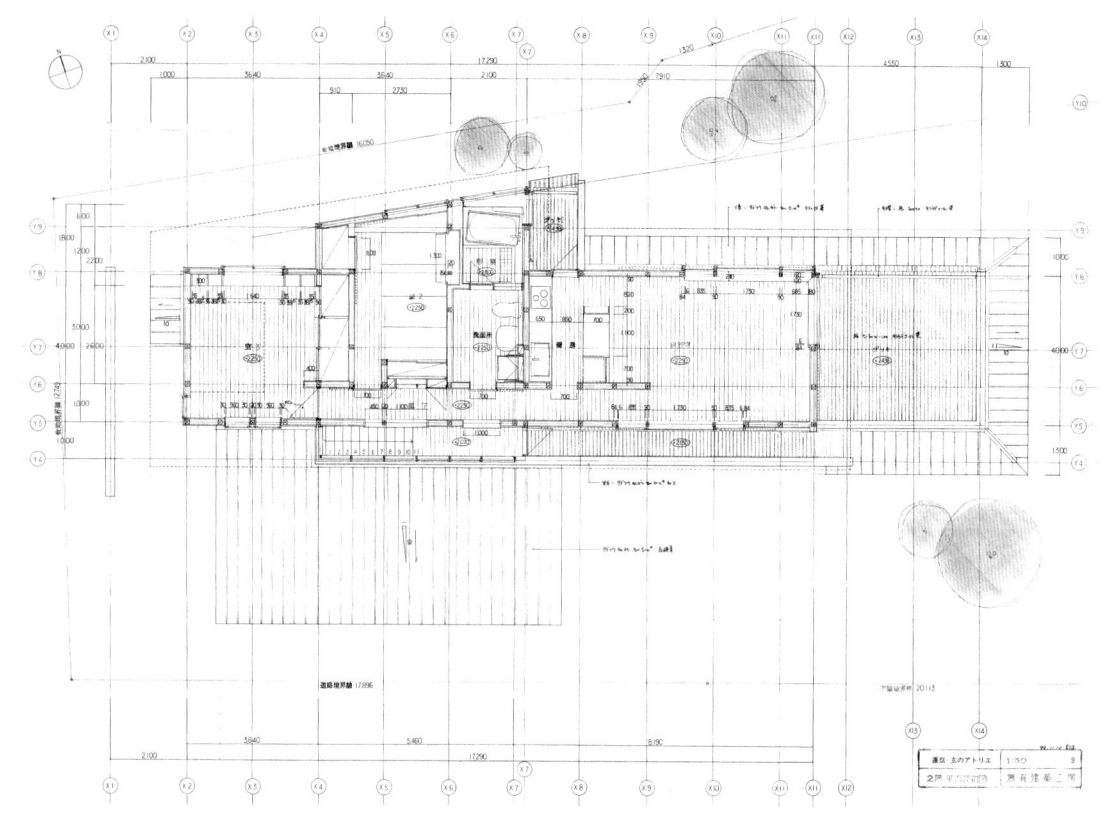

2階平面図　　Second-floor plan

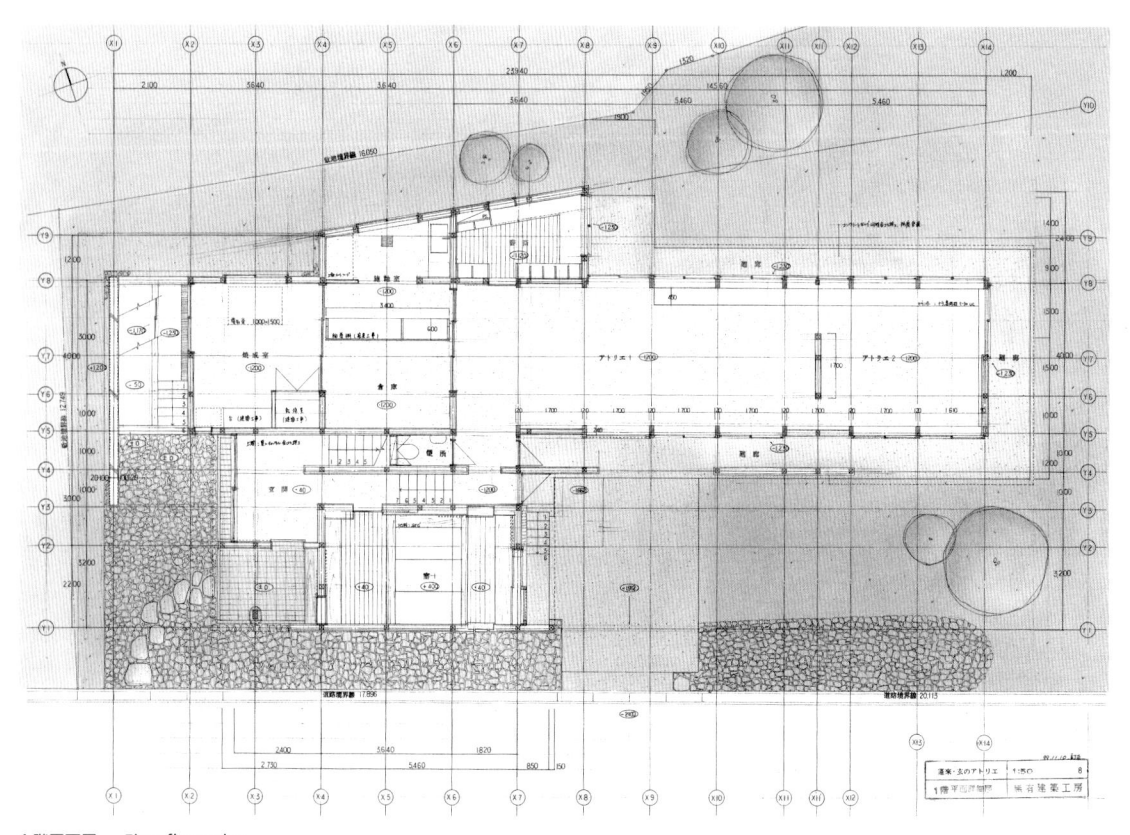

1階平面図　　First-floor plan

164

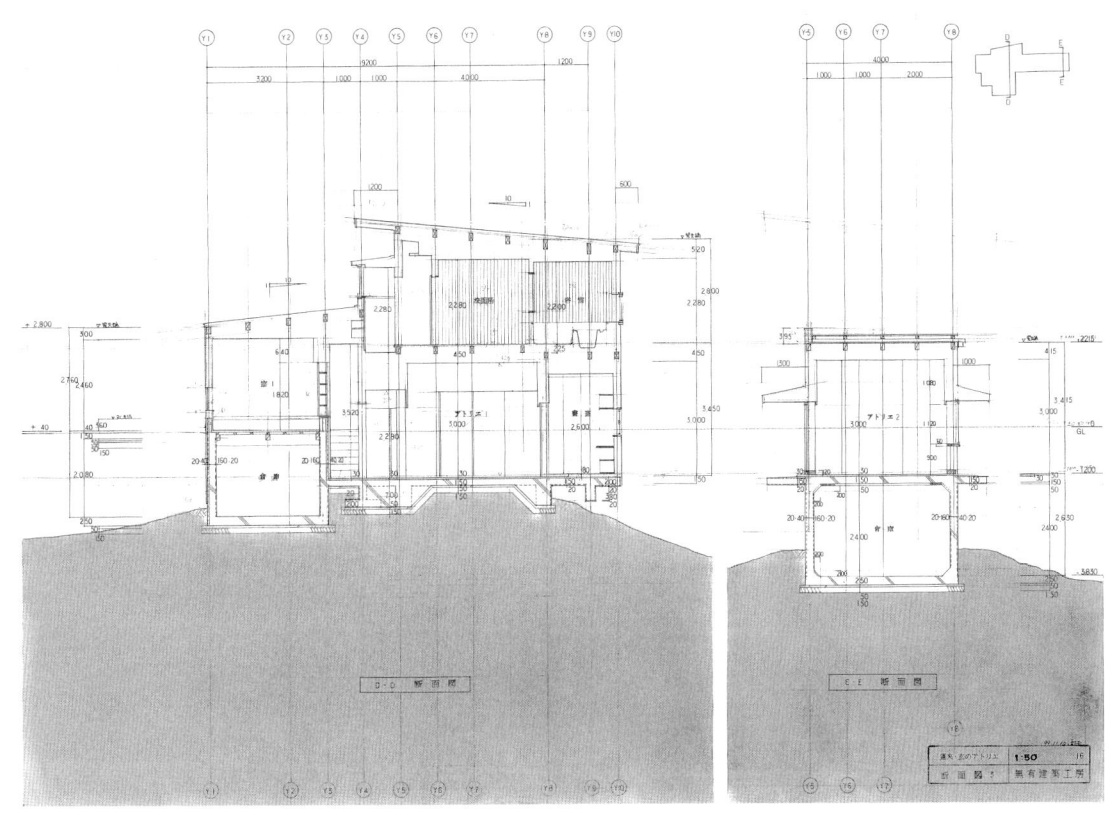

断面図　Section

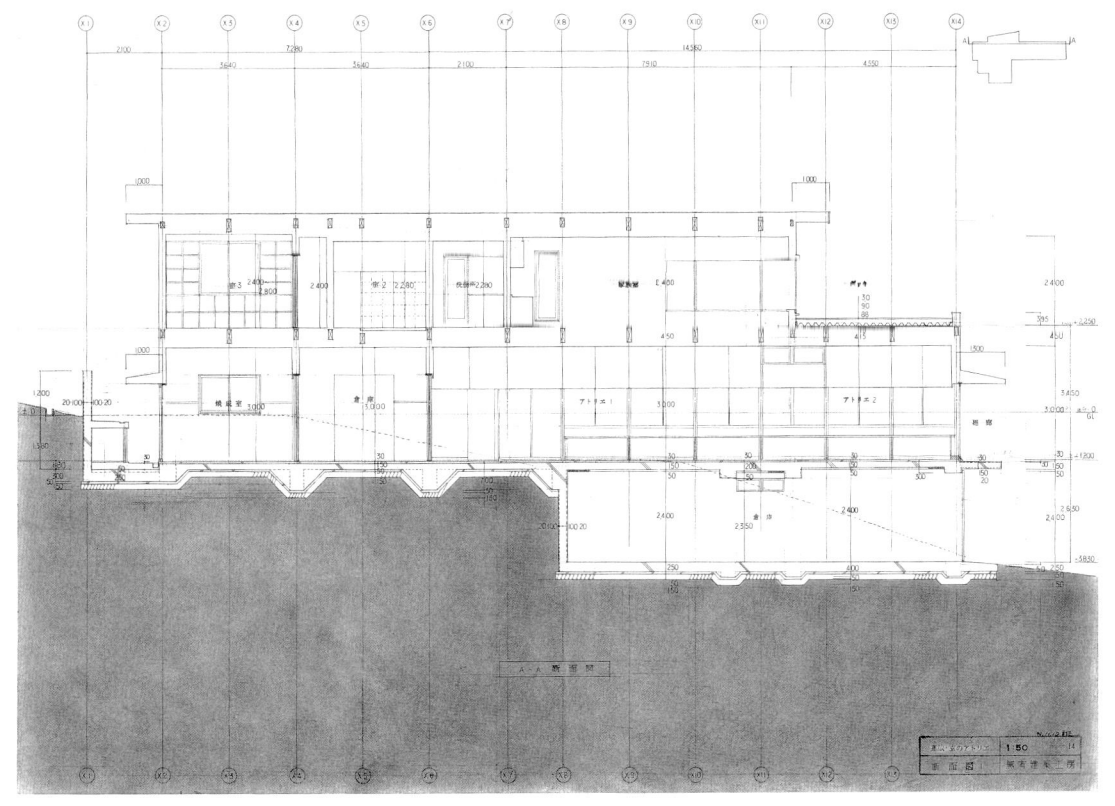

断面図　Section

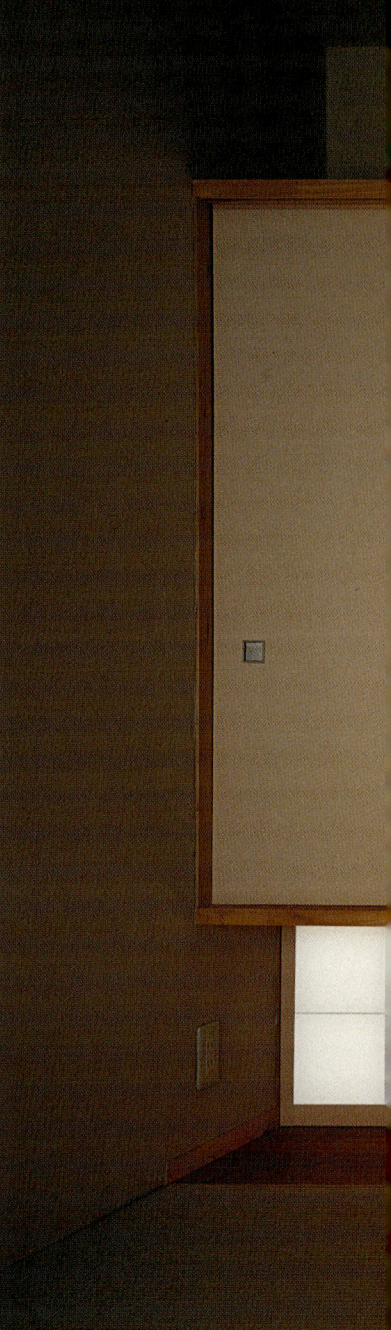

室2北・室2南を見る／内法のズレ、開口部の重なりによって
光の密度が操作され、奥行きをなす。

Views of the north and south side of Room 2:
Staggering the internal dimensions and layering
the openings controls the density of light and
adds depth to the space.

167 | Horai Atelier Kuro

2階デッキより地形と建築の関係性が一望できる。面台の高さに
延びるデッキが視界を調整し、パノラマの景色をほどよく切り取る。

From the second-floor deck, there is a sweeping view
of the connection between the topography and the
architecture. The deck, an extended and elevated surface,
controls the line of sight and frames the panoramic
view in a pleasing manner.

169 | Horai Atelier Kuro

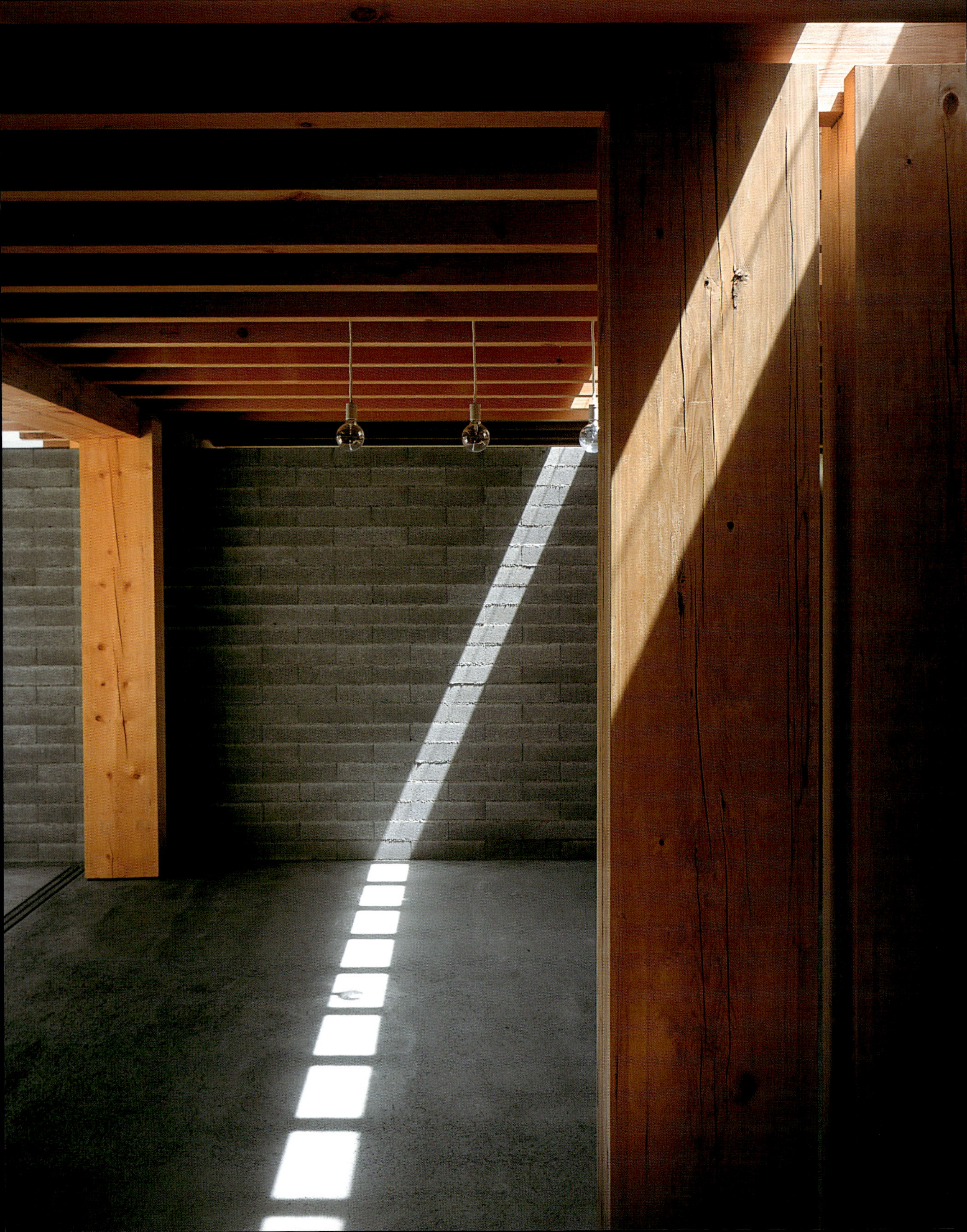

大阪府南部、臨海に浮かぶ関西国際空港の建設時に埋立て用の土砂を切り崩された阪南丘陵の一帯は、府の打ち出した跡地利用計画によって郊外のニュータウンへと開発分譲された。周囲を残された山並みが取り囲み、いまだ分譲中の空地が点在する未成熟な町である。その一角、三方を道路で囲まれた角地に敷地は位置する。

変わりゆく周辺環境、角地における人の視線に配慮し、隣家と道路に接する北側を2層分のL型の棟で囲い、街路に接する南側に高さを抑えた平屋の棟を配した。建物で一旦囲い取られた敷地は、屋上庭園によって失われた地面を取り戻し、残された余白は町へと開放される。さらに2棟の間で平面的・断面的なズレをつくり、そのスキマに生まれた立体的な内庭と中間領域は、壁・建具・柱の構成によって「内廻廊」と「外廻廊」に反転し、住空間を巡る。廻廊の結節点となる「間室」は上下の空間をつなぐと共に、土間を引き込むことで内外が錯綜し、室1と室4を離れとして意識させる。「外室」は家族のための外玄関となり、敷台は地続きの内庭と結界をつくると同時に、ふたつの棟を緊結する。内廻廊と外廻廊、間室と外室は軒下空間となって、内外を展開し、ここで巡りゆく生活に緊張感を与える。一方、すべての空間からズレ、内庭へと突き出した厨房は、あらゆる室や廻廊と視覚的につながり、平面の中核をなす。ズレと余白は成長する町と成長する家族の「間合い」をはかる仕掛けとなる。

こうした関係性は木とコンクリートの混構造の構成を骨格として現すことでさらに純化される。平屋の棟は屋根を垂直に支える大断面の木造架構と、屋根の下に水平に延びるブロック壁が拮抗し空間の方向性を示唆する。L型の棟はコンクリートの壁とスラブの上に木造の列柱が覆いかぶさり、洞窟のような空間を形成するが、屋根を直接支える2層分の通し柱が内庭へと開放し、天と地を意識的に結ぶ。がらんどうの空間を無心で駆け回る幼い子供たちも、いずれ成長し、与えられた空間の骨格を手掛かりに、それぞれの居場所とルールを見つけ出していくであろう。

箱作の家
Hakotsukuri House

This section of the Hannan Hills was leveled for use as landfill for Kansai International Airport and developed as a bedroom community. The area is dotted with lots in the process of being subdivided, and this residence stands on a corner with roads on three sides.

In view of the lot's position in the line of sight, the property was enclosed with a two-level, L-shaped wing on the north side and connected via an alley to a one-story house with a controlled height on the south side. A rooftop garden was created to recover some of the ground lost on the lot, and the remaining "empty space" was left open. By creating a flat, sectional gap between the two wings, the three-dimensional courtyard and intermediary space inverts the "inner corridor" and the "outer corridor" through the structure of the walls, fittings, and columns, and continues around the dwelling. The "intermediary room" that serves as the node for the corridors links the vertical space and while drawing in the earthen floor, blurs the boundary between interior and exterior, increasing one's awareness of the distance between Room 1 and Room 4. The "exterior space" functions as the entranceway, and the floored area creates a barrier to the courtyard, which is linked to the ground and joins the two wings. The inner and outer corridors, and intermediary and exterior spaces occupy a place under the eaves, and by developing the relationship between the interior and exterior, add a sense of tension. On the other hand, the kitchen, jutting out into the courtyard, is visually connected to each room, and forms the core of the plane. The gap between the wings and the empty space gauges the "distance" between the developing town and the family.

This relationship is further refined through the framework of the complex wood-and-concrete structure. In the one-story wing, the large, sectional wooden framework that supports the roof vertically and the block wall that stretches horizontally under the eaves create an antagonistic space. In the L-shaped wing, the concrete wall and the wooden colonnades on the slab hang down to create a cave-like space, but the through pillars on the second story that support the roof are open to the courtyard and connect the sky and the ground. The children at play in the hollow space will one day discover the rules for each living space provided by the residence's spatial structure.

南西立面／2層分の高さをもつL型の棟は敷地を囲い取り、内庭へと開かれる。平屋の棟は屋上庭園となり、2棟のズレに生まれた余白は町に開放される。

Southwest elevation: The two-story, L-shaped wing encloses the lot and opens onto a courtyard. The single-story wing is equipped with a rooftop garden and the empty space produced by the gap between the structures is open to the street.

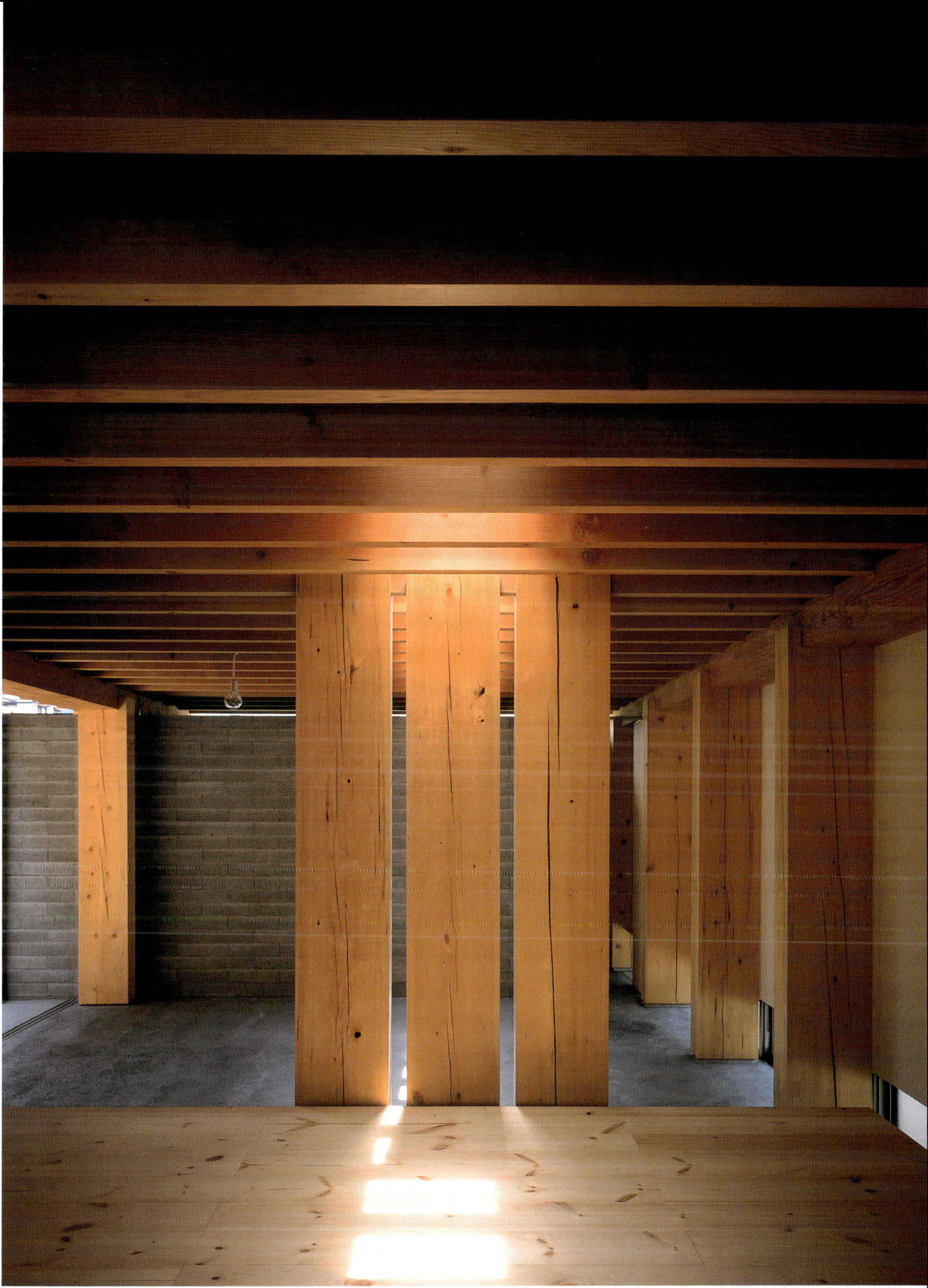

垂直ラインを構成する木造大断面の列柱と柱壁、水平ライン
を構成するブロック造の壁と化粧垂木が、自立しながら拮抗
し、剥き出しの素材が空間に力強さと透明感を与えている。

The vertical line created by the large-section wooden
colonnades and wall columns, and the horizontal
line created by the block walls and exposed rafters
imbue the space with strength through the free
yet antagonistic qualities of the bare materials.

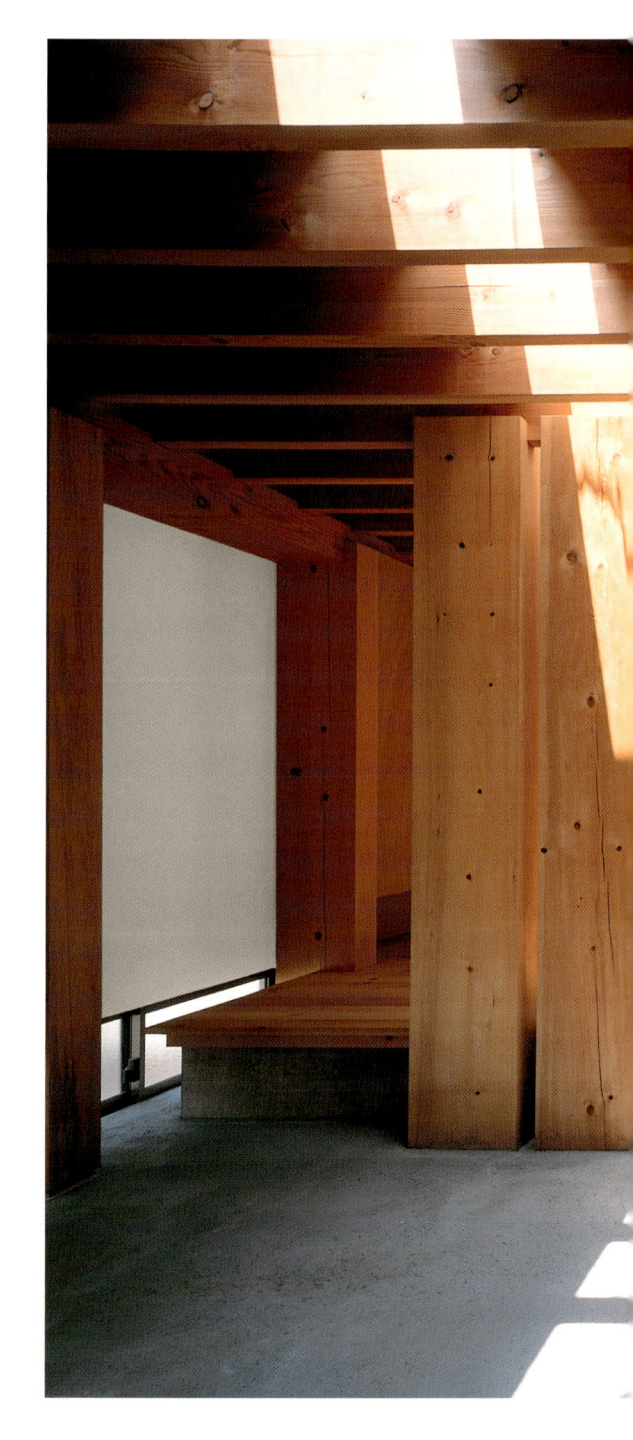

次頁：内廊下より外室を通して平屋の家族室棟を見返す／2棟のスキマには土間が引き込まれ、敷台は外室と内庭の結界となり2棟の架橋となって、生活に緊張感を与える。

Following page: Looking back at the single-story, family-room wing from below the inner corridor through Outer Room — The earthen floor draws together the gap between the two wings, and the low, broad step creates a barrier between the outer chamber and the courtyard, spanning the two wings and adding a sense of tension.

Hakotsukuri House

176

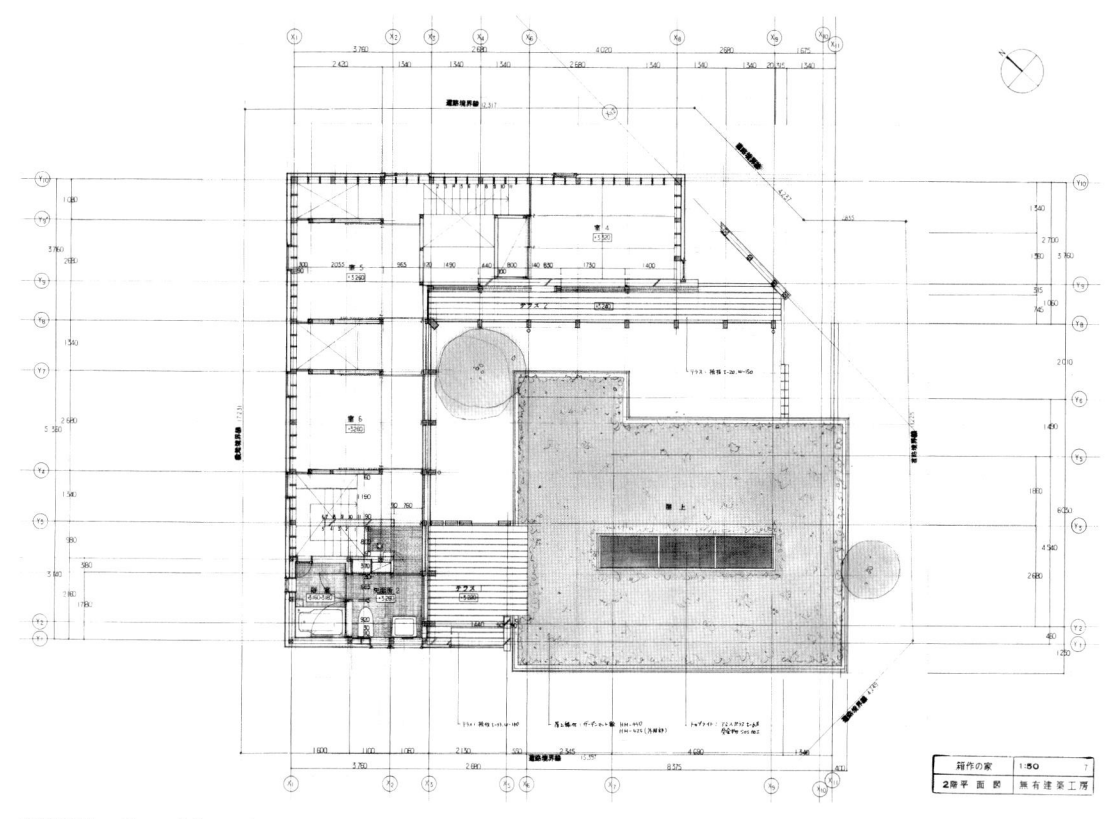

2 階平面図　　Second-floor plan

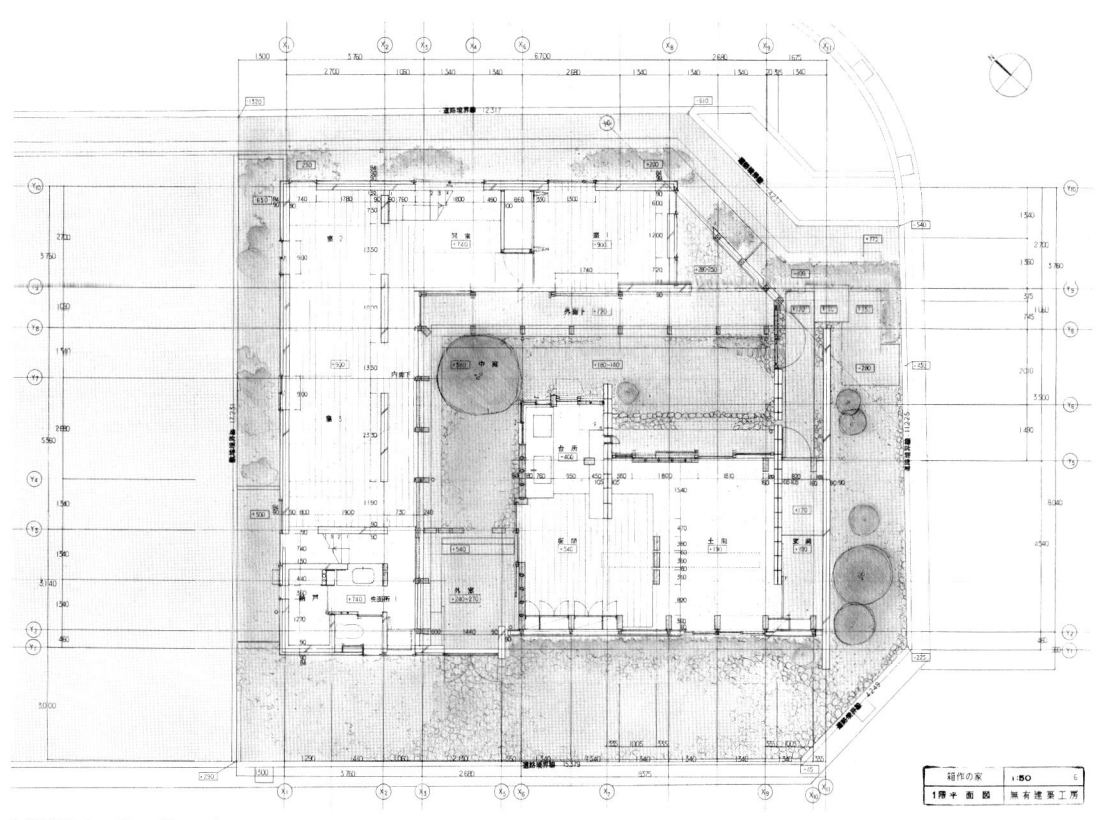

1 階平面図　　First-floor plan

177 | Hakotsukuri House

内廊下より外廊下を見る／壁際を走る建具と柱がつくる外廊下は内庭とわずかにレヴェル差をもち、平屋棟と間合いを取る。

View of outside corridor from inside corridor: The outside corridor, forming the fittings and columns along its walls, has a slightly higher level than the courtyard, establishing a sense of distance from the single-story wing.

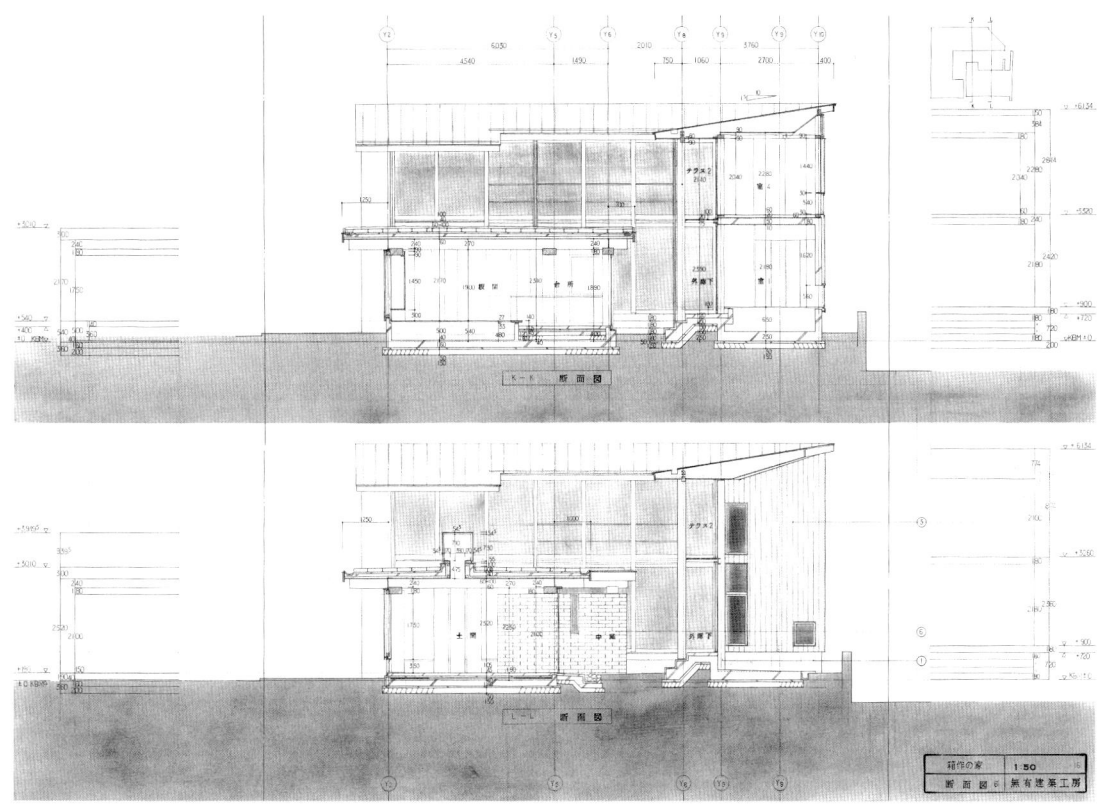

断面図　　Section

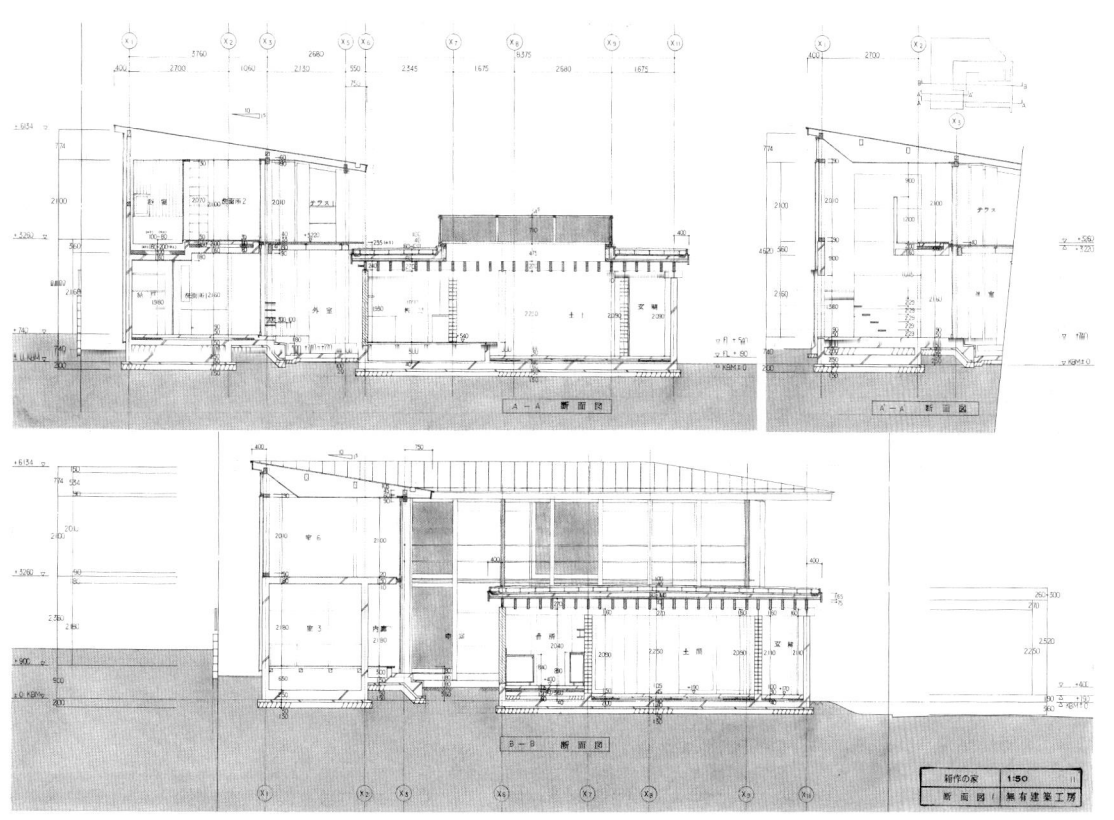

断面図　　Section

179 | Hakotsukuri House

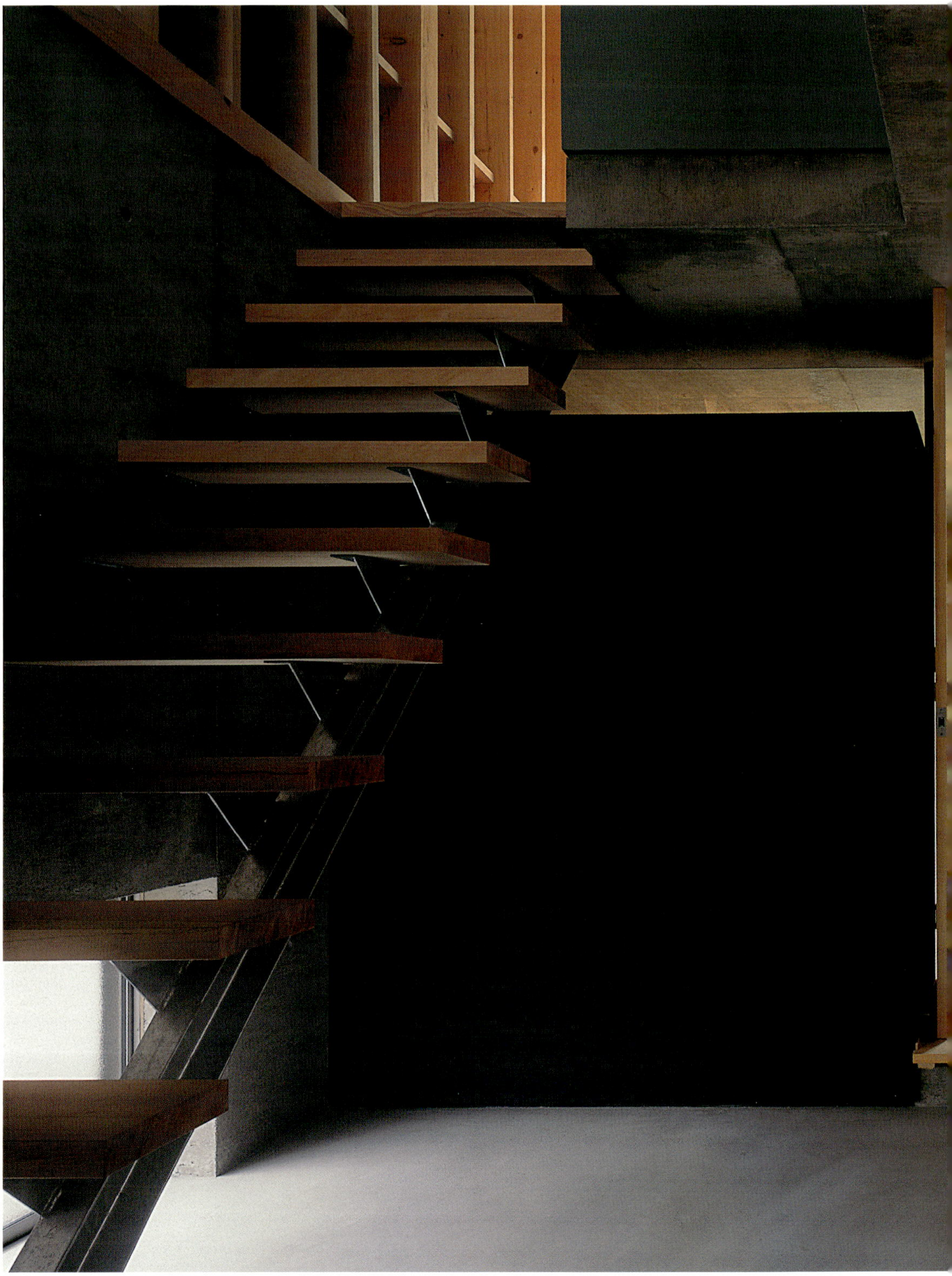

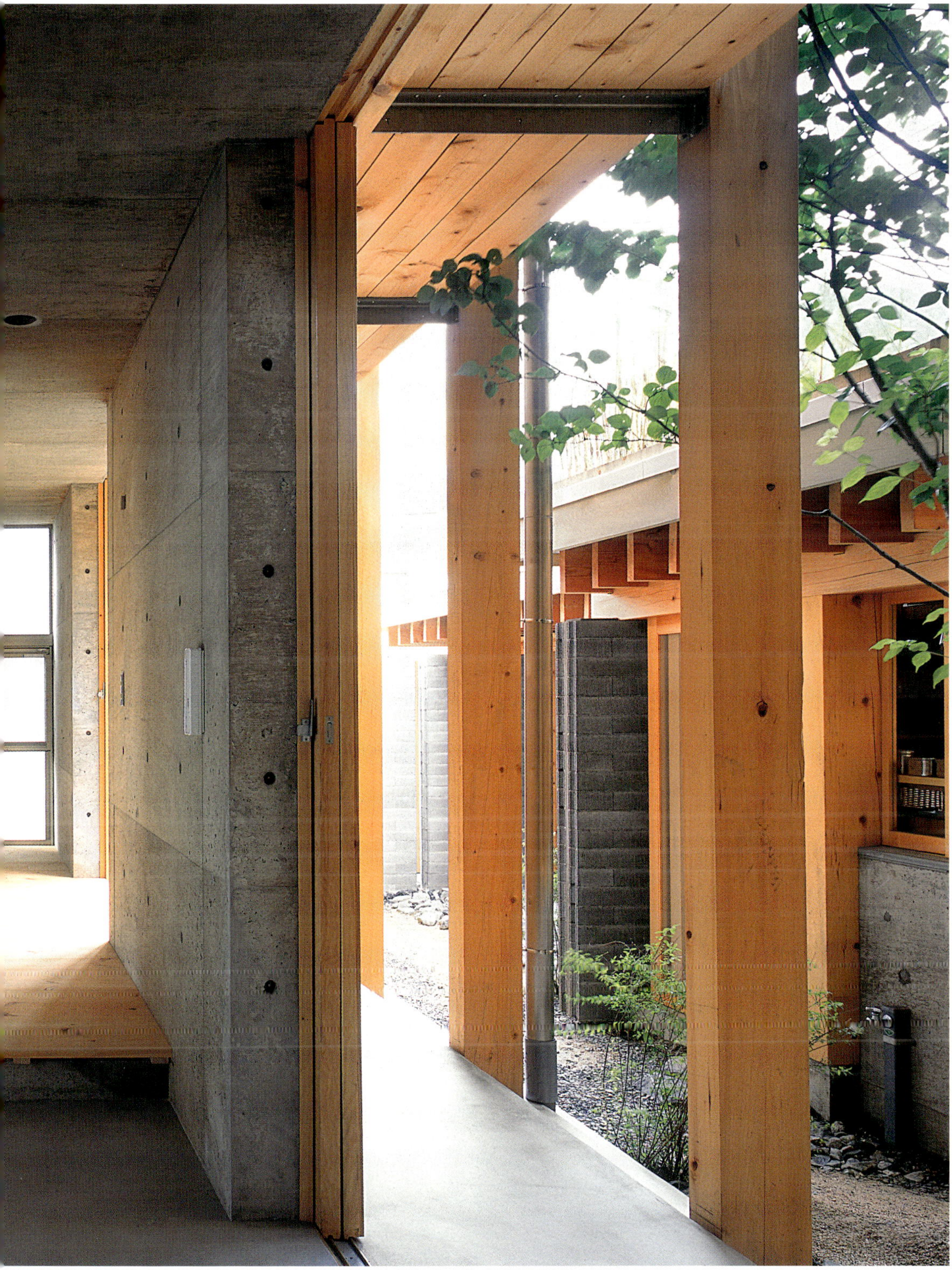

右：間室より内廻廊を見る／通し柱とその内側を走る建具、
スラブに抑え込まれたコンクリートの2枚の壁が内廻廊をつくり出す。

Right: View of inner corridor from intermediary room — The two concrete walls, restrained by the through columns, their inner fittings, and the slab, give shape to the inner corridor.

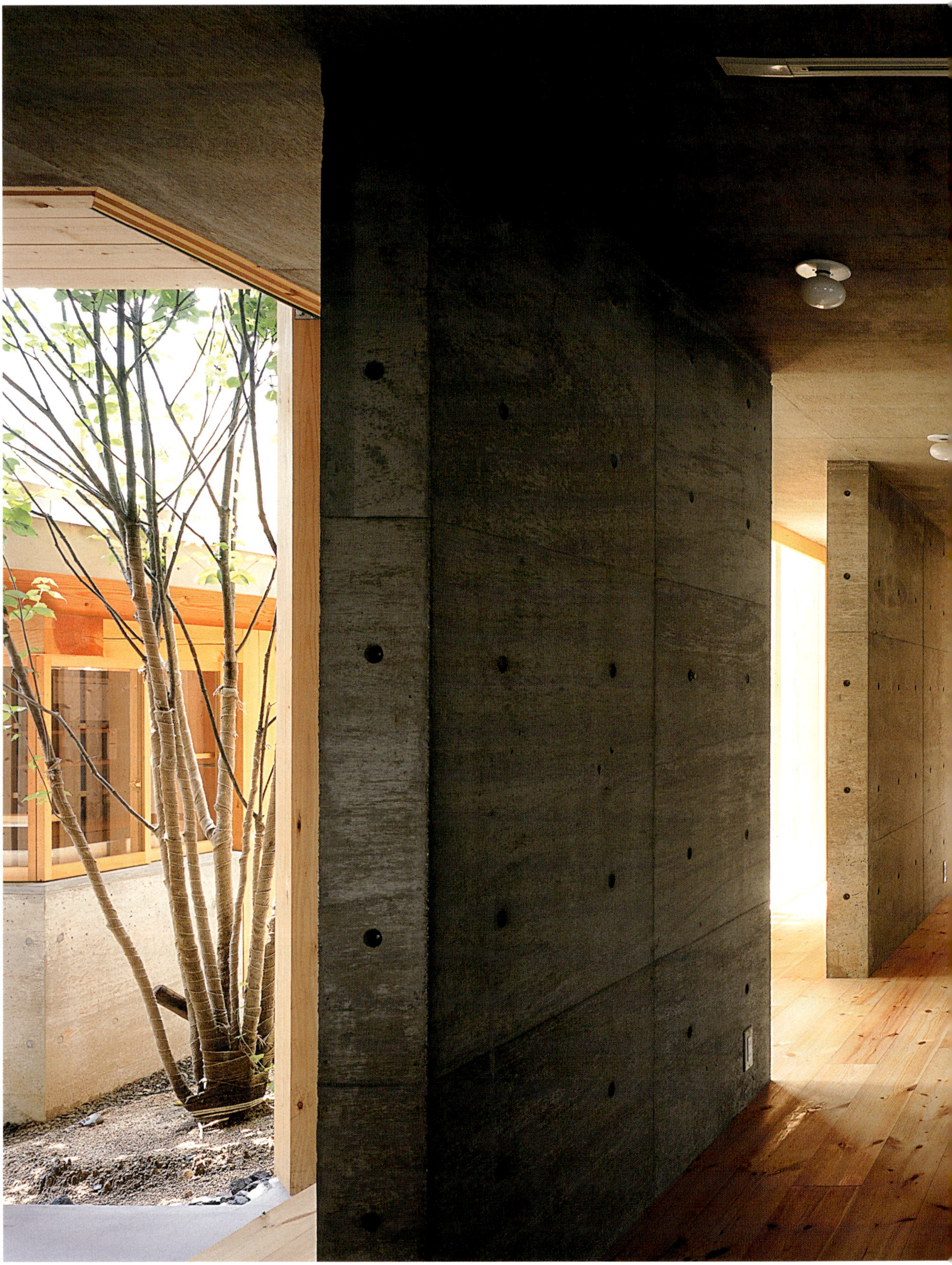

室2より室3を見る／2枚のコンクリートの壁は未分化ではあるが、洞窟のように室をおおらかに包み込む。スラブに穿たれた開口は吹抜になって上下階をつなぐ。内外が浸透し、子供たちの生活は庭へと溶け出していく。

View of Room 3 from Room 2: Though undifferentiated, the two concrete walls surround the cave-like room in a relaxed manner. The opening, penetrated by the slab, is an atrium connecting the upper and lower levels. Permeated with a sense of interior and exterior, the daily life of the resident children blends into the garden.

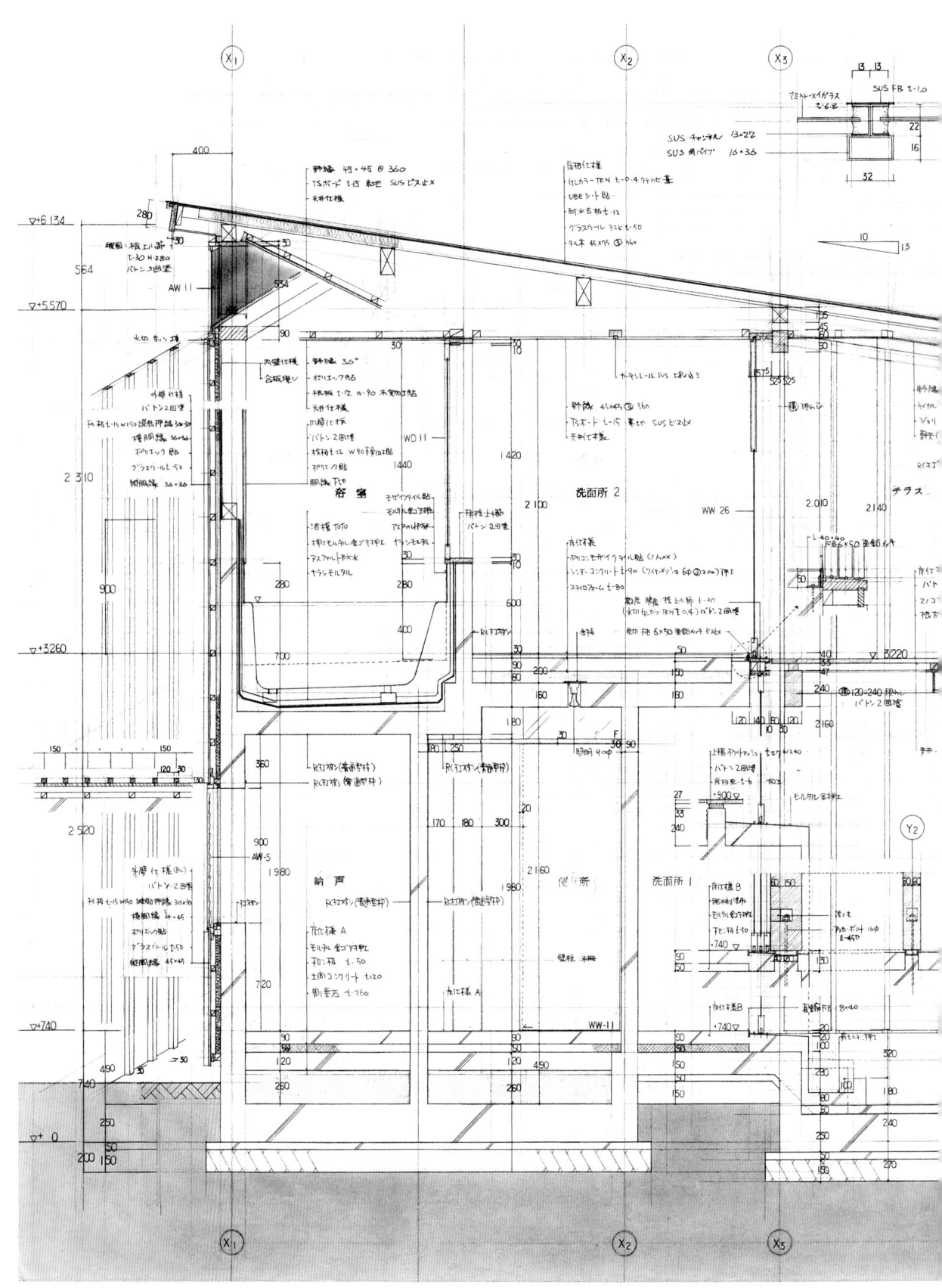

矩計詳細図　Detail drawing

Hakotsukuri House

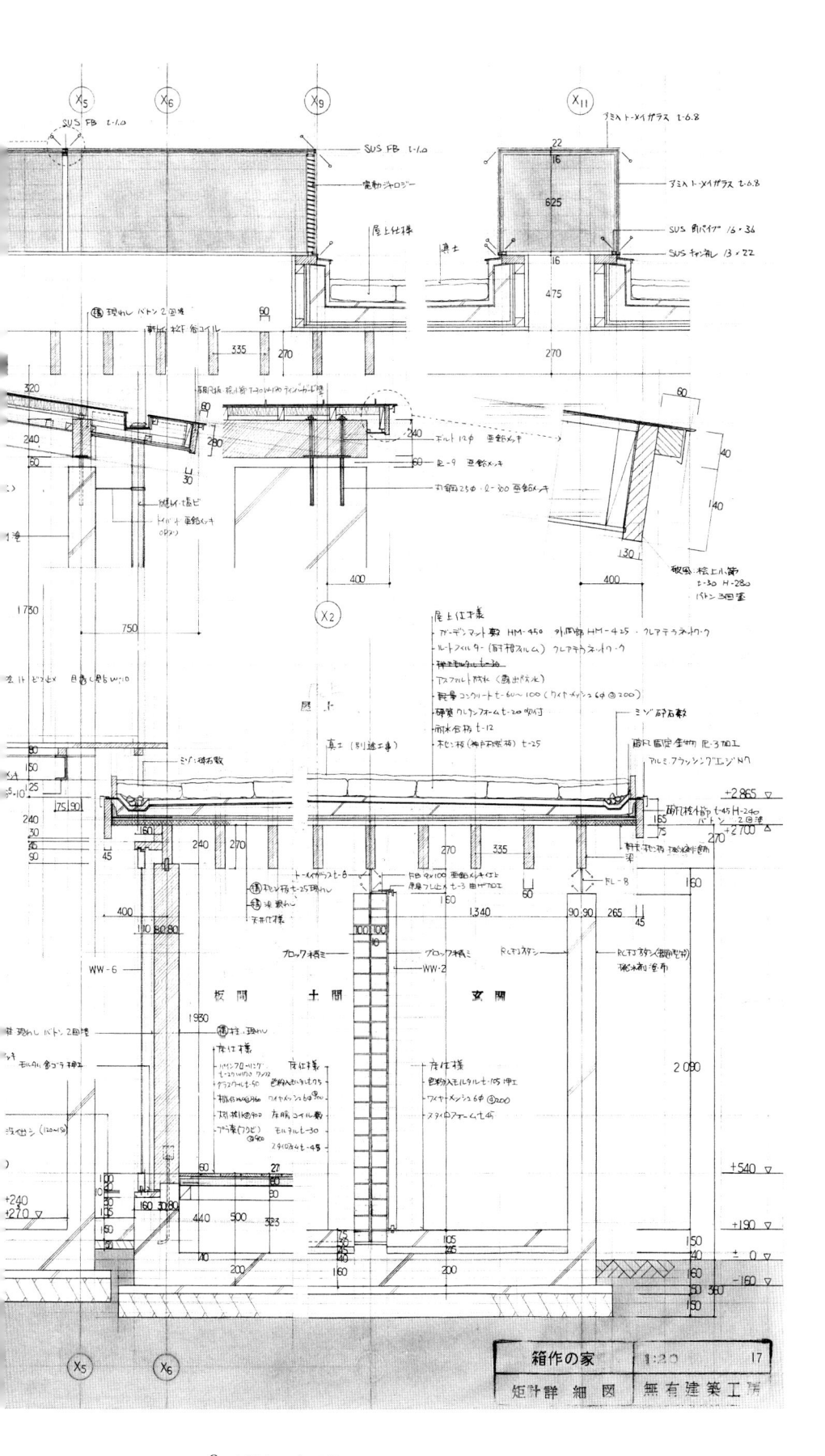

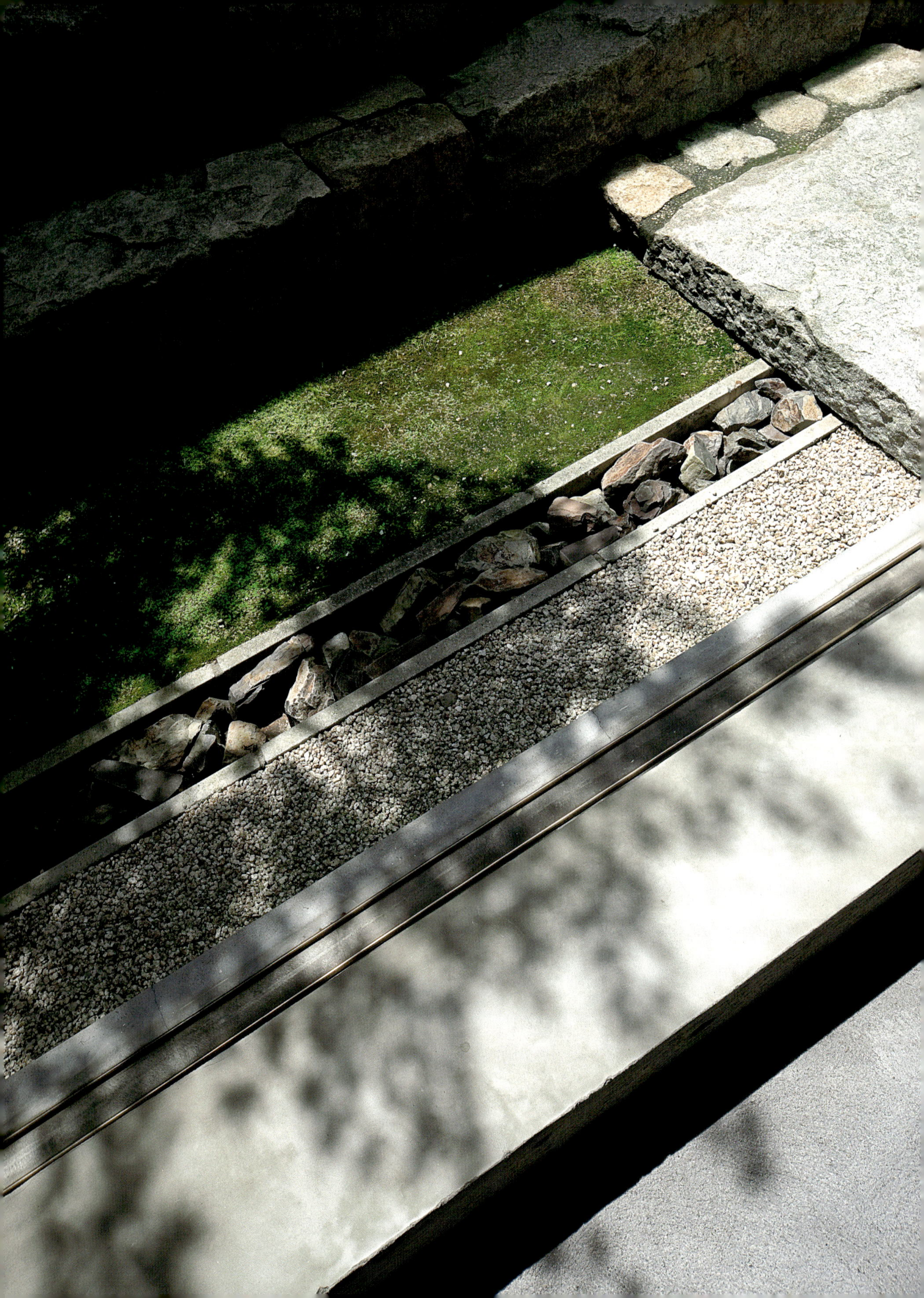

明石海峡を望む小高い丘の上の閑静な住宅街の一角。南東に二方道路をもち、高さ0.8〜3mの擁壁で囲われた敷地に建つ。南側の道路側に埋め込まれた既存のガレージは擁壁の一端を担い、西側の擁壁際には暗渠(あんきょ)になった水路が続く。この一帯は阪神大震災の際に施された擁壁の補強工事によって、そこら中にアースアンカーが地中貫通していた。盛土造成によって外周の擁壁天端が地盤面となり、ガレージ擁壁天端とはレヴェルを異にする。埋め込まれたガレージ擁壁を残し、アースアンカーの影響を受けることのない部分を探りながら、擁壁に負担をかけないように盛土の地盤面を掘り下げて建築を埋め込んでいる。既存地盤面の上をL型の棟が囲い取り、半層上がったガレージ擁壁の上に平屋の離れをもつ分棟型平面を形成する。ふたつの地盤のレヴェル差はL型の棟の内部に吸収し、立体的な廻遊動線を構成する。

　建物へは坂道を廻り込んでアプローチする。玄関の奥に穿たれた地窓から中庭の気配を感じ取りつつ、左手へ3段上がり、壁を折り返すと、ガラスを透過する光に満たされた階段が上階へと誘う。2階は厨房を中心に食堂・家族室・座室がL型に連続し、1本の自立柱と天井に連なる化粧垂木がこの空間をつなぎ留める。ここで初めて中庭へと開かれ、内に引き込まれた庭と、離れの屋根の水平ラインが視線を抑え込み、遠景の明石海峡へと意識をつなぐ。

　地階へ挿入された躯体と擁壁とのスキマに生まれたドライエリアは中庭までヴォイドを貫く。レヴェルのズレた2棟の間に段状に積まれた石組みは基壇をなし、離れに架かる屋根が稜線を深く切り取ることで、この中庭をより内なるものとして感じさせる。1階の室から土間へ一段床を落とし、土間から中庭へ敷居を立ち上げて結界をつくり、段状の石組み、半層分上がった離れの室4、そして空へと視線が連続する。こうして棟と棟、躯体と擁壁の狭間で中庭が立体的に巡り、平屋の離れを介して外界へと連続する。既存のふたつの地盤面に生じたレヴェル差によって、中庭を介して展開する分棟型平面に新たな関係性が生み出されたのである。

明石の家
Akashi House

On a hill overlooking the Akashi Strait, this lot is surrounded by a retaining wall with a height ranging from 0.8 to three meters. A preexisting underground garage on the south side serves as one end of the retaining wall. As part of some reinforcements made on the wall after an earthquake, earth anchors were inserted into the ground. By building an embankment, the crest of the peripheral wall became ground level – a different level from the garage wall. While searching for sections that hadn't been affected by the anchors, the ground level of the embankment was buried to avoid overloading the wall. On the embankment level, an L-shaped wing and a *buntogata* ("divided-ridge-style") plane were built with a detached, one-story wing on the half-story higher wall for the garage. The level difference between the foundations was absorbed within the L-shaped wing and a three-dimensional, "stroll-type" flow line was created.

While taking in the courtyard through a tectonic window in the rear of the entranceway, as one ascends the steps and turns back toward the wall, the stairs, bathed in natural light, invite them upstairs. With the kitchen at the center of the second floor, and the other rooms following the L shape of the structure, the exposed rafters, connecting one freestanding column and the ceiling, reign in the space. Here, for the first time, the residence opens out to the courtyard, and the horizontal line that runs between the eaves and the detached roof control the line of sight, bringing a distant view of the Akashi Strait into focus.

A void runs between the building frame and the retaining wall to the courtyard. Some stones piled in a stair-like formation between the two staggered wings serve as a platform, and the ridge line cut by the detached span of the roof makes the courtyard appear further inside. A continuous line of sight continues to the stones, the half-floor higher, detached Room 4, and the sky. The courtyard extends three-dimensionally through the narrow gap between the building frame and the retaining wall and connects to the outside world via the detached one-story wing. The difference between the preexisting ground levels produces a new relationship through the mediation of the courtyard.

玄関より中庭を垣間見ながら、左手へ導かれる。既存擁壁のレヴェル差を吸収する3段分の階段を上がり、折り返すと、光に満ちた階段室が上階へと誘う。

Looking through the walls toward the garden from the entrance, one is prompted toward the left. Climbing to the third step, which absorbs the level difference of the preexisting retaining wall, the sun-filled staircase invites one up to the next floor.

191 | Akashi House

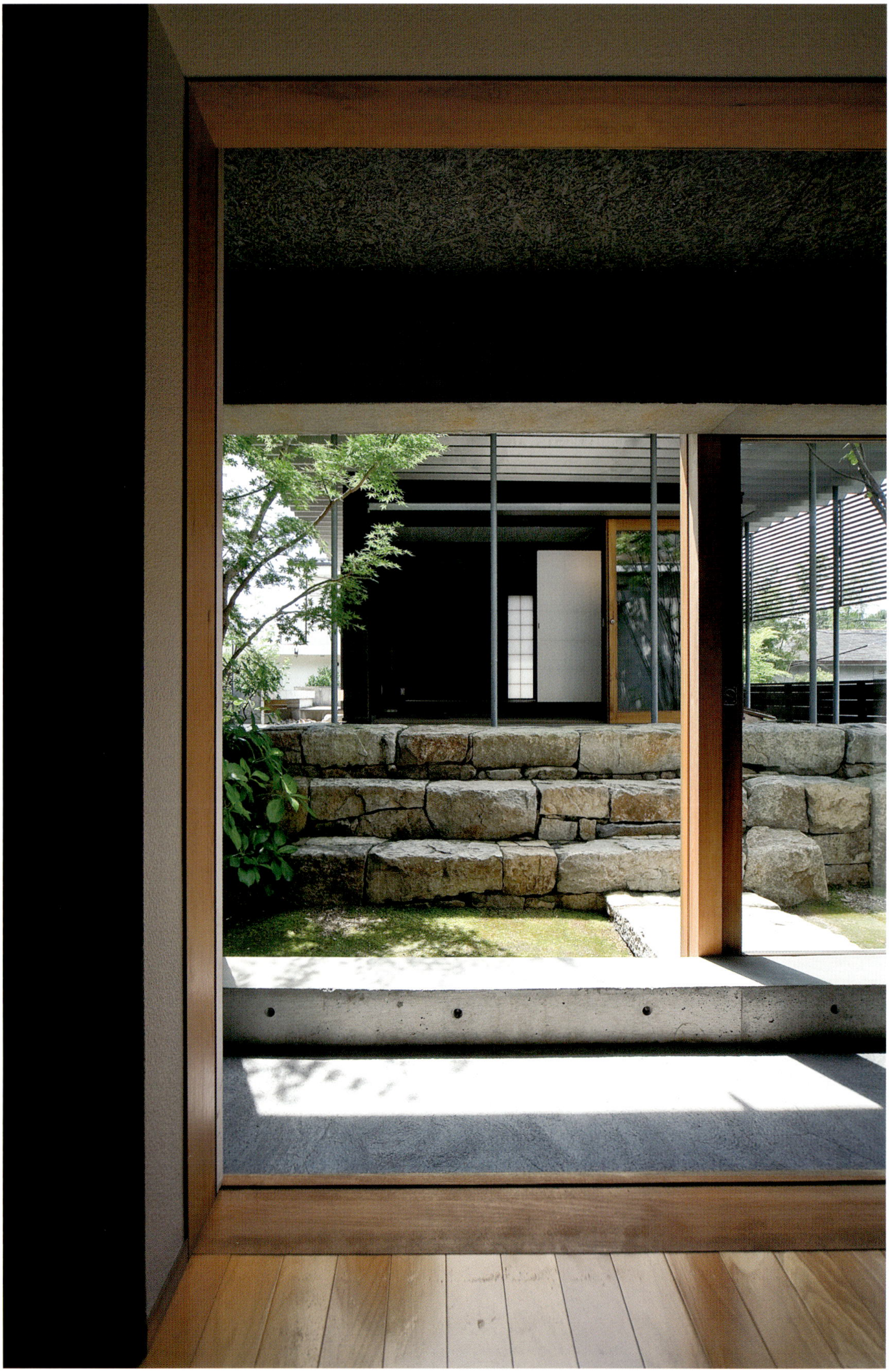

室3より段状の石組み越しに離れの棟を見る／床レヴェルが操作され、足元に立ち上げられた結界と内法を操作する垂壁が内外の領域を示唆しながら、視線を調整する。2棟が断面的にズレ、立体的な中庭が生まれた。

View of detached wing beyond the stone steps from Room 3: By altering the floor level, the barrier that rises up at one's feet and the vertical hanging wall, with controlled internal dimensions, indicate the interior and exterior, and limit the line of sight. Staggered sectionally, the two wings produce a three-dimensional courtyard.

Akashi House

離れの和室／玄（くろ）く塗り込まれた空間に最小限に抑え込まれた光が点在する。折板（せっぱん）の天井も陰翳のある空間では独特の質感を帯びる。限られた要素の中で美術や骨董とじっくりと向き合うための空間。

Detached Japanese-style room: The light that is sprinkled in the space, painted completely black, is kept to an absolute minimum, and the folded-plate ceiling adds a distinctive touch to this shadowy space which, with a limited number of elements, encourages a lengthy encounter with art and antiques.

194

195 | Akashi House

2階厨房・食堂・家族室・座室／内に引き込まれた庇が内法を調整し、連続する化粧垂木が厨房を介してL型に連続する家族室をひとつながりにつなぎ留める。建具と障子を壁の内外に引き込むことで、中庭に完全に開放される。

The second-floor kitchen, dining room, family room, and sitting room: Drawn into the space, the eaves control its internal dimensions and mediated by the kitchen, the exposed rafters create one continuous area with the living room following the wing's L-shape. Drawing the fittings and *shoji* in or out of the walls completely frees the courtyard.

197 | Akashi House

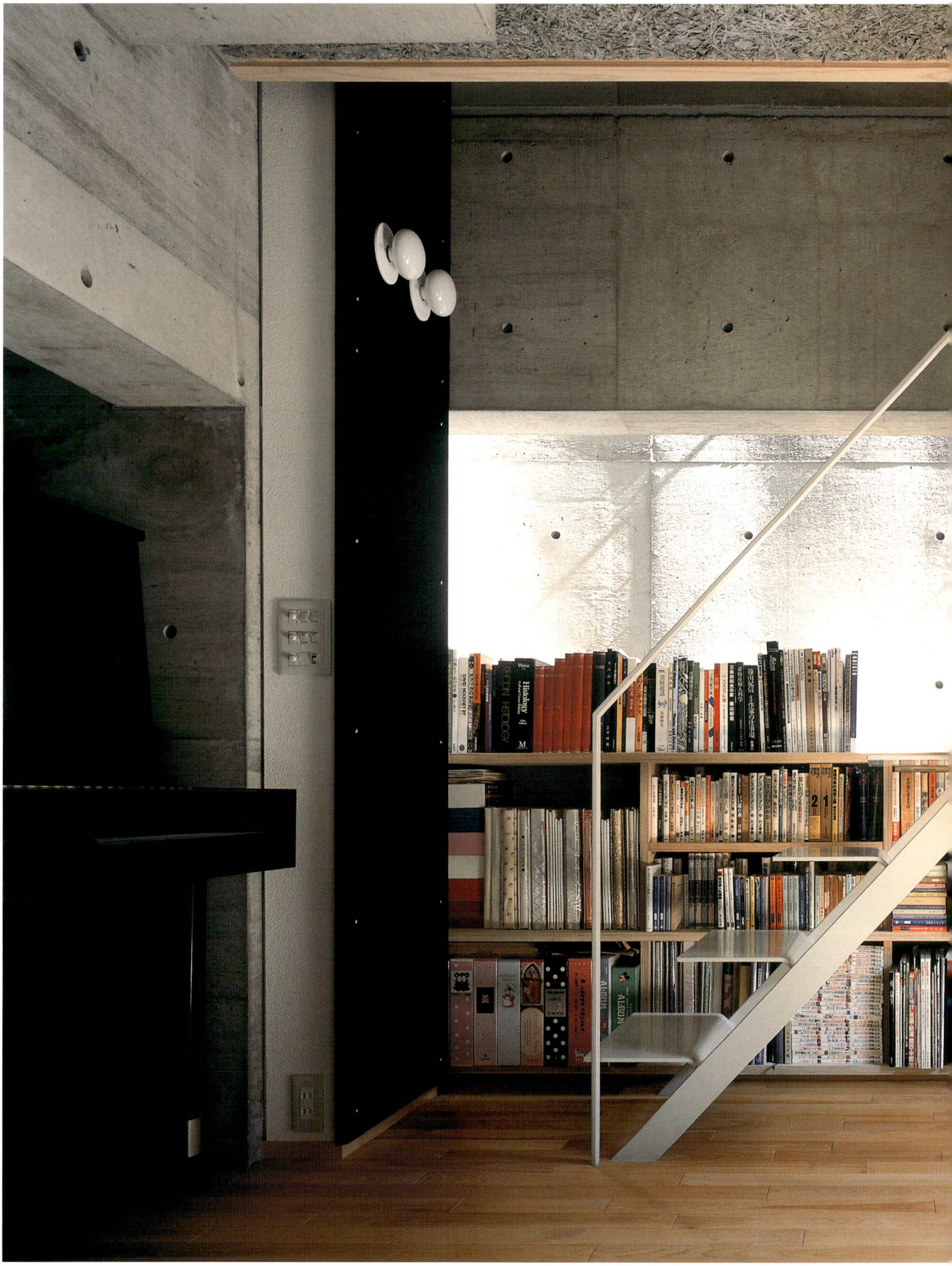

Akashi House

室2・階段・室1は動線状につながり、アースアンカーの影響を受けない唯一の場所に、地中へと埋め込まれた家族の趣味の空間がある。

Room 2, the staircase, and Room 1 are connected by the shape of the flow line, and the only place that isn't affected by the earth anchors is a space for the family to pursue their hobbies that is sunken in the ground.

Akashi House

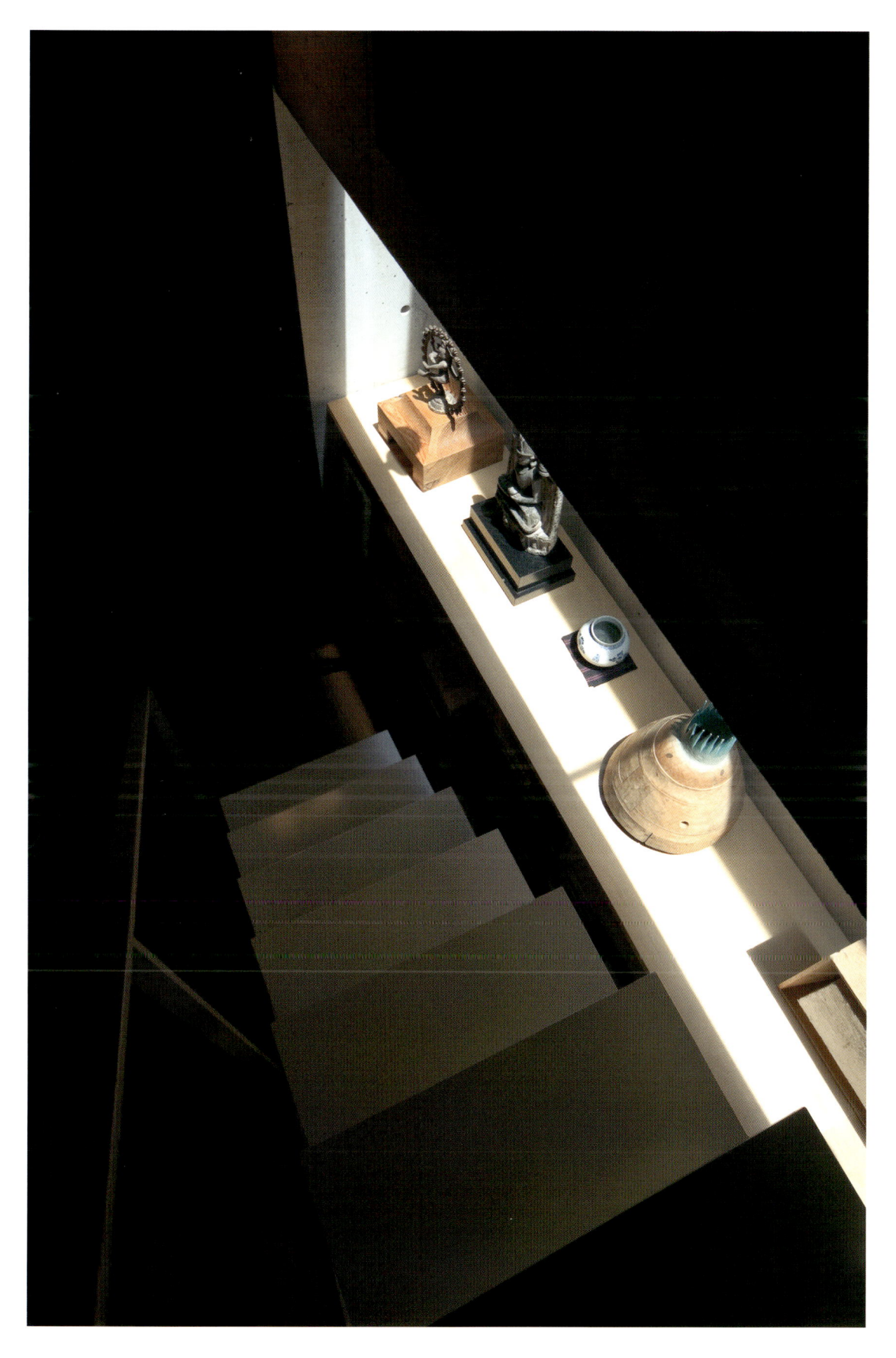

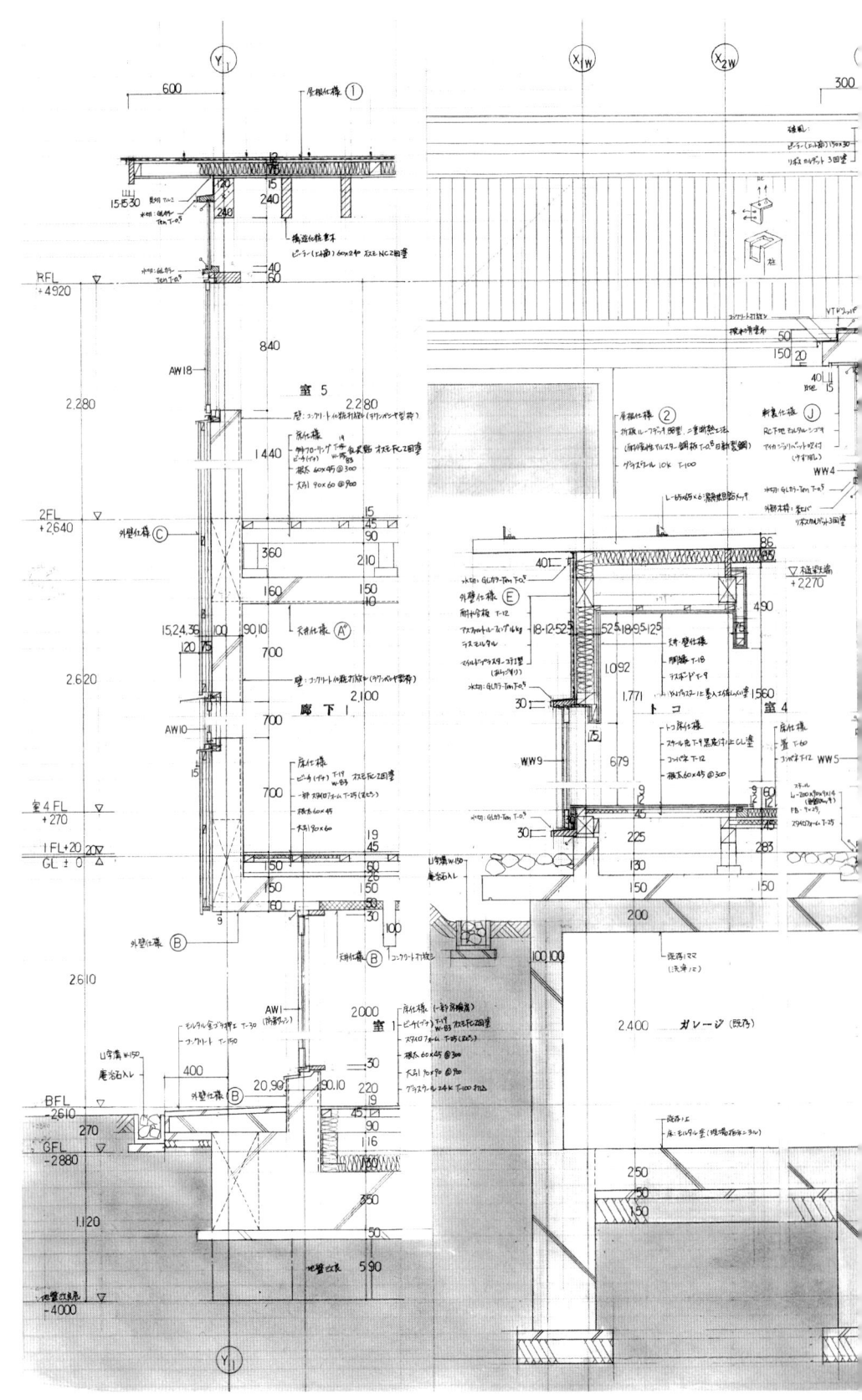

矩計詳細図　Detail drawing

明石の家 1:20 27
矩計詳細図 2 無有建築工房

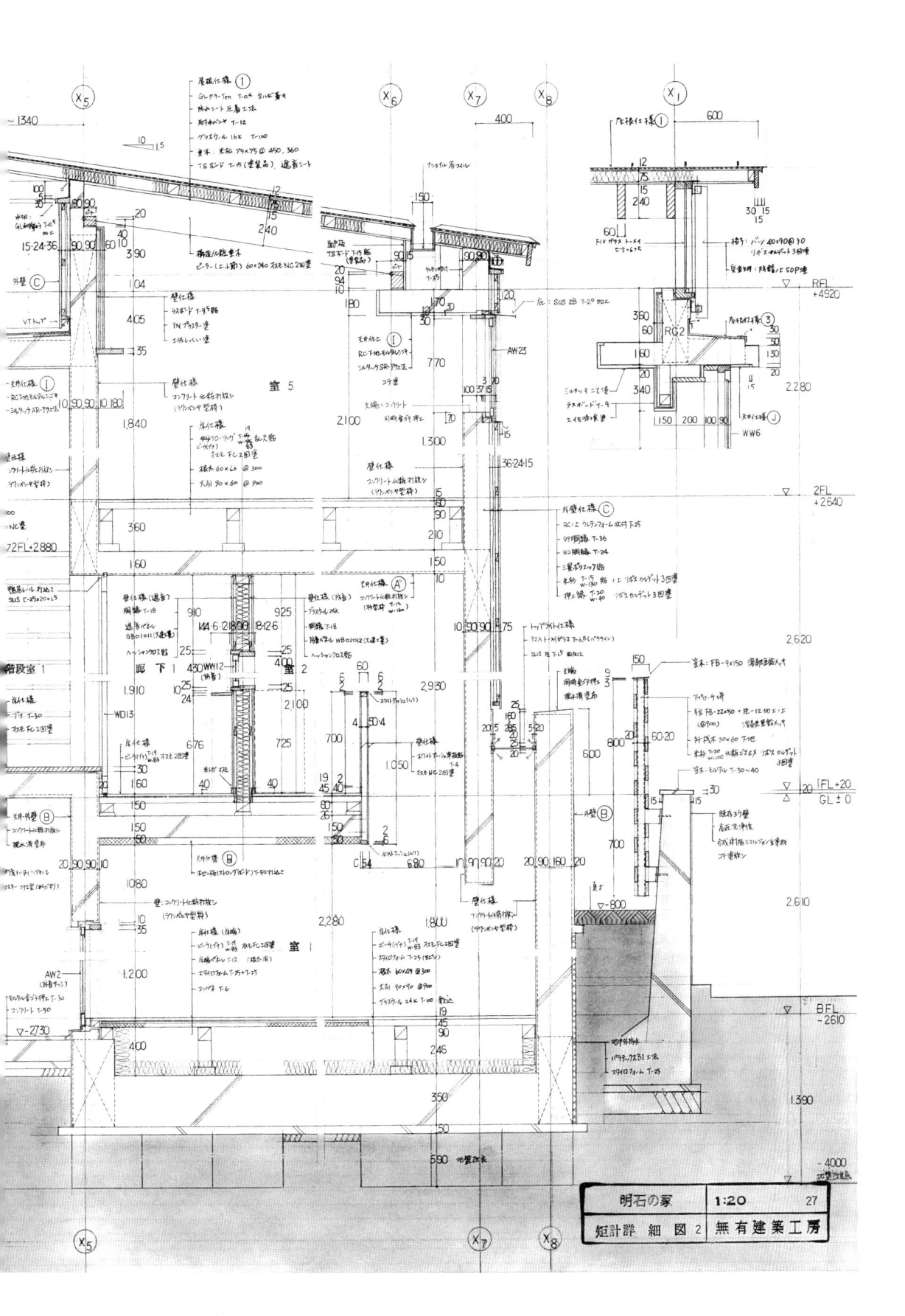

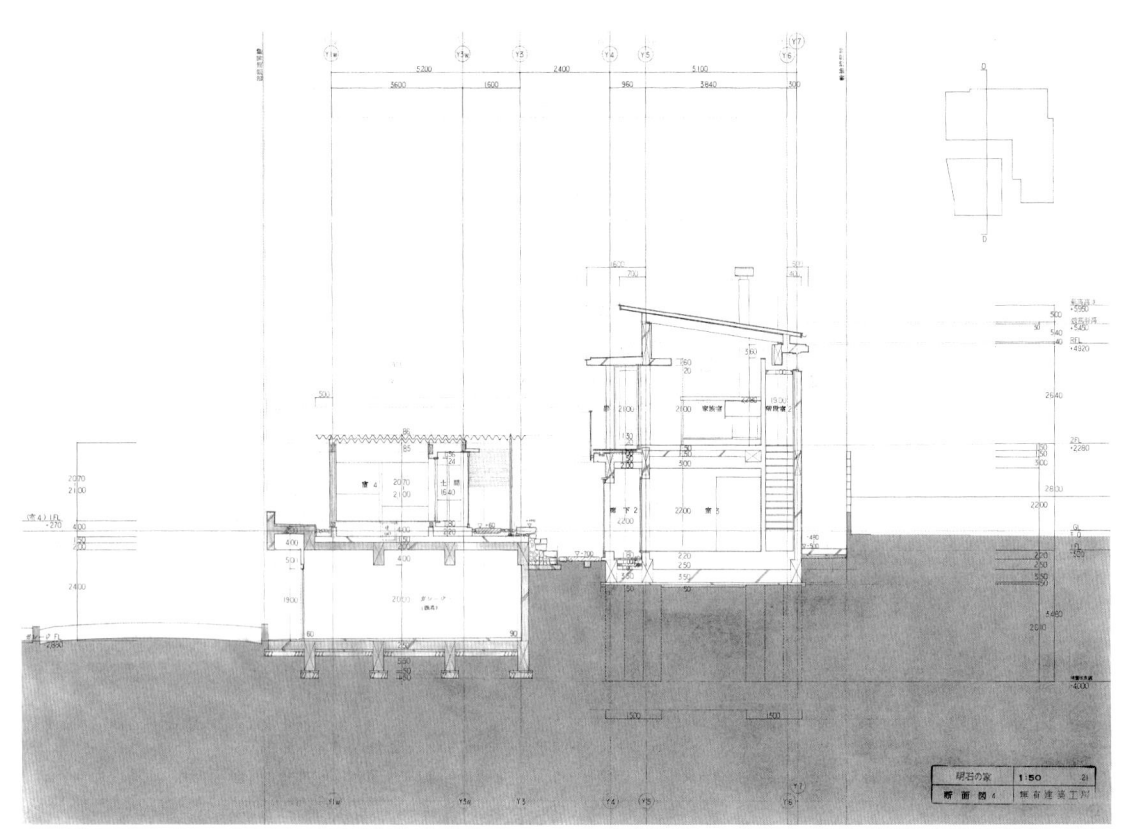

断面図　　Section

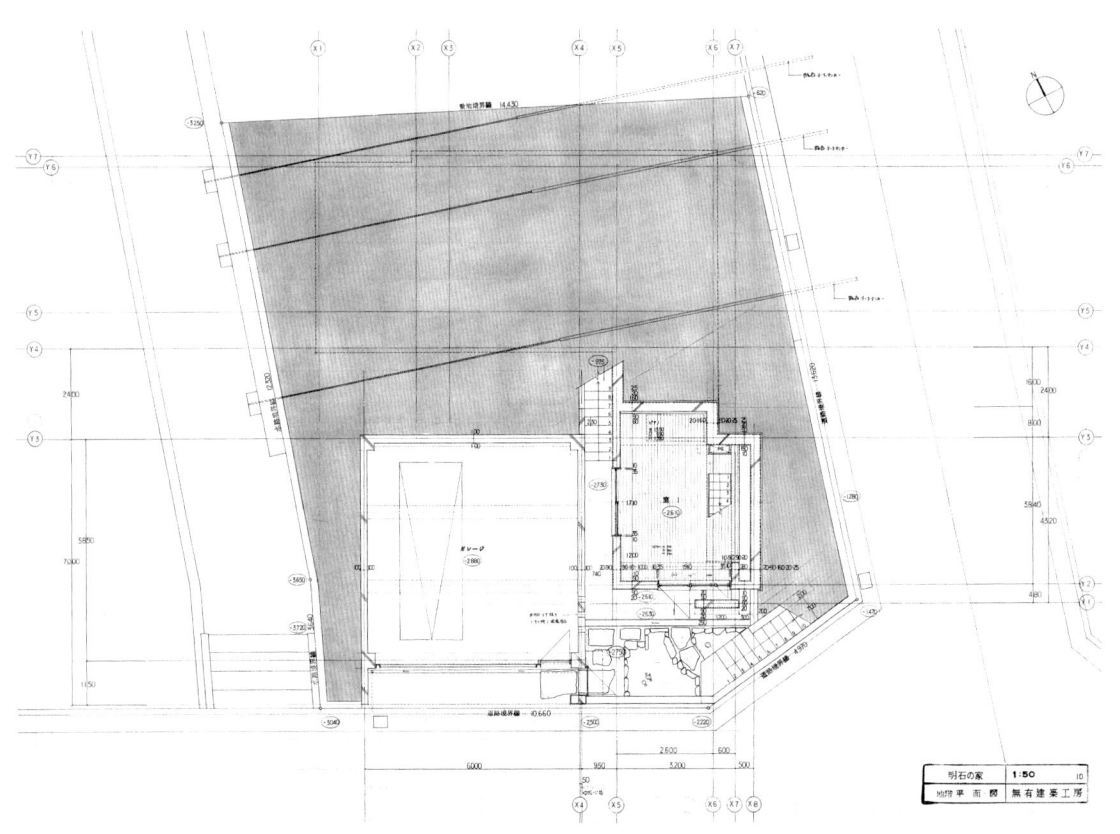

地階平面図　　Basement plan

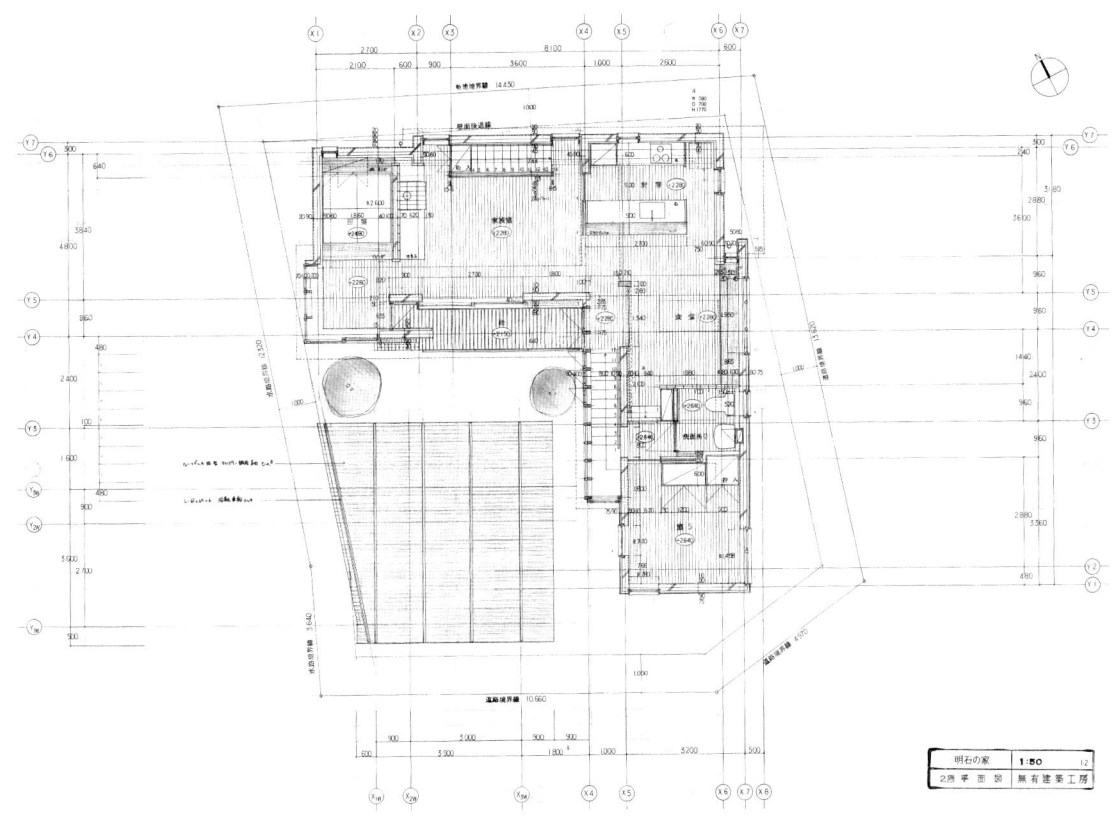

2階平面図　　Second-floor plan

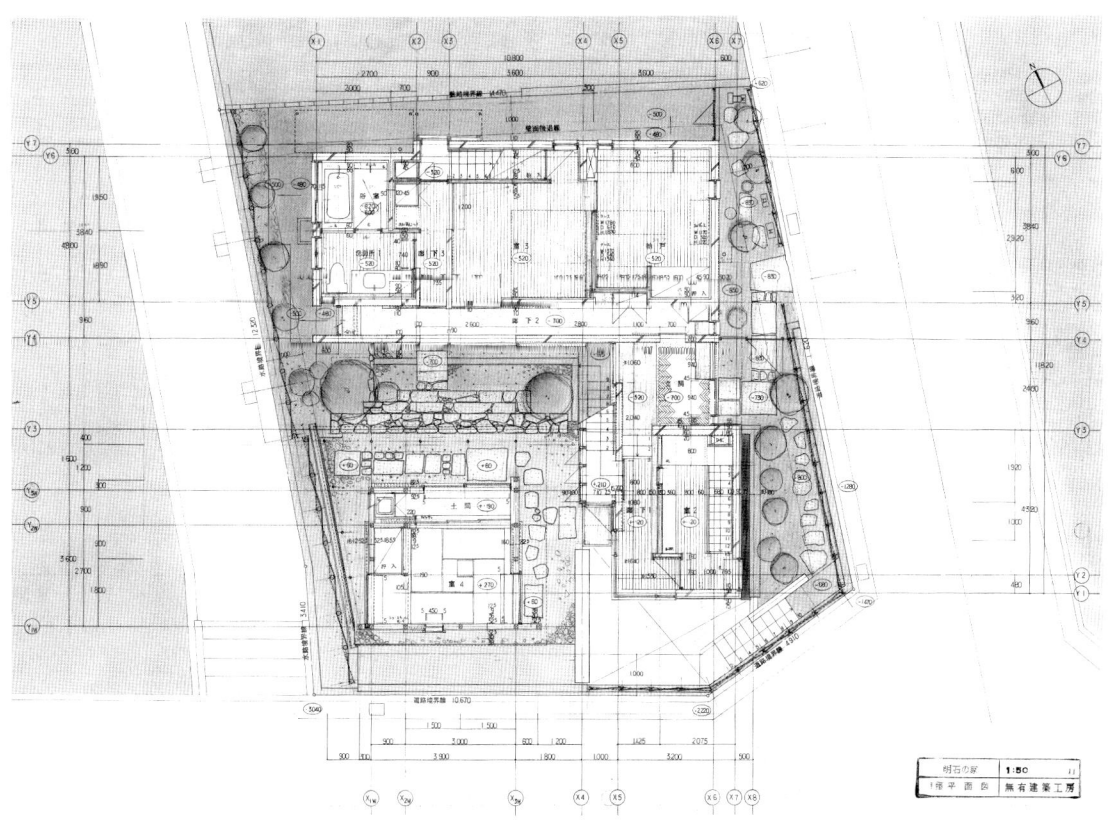

1階平面図　　First-floor plan

205 | Akashi House

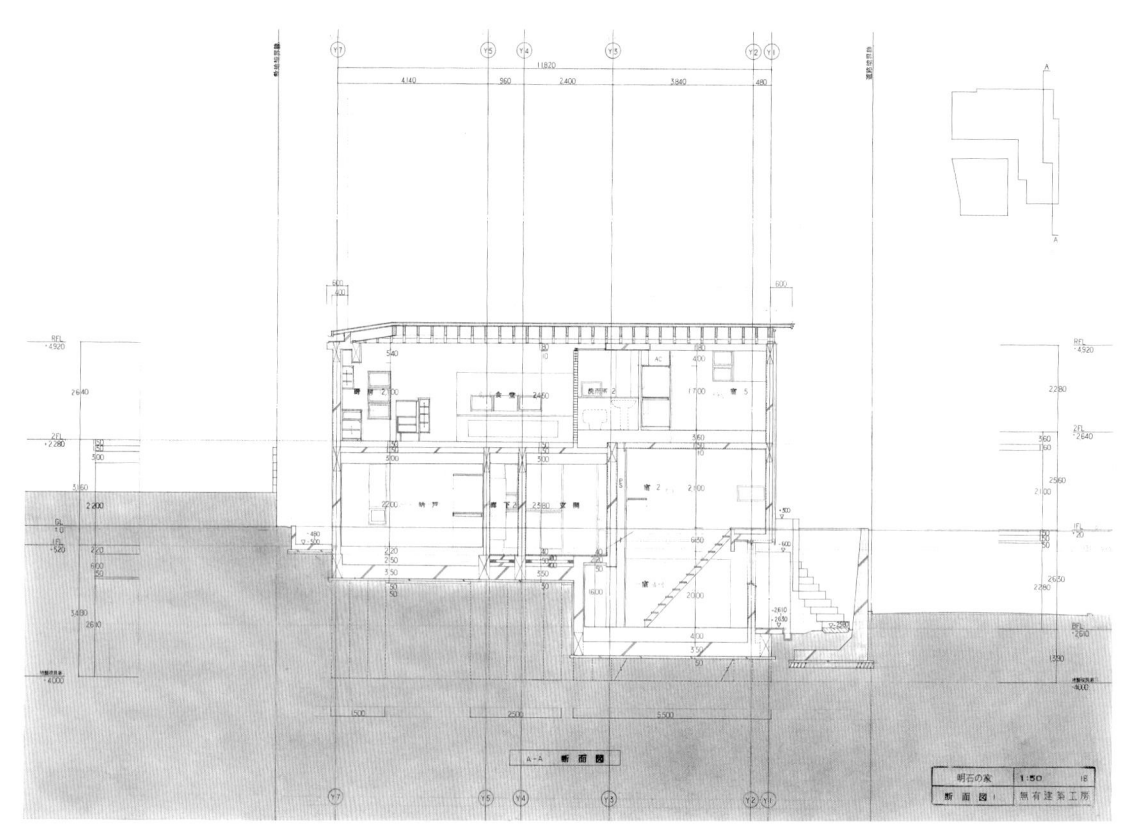

断面図　　Section

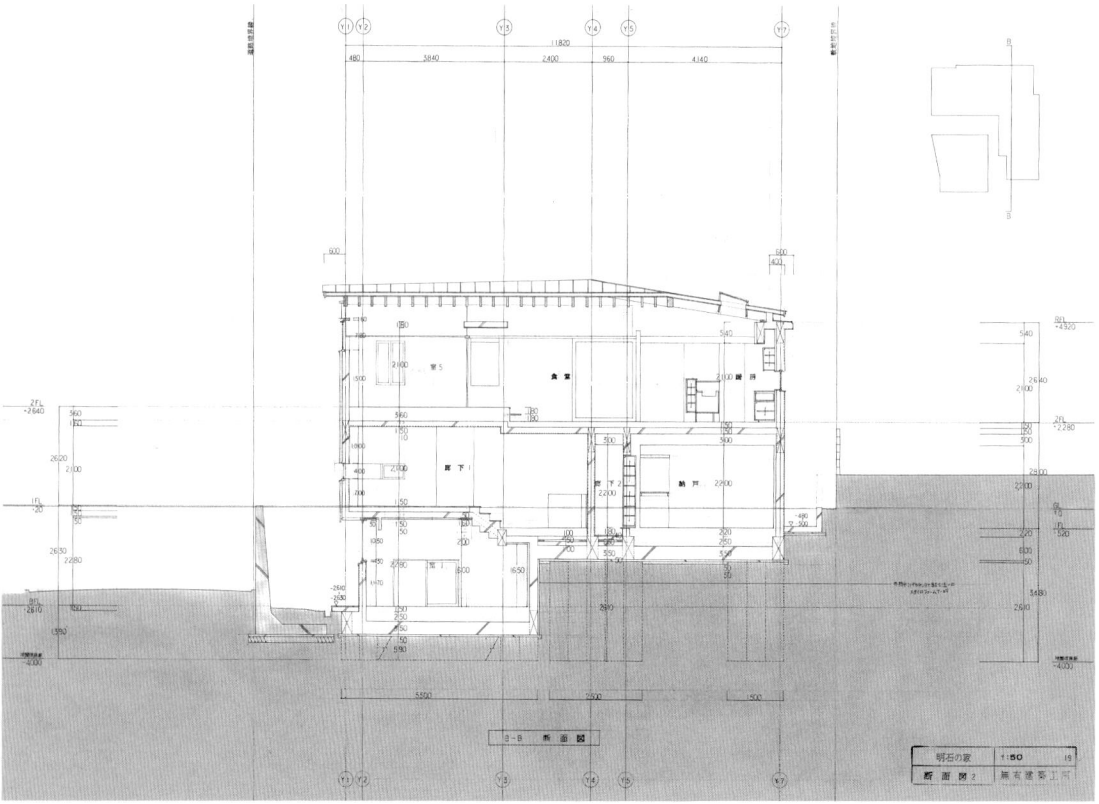

断面図　　Section

Akashi House

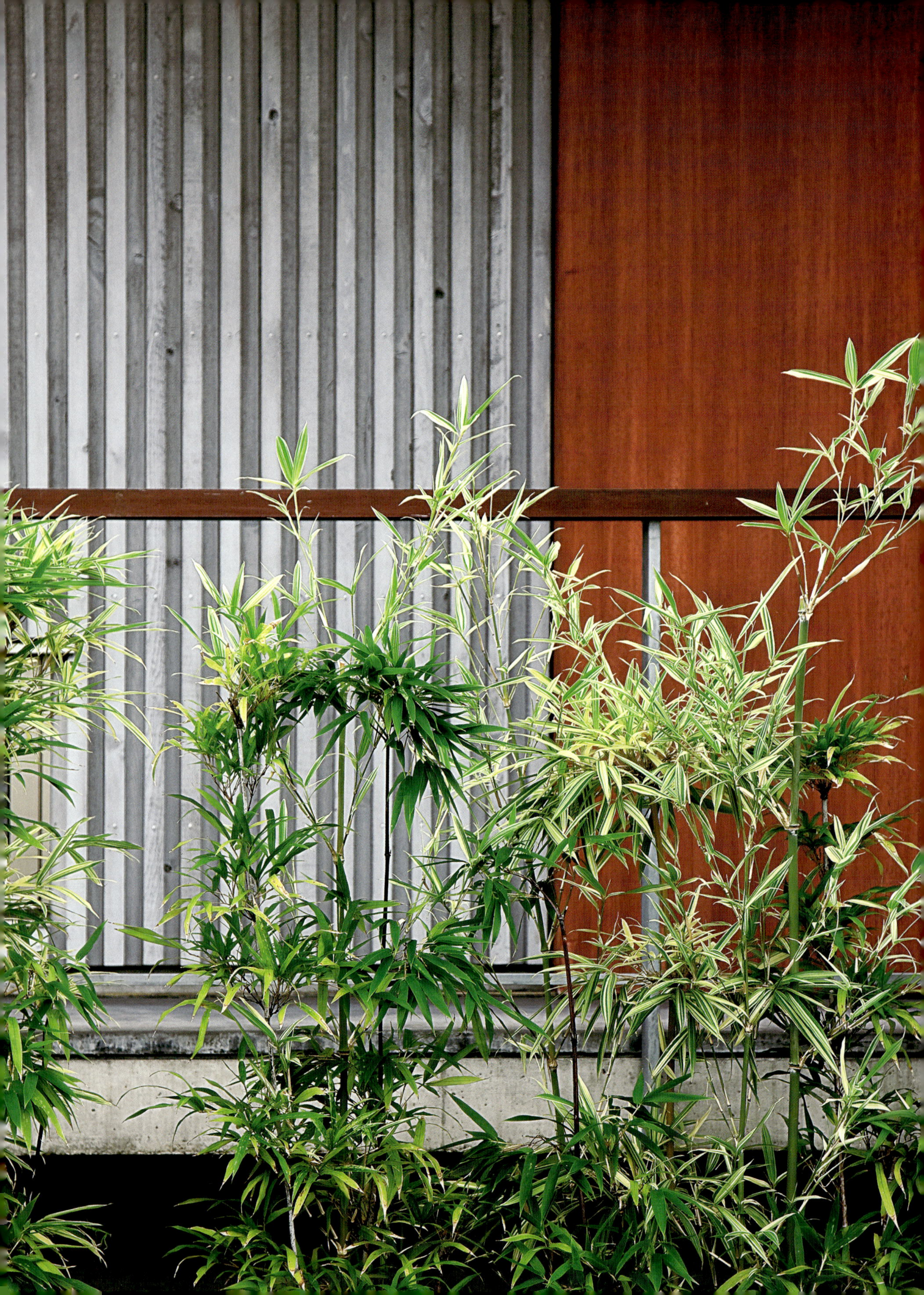

比叡山を望む京都市北部の閑静な住宅地の一角、風致地区における建築制限により建ぺい率40％、2層分の高さにヴォリュームを抑えられ、切妻の瓦屋根の連なる町並みの角地に、染織作家のアトリエと住居がつくられた。制作の場と生活がほどよく分節されながら、全体としてひとつの家型をなすように構成される。切妻屋根が表通りに対して平行に架かり、米杉板の押縁と内外を透かす格子が同ピッチで連続する陰翳ある外壁に、わずかな開口部だけを穿った家型の箱が控えて建つ。周囲には塀を建てず、建ぺい率の制限によって生まれた外側の余白をそのまま町へ開放している。

　均整のとれた切妻屋根のプロポーションとは対照的に、その箱の内には中庭が挿入され、敷地の裏手では屋根が切り欠かれ、家型の箱が密やかに空と関係を結ぶ。この内なる庭を中心に、小さなヴォリュームの中にアトリエと居住部分が間合いをもって対峙する。テキスタイルなどの大きな作品を掛けるために必要とされるアトリエの天井高が基準となり、スキップフロアの断面構成がとられ、中庭や外界に対してより立体的な視線の抜けと、緊張感のある関係が生まれる。

　3層にスキップする断面を階段や廊下、テラスなど、中庭を中心とした廻遊動線によって立体的につなぎ、それぞれ開口部の割り貫き方、床や天井のレヴェルを操作することで、景色の見え方を変化させ、路地や縁側、軒下空間に見立てられた廻遊空間が豊かなシーンを展開する。中庭を巡り、2階では比叡山の稜線を借景とした景色が待ち受け、家族室を巡って再び中庭へ引き寄せられると、遂には空へと突き抜ける。中庭の外を巡る格子戸は風や光を内へと導き、格子戸の外に残された余白は中庭と外室につながる裏手の通り路地となり、隣家に緑を提供する。風致によって制限を受けた住宅は手前にある余白を町へと開放し、家型を装いながら、風致によって残された遠くの余白を内部へと引き込んでいるのである。

岩倉の家
Iwakura House

In a quiet area in Kyoto with a view of Mt. Hiei, this combination atelier and dwelling was built for a dyer on a corner lot of a street lined with houses with tiled roofs and a controlled volume of two stories and 40-percent building coverage. While dividing the working and living spaces, the residence is a single entity. The gabled roof runs parallel to the street, and a house-shaped box stands on the other side of a small opening in a hatched wall with the same pitch as the red-cedar boards of the *osaebuchi* (horizontal bars) and a lattice door separating the interior and exterior. Without a wall around the perimeter, the blank exterior, a product of the coverage regulation, remains open to the street.

In contrast to the balanced proportions of the gabled roof, a courtyard is contained within the box, and in the rear of the site, the roof is notched and the house-shaped box forms a link with the sky. With the inner garden at the center, the atelier and dwelling area stand face-to-face in the small volume. As a high ceiling, necessary for hanging textiles, was a basic criterion, the atelier has a split-level, sectional structure, and the lack of a three-dimensional line of sight to the courtyard and the outside world adds a sense of tension.

By three-dimensionally linking the three-story, split-level sections with a "stroll-style" flow line and manipulating the way one passes through the openings and the levels of the floors and ceiling, one's view of the scenery is altered, and a "strolling" space engenders a rich variety of scenes. Circling the courtyard on the second floor, one enjoys the borrowed scenery of Mt. Hiei, and as one walks around the family room and is again drawn to the courtyard, the sky suddenly breaks through. Making one's way around the courtyard, the lattice door allows wind and light in, and the open space left outside the door serves as a rear passage connecting the courtyard and the outside.

This residence, developed on the basis of rules designed to maintain this district, leaves the empty space in front open, and while wearing the guise of a house, draws distant empty spaces preserved as part of the scenic area inside.

1階アトリエ1より中庭を見る／対峙する室は断面的にズレ、視線を違える。足元に透けて見えるのは半地階のアトリエ2。対峙する外室へ視線と風が抜ける。

View of courtyard from the first-floor atelier: Sectionally staggered, the opposing rooms have a different line of sight. Visible below is Atelier 2, which occupies the half-basement. One's line of sight and the wind are directed toward the outer room on the other side.

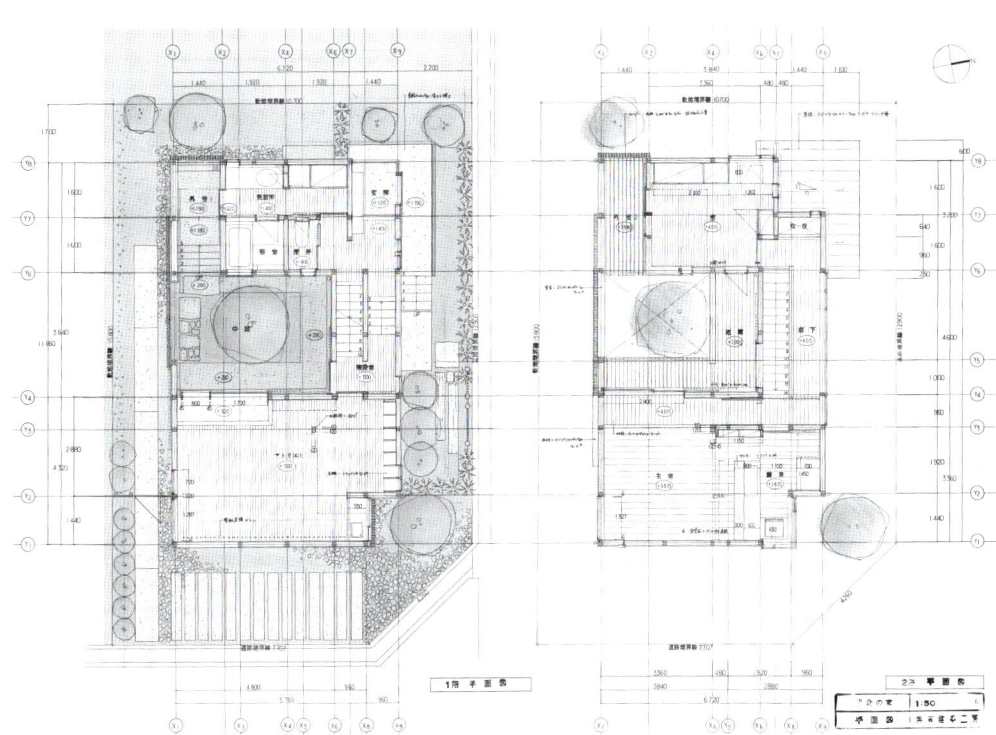

平面図　　Floor plan

211 | Iwakura House

左：外室1より中庭を介してアトリエ1を見る／格子戸を開くと隣地とのスキマに生まれた路地空間と相まって通り路地を形成する。
右：1階アトリエ1より中庭を見る／天井高に対し垂壁を落とし、低く抑えられた開口部は視線を足元へと誘う。

Left: View of Atelier 1 through courtyard from the outer room: When one opens the lattice door, an alley space, created by the gap between the house and the adjacent property, emerges along with a passage.
Right: View of courtyard from Atelier 1 —
By lowering the vertical hanging walls in relation to the height of the ceiling, the low, controlled opening directs the line of sight toward the ground.

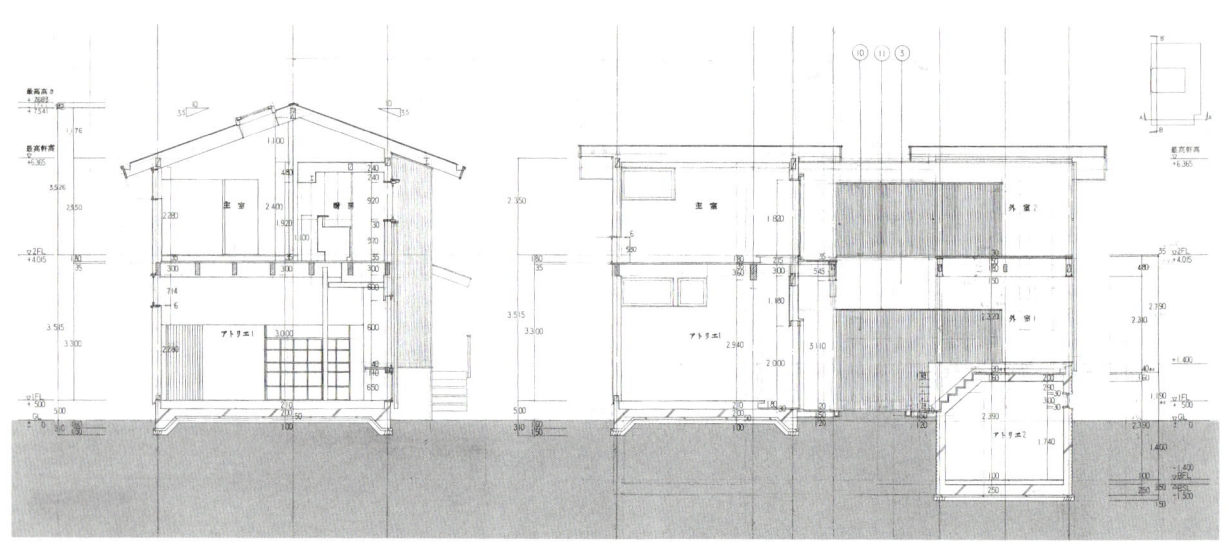

断面図　Section

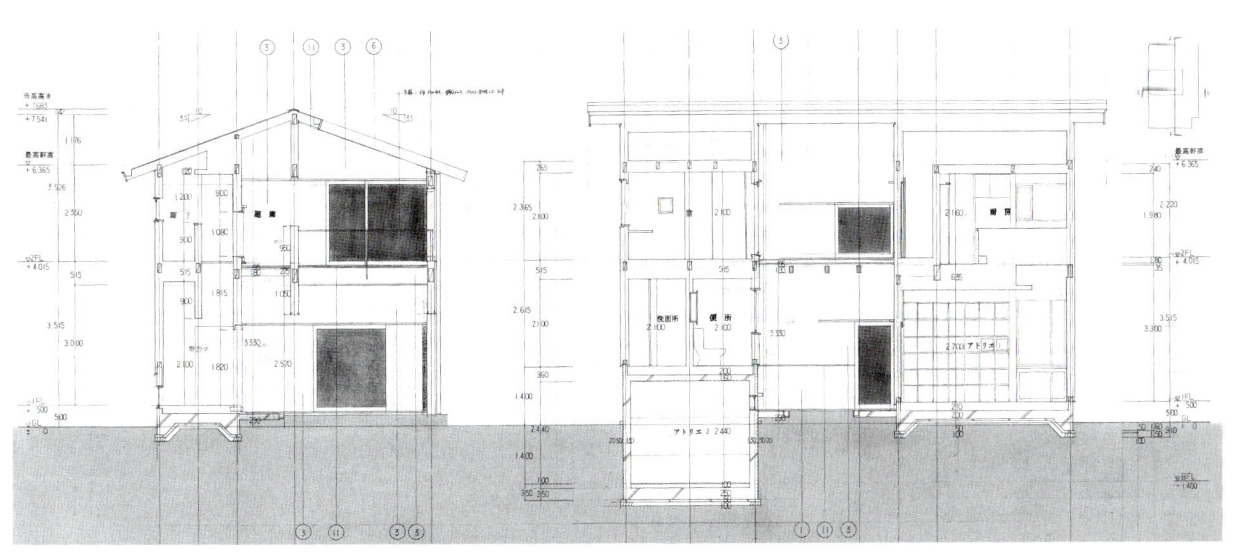

断面図　Section

213 | Iwakura House

階段室の構成／半階レヴェルのズレた階段と廊下、中庭のテラスが複雑な廻遊動線をつくる。それぞれ天井や床の高さ、開口部の高さを違えることで異なる景色を切り取り、廻遊動線はいつしか主室の縁に見立てられる。

Structure of the staircase: Staggered half a story, the stairs and corridor form a complex "stroll-style" flow line with the courtyard terrace. The varying heights of the ceilings, floors, and openings create different scenes and without realizing it, the flow line suddenly appears on the veranda in the main room.

216

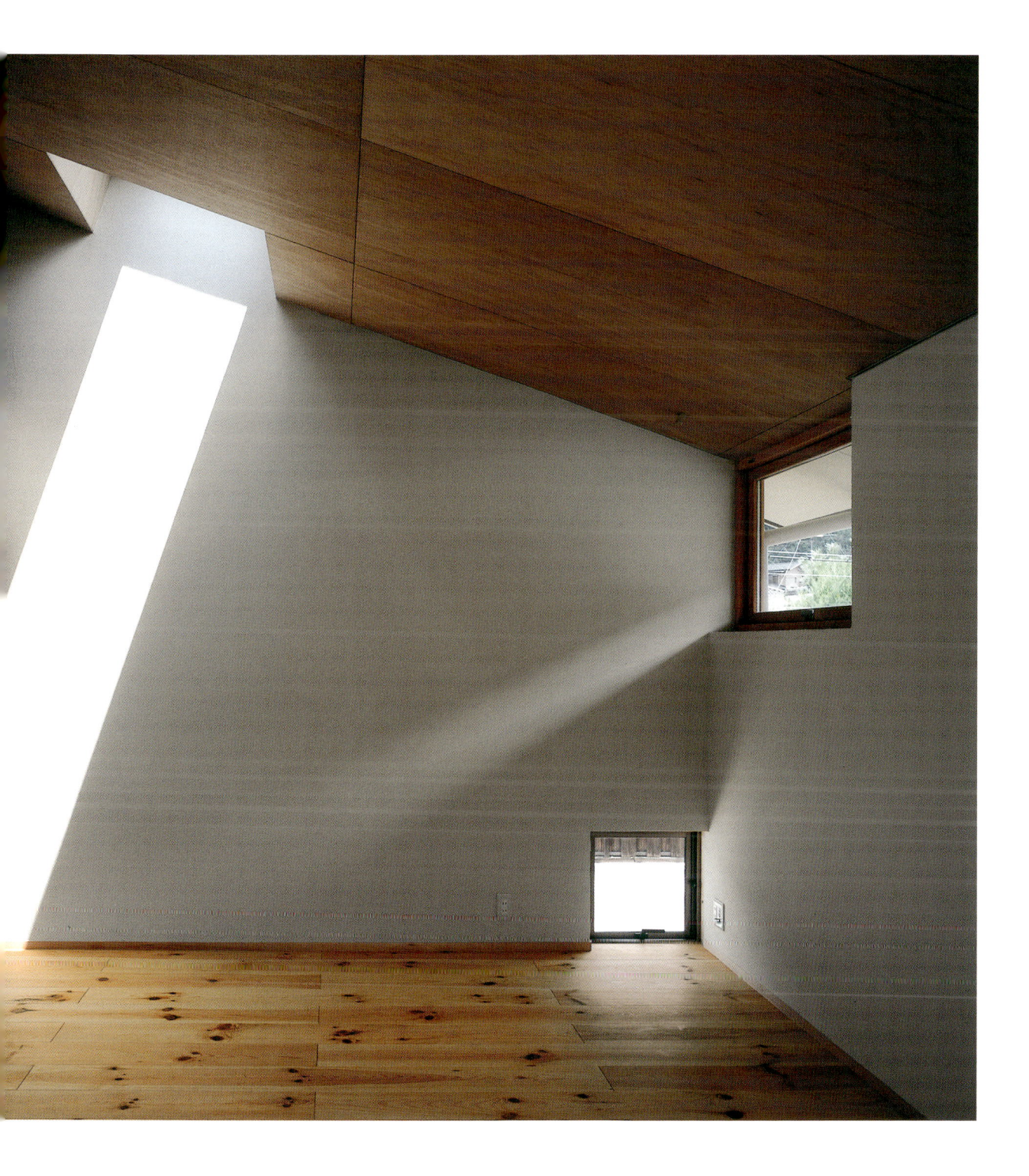

家型屋根の箱に中庭や外室が挿入され、屋根が切り込まれることで、内外が立体的につながる。外界から切り離されるように主室に点在させたマドから射し込む光は、生活に緊張感を取り戻す。

Placing the courtyard and outer room in the box of the house-shaped roof frames the roof and creates a three-dimensional relationship between the interior and exterior. The light that flows in through the windows, dotting the main room, seems detached from the outside world and brings a sense of tension back to daily life.

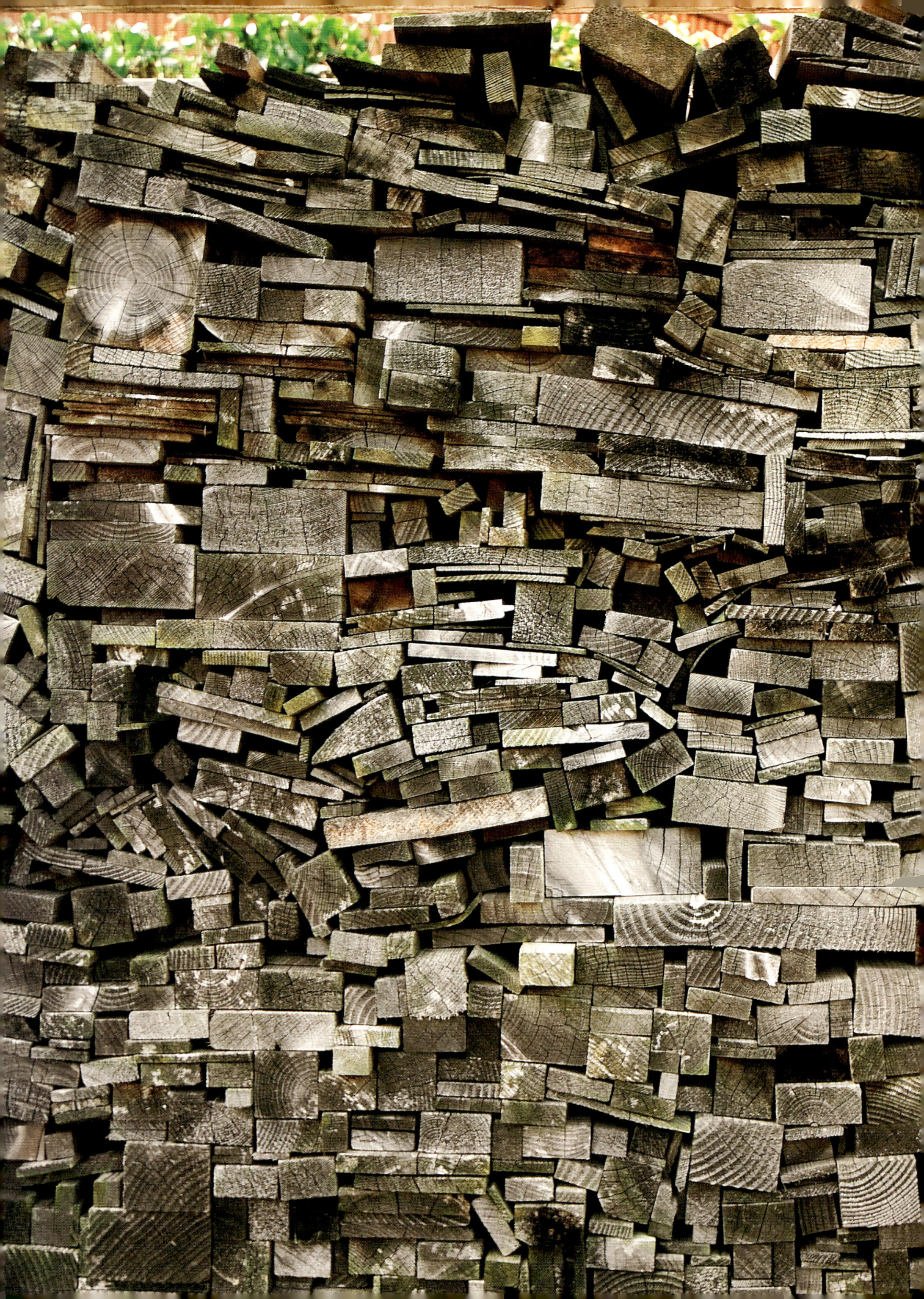

愛知県額田郡、渥美湾から6kmほどの気候の穏やかな地域に位置する。田畑や草地、水路や小山に囲まれたこの土地は比較的平穏な田舎の風景の中に建つ。両親の家の東隣の畑を埋め戻してできた敷地は、前面道路から12m入り込んだ旗竿状の形状をもち、いずれ宅地になる可能性のある北東の余白に対し領域を囲い取りながら、現状の水田の風景をほどよく透かし入れる。

　南北に敷地を3分割し、層の異なるふたつのヴォリュームを中庭を介して対峙させる。わずかな棟のズレによって重なった壁が周囲の視線を切り取り、そのスキマに光や風、視線の抜け道をつくり出す。北東に2層分立ち上がる壁は開口を極力控え、格子戸のスキマから風景を透かし見る。上に架かる屋根は宙に軽やかに浮かび、ハイサイドより光や風景を透かす。

　2層分の壁を正面に捉え、格子戸を開けると、長屋門のような吹きさらしの軒下空間が迎える。門をくぐると中庭の奥に平屋の棟が控え、化粧垂木の連続する軒下から敷台をまたいで家族室のある土間へ入る。土間の上に装置された床はわずか120mmの段差で浮かび、ここへ座り込むと視線が地面に吸い寄せられる。敷台は景色を囲い取る結界となり、地面との緊密な関係を意識させる。視線は地を這い、格子越しに水田や道路、山へと結ばれる。内外の床レベル、開口部、結界がわずかな寸法で操作されることで、生活の中に緊張感が生まれる。対する2層分の棟へは一旦雨ざらしの中庭へ出て、外室をくぐり抜けて辿り着く。わずか2室の内部空間が外部空間で接続する住宅は、土の中庭や外部のテラス、屋上庭園と従属的な関係をもちながら、その時々で変幻自在に使われ、かつての民家のような様相を見せる。

　この不便さの裏側に、内と外の豊かな関係が結ばれ、屋根の下に生まれた軒下空間、2階のヴォリュームの下に残された軒下空間と、雨や光を直接受ける庭が、生活に緊張感をもたらす。土の匂い立ち込める外部空間はしばしの間、子供たちの格好の遊び場としてにぎやかさを見せるであろう。

額田の家
Nukata House

Located in an area with a mild climate about six kilometers from a bay in Nukata, Aichi Prefecture, this plot is surrounded by fields, meadows, waterways, and hills. The flag lot is twelve meters back from the frontal road and though surrounded by empty spaces to the northeast that may become residential land, the rice-paddy-filled landscape is now quite open.

On a lot divided into three parts from north to south, two volumes with different levels are mediated by a courtyard. By slightly staggering the two wings, a layered wall prevents a direct line of sight from the outside and the gap between the two structures allows light, wind, and a line of sight inside. By limiting the opening in the wall, rising to the second story level on the northeast side, one is afforded a clear view of the scenery through the gaps in the lattice door.

As one faces the facade of the wall and opens the door, they arrive at a space under the eaves that is exposed to the wind much like the row-house gate. Passing through the gate, one finds a single-story wing beyond the courtyard and enters the earthen floor family-room area surrounded by a raised floor under the eaves with exposed rafters. With only a slight level difference (the floor rises about 120 millimeters above the earthen floor), when one sits here, their line of sight is drawn to the ground. The floor functions as a barrier to enclose the scenery and encourages an awareness of to the ground. One's line of sight next moves over the ground and arrives at the paddies, roads, and hills beyond the lattice door. Manipulating the floor level between the interior and exterior, the opening, and the barrier with miniscule differences in size gives rise to a sense of tension. Moving next into the rain-exposed courtyard toward the two-story wing, one passes through an outer room. Only the internal space of two rooms connects the residence via the external space, giving it the appearance of a traditional folk-style dwelling.

Daily life here is imbued with tension through the link between the interior and the exterior, the eave spaces under the roof and the volume of the second floor, and the garden, which is directly exposed to rain and wind. It won't be long before the external space, enveloped in the aroma of the earth, will be filled with the excitement of children playing.

旗竿の敷地をアプローチし、格子戸を開けると2階のヴォリュームの下に軒下空間が待ち受け、長屋門のように人を迎える。低く抑えられた空間が地平へと意識を呼ぶ。

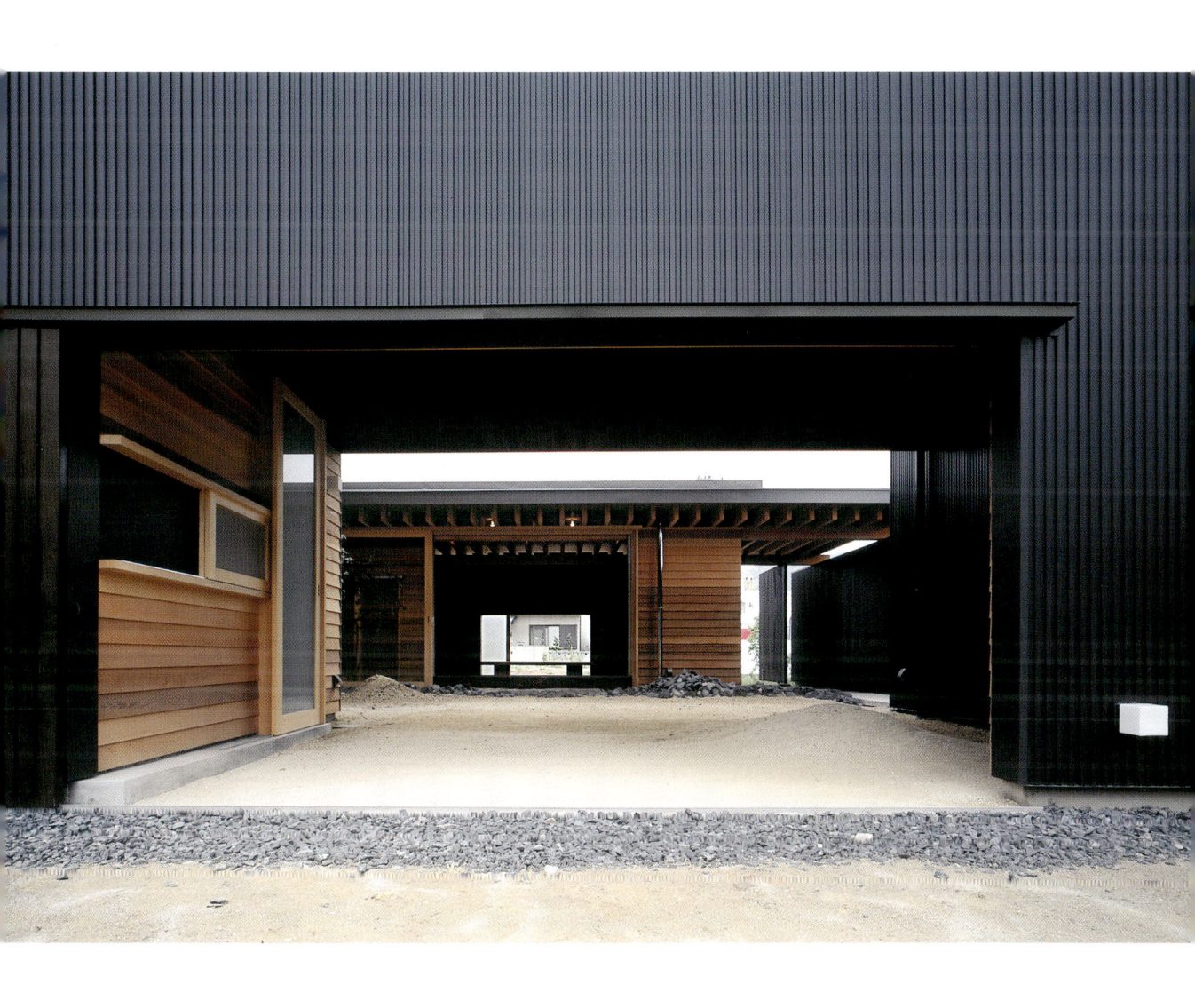

After approaching the flag lot and opening the lattice door, one finds a space under the eaves below the second-floor volume, and a welcoming row-house gate. The low, controlled space draws one's attention to the horizon.

左：軽やかに屋根を浮かべたエレヴェーションは北側隣地の水田に映し出され、格子戸、中庭、室1越しに、南側の水路の風景まで透かされる。
下：地面・土間・床のわずかなレヴェル差に敷台が結ぶ結界、連続する化粧垂木が見せる軒のラインが内と外の関係をつくる。
右：室2の足元に透かされ、土のまま残された外室3は緑化された平屋棟の屋上と関係を結ぶ。

Left: The elevation, which makes the roof seem to float lightly in the air, is reflected in the paddies on the lot that abuts the residence on the north side, and allows an unobstructed view of the waterway on the south side beyond the lattice door, courtyard, and Room 1.
Below: The barrier created by the entrance platform, linking the slight level differences of the ground, earthen-floor area, and floor, and the eaves, highlighted by the exposed rafters, establish a link between the interior and exterior.
Right: The clear view at foot level in Room 2 and Outer Room 3, with the ground left intact, creates a link to the rooftop greenery on top of the single-story wing.

Nukata House

左：水路側より室1・中庭・外室3を通し北側隣地を透かし見る／土間に直接敷かれた土台が敷台となって土間、床、庭とのわずかなレヴェル差に結界を結ぶ。

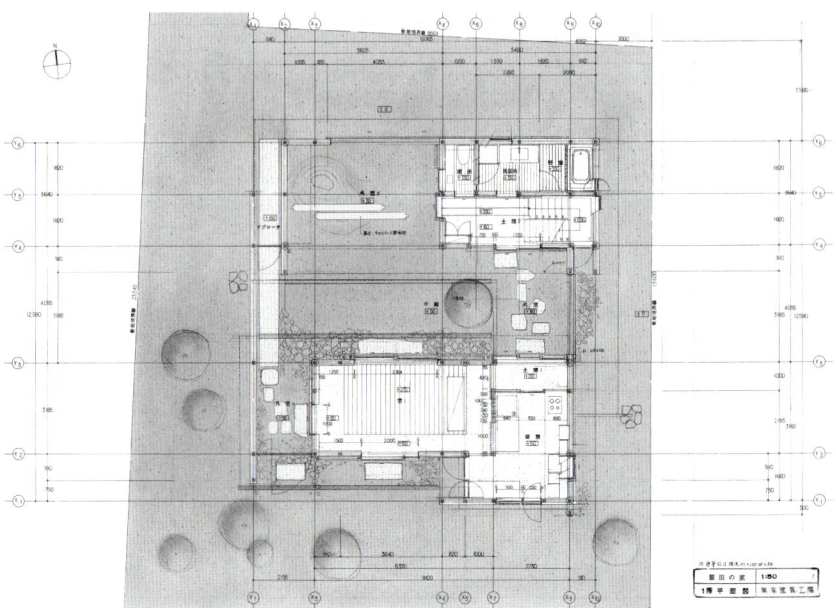

1階平面図　First-floor plan

224

Left: Unobstructed view of the abutting lot to the north through Room 1, courtyard, and Outer Room 3 from the waterway— The foundation, laid directly on the ground, acts as the entrance platform, forming a link to the barrier created by the slight level differences in the earthen floor, the floor, and the garden.

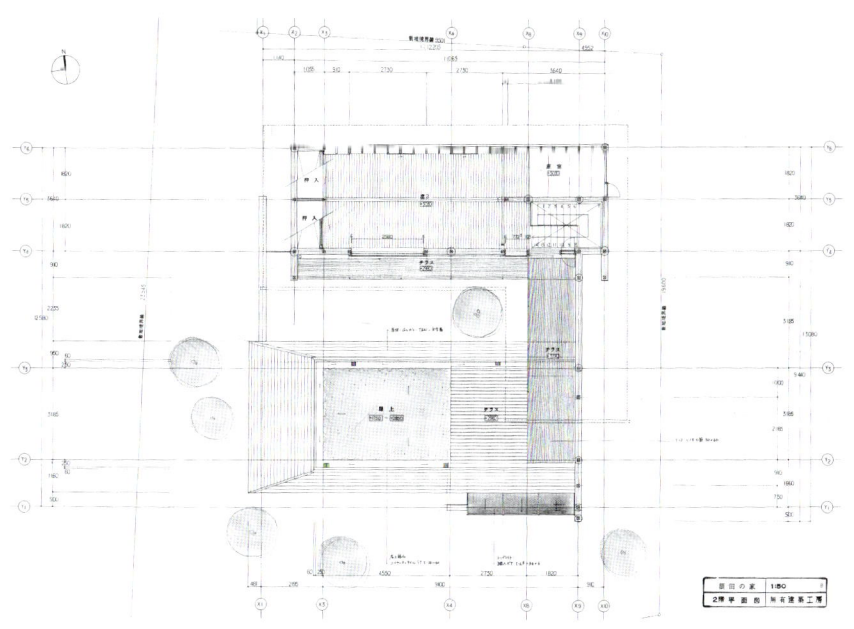

2階平面図　Second-floor plan

Nukata House

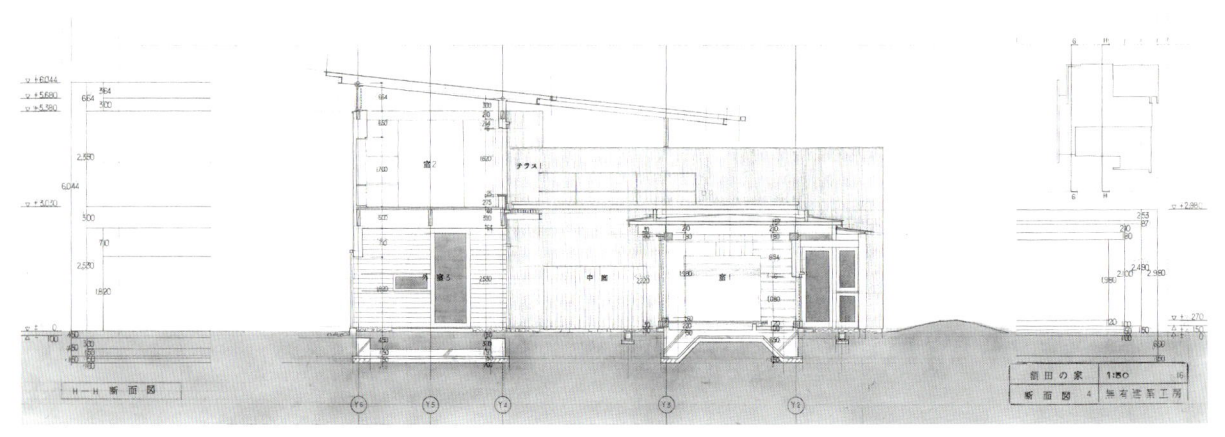

断面図　Section

敷地を3分割し、中庭を挟んで高さの異なる2棟が対峙する。2棟はL型に延びる薄い屋根とデッキによって結ばれ、屋上庭園は外室3や2階のハイサイドから北側の風景と連続する。

Dividing the property into three, the two wings, each with a different height, stand face to face on either side of the courtyard. They are connected by a thin roof that extends in an L shape and a deck, and the rooftop garden is linked to the scenery on the north side which is visible through Outer Room 3 and the high sidelights on the second floor.

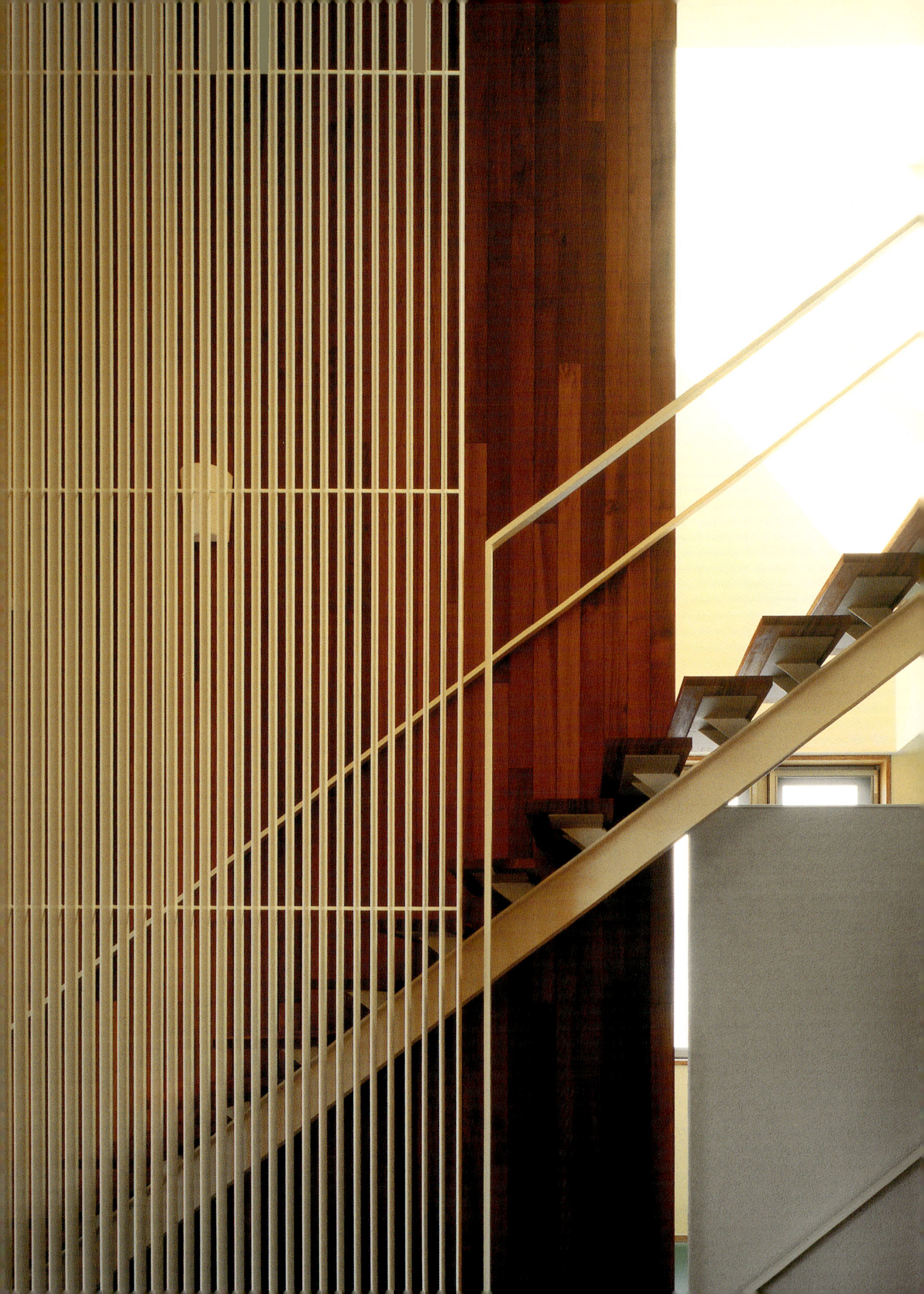

大阪府南部、南北に貫く紀州街道沿いに残る古くからの町並みと、新たな住宅地が混在し、いずれも秋になるとだんじり祭りのにぎわいで一色に包まれる岸和田の町。敷地は国道からひと筋入り込み、ほどよいスケールの路地を形成するT字路の突き当たりに位置する。東隣は空地となるが、南側にはとクスノキの大木が覆い茂る広い庭と泉南地域特有のシコロ葺屋根の格式ある屋敷をもつ隣家がある。風化したレンガ積の境界塀と豊かな緑が独特の雰囲気を醸し出す。

　T字路に面した町の懐柔、だんじりを中心とした祭事の場として独特なヴォリュームをもつこの住宅は、町家さながらに平面や立面を分割して構成することによって内と外、室と室の間合いがはかられる。タテ格子で構成されたガラスのスクリーンは視線を遮りながら光を透かしてヴォリュームを和らげ、コンクリートの外壁に映し出された小幅杉板型枠の表情が通りの様相に溶け込む。平面の中央に厚みのある壁が南北に貫かれ、ヴォリュームを2分割する。この壁を介しふたつの空間がネガポジの関係をもち、立体的に挿入されたヴォイドが内外を曖昧にする。

　1階では壁を介し「玄」と「白」の土間空間が反転する。「玄」の土間は薄暗いトンネル状の空間となり、南隣の庭を借景とする開口部からバウンドする光が、素材の色味やテクスチュアを彷彿とさせる。「白」の土間はガラスで構成された光に満ちた空間となり、色ガラスの垂木から落ちる幻想的な光に彩られる。陰翳に包まれた土間と、鮮やかな色彩と光に満ちた土間が寄り添い、外部へと意識が拡散する。

　上階では筒状の吹抜に柔らかな光が廻り込む漆喰塗の壁と、スリット状の吹抜から射し込む光に撫でられた粗壁の対比に、内とも外ともいえない空気が流れる。3層をつなぐ階段は吹抜となり、住空間全体に視線や空気が連続する。ヴォリュームに挿入された厚みのある壁と、ヴォリュームに割り貫かれた立体的なヴォイドが、領域を緩やかに分節しながら、おおらかな一室空間として透明性の高い廻遊式住居を形成するのである。

岸和田の家
Kishiwada House

Despite its mixture of old settlements along the Kishu Highway and new residential communities, Kishiwada, in southern Osaka Prefecture, is united by its *danjiri* (wooden float) festival every fall. One road off the highway, this lot is situated at the end of a T-junction. The boundary wall, made of weathered bricks, and the rich greenery lend the site a unique atmosphere.

While possessing the qualities of a traditional merchant's house, the residence divides the plane and the elevation surface, maintaining a good distance between the interior and exterior, and the rooms within it. Obstructing the line of sight, a glass screen allows light in, softening the volume and blending with the narrow, cedar-board frame projected on the concrete exterior wall. Running north-south through the center of the plane is a thick wall that produces two volumes. The spaces have a negative/positive relationship and give rise to a three-dimensional void which obscures the distinction between interior and exterior.

On the first floor, the wall-mediated "black" and "white" sections of the earthen floor are inverted. The "black" area, a dark, tunnel-like space, allows light to ricochet in through an opening, which provides a view of a borrowed landscape from the neighboring garden, and recalls the colors and textures of its materials. The "white" earthen floor is a glass-structured, light-filled space ornamented by the light that pours in through the colored-glass rafters. The combination of the static space enveloped in shadow and the kinetic space bathed in brilliant colors and light expands one's awareness of the exterior.

The upper floor, encompassing a contrast between plaster walls shrouded in soft light in a tubular atrium and rough-coated walls brushed with light streaming in through a slit-shaped atrium, is imbued with an air that is neither wholly interior nor exterior. While gently segmenting the property, the thick wall that divides the volume and the three-dimensional void that penetrates it give rise to a "stroll-style" residence with a high degree of transparency.

230

ヴォリュームの内へ引き込まれたアプローチは垂壁によって覆われ、人は濃密な空間へ誘われる。中へ入ると「玄」の土間が待ち受け、上階までつながっていく。

The approach, drawn within the volume, invites one into a covered, dense space via a hanging vertical wall. Once inside, one finds a "black" earthen floor that leads to the upper story.

南側隣地の庭と風化した境界塀を借景とし、対照的な明度・彩度をもった「玄」の土間と「白」の土間が寄り添う。「玄」の土間は陰翳のある空間にレンガのテクスチュアが彷彿とする。「白」の土間は色ガラスの垂木を透過して幻想的な光が落ちる。

With a borrowed landscape form the garden on the abutting lot to the south and a weathered boundary wall, two neighboring, earthen floor, one "black" and one "white," present contrasting amounts of light and color. The shadowy space in the "black" area has a brick-like texture. In the "white" area, light pours through colored-glass rafters.

ヴォリュームを2分割する厚みのある壁に門型に開口部が刳り貫かれる。粗く仕上げられたこの壁際にヴォイドとトップライトからもたらされる光によって、ヴォリュームの内にいながら内外を錯覚させる。

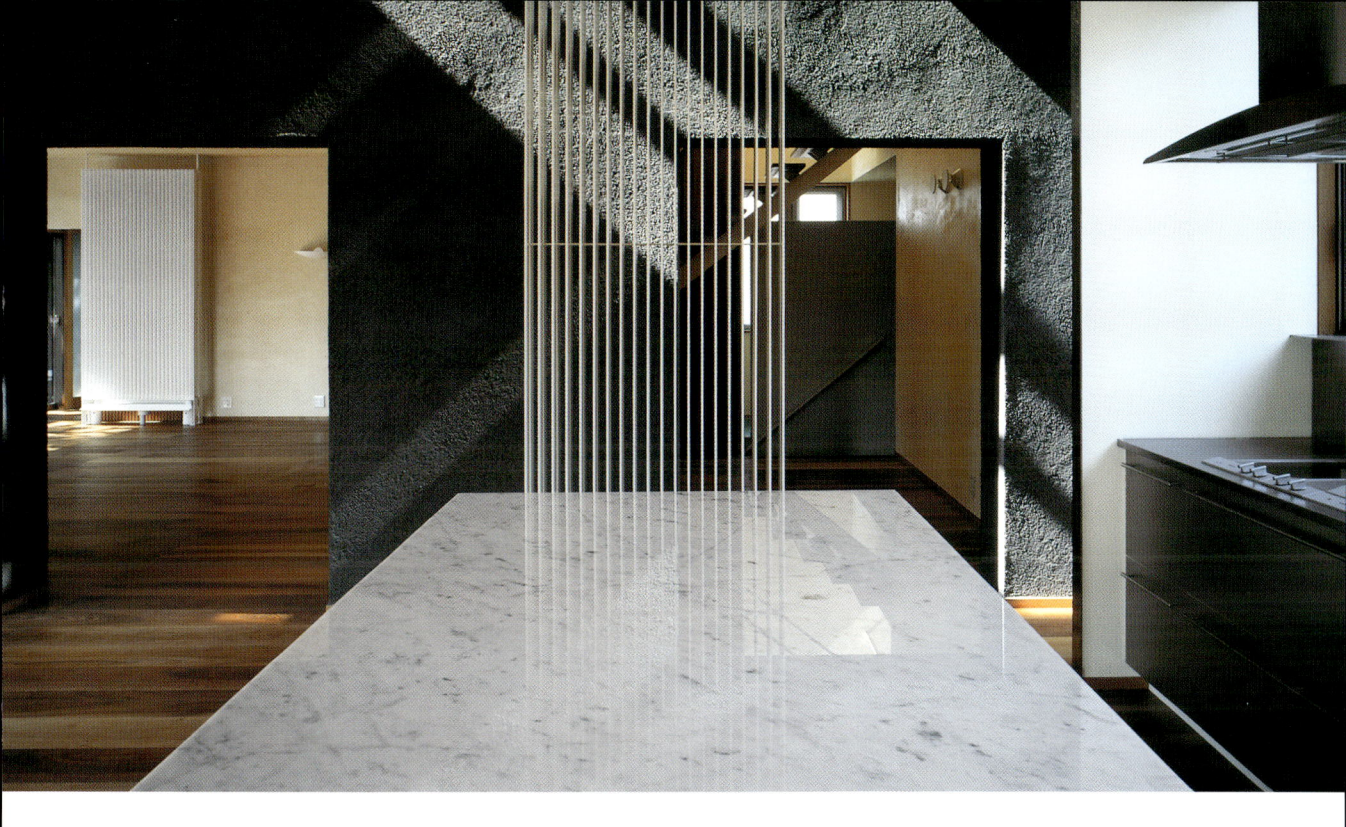

A gate-shaped opening leads through the thick wall that divides the volume into two. Along the roughly finished wall, the light that seeps in through the void and the skylight mixes one's sense of interior and exterior in the volume.

2 階平面図　　Second-floor plan

ヴォリュームを南北方向に2分割する壁に穿たれた開口部により、廻廊をもたす、室の連結で構成された平面に、新たな廻遊動線をつくる。

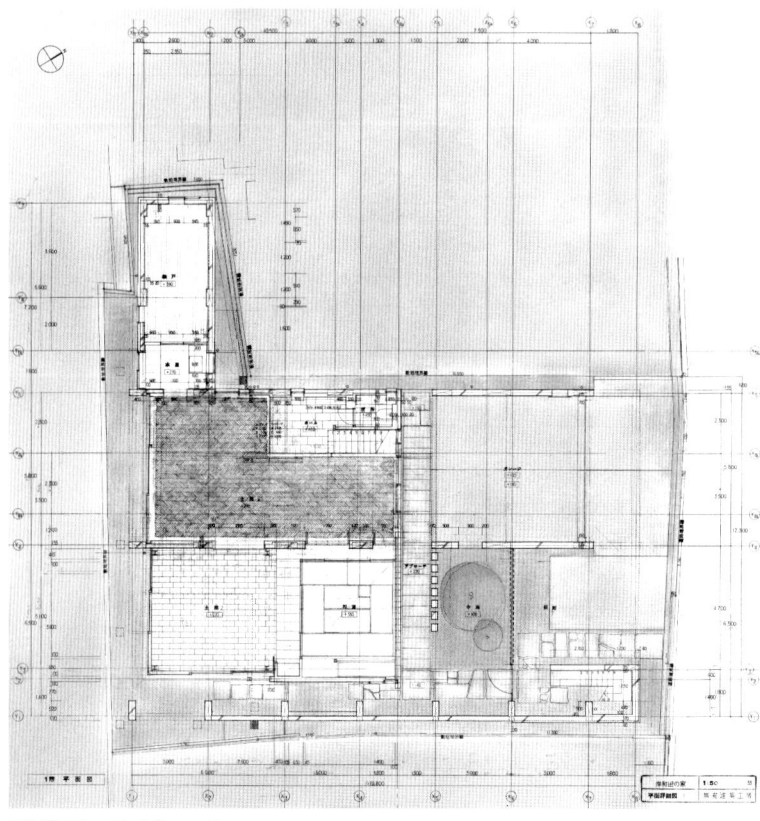

1 階平面図　　First-floor plan

236

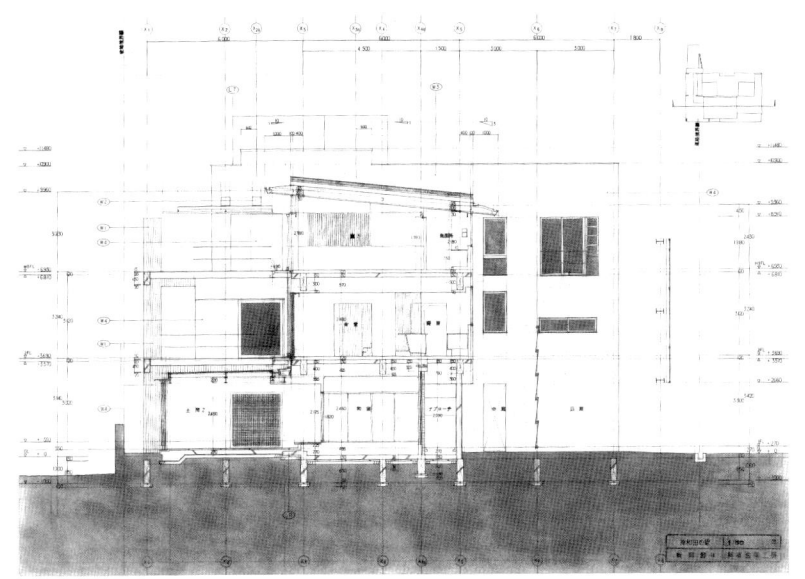

Without a corridor, the opening penetrating the north-south wall that divides the volume creates a new "stroll-style" flow line in the plane, which is structured out of connecting rooms.

断面図　Section

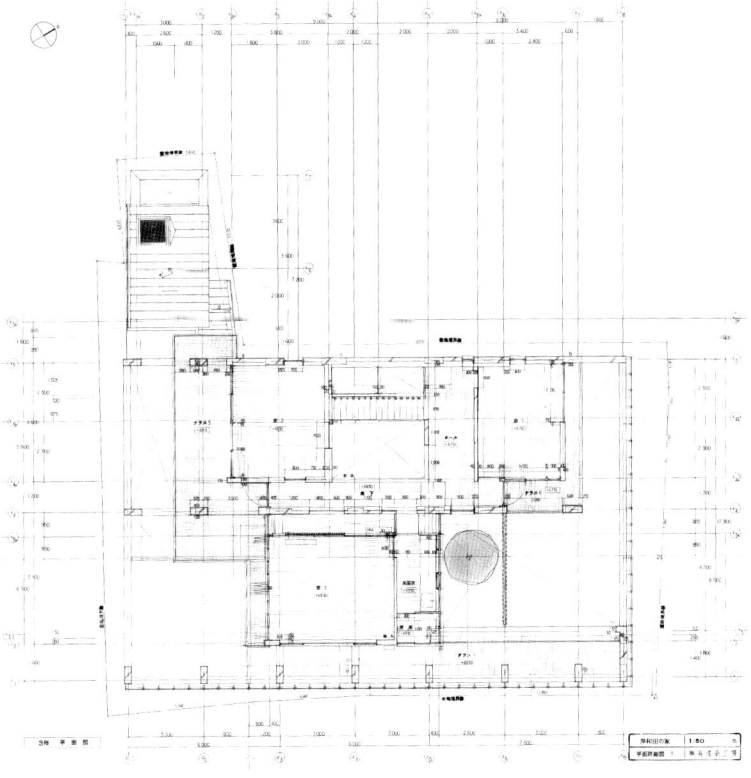

3階平面図　Third-floor plan

237 | Kishiwada House

階段室が3層の空間をつなぐヴォイドとなり、点在する室をつなぎ留める。
ヴォリュームに穿たれた開口部がヴォイドに立体的に交錯する。

The staircase acts as a void, connecting the spaces on all three levels, and bringing together the scattered rooms. The opening that penetrates the volume blends with the void in a three-dimensional manner.

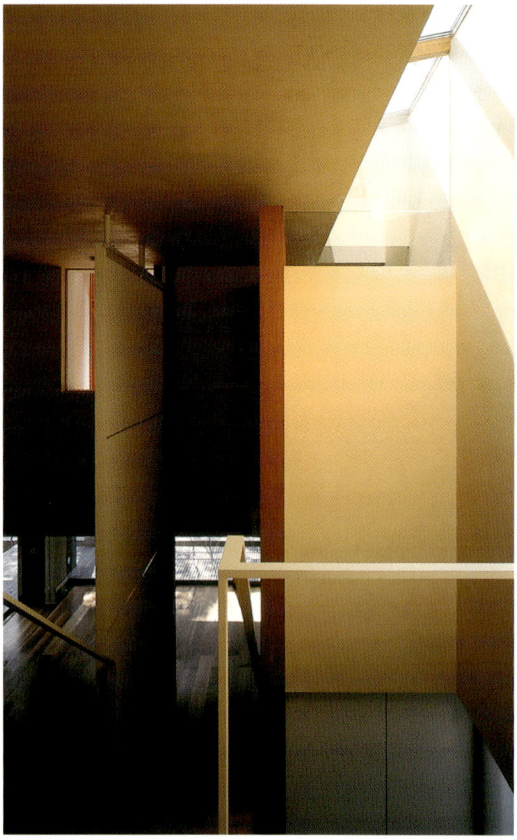

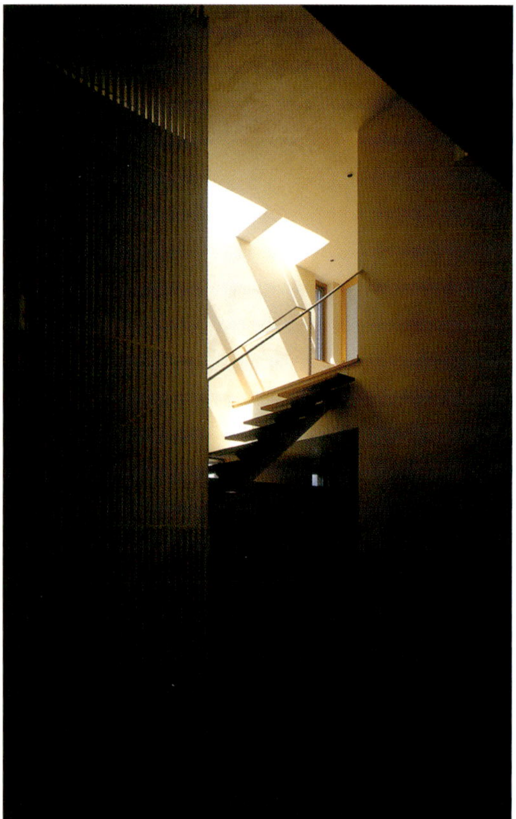

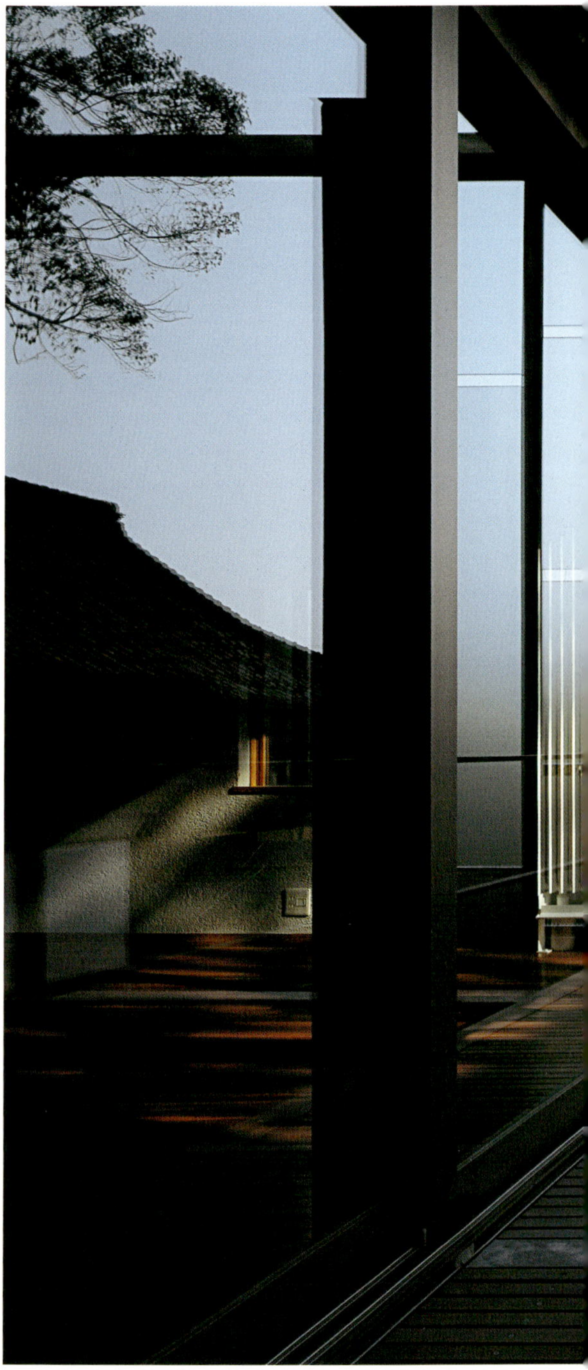

2階テラス／ガラスのスクリーンが周辺の視線を遮りながら、光だけを透過する。外部に架構するコンクリートの柱梁が、岸和田の町並みをフレーミングする。

Second-floor terrace: Discouraging the line of sight from outside, the glass screen only allows light in. The concrete columns and beams that structure the exterior frame the Kishiwada townscape.

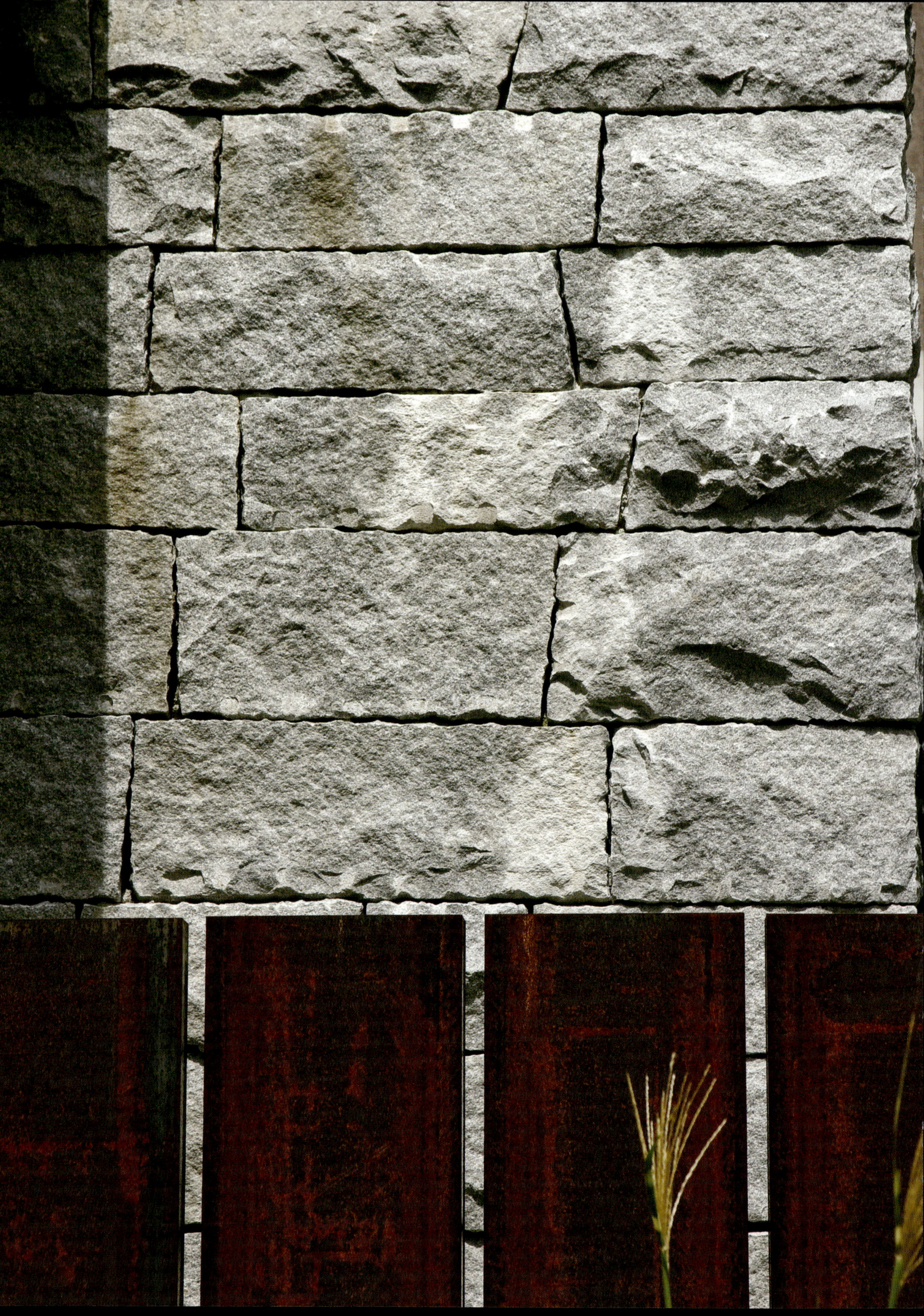

愛知県名古屋市南東部、縦横に流れる川の合間に緑地が点在し、平地と緩やかな丘陵地が続く。緑豊かな住宅地として、幹線道路や地下鉄の整備と共に広範囲にわたって区画整理されつつある新興の町である。3軒分の敷地を合筆したこの土地は、緩やかな坂道に沿って南北に40ｍの間口があり、ひな壇状のレヴェル差をもつ。道の向かいには落葉樹を主とした小高い森があり、季節ごとに景色を彩る。

　2世帯3世代のためのこの住まいは、2層分のT字型平面をもつ南棟と、3層分建ち上がる北棟が、1,500mmのレヴェル差をもって分棟型平面を形成する。配置・平面・断面が雁行し、そこへ立体的な庭が引き込まれることでファサードも分節され、スケールが調整される。面が重なり奥行きをなすエレヴェーションに、石、木、鉄、コンクリート、レンガなどの様々な素材が豊かな表情を見せ、引き込まれた庭の緑と重なりながら、向かいの森と風景を共有する。余白に生まれた5つの庭は個々の居場所とつながり、レヴェルが展開することで異なる景色が添えられる。半層分ズレた2棟の断面を生かし、開口部を操作することで、対峙する室の視線を調整しながら、庭の様相だけを内外に透過させる。2棟はブリッジや庭を介して接続し、入り組んだ動線が互いの領域と間合いを保ち、多世代の住まいにつかず離れずの関係をつくり出した。

　2棟は混構造で構成され、南棟は庇状に延びるコンクリートの水平スラブ、北棟はガレージを支えるコンクリートの門型フレームで対比的に基壇を形成し、その上に鉄骨で組まれた箱形のヴォリュームが載り、薄い小庇が空を切り込む。ヴォリュームを強く意識した空間は、100〜150mm角の鉄骨柱を土台の上に木造感覚で軽やかに組み上げることで構造を消し、素材の表情によって空間構成だけを浮かび上がらせる。こうしたヴォリュームの雁行によっていくつもの開口部が重なり合い、深い奥行きをもちながら、光や風、視線が内外を浸透し、分棟平面の中で家族の意識をつなぎ留めている。

乗鞍の家
Norikura House

In the southeast part of Nagoya, Aichi Prefecture, patches of green dot the land intercepted by rivers. This emerging community is part of a land readjustment project, and this lot, on a plot large enough for three houses, has a 40-meter frontage running north-south along a sloping road and a tiered level difference. Across the road is a forest that provides seasonal changes in scenery.

The residence, designed for two households, consists of a south wing with a two-story, T-shaped plane, and a rising three-story north wing, on a *buntogata* ("divided-ridge-style") plane with a level difference of 1,500 millimeters. The distribution, planes, and sections have an echelon structure, and by drawing the three-dimensional garden toward it, the facade is segmented and the scale controlled. To the elevation, with an added depth created by a layering of surfaces, a variety of materials create a rich expression, and overlap with the greenery in the garden. The gardens in the "empty spaces" are connected to each of the living areas, and by altering the level of each, provide unique scenery. Creating a section between the two wings, with a half-story gap between them, and manipulating the openings limits the line of sight from the opposing room, allowing only the garden to permeate both the interior and exterior. With the two wings connected via a bridge and garden, a complex flow line preserves the territory of each structure to realize a multi-generational dwelling that is neither completely united nor separated.

The complex structure of the residence is achieved through a horizontal concrete slab that extends in a peaked form in the south wing, and by contrast, a concrete, gate-style frame that supports the garage in the north wing. In addition, the residence incorporates a steel-framed, box-like volume with small, thin eaves that cut across the sky. In the space, the structures vanish through the use of 100-150-millimeter, square steel columns on the foundation that evoke the qualities of wood. While this echelon-structured volume juxtaposes several openings and adds depth to the residence, light, wind, and the line of sight permeate the space to anchor the family's awareness within the *buntogata* plane.

立面の構成／雁行するファサードに、コールテン鋼の塀、切石積みの壁、コンクリートの水平スラブが自立構成し、その上に薄い小庇に抑え込まれた板張りの箱が載る。

Elevation structure: In addition to the staggered facade, there are self-supporting structures such as a Corten steel fence, ashlar stone wall, and horizontal concrete slab. Atop the elevation is a boarded box with a form that is controlled by thin, small eaves.

245 | Norikura House

前頁：2階建ての南棟より3階建ての北棟へは敷地が1,500mm落ち込み、2棟も半層ずれる。
左：南棟1階和室より北棟を見る／コンクリート壁に穿たれた開口部は内法を抑え込まれ、半階分沈み込んだ北棟と開口部を違えながら、視線の抜けをつくる。

Preceding page: The site of the three-story north wing is 1,500 millimeters is lower than the two-story south wing, leading to a half-story difference in height.
Left: View of the north wing from Japanese-style room on first-floor of the south wing—The opening that penetrates the concrete wall controls the internal dimensions and while emphasizing the difference in the opening of the half-story-lower north wing, allows a clear line of sight.

Norikura House

北棟2階厨房より中庭を介して南棟を見る。北棟2階家族室2の上に室5がダイナミックに浮かぶ。L型に連続するヴォイドは土佐漆喰で塗り込められ、ヴォリュームと抜けを認識させる。

View of the south wing through the garden from the kitchen on the second floor of the north wing. Room 3, above Family Room 2 on the second-floor of the north wing, rises up in a dynamic way. The void, continuing in an L shape, is covered with Tosa plaster, calling attention to the volume and the gap.

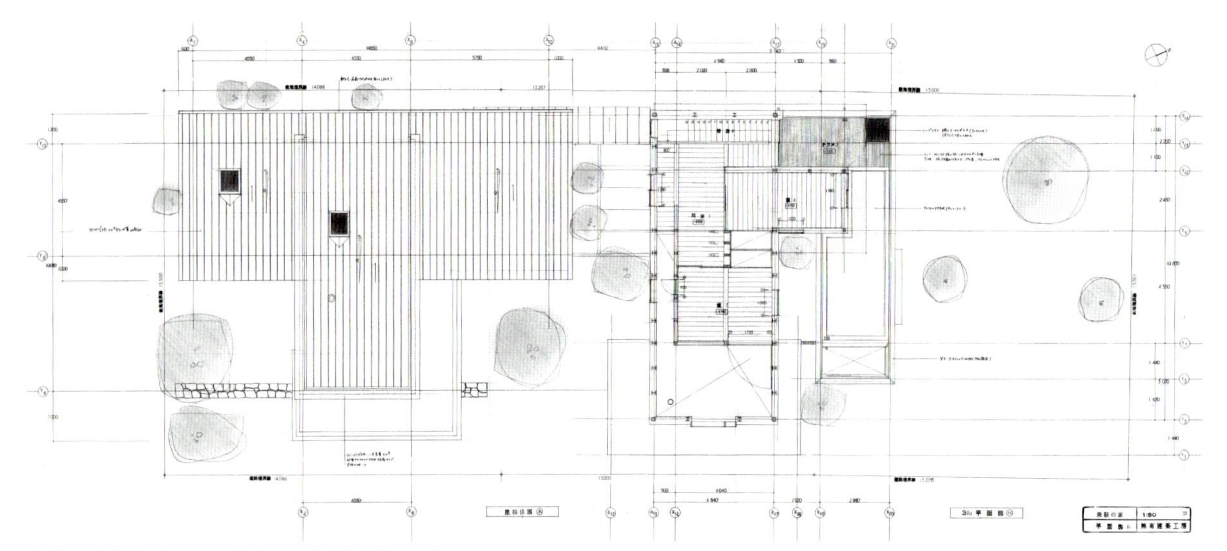

屋根伏図・3 階平面図　　Roof plan and Third-floor plan

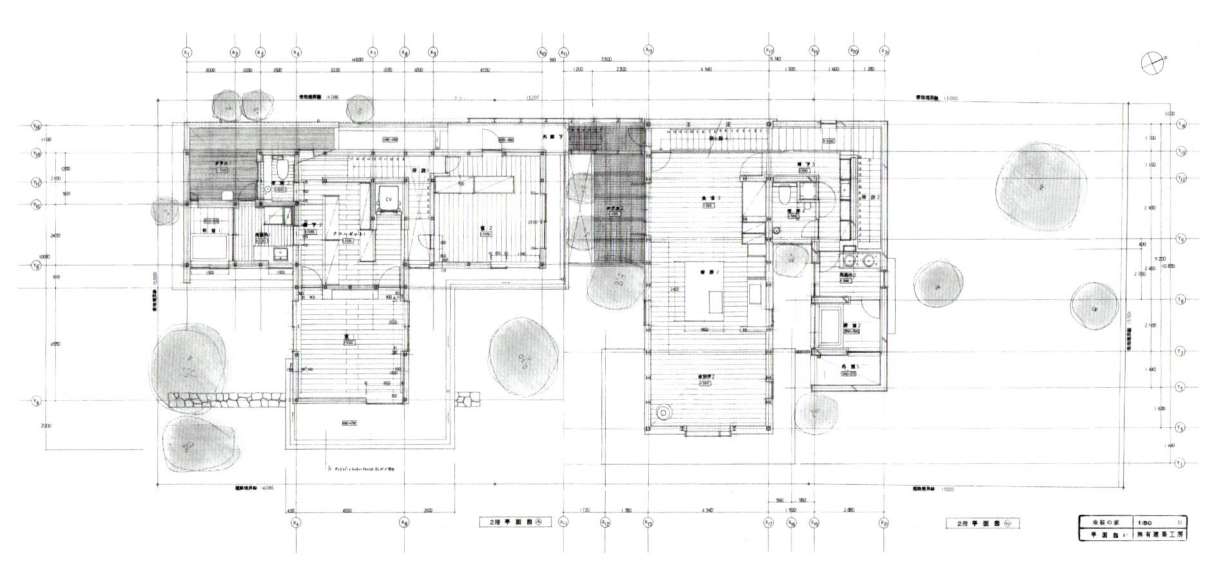

2 階平面図　　Second-floor plan

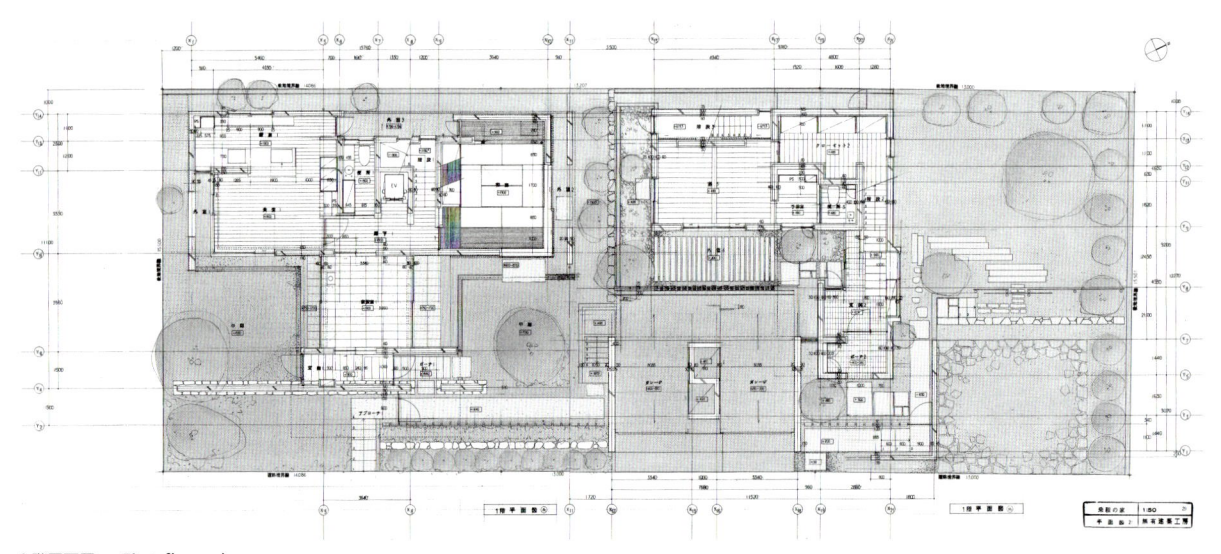

1 階平面図　　First-floor plan

250

251 | Norikura House

敷地断面のズレ、コンクリートの垂壁、全開放される建具、土間と畳の床レヴェルの関係は南棟和室と庭の関係を密実で豊かなものにする。

The staggered section of the site, the concrete hanging partition wall, the completely open fittings, and the levels of the earthen floor and the *tatami* floor produce an even richer relationship between the Japanese-style room in the south wing and the garden.

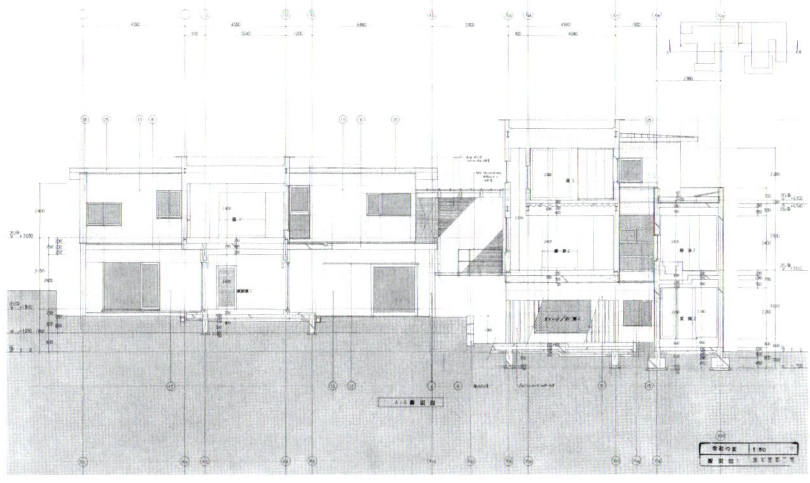

断面図　Section

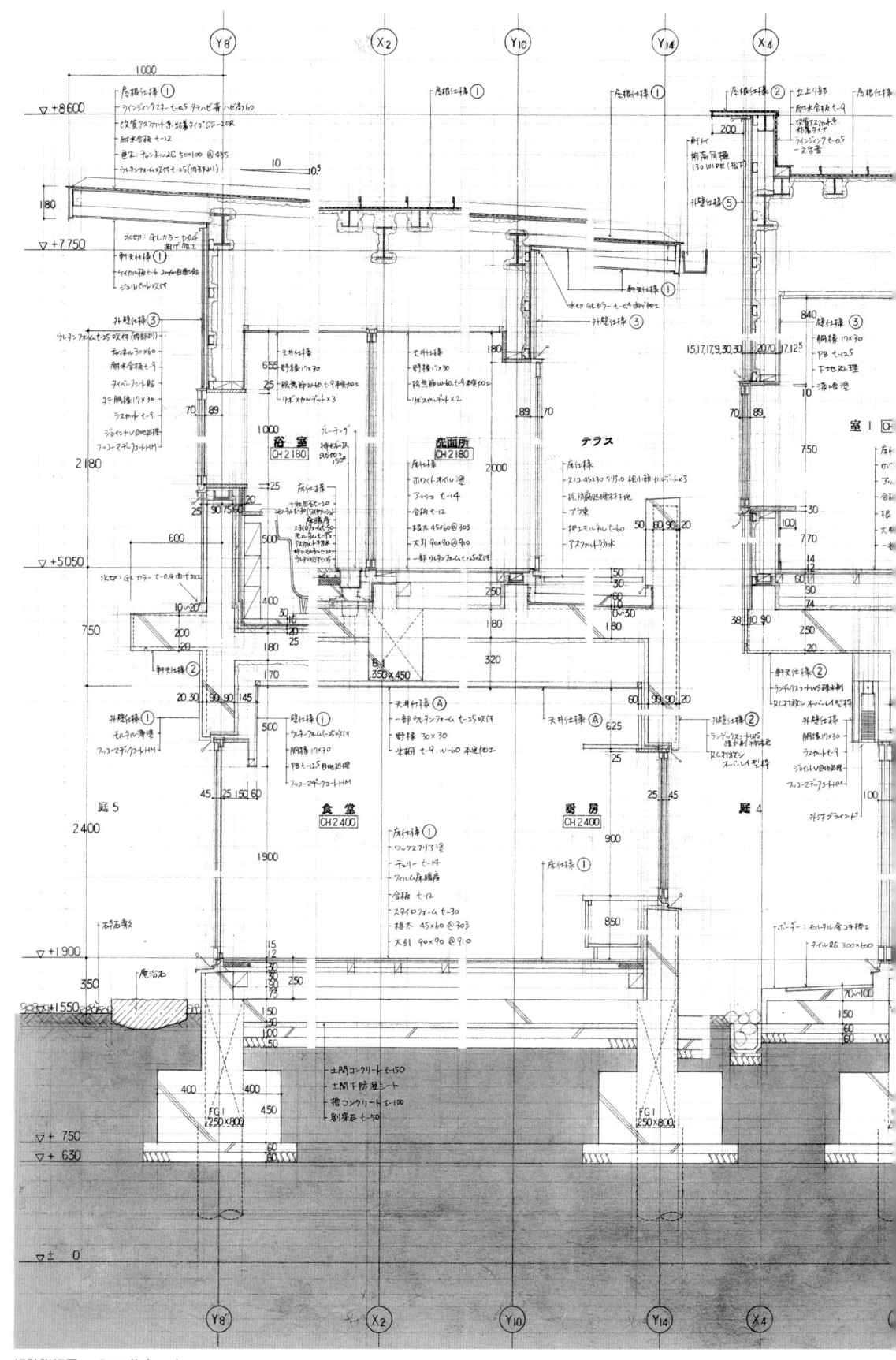

矩計詳細図　Detail drawing

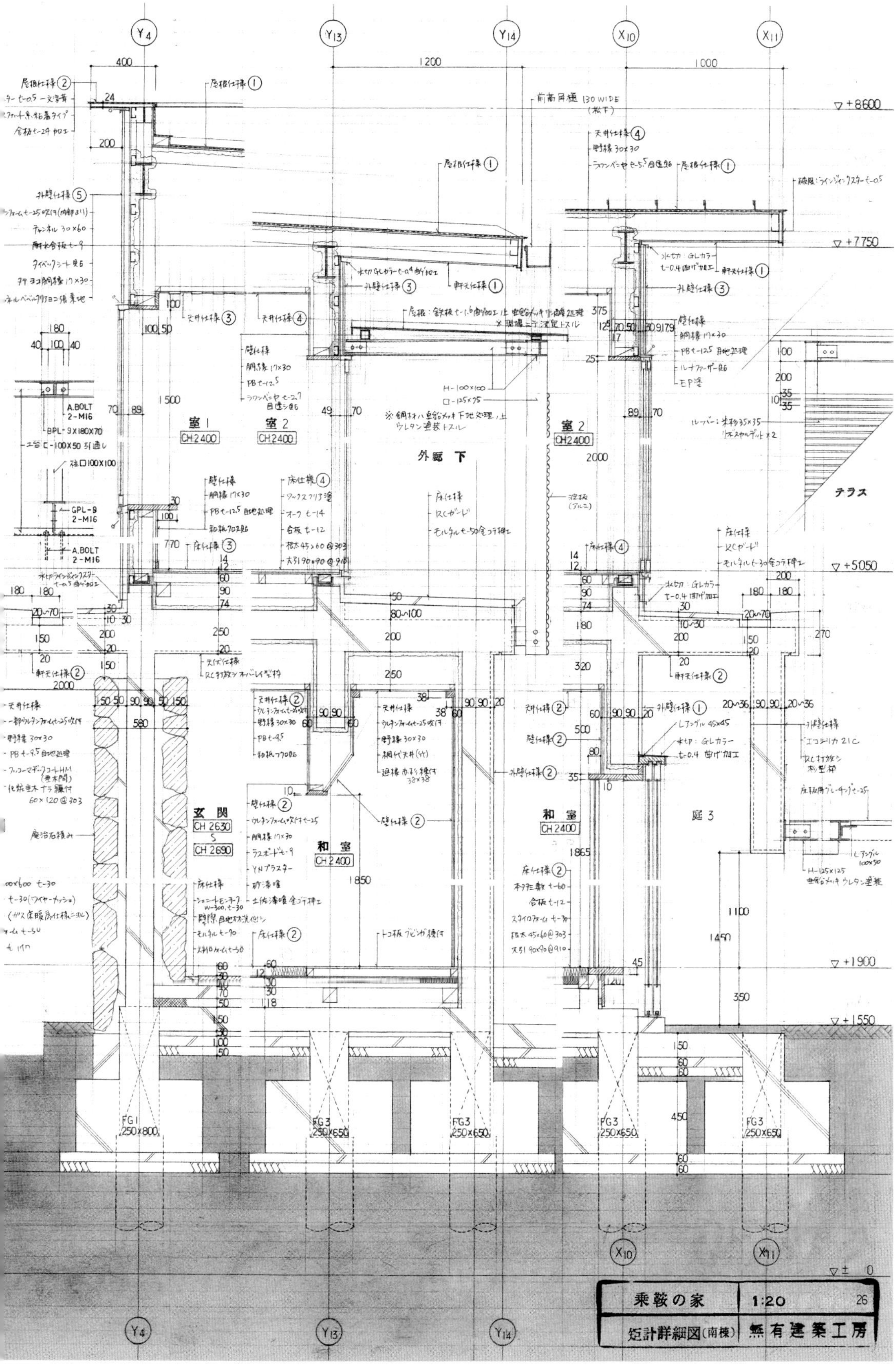
乗鞍の家
1:20
26
矩計詳細図(南棟)
無有建築工房
外廊下
室1
室2
玄関
和室
庭3
テラス

北棟と南棟はブリッジによってつながれ、雁行する棟配置により中庭がより立体的に展開する。

The two wings are connected via a bridge, and the echelon-style positioning of the structures gives the courtyard a stronger three-dimensional aspect.

Norikura House

兵庫県三田市、1980年代頃から千里に続く関西都心のベッドタウンとして、行政・医療・教育・商業と共に産業を引き込んだ多機能型の公園都市を形成するニュータウンの一角。起伏のある丘陵地を下り、ヘアピンカーブを曲がると高台のへさきに間口の広い敷地が並び、家々の連なりを背にして緑豊かなパノラマの景色を望む。

　一様に南面採光をとる家々の視線に配慮し、道路側に自立する壁を幾重に廻り込ませ、領域を囲い取る。自立壁は間口に対して適度に分節され、水平ラインを描く庇で抑え込む。そこから控えるように2枚の小さな屋根が架かり、エレヴェーションに奥行きをつくり出す。自立壁の内にはヴォリュームが凹凸し、そのスキマに入り組んだ路地空間とヴォイドが引き込まれ、外界との間合いをはかる。一旦中へ入るとコンクリートの壁柱によって支えられるピロティが足元を開放し、池や緑地から湿り気を帯びた風が通り抜ける。居住空間はすべて2階に担ぎ上げられ、上下階はスラブで一旦分節される。水平に連続するテラスと壁柱の連続はパノラマの景色へと視界を方向付ける。2階のヴォリュームは室のスケールに合わせて天井と屋根の高さを違え、水平の景色の拡がりに対し、意識を天空へと向かわせる。様々なスケールのヴォイドが視線や風の抜け、光の密度を操作し、1枚のスラブの上に、質の異なる居場所をつくり出す。

　大きな軒下空間を形成するピロティはしばしの間余白として残されるが、埋め戻した土の下に逆スラブの土間が打たれ、立上がりのついた人工地盤は将来組み込まれる新たな空間の受け皿となる。2階の床梁を横断面の逆スラブにすることで、床高を抑えながらピロティの天井高を確保し、スラブの水平ラインを強調する。2階小屋梁は縦断面にすることで、空間を垂壁で覆い内法を抑え込んでいる。木造の屋根は壁から透かされ、化粧垂木の合間より柔らかな光がもたらされる。構造が空間構成を際立たせ、そこへ様々な素材が組み込まれたとき、ピロティに浮かべられた住まいの中に、場の力が再現されるのである。

富士が丘の家
Fujigaoka House

The bedroom community of Sanda, Hyogo Prefecture was developed in the 1980s as a "park city" to attract governmental, educational, commercial, and industrial facilities. This residence, in the middle of some rolling hills, stands among a group of lots with a wide frontage and a verdant, panoramic landscape beyond a row of houses.

In view of the line of sight from the houses, all facing south, the property is layered with a free-standing wall and enclosed on the road side. The wall partitions the frontage, and the eaves, forming a horizontal line, control the space. Two small, restrained roofs straddle the lot and add depth to the elevation. The volume within the wall is uneven, and the alley space and void contained in the gap are drawn inside, maintaining a certain distance from the outside world. Upon entering the lot, one finds a piloti, supported by concrete wall columns, opening out in front of them as wind tinged with the moisture of the pond and greenery blow through the space. The living spaces are located on the second floor, and the stairs that lead between the upper and lower levels are segmented by a slab. The terrace, extending horizontally, and the line of wall columns direct one's gaze toward the panoramic landscape. The second-floor volume alters the height of the ceiling and the roof in accordance with the scale of the rooms and encourages one to gaze out at the sky. With a variety of dimensions, the void provides a gap for the line of sight and wind, and by limiting the density of light, produces living spaces with different qualities on a single slab.

Though often left as blank space, here, the piloti, giving form to the expanse under the eaves, is a reverse-slab, earthen floor below the backfilled ground; and the elevated artificial foundation is prepared to deal with any new spaces that might arise in the future. Using a cross-sectional reverse slab for the floor beams on the second story controls the distance between the surface of the floor and the ground while maintaining the piloti's distance from the floor to the ceiling and emphasizing the horizontal line of the slab. Using a vertical section for the roof-truss beams on the second floor allows the inner dimensions of the space to be controlled by the hanging partition walls. The wooden structure of the roof is visible, allowing soft light to stream in between the gaps in the exposed rafters. This emphasizes the spatial structure, and through the use of a variety of materials, the power of the place is reproduced within the residence, which rises upward via the piloti.

自立する壁と雁行するヴォリュームのスキマに、緊密なスケールの路地空間が生まれ、キャンティレバーの階段を介し2階へとアプローチは続く。薄暗い空間に射し込む光や、透過する光が訪れる者をゆっくりと誘う。

The gap between the free-standing wall and the echelon-structured volume gives rise to a dense alley space, and the approach to the second floor is mediated by a cantilevered staircase. The light, shooting into the dimly-lit space and permeating the area, slowly entices the visitor inside.

261 | Fujigaoka House

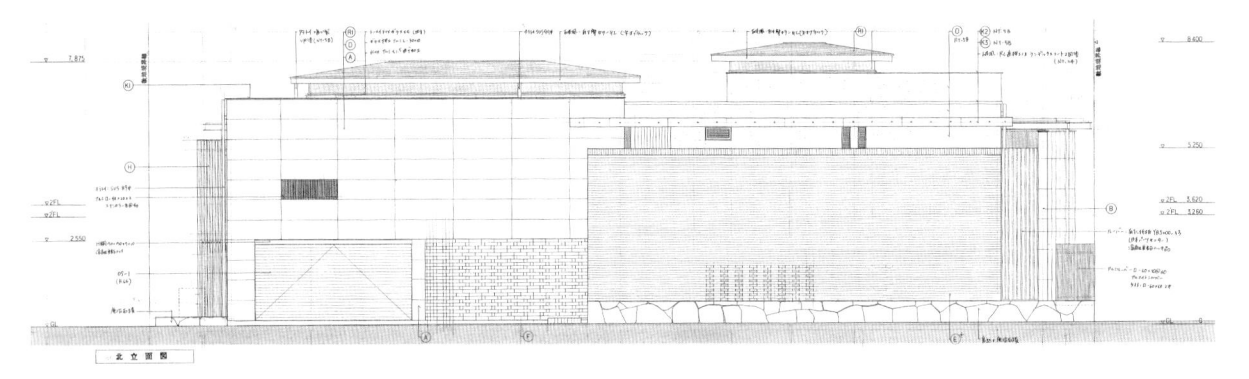

北立面図　　North elevation

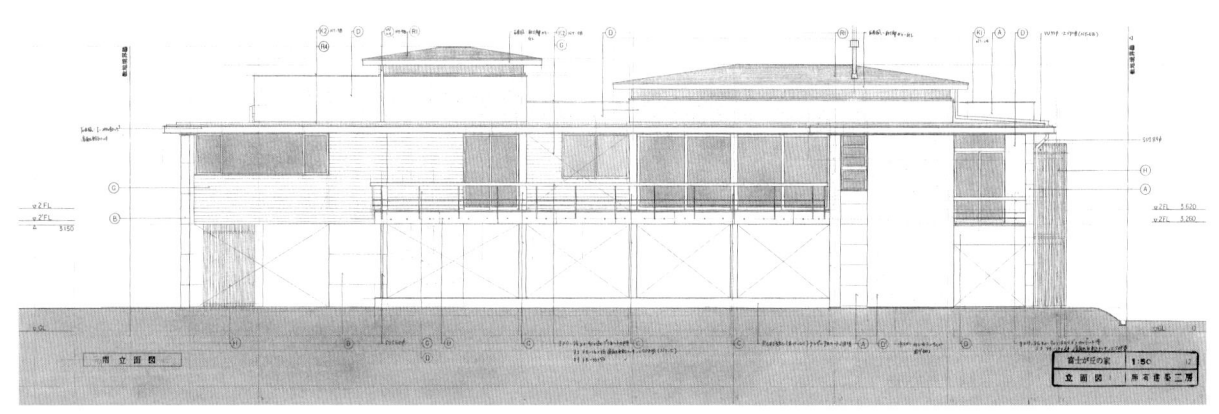

南立面図　　South elevation

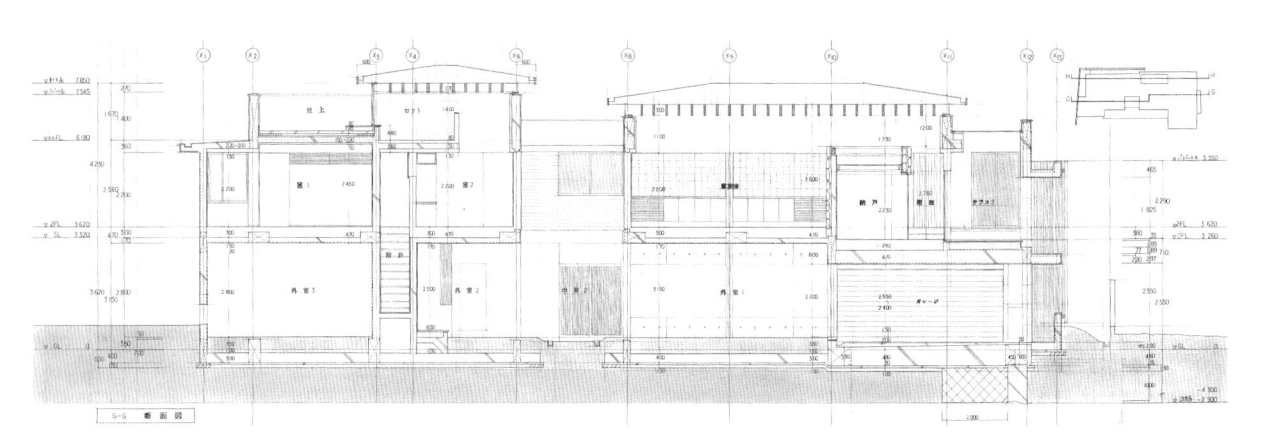

断面図　　Section

上：自立壁の中へ誘われると、コンクリートの壁柱が支えるピロティによって開放された空間が待ち受ける。
下：北側道路からレンガ積の自立する壁とヴォリュームのスキマに誘われる。

Above: Inside the free-standing wall, one is greeted by an open space created by a concrete-column-supported piloti.
Below: Entering from the alley on the north side, there is an inviting gap between the free-standing brick wall and the volume.

263 | Fujigaoka House

2階家族室は垂壁によって覆われた天井高の高い空間に化粧垂木の連続する屋根が架かり、垂木のスキマからもたらされる光がヴォリュームを優しく包み込む。正面に控える暖炉には庵治石が積まれ、トップライトの光になめされる。

The second-floor family room is straddled by a roof which connects the exposed rafters in the space with a high ceiling covered with a hanging partition wall. Light seeps in through the gaps in the rafters and gently envelops the volume. Aji stone is stacked around the hearth, with a restrained frontal view, and light pours in from the skylight.

Fujigaoka House

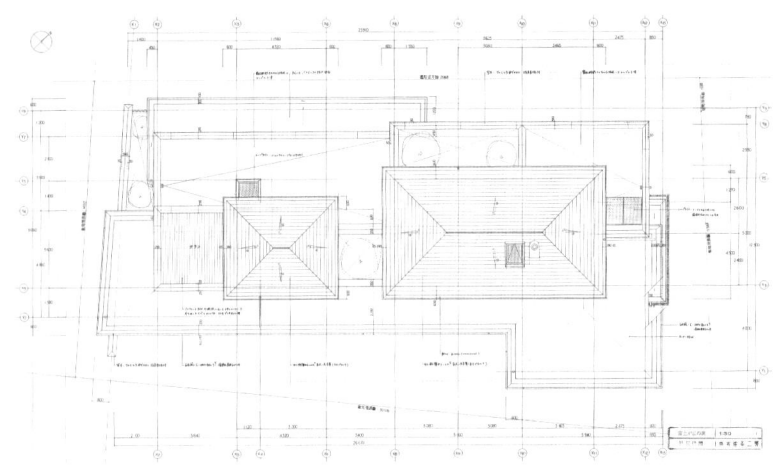

屋根伏図　　Roof plan

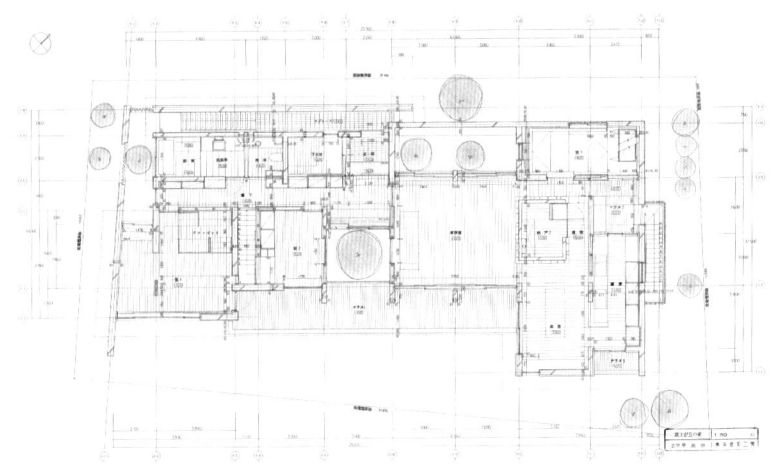

2階平面図　　Second-floor plan

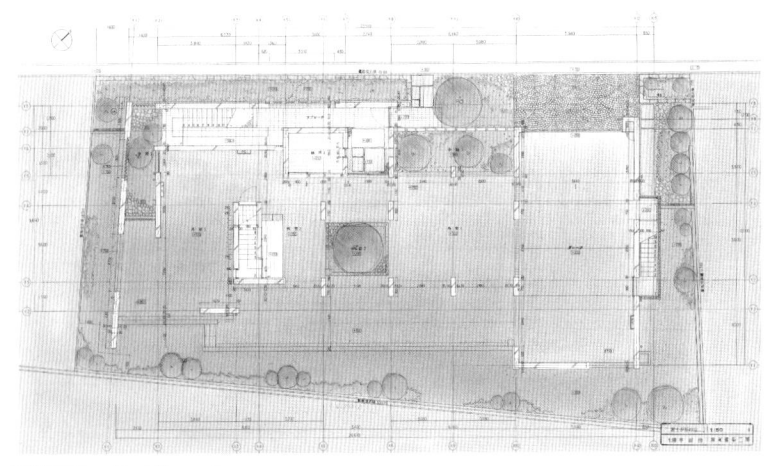

視覚的にはつながった食堂と家族室は、平面的に雁行し、レヴェルを違えることで、その領域を緩やかに分節する。

Visually linked, the dining room and family room, with a staggered planar configuration and different levels, softly segment the space.

1階平面図　　First-floor plan

267 | Fujigaoka House

左：室3より廻廊を見る。
右：室3西面を見る／玄（くろ）く塗り回された小間に、太鼓障子によって透過された光が点在し、銀揉みの天井に鈍い光が反射する。墨入土佐漆喰塗の壁の向こうに、庵治石積の壁、広葉樹の柱壁、化粧垂木の力強い骨格が際立つ。

Left: View of corridor from Room 3.
Right: View of west side of Room 3— Penetrating the *taiko shoji*, light is scattered around the small, black-painted space, and pure light is reflected off the silver rubbings on the ceiling. Rising up through the Tosa plaster walls, containing India ink, is the powerful structure of an Aji stone wall, a columned wall made with wood from broad-leaved trees, and exposed rafters.

269 | Fujigaoka House

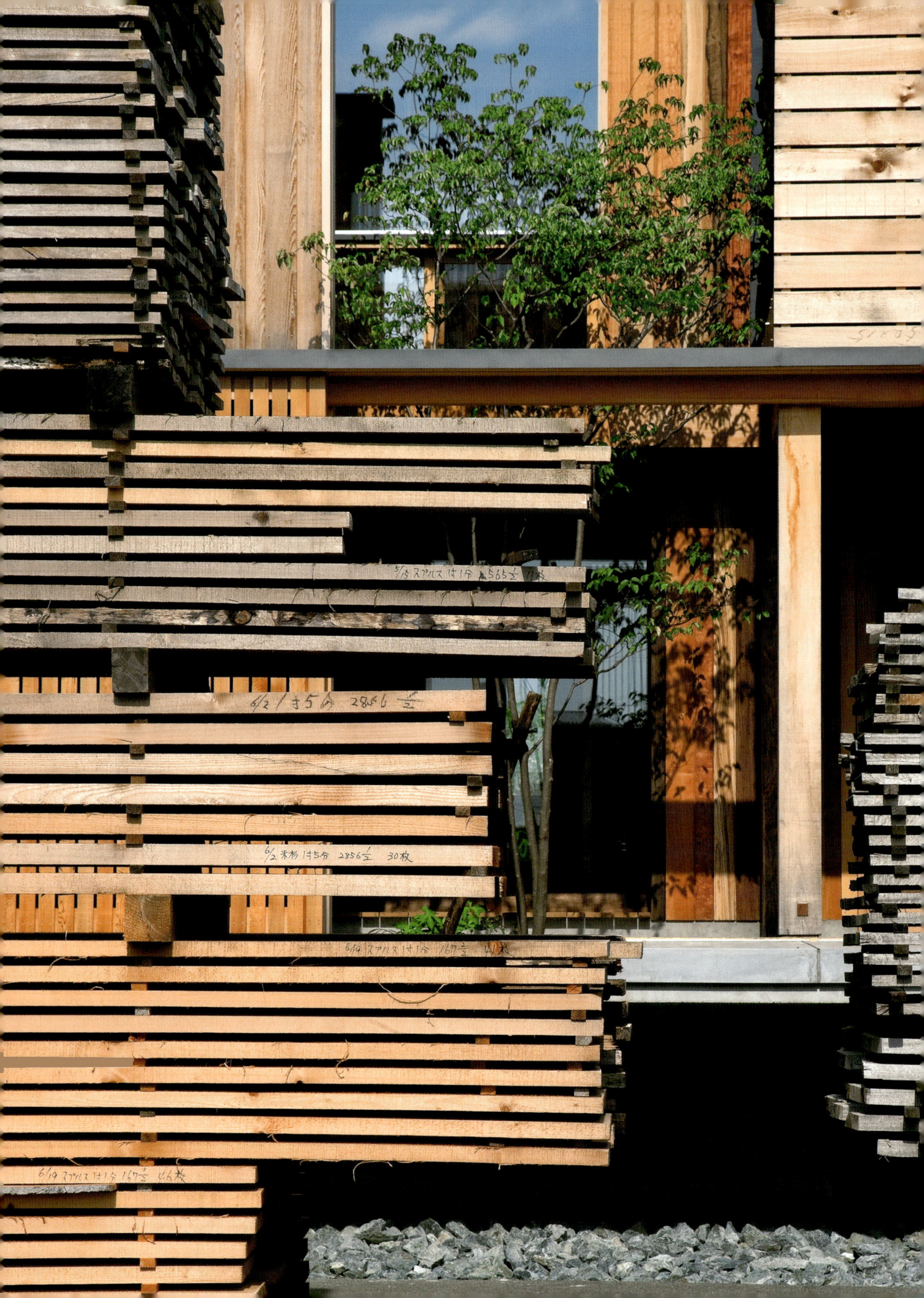

福岡県大川市、筑後川の流域に古くから家具や建具の加工場が並ぶ材木の町。時代と共にその市場は縮小しつつあるが、有明海への河口付近、木材の集積場の一角に大きな資材場を抱え、根強く営み続ける一軒の材木商があった。木のもつ本当の魅力を建築の力として引き出すことで、多くの人に伝えられないだろうか。そんな思いが出会いを呼び、この計画は始まった。

　住宅街とは一線を画す資材場の一角、道路から間口35m奥行き90mというとらえどころない敷地の中で、唯一手掛かりとなったのは筑後川を望む西側境界が堤防の土手によって地面から1.5m上がっていることであった。資材置場から住宅を切り離すようにコンクリートスラブで基壇を浮かし、堤防の高さまで1階の床レヴェルを上げて筑後川への眺望をとる。その上に田の字型平面を構成し、立体的なヴォイドを挿入して光や風の抜け道をつくりながら、空間に間合いをもたせ、1枚の大きな屋根によってそれらを再びつなぎ留める。

　この建築を木のもつ素材の力をもって表現し、木の可能性を再考するために、倉庫に眠ったままの木、中でもクセや個性が強く使いづらいとされる広葉樹を中心に 80種類の木を選び出した。長物の通し柱だけは丸太からの製材をやむなくしたが、端材も建具や縁甲板に転用し、ある材料をありのままの姿で使い切ることを心掛けた。鉋で削らず製材肌のままで使い、材寸も揃えない。そこには新たな大工の手技が加わる。使われる場所や見え方によって仕上げ方を変え、綺麗に仕上げないことで手間は掛かるが、眠ったままの木を再生させ、木のもつ魅力は格段に拡がりを見せた。外壁も荒削りの木を無塗装のまま使い、光や風の受け方の異なる4面の表情を厚みや仕上げ方によって変えた。陰翳を深く刻むディテールは、道路から大きく控え、川越しに見るこの建築のエレヴェーションを遠景にまで印象付ける。太陽と雨に晒された木は時が経つにつれ灰汁色に変化し、製材前の本来の姿へ還っていく。その深い表情は筑後川に沈む夕陽に照らし出され、材木の町の風景に馴染んでいくであろう。

大川の家
Okawa House

Okawa, Fukuoka Prefecture, is a lumber town that has long been home to furniture and fitting manufacturers along the Chikugo River. While the market has changed over the years, at least one lumber dealer has endured. This project was conceived with the aim of conveying the true charm of wood through the power of architecture.

With a frontage of 35 meters and a depth of 90 meters, the lot, beside a storage area that is demarcated from the residential neighborhood, rises 1.5 meters above ground level due to an embankment on the west boundary line that faces the river. Using a concrete slab as a platform to separate the residence from the storage area, the first story was elevated to the height of the embankment to create a view of the river. While constructing a grid-shaped plane with four equal sections, a three-dimensional void, and a gap for light and wind, "distance" was incorporated into the space and everything was unified under one large roof.

To express the power of wood as a material, 80 different varieties were selected from the lumber in the storehouse. An emphasis was placed on broad-leaved trees that are difficult to use (due to special characteristics) as a way of reconsidering the potential of wood. Only the wood for the long, straight columns was sawed out of logs, but even then, the remnants were saved for fittings and strip flooring. The surface of the milled wood was left unplaned and no attempt was made to arrange the pieces in terms of size. Though it was difficult to resist giving the wood a beautiful finish, altering the finishing method according to where it was going to be used or how it would be seen, and sticking to the material on hand dramatically increased the wood's charm. Using rough-hewn wood and no paint for the exterior walls created a variety of expressions, as each of the four surfaces is affected differently by light and wind, and varies in thickness and finish. The details of the structure, deeply enshrouded in shadow, make the elevation appear distant from the road. The wood, exposed to the sun and rain, has changed to ash gray with time, reverting to the appearance it had. These features are illuminated by the sun as it sinks over the river and are becoming a familiar part of the landscape in the town.

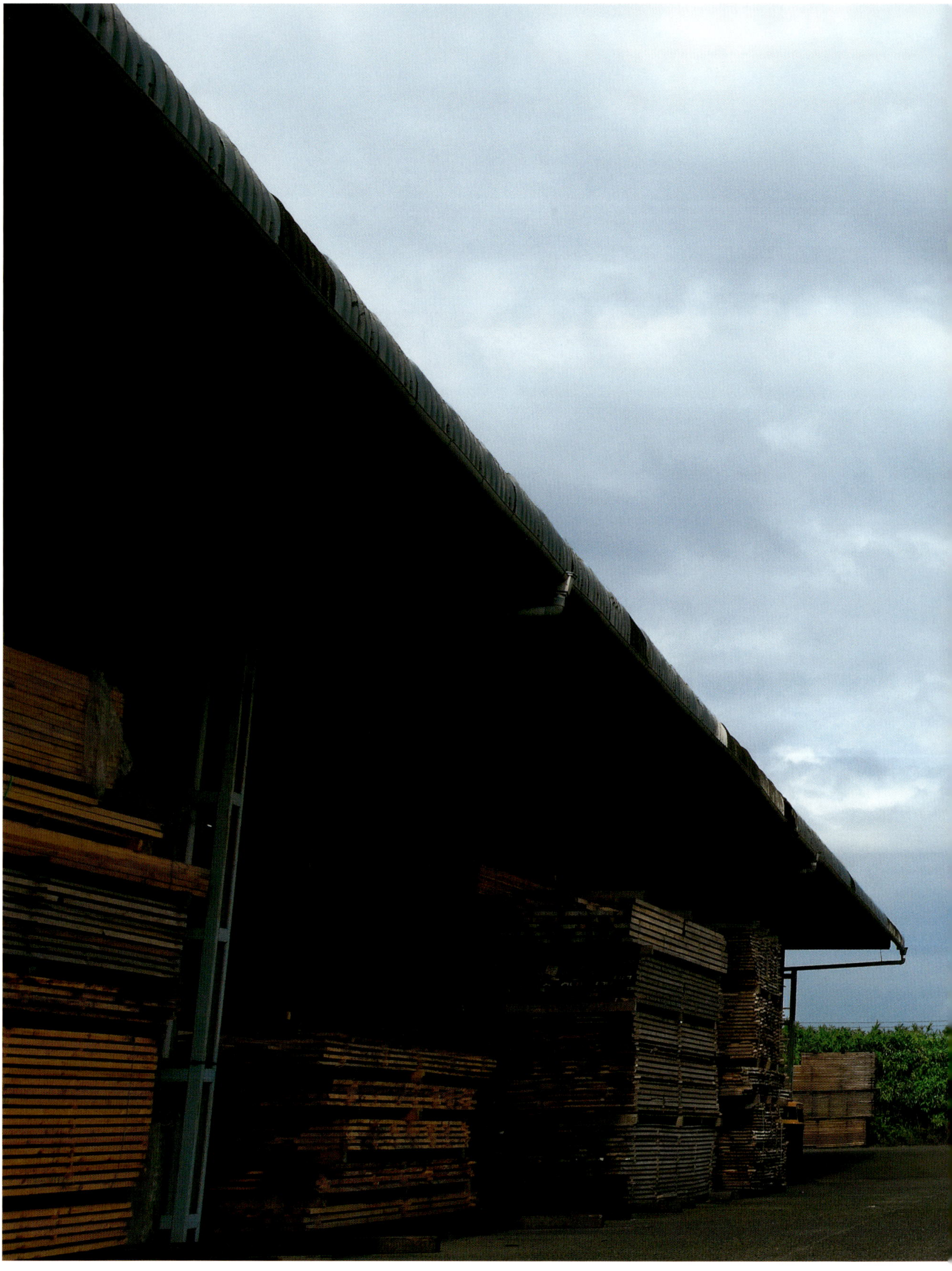

273 | Okawa House

274

外室1より玄関を見る／点在する室のスキマを縫い合わせるように雁行した半屋外空間が巡り、1枚の屋根の下に内外が浸透する。

View of entranceway from Outer Room 1: A half-outdoor space with a staggered structure unites the gaps between the scattered rooms with a strong sense of interior and exterior under a single roof.

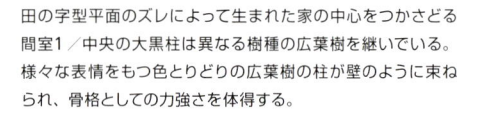

田の字型平面のズレによって生まれた家の中心をつかさどる
間室1／中央の大黒柱は異なる樹種の広葉樹を継いでいる。
様々な表情をもつ色とりどりの広葉樹の柱が壁のように束ね
られ、骨格としての力強さを体得する。

The product of a staggered grid-shaped plane, Intermediary Room 1 oversees the center of the house. The central column contains the legacy of wood from a variety of broad-leaved trees. As a group, the columns, made of various types of wood with a diverse range of expressions, unify the space like a wall, imparting a sense of strength as the main structure.

278

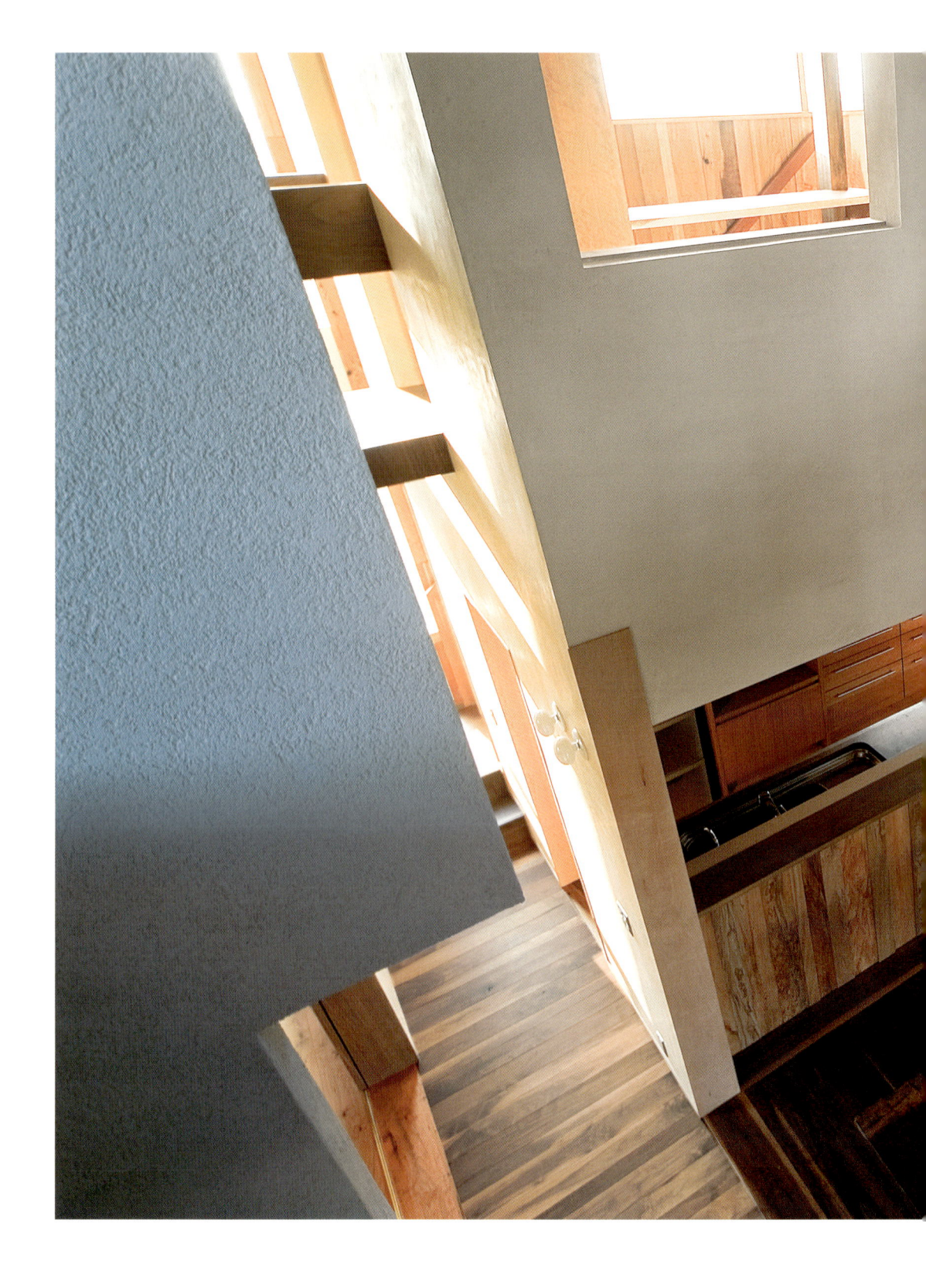

279 | Okawa House

280

Okawa House

上：家族室より間室1・外室2を見る／ヴォイドからもたらされた光が2枚の壁の間をすり抜け、奥行きと透明感を帯びる。
下：家族室より和室を見る／ヴォリュームの内へ引き込まれた外室が、室と室の間合いをはかり、内外を曖昧にする。

Above: View of Intermediary Room 1 and Outer Room 2 from the family room— The light that shines in through the void slips between the two walls imbuing the space with depth and transparency.
Below: View of Japanese-style room from the family room— The outer room, drawn inside the volume, establishes distance between the rooms and obscures the difference between the interior and exterior.

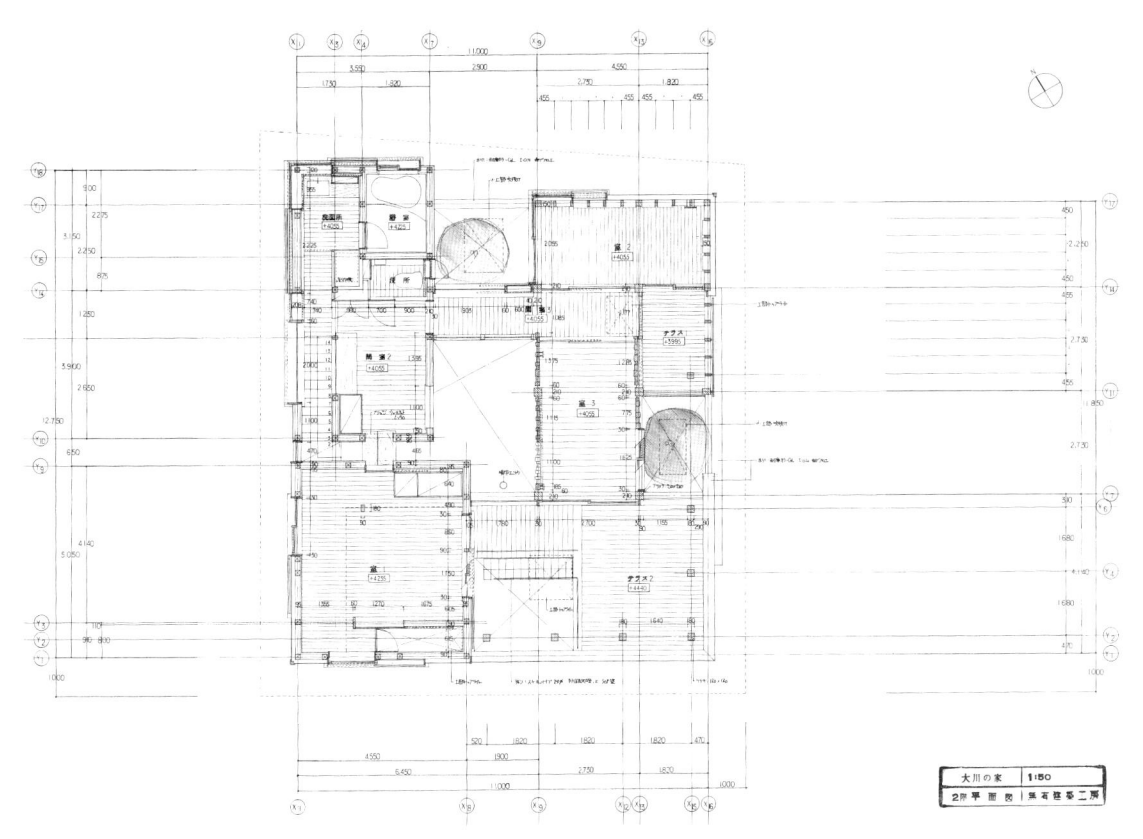

2階平面図　　Second-floor plan

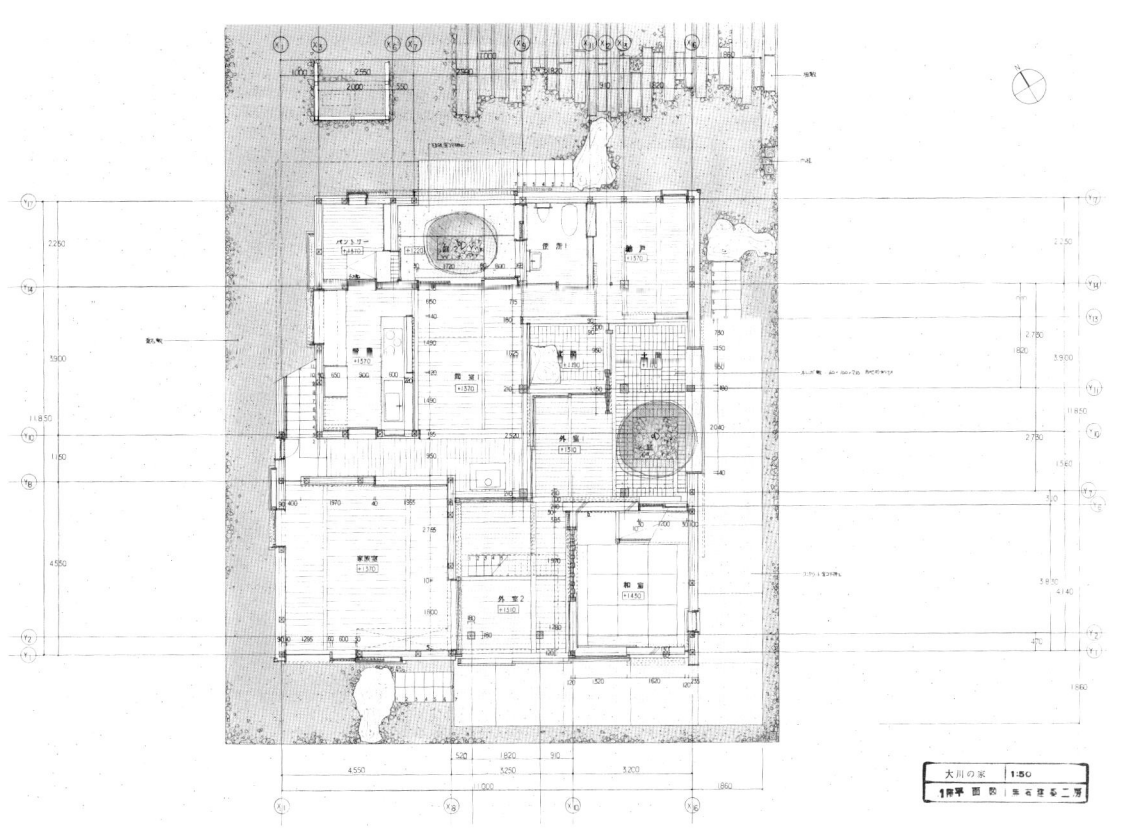

1階平面図　　First-floor plan

Okawa House

284

広葉樹の壁柱、墨入漆喰塗の壁、荒々しいコンクリート打ち放しの壁が重なり合う和室は、太鼓障子によって柔らかい光に包まれる。

Wall columns made of wood from broad-leaved trees, plaster walls containing India ink, and rough, exposed concrete walls are all juxtaposed in the Japanese-style room, bathed in gentle light that shines through the *taiko shoji*.

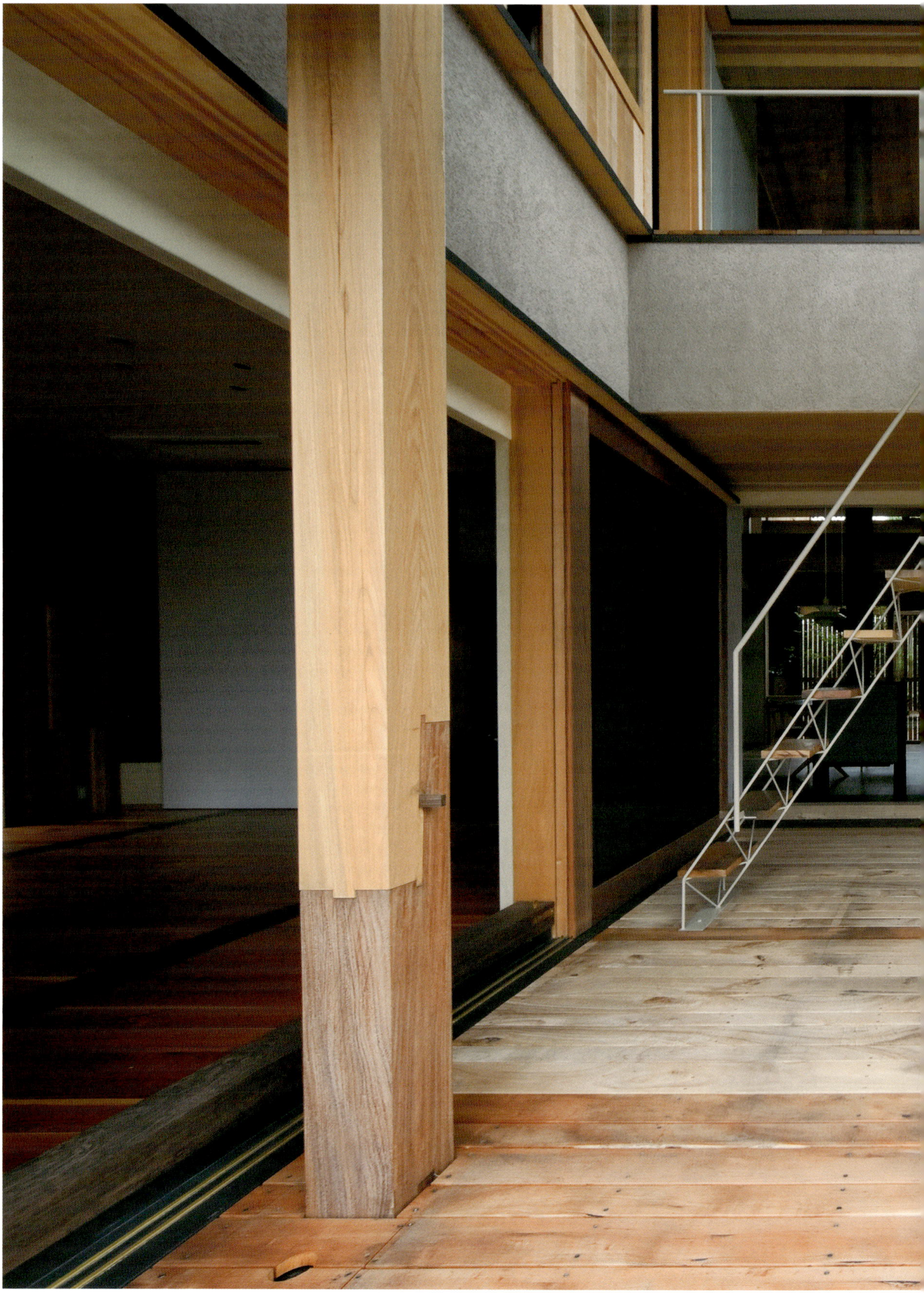

287 | Okawa House

階段より間室2を見る。

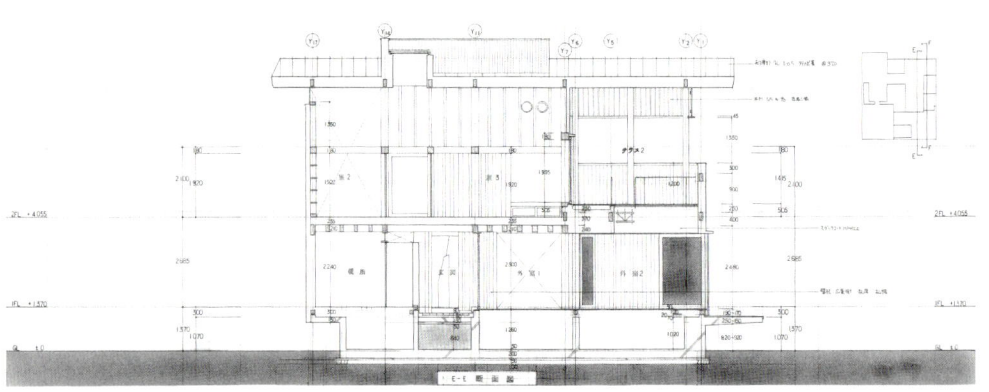

断面図　Section

View of Intermediary Room 2 from the staircase.

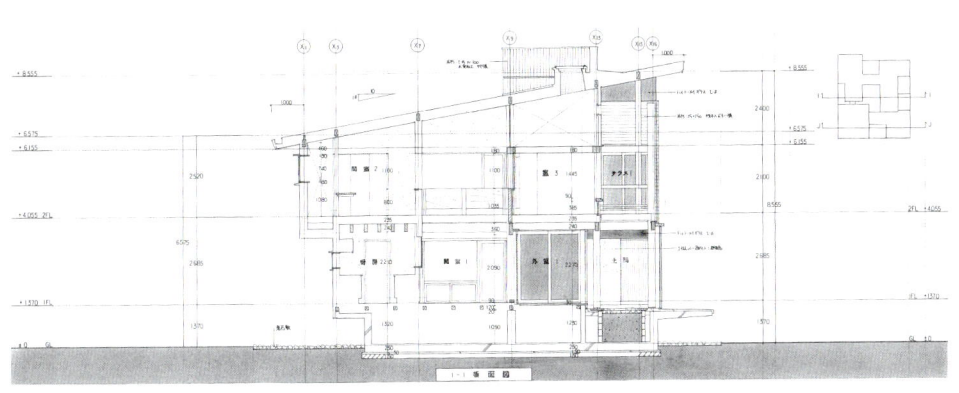

断面図　Section

広大な敷地に建つ正方形の平面に様々な方向から導かれる光は、漆喰塗の壁を撫でながら柔らかく反射し、入り組んだ架構のスキマに不均質に伝う。

Light, guided from a variety of directions of the square plane on this huge site, caresses the plaster walls as it is gently reflected and unevenly conveyed through the gaps in the complex structure.

291 | Okawa House

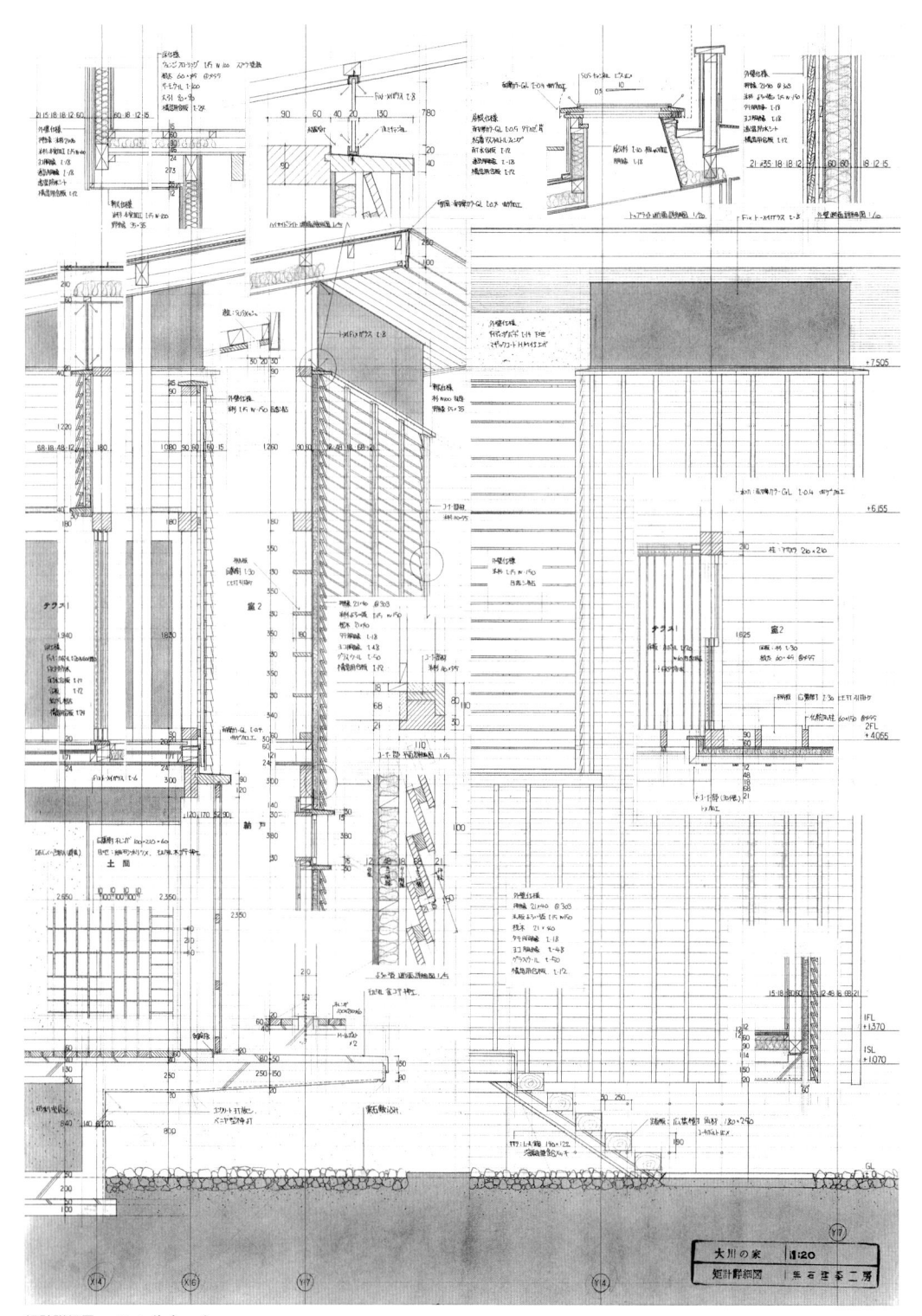

矩計詳細図　Detail drawing

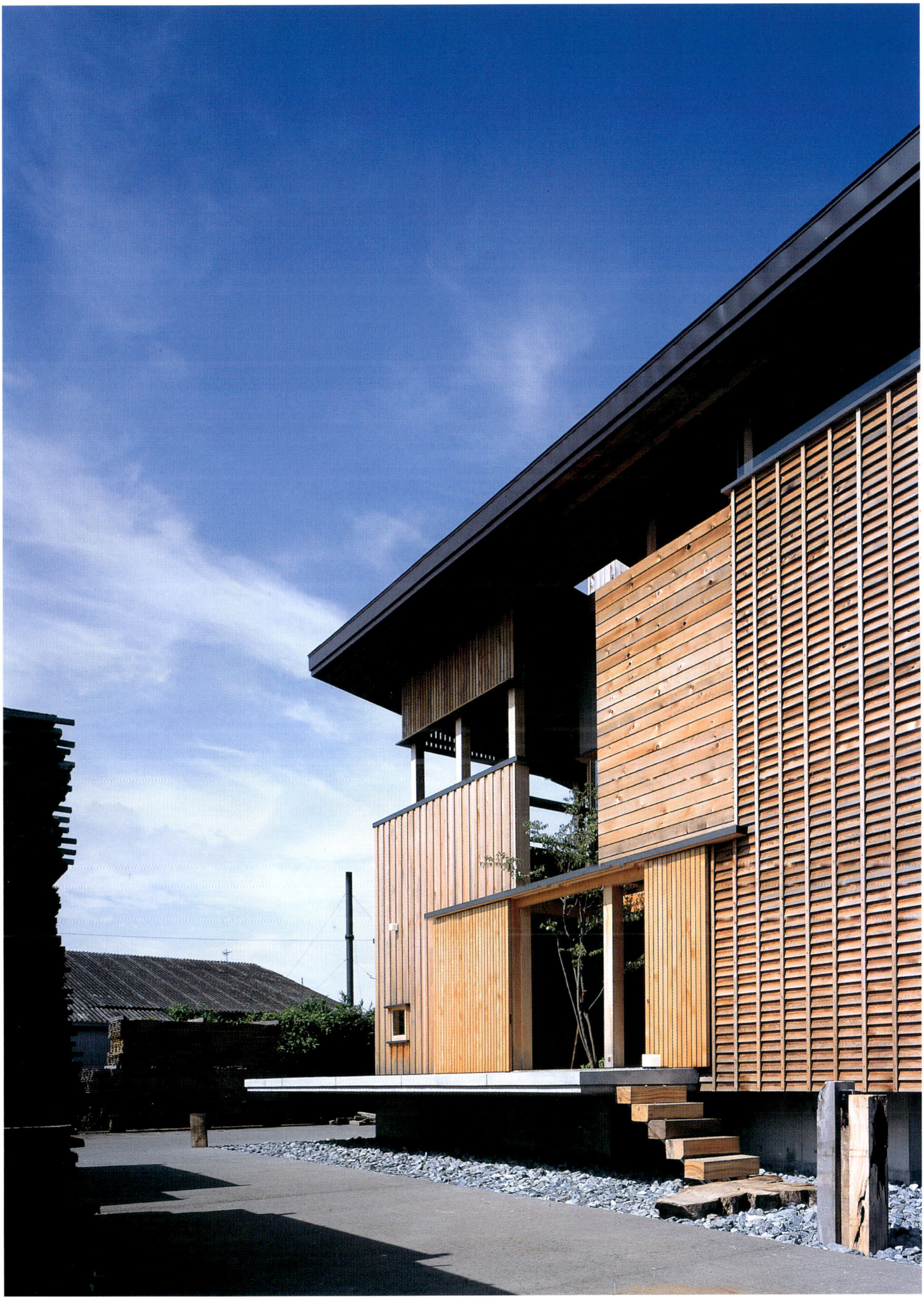

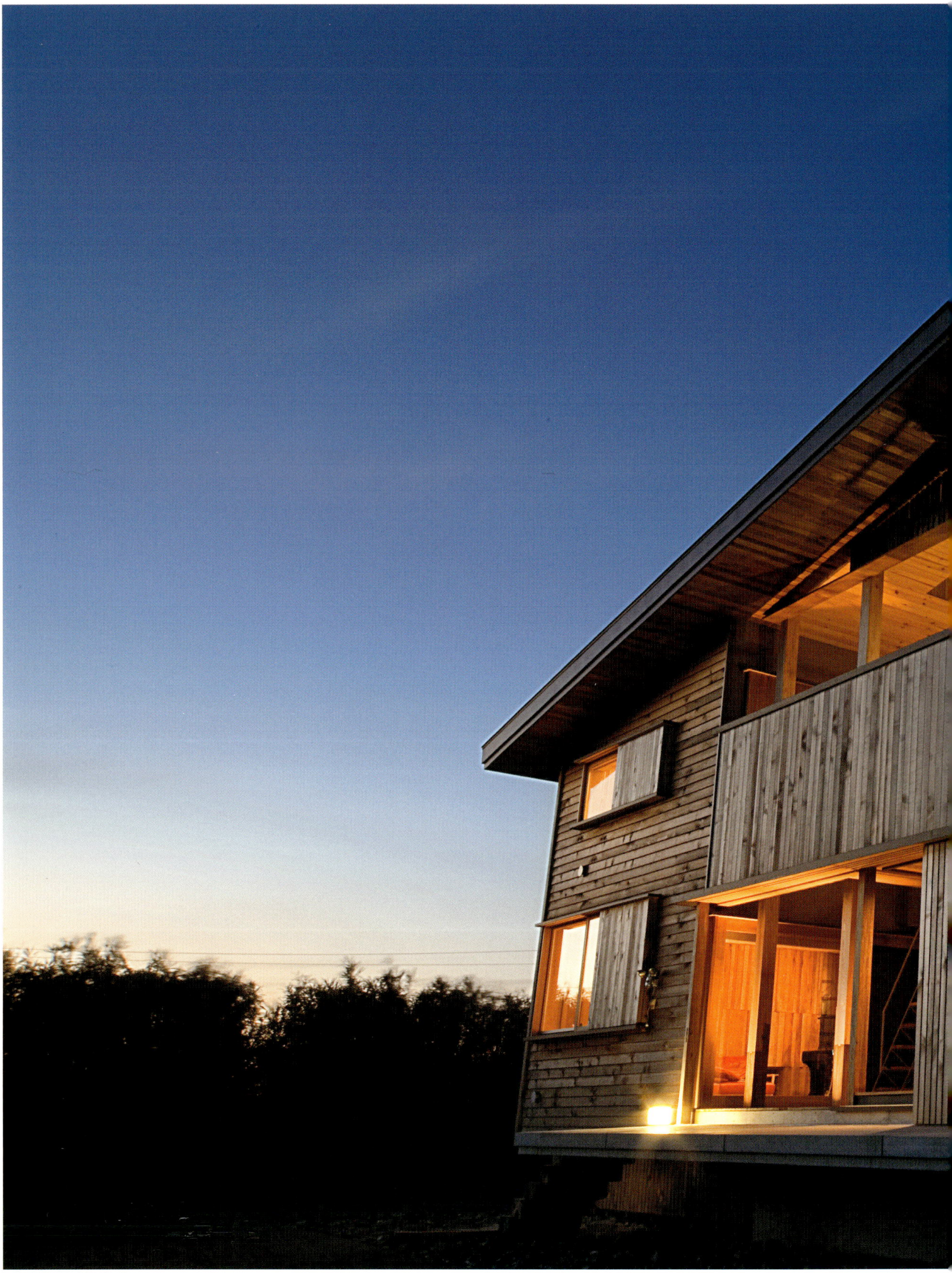

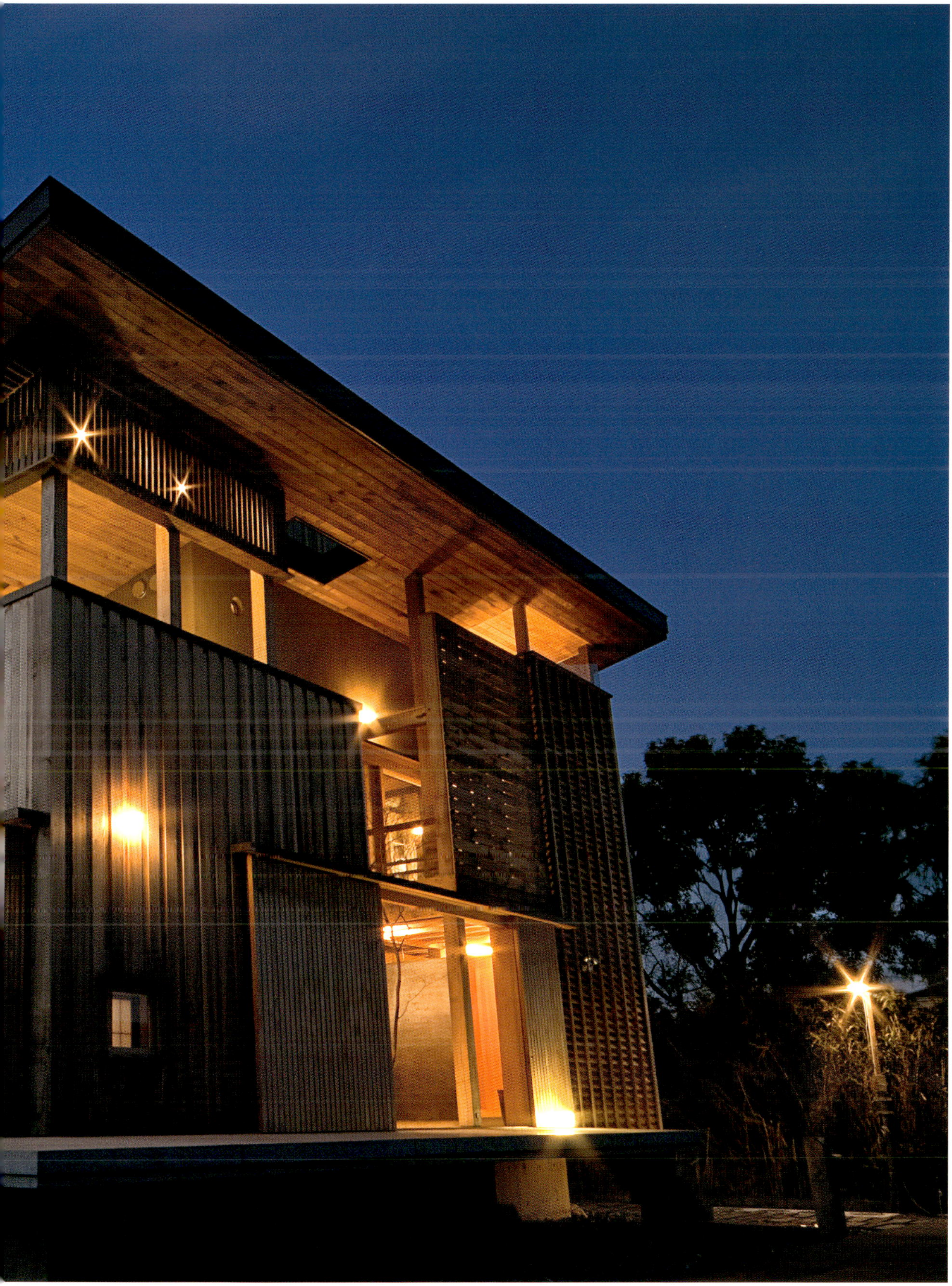

「建築」家・竹原義二

花田佳明　<神戸芸術工科大学教授>

浅薄な先入観

竹原義二は、石井修のもとでの修業期間を経て、1978年、30歳の若さで設計事務所・無有建築工房を開設した。そして住宅を中心に設計活動をおこない、現在までの約30年間に、個人住宅と若干の集合住宅を合わせ、およそ150棟の住まいを完成させてきた。

それらには通し番号が打たれている。

竹原作品を特集した『建築文化』1997年3月号には、その番号が1番から64番までの作品すべてを網羅したリストがあり、写真と建築概要が整然と並んでいる。それによれば、1番目の「勢野の家」の竣工が1978年、64番目の「山坂の家Ⅱ」の竣工が1996年。つまり18年間で64物件、1年に約3.6件のペースである。

その後、竹原が自邸「101番目の家」を発表したのが2002年。65番目から101番目までの37物件が6年間で竣工したことになる。1年に約6.2件のペースだ。

そして本作品集には、150番目までの作品データが掲載された。101番目の家の後、7年間で49物件、1年に7件のペースである。

これら150作品を通覧して驚くのは、完成度の一貫した高さと、それらをいくつかのスタイル、あるいは時期へと分類し区分することの難しさだ。変化があるとすれば、増加した年間竣工件数だけだとすら言いたくなる。

もちろん、敷地、規模、構造などに応じた差異はある。簡素な都市型住居から郊外の重厚な邸宅まで、テーマも意匠も多岐にわたる。コンクリート造、木造、鉄骨造を自在に使い分け、木や石や塗り物など素材の選択も意のままだ。

しかしそれらの違いは、時間軸に沿った「変化」ではなく、あくまでも共時的な「多様性」に見えてしまう。それほどに150作品のレヴェルは揃っており、あたかも最初からすべて竹原の頭の中にあったかのようだ。しかしこの多様性は、実際には30歳から60歳までの時間の中で生み出されており、彼の早熟ぶりと才能の安定性を示す証拠以外の何ものでもない。

こういった観察の先には、建築という外国語を異様な速度でマスターし、それを軽妙に操る会話の達人のような竹原像が浮かび上がる。

少なくとも私は、かつて『建築文化』1997年3月号を眺めながらこのような感想をもち、彼についてそれ以上考えることを怠っていた。しかし2003年8月、初めての竹原作品の、しかも自邸「101番目の家」の見学の機会を得て、この理解がいかに浅薄な先入観であり、自分の眼が節穴であったかということを思い知らされたのである。

「101番目の家」の衝撃

「101番目の家」に到着したのは午後の2時。研究室の学生10名ほどを連れていた。「学生の見学は30分にしてるけど、今日は特別」という竹原の甘い言葉のせいにしたい。はっと気付くと夜の8時になっていた。時が経つのを忘れるとはこういうことかと痛感し、6時間もの間、われわれはいったい何をしていたのかと、夢から覚めたときのような不思議な気分に包まれた。

内と外とが入れ子になった複雑な空間を、とにかく何度も上り下りし、あちこちの場所に立ってみたり座ってみたり。洞窟のような地下室では、スピーカーから流れるブルースに聴き入り、2階のテラスでは、次第に暮れていく空の色をぼんやりと眺めた。あろうことか学生のひとりは2階の座敷で寝入ってしまった。そんなことをしているうちに、あたりはすっかり闇に包まれていたのである。

何をしたわけでもない。しかし、たっぷりと何かをしたという実感が残る6時間。名付け難いさまざまな行為が空間によって誘発された。

このような、行為ともいえない居方を保証したものはいったい何か。

「101番目の家」を言葉で描くことは難しい。

敷地は大阪府豊中市の住宅地。面積は約100m²で、周囲には住宅が建て込み、現代日本のごく一般的な宅地である。ただし敷地の奥が1層分低い。構造はコンクリートと木の混構造。その中に廻遊性のある動線が組み込まれ、それに沿っていくつかの内部空間と外部空間が点在する。

しかし、こう書いてみても何も伝わらないなとつくづく思う。「101番目の家」の空間の質は、もっと別の要因によって決まっている。

太さや色合いの異なる広葉樹の柱列が、木ではなく鉄の塊にすら見える硬質性を漂わせる。それらがコンクリート梁の側面に取り付けられ、互いにずれを生み出しながら重なり合う特殊な混構造を構成する。柱の束はむしろ壁といってよいだろう。廻遊とはいうものの、途中の経路は階段、廊下、梯子と変化し、さらに内部、外部も入れ替わるから、さまざまな淀みが発生する。群島のように点在する内外の空間は、表面的な和の意匠を具体化するためのものではなく、空間相互の浸透や逆転という現象こそを重要視する竹原の住居観の空間化だと解釈できる。

おそらく「101番目の家」がもつ質感は、こういった操作、つまり、住居を構成するさまざまな要素がもつ一般的属性を否定する操作の集積によって生み出されているのだ。

しかも、これらの操作は互いに深く関わり合う。鉄のような印象の木の柱がつながることで壁をつくり、その壁が内外の空間を出入りして、それらの反転をさらに強く印象付けるといった具合にだ。

おそらくわれわれは、連鎖的につながるそういった空間構成の総合性を、分析的にではなく、まさに総合的に体感するために、6時間という長い時間と名付け難い行為とを要したのだ。

一方、その空間での竹原たちの暮らしぶりは、われわれの茫然自失の振る舞いをよそに、穏やかなリアリティに包まれていた。物があふれているのに違和感がない。それぞれの姿と場所が的確に定まり、すべてが空間の質を高めている。「こういう空間はこう使う、こういう空間からはこういう暮らしが生まれてくる」と、竹原一家が教えてくれているようだった。

つまり、「101番目の家」での6時間は、建築についての深い思考が、いかに革新的な空間と暮らしを生み出し得るかということを証明する無言の授業だったのである。

透明な論理

「101番目の家」の見学の後、私にはさらなる竹原体験が待っていた。

翌2004年に「101番目の家」を再訪し、彼へのインタヴューを記事にした[1]。また2006年には、彼の設計した「岸和田の家」を訪れて、その見学記を書いた[2]。さらに2008年には、4月にシンポジウムをやって竹原の住宅観を引き出すことを試み[3]、夏には「あけぼの学園 南楓亭」「永山園の家」「諏訪森町中の家」を見学し、竹原との座談会をおこなった[4]。

そのような体験を通してあらためて強く感じたのは、竹原の建築を貫く透明な論理の存在だ。

「岸和田の家」は一見ごく普通の戸建住宅の部屋配置なのだが、平面図をよく観察すれば、外部と見まがう1階の開放的な土間空間と2階の居間や食堂との間にガラスや扉がなく、それらが階段を介してひとつにつながっていることに気付くだろう。

私はうかつにもそのことを事前に見落とし、階段を昇る途中で2階の床に手が触れた瞬間、1階の土間空間と2階がつながっていることに気付き、「ここは外部？ この家の人は外で暮らしているのか？」と勘違いをしてうろたえた。

つまり「岸和田の家」の空間は、海の中に浮かぶ島のように、生活を支えるさまざまな場が、立体的につながる外部のような大空間の中に漂っているのだ。そこには、この家の濃密な意匠が生む印象とはまったく別の、クールで強い住居観の提示がある。

「あけぼの学園 南楓亭」では、構造形式に対する竹原の倫理観のようなものを教えられた。

豊かな木々に包まれた幼稚園の園舎改築の仕事である。竹原はその木立を見て、「地面から生えて枝を広げるツリーハウスをつくろう」と考えた。

そのために選ばれた方法が、木の柱を地面からの片持ち構造で立ち上げることだった。一番力のかかる根元を固めるために2階床下には梁を組み、それを1階部分のコンクリート壁にアンカーして固定する。すると2階の柱の先端部分はフリーになり、その上にふわりと屋根が載る。1階は、建具で囲って部屋とするが、いずれは撤去して柱だけが並ぶピロティにする。そのとき、片持ち柱が地面から生えたような風景が生まれ、園庭に茂る木々のメタファーになり、まさに「ツリーハウス」が出現するという計算だ。

竹原は「今流行の（笑）、ランダムな柱の立ち方も最初は考えてはみたものの、どうも今回はそれではないだろうと、すぐやめてしまいました。スチールにならざるを得なく、ツリーハウスからかけ離れてしまいますから」と語っている[4]。つまり彼は、文字通り「林のように」つくる直喩的な方法ではなく、より抽象的な変換を選んだのだ。そこには、前者の方法によって生まれるような関係を言葉との間につくる建築は、もはや構築物としての建築ではないという竹原の価値観が明快に示されている。

これらふたつのエピソードと「101番目の家」での観察からは、竹原の建築の背後に明晰な論理が存在することに気付かざるを得ないだろう。新しい構造形式、空間の質、住居観、生活像などを提示するための推進力としての論理である。

しかしそれらは、巧みな空間構成や素材選択の陰に隠れ、最前列には登場しない。竹原は、言葉と空間との二分法をよしとせず、両者が不可分な状態こそを設計目標とするからだ。論理が、まさに透明なベールとなって建物全体を覆っているのである。

総体化への強靭な意志

建築もひとつの言語体系だと考えるなら、それは、建築を構成する記号の配列規則を示す統辞論と、その記号と外部世界をつなぎ解釈を与える意味論と、建築が何らかの文脈の中で遂行する行為について語る実用論から構成されることになる。

多くのポレミックな建築家たちは、このうちのいずれかにおける操作に選択的な照準を絞り、他の建築家との差異を担った建築を「作品」として生産する。

しかしながら、そこにはさまざまなレヴェルでの無理も出る。機能上の犠牲、観念的空回り、建築の決定根拠の建築外的世界への依存などだ。

竹原の建築も、もちろん建築という言語体系の産物であり、他の建築家との差異をもつ。しかしその差異は、統辞論、意味論、実用論のいずれかに分類できるものではなく、むしろそのような分類の不可能性として特徴付けられるのだ。

本書のための取材時の「影響を受けた建築家は誰か」という問いに対し(5)、竹原は、篠原一男、白井晟一、石井修の名を挙げた。私には、これはきわめて興味深い答えだと思われた。

なぜならば、篠原一男は日本の伝統的空間の構造を抽象化したという点において統辞論的建築家であり、白井晟一はさまざまな文化的背景の中で形態や素材を決定したという点において意味論的建築家であり、石井修は自然や生活という広い視界の中で建築をとらえようとしたという点において実用論的建築家であるという図式化を前提にすれば、竹原の興味がこの3人に向いているという事実からは、彼の総合性の本質が浮かび上がってくるからだ。

もちろん、篠原一男も白井晟一も石井修も「総合的な」建築家だ。しかし、篠原は空間の形式化のために意味の豊穣さを、白井は空間の意味の深化のために生活のリアリティを、石井は空間の社会化のためにその形式性を、それぞれ最前列から外したと考えるなら、竹原は、まさにそのような欠損のない建築をつくろうとしているのであり、そこにこそ彼の総合性の本質があるといえるだろう。

つまり竹原は、統辞論、意味論、実用論を区別することなく、それらから成る建築という言語そのものを操作の対象とし、抽象にいたることのない強度とリアリティを兼ね備えた空間を探し続けてきたといえるのだ。

明らかにこれは、冒頭に書いた「会話の達人」にできる仕事でない。

むしろ竹原は、建築言語自体のルールの内容を深化させ運用を加速化することによって、「会話の達人」による「軽妙な会話」の対極にある、建築言語自体の新たな可能性の発見に挑んできたといえるだろう。その意味において、つまり建築を建築という言語によって考えることへの強い意志を貫いているという意味において、竹原はまさに「建築」家なのである。

(1) 「特集 建築家が自邸で問いかけるこれからの「住まい観」」『住宅建築』2004年8月号
(2) 花田佳明「泉州の町並みに浮かぶ島 「岸和田の家」に見る竹原義二の現在」
　　『新建築 住宅特集』2006年5月号
(3) JIA近畿支部住宅部会主催「建築家カタログvol.5 発刊記念講演会
　　竹原義二×坂本昭」(コーディネーター：花田佳明、2008年4月25日)
(4) 「特集 竹原義二 透明な技術の地平」『住宅建築』2008年8月号
(5) 2009年12月25日。藤森照信と筆者によるインタヴュー。

An Architect's Architect: Yoshiji Takehara

Yoshiaki Hanada
Professor, Kobe Design University

A Superficial Prejudice

Yoshiji Takehara set up his own practice, Moo Architect Workshop in 1978 at the age of just thirty, after apprenticing under Osamu Ishii. He has focused on designing houses and built approximately 150 individual residences and collective residences in the last thirty years.

Each project is given a serial number.

The March 1997 issue of *Kenchiku Bunka* gave systematic coverage to his projects numbered 1 to 64, complete with photos and descriptions. According to this, the first project, Seya House, was completed in 1978, and Yamasaka House II, the 64th project, was built in 1996. This means that he built 64 buildings in eighteen years, an average rate of 3.6 buildings a year.

He then presented his own house as House No. 101 in 2002. Thirty-seven buildings, numbering from 65 to 101, were completed in six years resulting in an annual rate of 6.2 projects.

This book presents data on Takehara's works up to the number 150. Since House No. 101, 49 houses have been completed in seven years, that is to say seven houses a year.

What surprises us when looking at these 150 projects is the high degree of consistent perfection throughout these works and the difficulties we face in attempting to classify them into categories such as style or period. I am tempted to say if there is a change, it is only in the number of projects completed per year.

Of course we can observe differences due to site, scale, and structure. The theme and design vary from simple urban residential buildings to dignified houses in the suburbs. He seems to know whether to use concrete, wood, or steel frame, and how to chose between materials such as wood, stone, and plaster.

However, these differences are not 'changes' that have occurred over time but represents a 'diversity' that has existed throughout. That is to say, the 150 projects have a consistent level of quality, as if they were lined up in Takehara's head from the beginning. However, this diversity, produced between the ages of 30 and 60, proves nothing more than the precociousness and reliability of his talent.

Beyond these observations, you can imagine Takehara being a person who learnt the foreign language called architecture quickly and managed to start conversing without any struggle.

At least I got such impression by flipping through the March 1997 issue of *Kenchiku Bunka* and neglected to think about him further. However, in August 2003, when I visited the House No. 101, his own house, which happened to be my first encounter with his work, I was made aware that the imaginary figure I had created of him was based upon a superficial prejudice. I had been blind.

The Impact of House No. 101

I arrived at House No. 101 at two o'clock in the afternoon. I brought along ten students from my laboratory.

It wasn't me, but rather Takehara kindly saying that "students are usually allowed to spend half-an-hour for visiting my projects but today is an exception" which led us to forget the time, until we suddenly realised it was eight in the evening. I realised what it was like to lose the sense of time, and could not really remember what we did for six hours. It felt strange, as if being waken up from a dream.

We went up and down again and again and sat down or stood up in the building's complex, nested space. We listen avidly to blues in a space like a cave in the basement floor, and we sat around and looked at the sky changing colour from the terrace on the second floor. One of the students even fell asleep. In short, we didn't realise it was already dark outside.

We didn't do anything special. However, that six hours felt like we did something good. The space spurred us to do all different kinds of activities which are hard to name.

What made us feel comfortable to spending time on doing nothing in particular?

It is difficult to describe House No. 101 in words.

The site is located in the residential area of Toyonaka City, Osaka. It is about 100 square meters and surrounded by other houses – it is a typical residential plot in contemporary Japan. Except that the site falls to the rear by one level. The structure is a hybrid of wood and concrete, and inside and outside spaces are scattered along the ambulatory circulation paths.

However, I know that writing this doesn't really convey anything. The spatial quality of House No. 101 is defined by other factors.

A row of columns in hardwoods of different thickness and colours looks more like iron than wood, exuding a steely aura. They are attached to concrete beams, creating a unique mixed structure through shifts and layerings. The bundle of columns is probably better described as a wall. The circulation is described as being ambulatory (*kaiyu*), but the flow changes from staircase to corridor to ladder, inside and outside spaces alternate as you navigate, and there are spaces where the flow stops. Rather than existing merely to invoke a superficially Japanese 'harmony', this archipelago of interior and exterior spaces can be interpreted as a demonstration of the importance placed on spatial interpenetration and reversals in giving concrete shape to Takehara's singular vision of dwelling.

It could be said that the texture of House No. 101 is created by this sort of manipulation – an accumulation of manipulations which deny the general attributes of the various elements of dwelling.

What is more, these manipulations are deeply interrelated. For example, the iron-like wooden columns make up a wall which weaves freely between inside and outside, giving an even stronger impression.

So, in order for us to thoroughly experience (rather than analyse) this integrated spatial structure linked together like a chain, it probably required a good six hours, along with various undefined activities.

Meanwhile, the way Takehara and his family inhabited the space was suffused with a quotidian calmness, in contrast to our wanderings around in a forgetful daze. The space is filled with stuff but not uncomfortable. The shape and place of each thing is perfectly apt, and contributes to raising the overall quality of the space. It was as if his family was telling us "we use this kind of space in this way – this kind of space offers this way of life."

In other words, the six hours at House No. 101 was a silent lesson showing how deep thinking in architecture yields progressive spaces and modes of dwelling.

A Clear Logic

After the visit to House No. 101 there was another Takehara experience awaiting me.

I revisited House No. 101 in 2004 and interviewed him for an article [1]. I also wrote about my visit to another of his projects, the Kishiwada House, in 2006 [2]. Furthermore, I organised a symposium intending to draw out his ideas on dwelling in April 2008 [3], and I conducted a talk event with him in the summer of that year after visiting the Akebono kindergarten "Nanputei", the Nagayamaen House, and the Suwamoricho Naka House.

Through these experiences what I felt strongly was the existence of a clear logic underlying Takehara's architecture.

The Kishiwada House at first sight seems to be organised according to a conventional layout, but on looking closer at its plan you begin to notice that there is neither glass nor doors between the ostensibly exterior large *doma* space on the ground floor and the living and dining space on the second floor, yet they are unified via a connecting staircase.

I was careless to overlook this earlier, and while ascending the staircase I found myself thinking "Is this an outside space? Are they living outside?" when I reached the second floor.

The space of the Kishiwada House can be described as islands floating in the sea – that is to say various spaces for living are floating in a large interconnected space. It represents a cool and robust view of living, totally different from the impression that the rich design of the house would give.

Akebono kindergarten "Nanputei" showed me Takehara's ethical understanding of structural form.

It was a renovation of a kindergarden surrounded by trees. Takehara was inspired by these trees and thought "let's build a treehouse, growing up from the ground, with spreading branches."

The method chosen to achieve this involved a structure of timber columns cantilevered from the ground. To strengthen the column bases where the stresses are greatest, beams were constructed under the second floor and affixed to the concrete walls of the ground level, using them as anchors. This freed the tips of the columns on the second floor allowing the roof to float on top. The ground floor spaces have been arranged as rooms with lightweight partitions, some of which will be removed eventually leaving the columns as a series of *piloti*. When that happens, the cantilevered columns will then be revealed as if they are growing from the ground, a metaphor designed to evoke the verdant stand of trees on the site, a genuine "tree house".

Takehara said: "I also contemplated the idea of having random columns, which is considered fashionable these days (*laughs*) – but soon gave up such an idea as it didn't feel right for this project. To do so, we could not have avoided using steel, which would have ended up being far from a treehouse."[4]. In other words, he didn't take a literal approach to build something as 'a forest' but rather chose an abstract transformation. This clearly shows Takehara's sense of values, regarding architecture that builds its relationship with words as seen in the former approach is no longer an architecture understood as built structure.

From these two episodes, and from our observations at the House No. 101, one can't help concluding that a clear logic informs Takehara's architecture. It is this logic that provides the impetus for new structural forms, spatial qualities, modes of dwelling, and images of life.

However, these are hidden behind ingenious spatial arrangements or material choices rather than being positioned front and centre. Takehara would not be satisfied with the dichotomy between words and spaces, aiming rather to design architecture in which these form an indivisible whole. The theory becomes a transparent veil covering the whole building.

Commitment to the Whole

If we regard architecture as a linguistic system, it can be seen as consist of *syntax*, indicating the rules for the arrangement of architectural codes; *semantics*, giving the interpretations that relate such codes to the outside world; and *pragmatics*, describing the actions enacted by architecture under some particular context.

Most polemical architects focus selectively on one of these categories and produce architecture as "works" that aim to differentiate themselves from the works of others.

However, there are irrationalities at various levels with this. These include functional sacrifices, empty conceptual speculations, and basing architectural decisions on things beyond architecture's purview.

Takehara's architecture is of course also a product of the linguistic system that is architecture, and his work is also different from others. However, this difference can't be classified into the categories of syntax, semantics, or pragmatics, but is rather characterised by the impossibility of such classification.

When I interviewed him for this piece, I asked him "Who are the architects who have influenced you?"[5] In response he gave the names Kazuo Shinohara, Sei'ichi Shirai, and Osamu Ishii. I found this answer extremely interesting.

Kazuo Shinohara is an architect of syntax, working with abstractions of traditional Japanese space. Sei'ichi Shirai is an architect of semantics, defining various forms and materials amongst diverse cultural backgrounds. Osamu Ishii is an architect of pragmatics, who tries to position architecture within the wider perspectives of nature and lifestyle. Assuming this schematic outline is right, the fact that Takehara's interests are directed towards these different architects helps us find the substance of his integration.

Of course, Shinohara, Shirai, and Ishii are all "integrated" architects too. However, if we consider that Shinohara abandoned richness of meaning in order to formalise space; Shirai left the reality of life in order to deepen spatial meaning; and Ishii missed spatial formalisation in order to give space social content, we can say that it is Takehara who tries to build without any of these deficits and it is precisely here that we find the essence of his synthesis.

In other words, Takehara doesn't distinguish between syntax, semantics, and pragmatics. Rather, he makes his field of operation the language of architecture itself, pursuing a space that has both reality and a strength that does not admit of 'abstraction.'

It is clear that this can not be handled by a 'master of conversation'.

It could be argued rather that Takehara has taken on the challenge of discovering new possibilities within the language of architecture itself by deepening the content of its rules and speeding its implementation, a position diametrically opposed to the 'witty banter' of a 'master of conversation.'

In this sense then – the sense in which he is resolutely carrying out a thinking through of architecture via the language of architecture itself – Takehara is a truly an 'architect's architect'.

Footnotes

1. "Special Issue: Architects' 'sense of dwelling' from analysis of their own houses." *Jutaku Kenchiku*, August 2004.
2. Hanada Yoshiaki, "An island floating in the Senshu townscape: Takehara Yoshiji as seen through "Kishiwada House." Shinkenchiku *Jutaku-tokushu*, May 2006.
3. "Takehara Yoshiji and Sakamoto Akira: Symposium Commemorating Publication of *Kenchikuka Katarogu* vol.5," organised by Housing Section, Kinki Regional Chapter, JIA. (Co-ordinator: Hanada Yoshiaki, 25 April 2008).
4. "Special Issue: Takehara Yoshiji – The Horizon of Lucid Technique". *Jutaku Kenchiku*, August 2008.
5. Author's interview with Terunobu Fujimori, 25 December 2009.

作品データ
Information on Works

凡例

No. 作品名 竣工 Completion Date
　　　Project Name
①所在地　Location
②用途　Principal Use
③主体構造　Main Structure
　　　W＝木造　Wooden Construction
　　　RC＝鉄筋コンクリート造　Reinforced Concrete
　　　CB＝コンクリートブロック造　Concrete Block
　　　SRC＝鉄骨鉄筋コンクリート造
　　　　　Steel-Framed Reinforced Concrete
④規模　Scale of Building
⑤敷地面積　Site Area
⑥建築面積　Building Area
⑦延床面積　Total Floor Area

No.1　勢野の家　1978
　　　Seya House
①奈良県生駒郡　Ikoma-gun, Nara
②専用住宅　Dwelling House
③W　④地上2階　2 stories
⑤186.71㎡　⑥90.13㎡　⑦90.13㎡

No.2　伊庭宇台の家　1979
　　　Ibajidai House
①滋賀県神崎郡　Kanzaki-gun, Shiga
②専用住宅　Dwelling House
③W　④地上2階　2 stories
⑤132.43㎡　⑥54.80㎡　⑦88.56㎡

No.3　帝塚山中町の家　1979
　　　Tezukayama Nakamachi House
①大阪市住吉区　Sumiyoshi-ku, Osaka-shi
②専用住宅　Dwelling House
③W　④地上2階　2 stories
⑤68.77㎡　⑥56.63㎡　⑦91.82㎡

No.4　忍海の家　1980
　　　Oshimi House
①奈良県北葛城郡　Kita Katsuragi-gun, Nara
②専用住宅　Dwelling House
③RC＋W　④地上2階　2 stories
⑤327.35㎡　⑥102.00㎡　⑦131.18㎡

No.5　岸和田の家　1980
　　　Kishiwada House
①大阪府岸和田市　Kishiwada-shi, Osaka
②専用住宅　Dwelling House
③W　④地上2階　2 stories
⑤116.59㎡　⑥69.31㎡　⑦92.92㎡

No.6　港晴の家　1980
　　　Kosei House
①大阪市港区　Minato-ku, Osaka-shi
②専用住宅　Dwelling House
③W　④地上2階　2 stories
⑤67.35㎡　⑥57.85㎡　⑦121.52㎡

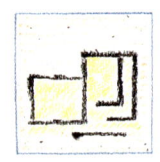

No.7　和泉砂川の家　1980
　　　Izumi Sunagawa House
①大阪府泉南市　Sennan-shi, Osaka
②専用住宅　Dwelling House
③RC＋W　④地上2階　2 stories
⑤118.43㎡　⑥73.56㎡　⑦116.43㎡

No.8　三木の家　1981
　　　Miki House
①兵庫県三木市　Miki-shi, Hyogo
②専用住宅　Dwelling House
③W　④地上2階　2 stories
⑤265.32㎡　⑥27.87㎡　⑦47.19㎡

No.9　当麻の家　1981
　　　Taima House
①奈良県北葛城郡　Kita Katsuragi-gun, Nara
②住宅＋店舗　House and Shop
③W　④地上2階　2 stories
⑤133.89㎡　⑥74.60㎡　⑦120.41㎡

No.10　北楠葉の家　1982
　　　Kita Kuzuha House
①大阪府枚方市　Hirakata-shi, Osaka
②専用住宅　Dwelling House
③W　④地上2階　2 stories
⑤102.71㎡　⑥48.82㎡　⑦82.37㎡

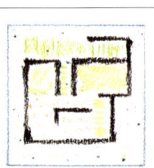

No.11　有里の家　1982
　　　Arisato House
①奈良県生駒市　Ikoma-shi, Nara
②専用住宅　Dwelling House
③W　④地上2階　2 stories
⑤114.60㎡　⑥63.61㎡　⑦101.59㎡

No.12　粉浜の家Ⅰ　1983
　　　Kohama House Ⅰ
①大阪市住之江区　Suminoe-ku, Osaka-shi
②専用住宅　Dwelling House
③W　④地上2階　2 stories
⑤82.99㎡　⑥65.21㎡　⑦112.03㎡

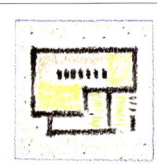

No.13　西明石の家　1983
　　　Nishi Akashi House
①兵庫県明石市　Akashi-shi, Hyogo
②専用住宅　Dwelling House
③RC＋W　④地上2階　2 stories
⑤198.37㎡　⑥100.29㎡　⑦173.97㎡

306

No.14 延命湯 1983
Enmeiyu
①大阪市福島区　Fukushima-ku, Osaka-shi
②銭湯＋住宅　Public Bath and House
③RC　④地上3階　3 stories
⑤271.17㎡　⑥221.99㎡　⑦374.26㎡

No.15 長岡京の家 1984
Nagaokakyo House
①京都府長岡京市　Nagaokakyo-shi, Kyoto
②専用住宅　Dwelling House　③RC／W
④地下1階 地上2階　basement, 2 stories
⑤213.36㎡　⑥81.85㎡　⑦143.99㎡

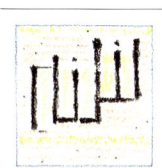

No.16 STEP HOUSE SUMINODO 1984
STEP HOUSE SUMINODO
①大阪府大東市　Daito-shi, Osaka
②長屋5戸　Five-Unit Row House
③W　④地上2階　2 stories
⑤285.99㎡　⑥162.00㎡　⑦450.20㎡

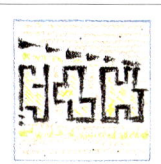

No.17 STEP HOUSE Ⅱ 1985
STEP HOUSE Ⅱ
①大阪府東大阪市　Higash Osaka-shi, Osaka
②専用住宅　Dwelling House
③W　④地上2階　2 stories
⑤98.70㎡　⑥63.014㎡　⑦114.45㎡

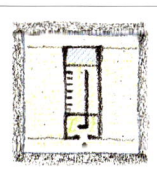

No.18 粉浜の家Ⅱ 1985
Kohama House Ⅱ
①大阪市住之江区　Suminoe-ku, Osaka-shi
②専用住宅　Dwelling House
③W＋RC　④地上2階　2 stories
⑤36.30㎡　⑥30.71㎡　⑦69.77㎡

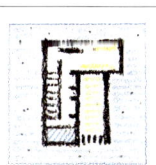

No.19 深井中町の家 1985
Fukai Nakamachi House
①大阪府堺市　Sakai-shi, Osaka
②専用住宅　Dwelling House
③RC　④地上2階　2 stories
⑤96.92㎡　⑥54.40㎡　⑦89.16㎡

No.20 本田外科・胃腸科 1986
Honda Clinic
①兵庫県芦屋市　Ashiya-shi, Hyogo
②医院　Clinic
③RC　④地上2階　2 stories
⑤202.73㎡　⑥111.81㎡　⑦207.69㎡

No.21 阿弥の家 1986
Ami House
①大阪府南河内郡　Minami Kawachi-gun, Osaka
②専用住宅　Dwelling House
③W／S　④地上2階　2 stories
⑤144.98㎡　⑥53.00㎡　⑦78.81㎡

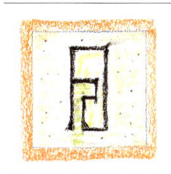

No.22 ドムス北長狭 1987
Domus Kitanagasa
①兵庫県神戸市　Kobe-shi, Hyogo
②賃貸共同住宅＋住宅　Public Housing and House　③S
④地下1階 地上5階　basement, 5 stories
⑤83.22㎡　⑥76.63㎡　⑦319.51㎡

No.23 依羅通りの家 1987
Yosamidori House
①大阪市住吉区　Sumiyoshi-ku, Osaka-shi
②専用住宅　Dwelling House
③W　④地上2階　2 stories
⑤98.04㎡　⑥57.60㎡　⑦97.31㎡

No.24 塗屋造の家 1987
Nuriyazukuri House
①大阪府東大阪市　Higashi Osaka-shi, Osaka
②専用住宅　Dwelling House
③W　④地上2階　2 stories
⑤123.76㎡　⑥67.96㎡　⑦117.25㎡

No.25 石丸の家 1988
Ishimaru House
①大阪府箕面市　Minoh-shi, Osaka
②専用住宅　Dwelling House　③RC
④地下1階 地上2階　basement, 2 stories
⑤252.9㎡　⑥134.55㎡　⑦286.72㎡

No.26 南山栗平の山荘 1988
Minamiyama Kuridaira Cottage
①長野県芽野市　Chino-shi, Nagano
②別荘　Weekend House　③W
④地下1階 地上2階　basement, 2 stories
⑤11026.96㎡　⑥115.15㎡　⑦125.72㎡

No.27 西中島の家 1988
Nishi Nakajima House
①大阪府淀川区　Yodogawa-ku, Osaka-shi
②専用住宅　Dwelling House
③W＋CB　④地上2階　2 stories
⑤90.31㎡　⑥52.70㎡　⑦101.40㎡

No.28 マニフェスト楠町 1988
Manifesto Kusunokicho
①兵庫県芦屋市　Ashiya-shi, Hyogo
②専用住宅　Dwelling House
③RC　④地上3階　3 stories
⑤271.87㎡　⑥129.50㎡　⑦281.72㎡

No.29 千里山の家 1989
Senriyama House
①大阪府吹田市　Suita-shi, Osaka
②専用住宅　Dwelling House　③RC
④地下1階 地上2階　basement, 2 stories
⑤272.45㎡　⑥108.54㎡　⑦257.57㎡

No.30 寿町の家 1989
Kotobukicho House
① 大阪府吹田市 Suita-shi, Osaka
② 専用住宅 Dwelling House
③ CB／RC ④ 地上2階 2 stories
⑤ 155.06㎡ ⑥ 92.22㎡ ⑦ 180.42㎡

No.31 本庄町の家 1989
Honjocho House
① 兵庫県西宮市 Nishinomiya-shi, Hyogo
② 専用住宅 Dwelling House ③ RC
④ 地下1階 地上2階 basement, 2 stories
⑤ 212.55㎡ ⑥ 105.06㎡ ⑦ 198.77㎡

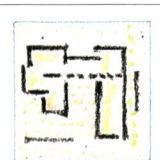

No.32 吉見ノ里の家 1990
Yoshiminosato House
① 大阪府泉南郡 Sennan-gun, Osaka
② 専用住宅 Dwelling House
③ RC ④ 地上2階 2 stories
⑤ 577.59㎡ ⑥ 169.87㎡ ⑦ 249.95㎡

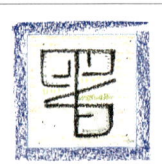

No.33 石壁の家 1991
Ishikabe House
① 兵庫県神戸市 Kobe-shi, Hyogo
② 共同住宅 (3戸) Apartment Complex (3 Units) ③ RC
④ 地下1階 地上2階 basement, 2 stories
⑤ 997.53㎡ ⑥ 497.36㎡ ⑦ 1114.68㎡

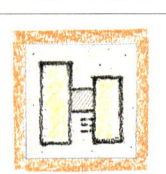

No.34 ノースタワービル 1991
North Tower Bldg.
① 大阪市北区 Kita-ku, Osaka-shi
② 賃貸共同住宅＋事務所 Public Housing and Office ③ SRC／RC
④ 地下1階 地上10階 basement, 10 stories
⑤ 263.85㎡ ⑥ 168.97㎡ ⑦ 1517.61㎡

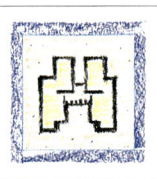

No.35 ドムス壱分 1991
Domus Ichibu
① 奈良県生駒市 Ikoma-shi, Nara
② 賃貸共同住宅＋住宅 Public Housing and House
③ RC ④ 地上3階 3 stories
⑤ 1116.14㎡ ⑥ 240.05㎡ ⑦ 585.76㎡

No.36 御崎の家Ⅰ 1991
Misaki House Ⅰ
① 大阪市住之江区 Suminoe-ku, Osaka-shi
② 専用住宅 Dwelling House
③ S ④ 地上3階 3 stories
⑤ 64.44㎡ ⑥ 43.61㎡ ⑦ 108.08㎡

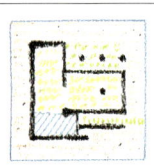

No.37 御園の家 1991
Misono House
① 兵庫県尼崎市 Amagasaki-shi, Hyogo
② 専用住宅 Dwelling House
③ W ④ 地上3階 3 stories
⑤ 103.93㎡ ⑥ 50.14㎡ ⑦ 92.17㎡

No.38 大矢医療機器ビル 1991
Oya Medical Equipment Bldg.
① 大阪市東成区 Higashinari-ku, Osaka-shi
② 事務所 Office
③ S ④ 地上4階 4 stories
⑤ 83.88㎡ ⑥ 72.00㎡ ⑦ 286.38㎡

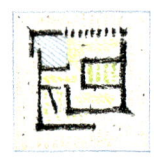

No.39 真法院町の家 1992
Shinpoincho House
① 大阪市天王寺区 Tennoji-ku, Osaka-shi
② 専用住宅 Dwelling House
③ RC／S ④ 地上3階 3 stories
⑤ 181.42㎡ ⑥ 72.58㎡ ⑦ 282.35㎡

No.40 山坂の家Ⅰ 1992
Yamasaka House Ⅰ
① 大阪市東住吉区 Higashi Sumiyoshi-ku, Osaka-shi
② 専用住宅 Dwelling House
③ RC／S ④ 地上3階 3 stories
⑤ 148.92㎡ ⑥ 87.24㎡ ⑦ 225.08㎡

No.41 玉串川の家 1992
Tamakushigawa House
① 大阪府八尾市 Yao-shi, Osaka
② 専用住宅 Dwelling House
③ W ④ 地上2階 2 stories
⑤ 267.52㎡ ⑥ 132.77㎡ ⑦ 162.48㎡

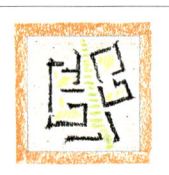

No.42 ドムス桜ヶ丘 1993
Domus Sakuragaoka
① 大阪府箕面市 Minoh-shi, Osaka
② 賃貸共同住宅 Public Housing
③ RC ④ 地上2階 2 stories
⑤ 405.68㎡ ⑥ 197.18㎡ ⑦ 328.08㎡

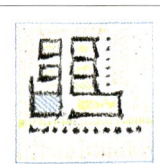

No.43 印田の家 1993
Inda House
① 大阪府枚方市 Hirakata-shi, Osaka
② 専用住宅 Dwelling House
③ W ④ 地上2階 2 stories
⑤ 375.17㎡ ⑥ 114.01㎡ ⑦ 156.45㎡

No.44 千里園の家 1993
Senrien House
① 大阪府豊中市 Toyonaka-shi, Osaka
② 専用住宅 Dwelling House
③ RC／W ④ 地上2階 2 stories
⑤ 473.47㎡ ⑥ 230.30㎡ ⑦ 323.37㎡

No.45 小路の家 1993
Shoji House
① 大阪市生野区 Ikuno-ku, Osaka-shi
② 専用住宅 Dwelling House
③ W ④ 地上3階 3 stories
⑤ 62.94㎡ ⑥ 36.19㎡ ⑦ 95.18㎡

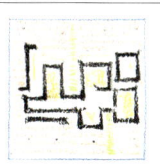

No.46 久御山の家 1993
Kumiyama House
①京都府久世郡 Kuse-gun, Kyoto
②専用住宅 Dwelling House
③RC／W ④地上2階 2 stories
⑤509.09㎡ ⑥281.25㎡ ⑦376.42㎡

No.47 鴻ノ巣の家 1993
Tonnosu House
①和歌山県西牟婁郡 Nishimuro-gun, Wakayama
②別荘 Weekend House ③RC
④地下1階 地上2階 basement, 2 stories
⑤983.49㎡ ⑥317.02㎡ ⑦383.55㎡

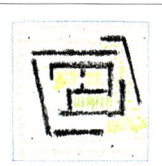

No.48 住吉山手の家 1993
Sumiyoshi Yamate House
①兵庫県神戸市 Kobe-shi, Hyogo
②専用住宅 Dwelling House ③RC＋W
④地下1階 地上2階 basement, 2 stories
⑤241.28㎡ ⑥94.37㎡ ⑦188.27㎡

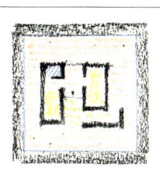

No.49 御崎の家Ⅱ 1994
Misaki House Ⅱ
①大阪市住之江区 Suminoe-ku, Osaka-shi
②専用住宅 Dwelling House
③W＋RC／S ④地上2階 2 stories
⑤176.27㎡ ⑥88.39㎡ ⑦133.75㎡

No.50 朱雀の家 1994
Suzaku House
①奈良県奈良市 Nara-shi, Nara
②専用住宅 Dwelling House
③RC／S ④地上2階 2 stories
⑤327.46㎡ ⑥106.26㎡ ⑦157.62㎡

No.51 鶴ヶ丘の家 1995
Tsurugaoka House
①大阪市東住吉区 Higashi Sumiyoshi-ku, Osaka-shi
②専用住宅 Dwelling House
③W ④地上2階 2 stories
⑤369.52㎡ ⑥154.08㎡ ⑦247.82㎡

No.52 ドムス柿木Ⅰ 1995
Domus Kakinoki Ⅰ
①大阪市大東市 Daito-shi, Osaka
②賃貸共同住宅 Public Housing
③RC ④地上2階 2 stories
⑤106.96㎡ ⑥120.51㎡ ⑦213.38㎡

No.53 ドムス羽衣 1995
Domus Hagoromo
①大阪府高石市 Takaishi-shi, Osaka
②賃貸共同住宅 Public Housing
③RC ④地上3階 3 stories
⑤701.01㎡ ⑥268.45㎡ ⑦673.47㎡

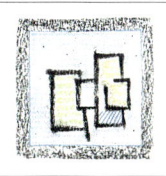

No.54 真弓の家 1995
Mayumi House
①奈良県生駒市 Ikoma-shi, Nara
②専用住宅 Dwelling House ③S／RC
④地下1階 地上3階 basement, 3 stories
⑤186.86㎡ ⑥100.92㎡ ⑦166.86㎡

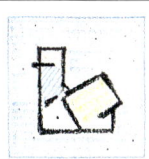

No.55 城山町の家 1995
Shiroyamacho House
①大阪府豊中市 Toyonaka-shi, Osaka
②専用住宅 Dwelling House
③RC ④地上3階 3 stories
⑤135.45㎡ ⑥55.09㎡ ⑦121.62㎡

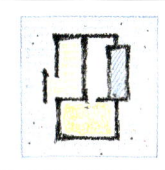

No.56 粉浜の家Ⅲ 1995
Kohama House Ⅲ
①大阪市住之江区 Suminoe-ku, Osaka-shi
②専用住宅 Dwelling House
③S ④地上4階 4 stories
⑤167.99㎡ ⑥97.02㎡ ⑦244.85㎡

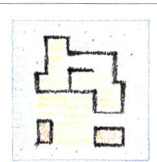

No.57 帝塚山の家 1995
Tezukayama House
①大阪市阿倍野区 Abeno-ku, Osaka-shi
②専用住宅 Dwelling House
③RC ④地上3階 3 stories
⑤327.76㎡ ⑥119.37㎡ ⑦267.86㎡

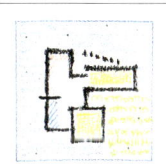

No.58 宝山町の家 1995
Hozancho House
①大阪府豊中市 Toyonaka-shi, Osaka
②専用住宅 Dwelling House
③W／RC ④地上2階 2 stories
⑤316.77㎡ ⑥114.73㎡ ⑦139.25㎡

No.59 田辺の家 1995
Tanabe House
①大阪市東住吉区 Higashi Sumiyoshi-ku, Osaka-shi
②専用住宅 Dwelling House
③S ④地上4階 4 stories
⑤114.44㎡ ⑥68.33㎡ ⑦231.14㎡

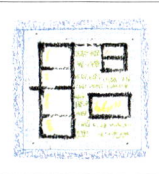

No.60 アルディア巨椋 1995
Aldia Ogura
①京都府宇治市 Uji-shi, Kyoto
②賃貸共同住宅 Public Housing
③RC ④地上6階 6 stories
⑤1868.00㎡ ⑥577.26㎡ ⑦2551.07㎡

No.61 恵我之荘の家 1996
Eganosho House
①大阪府羽曳野市 Habikino-shi, Osaka
②専用住宅 Dwelling House
③W ④地上2階 2 stories
⑤159.63㎡ ⑥85.78㎡ ⑦136.04㎡

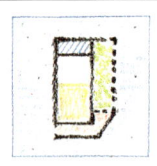

No.62　向陵中町の家　1996
　　　Koryo Nakamachi House
①大阪府堺市　Sakai-shi, Osaka
②専用住宅　Dwelling House
③W＋RC　④地上3階　3 stories
⑤65.70㎡　⑥42.61㎡　⑦92.38㎡

No.63　魚崎北町の家　1996
　　　Uozaki Kitamachi House
①兵庫府神戸市　Kobe-shi, Hyogo
②専用住宅　Dwelling House
③RC　④地上2階　2 stories
⑤132.51㎡　⑥77.71㎡　⑦147.77㎡

No.64　山坂の家Ⅱ　1996
　　　Yamasaka House Ⅱ
①大阪市東住吉区　Higashi Sumiyoshi-ku, Osaka-shi
②専用住宅　Dwelling House
③RC／S　④地上3階　3 stories
⑤116.41㎡　⑥68.20㎡　⑦165.29㎡

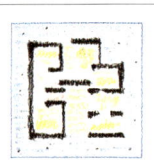

No.65　浜松の家　1997
　　　Hamamatsu House
①静岡県浜松市　Hamamatsu-shi, Shizuoka
②専用住宅　Dwelling House
③RC　④地上3階　3 stories
⑤380.16㎡　⑥196.60㎡　⑦422.29㎡

No.66　南河内の家　1997
　　　Minami Kawachi House
①大阪府富田林市　Tondabayashi-shi, Osaka
②専用住宅　Dwelling House
③W　④地上2階　2 stories
⑤300.66㎡　⑥88.14㎡　⑦139.43㎡

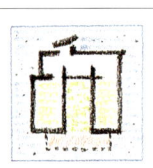

No.67　緑丘の家　1997
　　　Midorigaoka House
①大阪府豊中市　Toyonaka-shi, Osaka
②専用住宅　Dwelling House　③RC／S
④地下1階 地上2階　basement, 2 stories
⑤255.01㎡　⑥101.54㎡　⑦259.03㎡

No.68　ハルナ保育園　1997
　　　Haruna Nursery School
①奈良県香芝市　Kashiba-shi, Nara
②保育所　Nursery
③S　④地上2階　2 stories
⑤1026.11㎡　⑥421.39㎡　⑦641.16㎡

No.69　目神山の家　1997
　　　Megamiyama House
①兵庫県西宮市　Nishinomiya-shi, Hyogo
②専用住宅　Dwelling House　③RC
④地下1階 地上2階　basement, 2 stories
⑤1501㎡　⑥321.46㎡　⑦500.97㎡

No.70　東広島の家　1997
　　　Higashi Hiroshima House
①広島県東広島市　Higashi Hiroshima-shi, Hiroshima
②専用住宅　Dwelling House
③W　④地上2階　2 stories
⑤525.31㎡　⑥181.24㎡　⑦232.72㎡

No.71　ドムス柿木Ⅱ　1997
　　　Domus Kakinoki Ⅱ
①大阪府大東市　Daito-shi, Osaka
②賃貸共同住宅＋住宅　Public Housing and House
③RC　④地上3階　3 stories
⑤1087.09㎡　⑥232.02㎡　⑦497.57㎡

No.72　法園寺　1997
　　　Hoonji Temple
①大阪府池田市　Ikeda-shi, Osaka
②客殿＋庫裡　Reception Hall and Monks' Quarters　③S＋RC＋W
④地下1階 地上2階　basement, 2 stories
⑤1832.11㎡　⑥734.64㎡　⑦951.72㎡

No.73　広陵町の家　1997
　　　Koryocho House
①奈良県北葛城郡　Kita Katsuragi-gun, Nara
②専用住宅　Dwelling House
③W／RC　④地上2階　2 stories
⑤235.88㎡　⑥86.47㎡　⑦133.60㎡

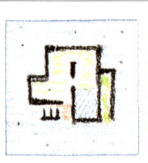

No.74　大阪府住宅供給公社リフォーム事業　1997
　　　Osaka Prefecture Rental Housing Renovation Project
①大阪府豊中市／堺市　Toyonaka-shi/Sakai-shi, Osaka
②公社賃貸共同住宅　Public Housing　③RC
④地上5階　5 stories　⑦44.57㎡ (5 types)

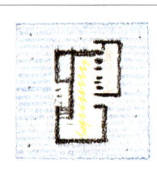

No.75　東園田の家　1997
　　　Higashi Sonoda House
①兵庫県尼崎市　Amagasaki-shi, Hyogo
②専用住宅　Dwelling House
③S＋W　④地上3階　3 stories
⑤73.54㎡　⑥42.19㎡　⑦109.43㎡

No.76　地域農業総合管理センター　1997
　　　Regional Agricultural Integrated Management Center
①和歌山県和歌山市　Wakayama-shi, Wakayama
②事務所＋研修室　Office and Training Room
③RC／S　④地上2階　2 stories
⑤1449.80㎡　⑥813.30㎡　⑦1225.71㎡

No.77　城崎の家　1997
　　　Kinosaki House
①兵庫県城崎郡　Kinosaki-gun, Hyogo
②専用住宅　Dwelling House
③S＋W　④地上3階　3 stories
⑤110.89㎡　⑥86.77㎡　⑦255.43㎡

No.78　法円坂の家　1997
　　　　Hoenzaka House
①大阪市中央区　Chuo-ku, Osaka-shi
②専用住宅　Dwelling House
③RC／W　④地上3階　3 stories
⑤78.02㎡　⑥58.70㎡　⑦170.00㎡

No.79　新千里南町の家　1997
　　　　Shinsenri Minamimachi House
①大阪府豊中市　Toyonaka-shi, Osaka
②専用住宅　Dwelling House　③RC
④地下1階 地上2階　basement, 2 stories
⑤355.37㎡　⑥127.02㎡　⑦333.17㎡

No.80　日ノ下商店高井田倉庫　1998
　　　　Hinoshita Shoten Takaida
　　　　Warehouse
①大阪府東大阪市　Higashi Osaka-shi, Osaka
②倉庫＋事務所　Storage and Office
③S＋RC　④地上1階　1 story
⑤913.24㎡　⑥697.45㎡　⑦762.4㎡

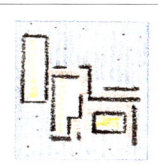

No.81　マツ勘社屋　1998
　　　　Matsukan Office
①福井県小浜市　Obama-shi, Fukui
②事務所＋倉庫＋アトリエ　Office, Storage
　Room, and Atelier
③S＋RC　④地上2階　1 story
⑤1306.05㎡　⑥989.96㎡　⑦594.07㎡

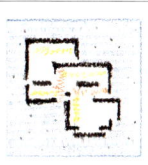

No.82　一宮の家　1998
　　　　Ichinomiya House
①兵庫県津名郡　Tsuna-gun, Hyogo
②店舗＋住宅　Shop and House
③RC＋W　④地上2階　2 stories
⑤183.05㎡　⑥79.14㎡　⑦166.71㎡

No.83　日ノ下商店事務所・社宅　1998
　　　　Hinoshita Shoten Office/Company
　　　　Housing
①大阪府東大阪市　Higashi Osaka-shi, Osaka
②事務所＋社宅　Office and Company Housing
③RC＋W　④地上3階　3 stories　⑤139.04㎡
⑥82.73㎡　⑦214.92㎡

No.84　千里丘の家　1998
　　　　Senrioka House
①大阪府吹田市　Suita-shi, Osaka
②専用住宅　Dwelling House
③RC＋W　④地上3階　3 stories
⑤174.33㎡　⑥71.49㎡　⑦157.92㎡

No.85　沢之町の家　1998
　　　　Sawanocho House
①大阪市住吉区　Sumiyoshi-ku, Osaka-shi
②専用住宅　Dwelling House
③RC＋W　④地上3階　3 stories
⑤61.24㎡　⑥41.91㎡　⑦100.50㎡

No.86　天神橋の家　1998
　　　　Tenjinbashi House
①大阪市北区　Kita-ku, Osaka-shi
②専用住宅　Dwelling House
③RC　④地上6階　6 stories
⑤84.29㎡　⑥66.35㎡　⑦351.62㎡

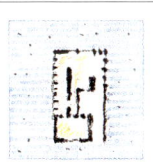

No.87　夙川の家　1999
　　　　Shukugawa House
①兵庫県西宮市　Nishinomiya-shi, Hyogo
②専用住宅　Dwelling House
③W　④地上3階　3 stories
⑤66.48㎡　⑥38.86㎡　⑦87.76㎡

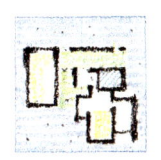

No.88　武蔵小金井の家　1998
　　　　Musashi Koganei House
①東京都小金井市　Koganei-shi, Tokyo
②専用住宅　Dwelling House　③RC＋W
④地下1階 地上2階　basement, 2 stories
⑤156.16㎡　⑥61.95㎡　⑦124.28㎡

No.89　泉北の家　1999
　　　　Semboku House
①大阪府堺市　Sakai-shi, Osaka
②専用住宅（増築）　Dwelling House
　（Expansion）
③W／RC　④地上1階　1 story
⑤272.58㎡　⑥43.01㎡　⑦36.86㎡

No.90.1　土と陶の工房 美乃里（アトリエ棟）
　　　　　1999
　　　　　Atelier Earthenware Minori
①大阪府八尾市　Yao-shi, Osaka　②アトリエ
　Atelier　③RC＋W　④地上2階　2 stories
⑤1148.96㎡　⑥327.87㎡　⑦315.31㎡

No.90.2　土と陶の工房 美乃里（住宅棟）　1999
　　　　　Atelier Earthenware Minori
　　　　　(House)
①大阪府八尾市　Yao-shi, Osaka
②専用住宅　Dwelling House
③RC＋W　④地上3階　3 stories
⑤1148.96㎡　⑥78.58㎡　⑦155.07㎡

No.91　海椿葉山　1999
　　　　Umitsubaki Hayama
①和歌山県西牟婁郡　Nishimuro-gun,
　Wakayama
②旅館　Japanese Inn
③W＋RC　④地上1階　1 story
⑤1532.70㎡　⑥519.12㎡　⑦502.39㎡

No.92　日ノ下商店ビル　1999
　　　　Hinoshita Shoten Bldg.
①大阪市中央区　Chuo-ku, Osaka-shi
②住宅＋貸事務所　House and Rental Office
③RC　④地上5階　5 stories
⑤429.20㎡　⑥289.08㎡　⑦1083.62㎡

No.93　比叡平の家　2000
　　　　Hieidaira House
①滋賀県大津市　Otsu-shi, Shiga
②専用住宅　Dwelling House
③RC＋W　④地上2階　2 stories
⑤394.66㎡　⑥102.70㎡　⑦170.98㎡

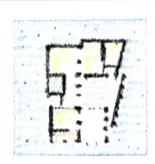

No.94　甲子園六番町の家　2000
　　　　Koshien Rokubancho House
①兵庫県西宮市　Nishinomiya-shi, Hyogo
②専用住宅　Dwelling House
③W　④地上2階　2 stories
⑤224.89㎡　⑥105.20㎡　⑦206.82㎡

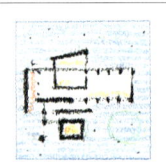

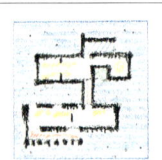

No.95　蓬萊・玄のアトリエ　2000
　　　　Horai Atelier Kuro
①滋賀県志賀郡　Shiga-gun, Shiga
②アトリエ＋住宅　Atelier and House
③RC＋W
④地下1階 地上2階　basement, 2 stories
⑤657.00㎡　⑥156.46㎡　⑦274.40㎡

No.96　鷲林寺南町の家　2000
　　　　Jurinji Minamimachi House
①兵庫県西宮市　Nishinomiya-shi, Hyogo
②専用住宅　Dwelling House　③RC＋W
④地下1階 地上1階　basement, 1 story
⑤868.85㎡　⑥300.76㎡　⑦399.63㎡

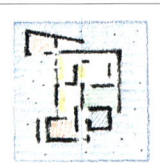

No.97　大渕の家　2000
　　　　Obuchi House
①奈良県奈良市　Nara-shi, Nara
②専用住宅　Dwelling House　③RC＋W
④地下1階 地上2階　basement, 2 stories
⑤312.75㎡　⑥122.07㎡　⑦284.54㎡

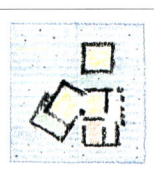

No.98　東豊中の家　2001
　　　　Higashi Toyonaka House
①大阪府豊中市　Toyonaka-shi, Osaka
②専用住宅　Dwelling House
③W　④地上2階　2 stories
⑤185.69㎡　⑥67.55㎡　⑦114.80㎡

No.99　箱作の家　2001
　　　　Hakotsukuri House
①大阪府阪南市　Hannan-shi, Osaka
②専用住宅　Dwelling House
③RC＋W　④地上2階　2 stories
⑤297.30㎡　⑥130.07㎡　⑦184.75㎡

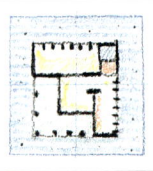

No.100　菜畑の家　2001
　　　　Nabata House
①奈良県生駒市　Ikoma-shi, Nara
②専用住宅　Dwelling House
③W　④地上2階　2 stories
⑤75.92㎡　⑥130.07㎡　⑦115.20㎡

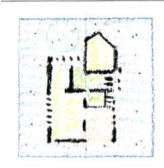

No.101　101番目の家　2002
　　　　House No.101
①大阪府豊中市　Toyonaka-shi, Osaka
②専用住宅　Dwelling House　③RC＋W
④地下1階 地上2階　basement, 2 stories
⑤108.90㎡　⑥65.22㎡　⑦156.21㎡

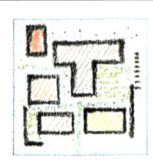

No.102　真上町の家　2001
　　　　Magamicho House
①大阪府高槻市　Takatsuki-shi, Osaka
②専用住宅　Dwelling House
③W／RC　④地上2階　2 stories
⑤413.28㎡　⑥230.49㎡　⑦375.60㎡

No.103　加守町の家　2001
　　　　Kamoricho House
①大阪府岸和田市　Kishiwada-shi, Osaka
②専用住宅　Dwelling House
③RC　④地上2階　2 stories
⑤101.54㎡　⑥57.15㎡　⑦109.46㎡

No.104　明石の家　2001
　　　　Akashi House
①兵庫県明石市　Akashi-shi, Hyogo
②専用住宅　Dwelling House　③RC＋W
④地下1階 地上2階　basement, 2 stories
⑤228.41㎡　⑥100.47㎡　⑦217.97㎡

No.105　高柳の家　2001
　　　　Takayanagi House
①大阪府寝屋川市　Neyagawa-shi, Osaka
②専用住宅　Dwelling House
③W　④地上3階　3 stories
⑤48.56㎡　⑥29.00㎡　⑦84.73㎡

No.106　あなん・花の木　2001
　　　　Anan Hananoki
①徳島県阿南市　Anan-shi, Tokushima
②店舗＋住宅　Shop and House
③RC＋W　④地上2階　2 stories
⑤395.98㎡　⑥225.02㎡　⑦312.67㎡

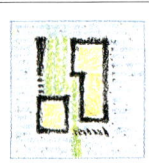

No.107　大社町の家　2001
　　　　Taishacho House
①兵庫県西宮市　Nishinomiya-shi, Hyogo
②専用住宅　Dwelling House
③W＋S　④地上2階　2 stories
⑤99.75㎡　⑥59.82㎡　⑦122.88㎡

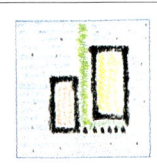

No.108　別所町の家　2002
　　　　Besshocho House
①大阪府岸和田市　Kishiwada-shi, Osaka
②専用住宅　Dwelling House
③W　④地上2階　2 stories
⑤112.64㎡　⑥59.42㎡　⑦113.36㎡

No.109　岩倉の家　2002
　　　　Iwakura House
①京都府京都市　Kyoto-shi, Kyoto
②専用住宅　Dwelling House　③W＋RC
④地下1階 地上2階　basement, 2 stories
⑤164.85㎡　⑥64.57㎡　⑦122.74㎡

No.110　朝日ヶ丘の家　2002
　　　　Asahigaoka House
①兵庫県芦屋市　Ashiya-shi, Hyogo
②専用住宅　Dwelling House　③RC
④地下1階 地上3階　basement, 3 stories
⑤280.00㎡　⑥110.72㎡　⑦275.75㎡

No.111　都島の家　2002
　　　　Miyakojima House
①大阪市都島区　Miyakojima-ku, Osaka-shi
②専用住宅　Dwelling House
③RC　④地上3階　3 stories
⑤192.91㎡　⑥112.43㎡　⑦247.97㎡

No.112　河内山本の家　2003
　　　　Kawachi Yamamoto House
①大阪府八尾市　Yao-shi, Osaka
②専用住宅　Dwelling House
③W　④地上2階　2 stories
⑤491.20㎡　⑥165.31㎡　⑦240.93㎡

No.113　あけぼの大門保育園　2003
　　　　Akebono Daimon Nursery School
①奈良県香芝市　Kashiba-shi, Nara
②保育所　Nursery
③RC＋S＋W　④地上2階　2 stories
⑤7799.95㎡　⑥737.33㎡　⑦984.58㎡

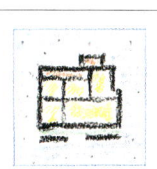

No.114　上賀茂の家　2003
　　　　Kamigamo House
①京都府京都市　Kyoto-shi, Kyoto
②専用住宅　Dwelling House
③W　④地上2階　2 stories
⑤796.32㎡　⑥322.78㎡　⑦274.00㎡
(Renovation area)

No.115　大福保育園　2003
　　　　Ofuku Nursery School
①岡山県岡山市　Okayama-shi, Okayama
②保育所　Nursery
③RC／W／S　④地上1階　1 story
⑤3269.12㎡　⑥1175.21㎡　⑦996.29㎡

No.116　芦屋の家　2003
　　　　Ashiya House
①兵庫県芦屋市　Ashiya-shi, Hyogo
②専用住宅　Dwelling House　③W／RC
④地下1階、地上2階　basement, 2 stories
⑤397.29㎡　⑥192.27㎡　⑦289.65㎡

No.117.1　SOBRIO GARDEN A　2003
　　　　　SOBRIO GARDEN A
①岡山県岡山市　Okayama-shi, Okayama
②店舗　Shop　③S＋RC
④地上1階の一部改装　1 story (partial renovation)　⑤445.00㎡　⑥291.86㎡
⑦139.22㎡ (Renovation area)

No.117.2　SOBRIO GARDEN B　2003
　　　　　SOBRIO GARDEN B
①岡山県岡山市　Okayama-shi, Okayama
②店舗　Shop
③S　④地上1階　1 story
⑤330.60㎡　⑥137.50㎡　⑦228.42㎡

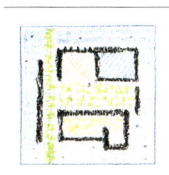

No.118　額田の家　2004
　　　　Nukata House
①愛知県額田郡　Nukata-gun, Aichi
②専用住宅　Dwelling House
③W／S　④地上2階　2 stories
⑤434.30㎡　⑥102.17㎡　⑦132.59㎡

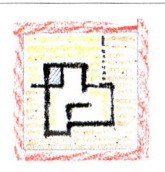

No.119　オサダ整形外科クリニック　2004
　　　　Osada Orthopedic Clinic
①大阪府堺市　Sakai-shi, Osaka
②診療所＋住宅　Clinic and House
③S　④地上3階　3 stories
⑤380.26㎡　⑥227.92㎡
⑦229.88㎡ (Expansion area)

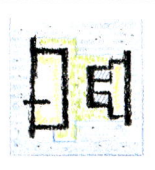

No.120　御宿の家　2004
　　　　Onjuku House
①千葉県夷隅郡　Isumi-gun, Chiba
②専用住宅　Dwelling House
③W＋RC／S　④地上1階　1 story
⑤730.63㎡　⑥117.33㎡　⑦104.55㎡

No.121　福島の家　2004
　　　　Fukushima House
①大阪市福島区　Fukushima-ku, Osaka-shi
②専用住宅　Dwelling House
③S　④地上3階　3 stories
⑤111.97㎡　⑥79.92㎡　⑦215.10㎡

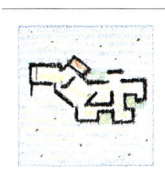

No.122　あやの台保育園・幼稚園　2005
　　　　Ayanodai Nursery School & Kindergarten
①和歌山県橋本市　Hashimoto-shi, Wakayama
②幼稚園＋保育所（認定こども園）　Nursery and Kindergarten　③S
④地上1階　1 story　⑤3506.40㎡
⑥1370.46㎡　⑦1277.35㎡

No.123　松茂町第二体育館　2005
　　　　Matsushigecho Second Gymnasium
①徳島県板野郡　Itano-gun, Tokushima
②体育館　Gymnasium
③RC／S／W　④地上1階　1 story
⑤6038.00㎡　⑥1902.22㎡　⑦1690.87㎡

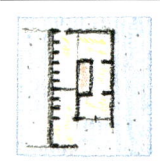

No.124　粉浜の家Ⅳ　2005
　　　　　Kohama House Ⅳ
①大阪市住之江区　Suminoe-ku, Osaka-shi
②住宅＋アトリエ　House and Atelier
③W　④地上2階　2 stories
⑤78.94㎡　⑥59.94㎡　⑦105.30㎡

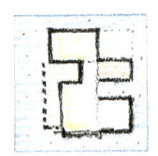

No.125　北恩加島の家　2005
　　　　　Kita Okajima House
①大阪市大正区　Taisho-ku, Osaka-shi
②住宅＋事務所　House and Office
③S　④地上3階　3 stories
⑤108.38㎡　⑥64.88㎡　⑦162.59㎡

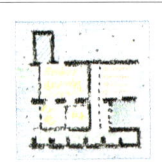

No.126　岸和田の家　2005
　　　　　Kishiwada House
①大阪府岸和田市　Kishiwada-shi, Osaka
②専用住宅　Dwelling House
③RC／S　④地上3階　3 stories
⑤340.70㎡　⑥208.44㎡　⑦430.04㎡

No.127.1　OPEN SPACE LEGATO
　　　　　デイサービスセンターらく　2005
　　　　　Daycare Center Raku
①滋賀県湖南市　Konan-shi, Shiga
②高齢者・障害者総合デイサービスセンター
　Daycare Center　③W　④地上1階　1 story
⑤4051.32㎡　⑥1003.30㎡　⑦852.53㎡

No.127.2　OPEN SPACE LEGATO
　　　　　オープンスペースれがーと　2005
　　　　　Open Space Legato
①滋賀県湖南市　Konan-shi, Shiga　②地域交流レスパイトスペース　Regional Respite Center　③RC＋W　④地上2階　2 stories
⑤1425.08㎡　⑥306.97㎡　⑦441.74㎡

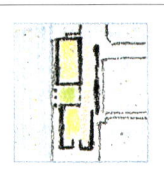

No.128　粉浜の家Ⅴ　2005
　　　　　Kohama House Ⅴ
①大阪市住之江区　Suminoe-ku, Osaka-shi
②専用住宅　Dwelling House
③W　④地上2階　2 stories
⑤63.26㎡ (Expansion area)
⑥95.33㎡　⑦86.91㎡ (Expansion area)

No.129.1　mia via GNOTI　2005
　　　　　mia via GNOTI
①大阪府吹田市　Suita-shi, Osaka
②商業施設（結婚式場）　Wedding Hall　③RC
④地下1階地上1階　basement, 1 story
⑤11626.76㎡　⑥371.10㎡　⑦225.89㎡

No.129.2　mia via 集会棟　2005
　　　　　mia via GALLERY
①大阪府吹田市　Suita-shi, Osaka
②商業施設（結婚式場）　Wedding Hall
③S　④地上2階　2 stories
⑤11626.76㎡　⑥658.56㎡　⑦922.05㎡

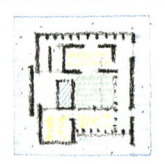

No.130　宮ノ谷の家　2005
　　　　　Miyanotani House
①京都府城陽市　Joyo-shi, Kyoto
②専用住宅　Dwelling House
③RC＋W　④地上2階　2 stories
⑤295.87㎡　⑥144.04㎡　⑦209.51㎡

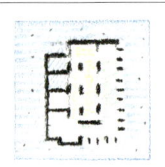

No.131　えぽハウス　2006
　　　　　Epo House
①北海道空知郡　Sorachi-gun, Hokkaido
②障害者通所施設・地域生活支援センター
　Daycare & Regional Support Center for
　the Disabled　③W　④地上2階　2 stories
⑤618.75㎡　⑥257.22㎡　⑦402.84㎡

No.132　新蔵の家　2006
　　　　　Shinkura House
①徳島県徳島市　Tokushima-shi, Tokushima
②専用住宅　Dwelling House
③W　④地上2階　2 stories
⑤819.58㎡　⑥129.36㎡　⑦196.89㎡

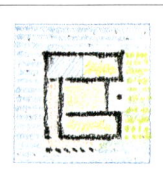

No.133　トヨタすまいるライフ 雅　2006
　　　　　Toyota Smile Life Miyabi
①愛知県岡崎市　Okazaki-shi, Aichi
②専用住宅（モデルハウス）　Dwelling House
　(Model Home)
③W　④地上2階　2 stories
⑤210.93㎡　⑥92.78㎡　⑦143.26㎡

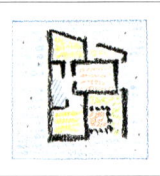

No.134　弁天町の家　2006
　　　　　Bentencho House
①大阪市港区　Minato-ku, Osaka-shi
②専用住宅　Dwelling House
③S　④地上4階　4 stories　⑤109.37㎡
⑥75.61㎡　⑦214.49㎡

No.135　北畠の家　2006
　　　　　Kitabatake House
①大阪市阿倍野区　Abeno-ku, Osaka-shi
②専用住宅　Dwelling House　③W／RC
④地下1階 地上2階　basement, 2 stories
⑤254.80㎡　⑥101.88㎡　⑦173.06㎡

No.136　深谷の家　2007
　　　　　Fukaya House
①埼玉県深谷市　Fukaya-shi, Saitama
②専用住宅　Dwelling House
③RC＋W　④地上3階　3 stories
⑤723.24㎡　⑥276.16㎡　⑦219.46㎡

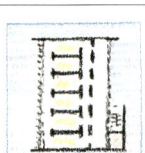

No.137　プライムアーバン江坂Ⅱ　2007
　　　　　Prime Urban Esaka Ⅱ
①大阪府吹田市　Suita-shi, Osaka
②賃貸共同住宅　Public Housing
③RC　④地上11階　11 stories
⑤441.77㎡　⑥217.20㎡　⑦1783.83㎡

314

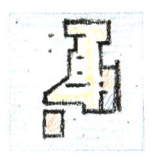

No.138　諏訪森町中の家　2007
　　　　Suwanomoricho Naka House
①大阪府堺市　Sakai-shi, Osaka
②専用住宅　Dwelling House
③W　④地上2階　2 stories
⑤406.3㎡　⑥152.87㎡　⑦253.74㎡

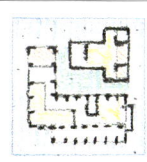

No.139.1　ゆうかり保育園　2007
　　　　Yukari Nusery School
①鹿児島県鹿児島市　Kagoshima-shi, Kagoshima
②保育所　Nursery
③RC＋W　④地上2階　2 stories
⑤947.59㎡　⑥494.50㎡　⑦637.84㎡

No.139.2　ゆうかりデイサービスセンター　2007
　　　　Yukari Daycare Center
①鹿児島県鹿児島市　Kagoshima-shi, Kagoshima　②高齢者・障害者総合デイサービスセンター　Daycare Center
③W　④地上2階　2 stories
⑤387.95㎡　⑥169.15㎡　⑦273.47㎡

No.140　諏訪森町東の家　2007
　　　　Suwanomoricho Higashi House
①大阪府堺市　Sakai-shi, Osaka
②専用住宅　Dwelling House
③RC／W　④地上2階　2 stories
⑤205.30㎡　⑥102.49㎡　⑦203.09㎡

No.141　乗鞍の家　2007
　　　　Norikura House
①愛知県名古屋市　Nagoya-shi, Aichi
②専用住宅　Dwelling House
③RC＋S　④地上3階　3 stories
⑤622.92㎡　⑥240.88㎡　⑦420.18㎡

No.142.1　あけぼの学園 南楓亭　2007
　　　　Akebono Kindergarten "Nanputei"
①大阪府豊中市　Toyonaka-shi, Osaka
②幼稚園＋保育所　Nursery and Kindergarten
③W＋RC　④地上2階　2 stories
⑤1527.41㎡　⑥71.61㎡　⑦110.86㎡

No.142.2　あけぼの学園 風の棟　2007
　　　　Akebono Kindergarten "Kaze no To"
①大阪府豊中市　Toyonaka-shi, Osaka　②幼稚園＋保育所（認定こども園）　Nursery and Kindergarten　③S　④地上4階　4 stories
⑤1527.41㎡　⑥446.23㎡　⑦1066.70㎡

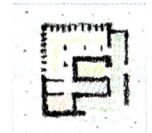

No.143　小倉町の家　2008
　　　　Oguracho House
①大阪府枚方市　Hirakata-shi, Osaka
②専用住宅　Dwelling House
③W　④地上2階　2 stories
⑤152.20㎡　⑥85.13㎡　⑦132.77㎡

No.144　一宮の家Ⅱ　2008
　　　　Ichinomiya House Ⅱ
①兵庫県津名郡　Tsuna-gun, Hyogo
②専用住宅　Dwelling House
③W　④地上2階　2 stories
⑤178.68㎡　⑥50.18㎡　⑦94.94㎡

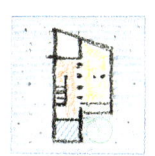

No.145　永山園の家　2008
　　　　Nagayamaen House
①大阪府堺市　Sakai-shi, Osaka
②専用住宅　Dwelling House
③W／RC　④地上3階　3 stories
⑤135.95㎡　⑥53.06㎡　⑦132.60㎡

No.146　愛成学園 メイプルガーデン　2010
　　　　Aisei Gakuen Maple Garden
①東京都中野区　Nakano-ku, Tokyo
②障害者支援施設　Support Facility for the Disabled
③RC　④地上3階　3 stories
⑤2167.07㎡　⑥823.32㎡　⑦2189.69㎡

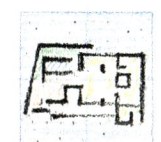

No.147　富士が丘の家　2009
　　　　Fujigaoka House
①兵庫県三田市　Sanda-shi, Hyogo
②専用住宅　Dwelling House
③RC／W　④地上2階　2 stories
⑤464.54㎡　⑥229.67㎡　⑦391.39㎡

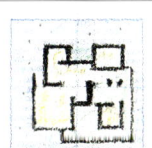

No.148　大川の家　2009
　　　　Okawa House
①福岡県大川市　Okawa-shi, Fukuoka
②専用住宅　Dwelling House
③W　④地上2階　2 stories
⑤1365.11㎡　⑥133.54㎡　⑦204.99㎡

No.149　山本町北の家　2009
　　　　Yamamotocho Kita House
①大阪府八尾市　Yao-shi, Osaka
②住宅＋事務所　House and Office
③W　④地上2階　2 stories
⑤192.41㎡　⑥101.78㎡　⑦182.27㎡

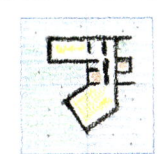

No.150　釼谷庵　2010
　　　　Kentanian
①兵庫県芦屋市　Ashiya-shi, Hyogo
②専用住宅　Dwelling House
③W／RC／S
④地下1階 地上2階　basement, 2 stories
⑤543.43㎡　⑥154.17㎡　⑦276.66㎡

Information on Works

竹原義二
Yoshiji Takehara

略歴
1948　徳島県生まれ
1971　大阪市立大学富樫研究室を経て石井修／
　　　美建・設計事務所勤務
1978　無有建築工房設立
2000-　大阪市立大学大学院生活科学研究科教授

主な受賞歴
1984　渡辺節賞（延命湯）
1992　日本建築士会連合会賞優秀賞（吉見ノ里の家）
1996　第9回 村野藤吾賞（鴻ノ巣の家）
1997　第4回 関西建築家大賞
　　　（宝山町の家、山坂の家Ⅱ、広陵町の家）
1999　日本建築学会作品選奨（東広島の家）
2000　JCDデザイン賞優秀賞（海椿葉山）
2001　日本建築学会作品選奨（土と陶の工房 美乃里）
2002　日本建築学会作品選奨（海椿葉山）
2003　第12回 甍賞経済産業大臣賞（海椿葉山）
2004　第1回 木の建築（101番目の家）
2004　日本建築学会作品選集（101番目の家）
2005　第1回「(社)日本建築家協会優秀建築選2005」
　　　（箱作の家、101番目の家、大福保育園）
2006　第5回 芦原義信賞奨励賞（mia via GNOTI）
2007　日本建築学会作品選奨（松茂町第二体育館）
2007　第3回「(社)日本建築家協会優秀作品選2007」
　　　（OPEN SPACE れがーと、岸和田の家）
2008　第4回「こども環境学会賞」こども環境デザイン賞
　　　（あけぼの学園 南楓亭）
2009　第5回「(社)日本建築家協会優秀作品選2009」
　　　（乗鞍の家、深谷の家）
2009　第8回 日本建築美術工芸協会芦原義信賞
　　　（豊崎長屋）

著書
　　　『無有』（学芸出版社 2007年）

展覧会
　　　「100＋1のイエ」
　　　建築家 竹原義二×写真家 絹巻豊（2007年）
　　　「繊細」日本建築展 巡回展

Profile
1948　Born in Tokushima, Japan
1971　Studied at Togashi Research Laboratory, Osaka City University
　　　Worked at Osamu Ishii Biken Architectural Design Office
1978　Founded Moo Architect Workshop
2000-　Professor at Graduate School of Human Life Science, Osaka City University

Principal Awards
1984　Setsu Watanabe Prize (Enmeiyu)
1992　Japan Federation of Architects & Building Engineers Association Award for Excellence (Yoshiminosato House)
1996　9th Togo Murano Award (Tonnosu House)
1997　4th Kansai Architects Grand Prix (Hozancho House, Yamasaka House II, Koryocho House)
1999　Architectural Institute of Japan Encouragement Prize (Higashi Hiroshima House)
2000　Japanese Society of Commercial Space Designers' Award for Excellence (Umitsubaki Hayama)
2001　Architectural Institute of Japan Encouragement Prize (Atelier Earthenware "Minori")
2002　Architectural Institute of Japan Encouragement Prize (Umitsubaki Hayama)
2003　12th Iraka Award; Economy, Trade, and Industry Minister's Prize (Umitsubaki Hayama)
2004　1st Wood Architecture Award (House No. 101)
2004　Collected Works of the Architectural Institute of Japan (House No. 101)
2005　1st Japan Institute of Architects Award for Excellence 2005 (Hakotsukuri House, House No. 101, Ofuku Nursery School)
2006　5th Ashihara Yoshinobu Encouragement Award (Mia Via GNOTI)
2007　Architectural Institute of Japan Encouragement Prize (Matsushigecho Second Gymnasium)
2007　3rd Japan Institute of Architects Award for Excellence 2007 (OPEN SPACE LEGATO, Kishiwada House)
2008　4th Association for Children's Environment Design Award (Akebono Kindergarten "Nanputei")
2009　5th Japan Institute of Architects Award for Excellence 2009 (Norikura House, Fukaya House)
2009　Japan Association of Artists, Craftsmen & Architects Ashihara Yoshinobu Award (Toyosaki Row House)

Published Work
Moo (Absence/Presence) (Gakugei Shuppansha, 2007)

Exhibitions
100 + 1 Houses: The Architect Yoshiji Takehara and the Photographer Yutaka Kinumaki (2007)
Sensai: Japanese Architecture Exhibition

クレジット
Credits

写真	絹巻豊（絹巻豊写真事務所）
図版	無有建築工房
英訳	クリストファー・スティヴンス 作品解説、図版キャプション、 巻末データ他 ジュリアン・ウォラル pp. 006-025, pp. 138-145, pp. 296-305
協力	
構造設計	GAL構造事務所／豊島英雄 建築力学研究所工楽舎／細川悟 下山建築設計室／下山聡
設備設計	アサヒ設備設計／中脇康彦 南都設計／中森光男
建築施工	あめりか屋 飯田工務店 加藤組 熊倉建匠 SEEDS・CASA 友八工務店 中谷工務店 西村建築工房 日興
家具	家倶家／吉弘良太 カスタム工房／長谷川邦男
外構	山中三方園／山中晃

Photographs
Yutaka Kinumaki (Yutaka Kinumaki Photo Studio)

Drawings
MOO Architect Workshop

English Translations
Christopher Stephens:
Descriptions of Works, Captions, Publishing Information
Julian Worrall:
pp. 006-025, pp. 138-145 and pp. 296-305

In Cooperation With

Structural Design
GAL Structural Design Office: Hideo Toyoshima
Kogakusha Structural Design Office: Satoru Hosokawa
Shimoyama Structural Design Office: Satoru Shimoyama

Facility Design
Asahi Mechanical Engineering: Yasuhiko Nakawaki
Nanto Electrical Engineering: Mitsuo Nakamori

Construction
Amerikaya Architecture
Iida Construction Company
Katougumi
Kumakura Kensho
Seeds Casa
Tomohachi Construction Company
Nakatani Construction Company
Nishimura Construction Company
Nikko, Inc.

Furniture
Kaguya: Ryota Yoshihiro
Custom-Kb: Kunio Hasegawa

Exterior
Yamanaka Sanpohen: Akira Yamanaka

無有建築工房
MOO Architect Workshop

竹原義二	Yoshiji Takehara
清水佳代	Kayo Shimizu
玉井 淳	Atsushi Tamai
竹内洋子	Yoko Takeuchi
田野宏昌	Hiromasa Tano
志水直人	Naoto Shimizu
木林えりか	Erika Kibayashi
武景晃弘	Akihiro Takenaga
岡本知樹	Tomoki Okamoto
竹原和子	Kazuko Takehara
池田和雄	Kazuo Ikeda
小河原一郎	Ichiro Ogahara
岡本進一	Shinichi Okamoto
栗山立巳	Tatsumi Kuriyama
今岡一哉	Kazuya Imaoka
小山隆治	Ryuji Koyama
清水寛仁	Kanji Shimizu
石原正明	Masaaki Ishihara
梶 純子	Junko Kaji
由布真喜男	Makio Yufu
松本直樹	Naoki Matsumoto
矢田朝士	Asashi Yada
木下 洋	Hiroshi Kinoshita
岸下真理	Shinri Kishishita
荒谷省午	Shogo Aratani
平田玲子	Reiko Hirata
酒井康成	Yasunari Sakai
丸山泰正	Yasumasa Maruyama
去来川仁美	Hitomi Isagawa
清水敦子	Atsuko Shimizu

竹原義二の住宅建築

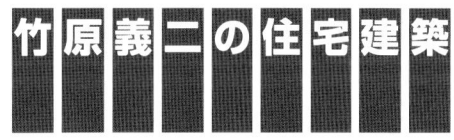

Yoshiji Takehara: Residential Architecture

2010年4月10日　　初版第1刷発行
2018年3月20日　　初版第3刷発行

著者　————————　竹原義二

写真　————————　絹巻　豊

発行者　———————　加藤　徹

ブックデザイン　———　太田徹也

印刷・製本　—————　大日本印刷株式会社

発行所　———————　TOTO出版（TOTO株式会社）

〒107-0062 東京都港区南青山1-24-3
TOTO乃木坂ビル2F
［営業］tel. 03-3402-7138
　　　　fax. 03-3402-7187
［編集］tel. 03-3497-1010
URL. https://jp.toto.com/publishing

落丁本・乱丁本はお取り替えいたします。
本書の全部又は一部に対するコピー・スキャン・デジタル化等の無断複製行為は、著作権法上での例外を除き禁じます。
本書を代行業者等の第三者に依頼してスキャンやデジタル化することは、たとえ個人や家庭内での利用であっても著作権上認められておりません。
定価はカバーに表示してあります。

©2010 Yoshiji Takehara, Yutaka Kinumaki
Printed in Japan
ISBN978-4-88706-310-5